The Reagan Wars

The Reagan Wars

A Constitutional Perspective on War Powers and the Presidency

David Locke Hall

Westview Press

BOULDER • SAN FRANCISCO • OXFORD

Copyright © 1991 by Westview Press, Inc.

Published in 1991 in the United States of America by Westview Press, Inc., 5500 Central Avenue, Boulder, Colorado 80301, and in the United Kingdom by Westview Press, 36 Lonsdale Road, Summertown, Oxford OX2 7EW

Library of Congress Cataloging-in-Publication Data
Hall, David Locke.
  The Reagan wars : a constitutional perspective on war powers and
the presidency / David Locke Hall.
    p. cm.
  Includes bibliographical references and index.
  ISBN 0-8133-1198-5
  1. War and emergency powers—United States. 2. Executive power—
United States. 3. United States—Constitutional law. 4. United
States—Foreign relations—1981–1989. 5. Reagan, Ronald.
I. Title.
KF5060.H35 1991
342.73′0412—dc20
[347.302412]
                91-13127
                CIP

Printed and bound in the United States of America

The paper used in this publication meets the requirements of the American National Standard for Permanence of Paper for Printed Library Materials Z39.48-1984.

10   9   8   7   6   5   4   3   2   1

Contents

Maps

Preface

President Reagan's term in office was characterized by what has been called a "compellent diplomacy."[1] His aggressive foreign policy was a result of what one Chief of Naval Operations described as an "era of violent peace."[2] Punctuating the cycles of this violent peace during the Reagan years were four significant episodes of military force ordered by the President. This book explores the question of whether Reagan's use of the military in these four situations was constitutional. Those who believe that the issue of the constitutionality of the President's use of force is a purely academic exercise will have no interest in this book, which is written for those who believe in the rule of law.

David Locke Hall

Notes

1. Huntington, "Coping with the Lippmann Gap," 66 FOREIGN AFFAIRS 453, 463 (1988). *See also* B. BLECHMAN AND S. KAPLAN, FORCE WITHOUT WAR (1978).

2. Watkins, "The Maritime Strategy," U.S. Naval Institute PROCEEDINGS (January 1986 Supplement).

Wellington thrashed Bonaparte,
as ev'ry child can tell,
The House of Peers,
throughout the war,
Did nothing in particular,
And did it very well:
Yet Britain set the world a-blaze
In good King George's glorious days!

—Gilbert and Sullivan,
"When Britain Ruled the Waves,"
Iolanthe (or the Peer and the Peri)

Introduction

The King (in disguise): Methinks I could not die anywhere so contented as in the King's company, his cause being just. . . .

Williams (a soldier): But if the cause be not good, the King himself hath a heavy reckoning to make when all those legs and arms and heads, chopped off in a battle, shall join together at the latter day and cry all, 'We died at such a place,' some swearing, some crying for a surgeon, some upon their wives left poor behind them. . . .

—W. Shakespeare, KING HENRY V

On more than a hundred occasions since the Constitutional Convention of 1787, Presidents have waged war without a congressional declaration.[1] The issue of whether a declaration of war is necessary to empower the President to wage war received special scrutiny during the undeclared war in Vietnam.[2] Some commentators have argued that the President's use of force in Vietnam was not lawful, because it was not congressionally authorized. Others, including several courts,[3] have insisted that the President's use of force in Vietnam was authorized by the Tonkin Gulf Resolution,[4] as well as numerous appropriations and draft enactments.[5] Even those who contend that the Vietnam War was unconstitutional acknowledge that at least some aspects of the war, such as its financing, were authorized by Congress.[6] For these critics, the argument that the Vietnam War was unconstitutional is based solely on the absence of a declaration of war.

Since the Vietnam War, the debate has been revisited on each occasion of presidential war-making. Unfortunately, these debates, though intensive, have been too short-lived to produce any resolution. Interest in debating the fine points of the war powers wanes after the conclusion of a military operation. Other issues arise and demand attention, leaving the war powers question in limbo, awaiting resurrection on the next occasion of presidential war-making.

Opponents of war-making by President Reagan have argued that, since Congress alone is empowered to declare war, the President exceeds the scope of his constitutional authority by employing force abroad without a declaration of war.[7] Proponents of President Reagan's actions have

1

claimed that his authority as the nation's chief executive and as Commander-in-Chief of the armed forces justifies his actions.[8] Superimposed over these constitutional debates have been statutory wrangles about whether the President complied with the requirements of the War Powers Resolution,[9] which was enacted after the Vietnam War in 1973. Some observers have found the legal issues to be either overwhelming or irrelevant; after the Grenada intervention, the *Wall Street Journal* wished the lawyers would "shut up."[10] At stake in these debates, however, is not only the question of whether a particular belligerent act by the President is constitutionally authorized, but also the broader issue of how seriously the Constitution is to be treated in determining the distribution of the war powers.

One of the sources of confusion and incoherency in the post-Vietnam war powers debates has been the failure of many participants to distinguish the question of whether the President's actions were lawful from the question of whether they were wise.[11] This book is about the former; it seeks to determine whether the circumstances under which the Constitution permits unilateral presidential war-making were present when President Reagan waged war between 1980 and 1988. It will show that, given the breadth of the President's war powers under the Constitution, each of President Reagan's military involvements was lawful. Thus the constitutional balance of war powers will be seen to favor the President in the short term and Congress in the long run. This balance of constitutional powers will lead to political equilibrium only by means of a clash of wills between the President and Congress.

The first section of the book will describe the constitutional balance of war powers. The views of the Framers and the courts on the issue of presidential war-making will be presented along with an explanation for the reluctance of the courts to address the issue. The War Powers Resolution will be criticized as an unsuccessful attempt to adjust the balance of war powers in favor of Congress.

The second section of this book will describe instances of presidential war-making from 1980 to 1988. The following episodes will be covered: the 1982–1984 deployment of U.S. Marines to Lebanon; the 1983 intervention in Grenada; the 1986 air strikes against Libya from the Gulf of Sidra; and the Persian Gulf operations in 1987 and 1988.[12] This book does not seek to analyze all of President Reagan's foreign policy actions. Beyond the scope of this book's coverage, for example, are President Reagan's policies in Central America and the so-called "Iran-Contra" affair.[13] Although such policies and events raised numerous interesting legal issues, they did not involve a unilateral presidential decision to commit U.S. forces to combat.

This book seeks to show that all four instances of war-making by President Reagan were undertaken within the scope of the President's broad, but not unlimited, war powers. The conclusion that President Reagan's use of force was lawful does not imply the wisdom of such military operations. Thus this book seeks to be something other than an *apologia* or a legal brief for President Reagan. The legal analysis presented here does not apply exclusively to President Reagan or Republican presidents. The legal rules apply with equal force to President Carter's hostage rescue mission in Iran, President Kennedy's use of the military in Vietnam, President Truman's use of force in Korea, and President Roosevelt's use of the military in World War II prior to the U.S. declaration of war. The ultimate conclusion of this book is that, regardless of how the war powers are allocated, they are allocated by the Constitution and not by political expediency. The war powers equilibrium between the President and Congress is not determined by transient political popularity but by deliberate reference to the meaning of the Constitution.

Notes

1. *See, e.g.,* "War Without Declaration: A Chronological List of 199 Military Hostilities Abroad Without a Declaration of War, 1798–1972," 119 CONG. REC. 25,066–25,076 (1973); U.S. Congress, House of Representatives, Committee on International Relations, "Background Information on the Use of U.S. Armed Forces in Foreign Countries," 94th Cong., 1st Sess. (1975); Emerson, "War Powers Legislation," 74 W.VA. L. REV. 53, 88–119 (1972) (199 uses of force); U.S. Congress, House of Representatives, Committee on Foreign Affairs, "Background Information on the Use of United States Armed Forces in Foreign Countries," 91st Cong., 2d Sess., 44–46, 59 (1970); Historical Studies Div., Bureau of Public Affairs, Dept. of State, "Armed Actions Taken By the United States Without a Declaration of War, 1789–1967," (Research Project No. 806A August 1967); Schaffter and Matthews, "The Powers of the President as Commander in Chief of the Army and Navy of the United States," U.S. Congress, House of Representatives, Doc. No. 443, 84th Cong., 2d Sess., 6–7, 9–10 (1953); E. CORWIN, THE CONSTITUTION AND WHAT IT MEANS TODAY 126 (1958); J. ROGERS, WORLD POLICING AND THE CONSTITUTION 45–55 (1945).

2. *See, e.g.,* A. SCHLESINGER, THE IMPERIAL PRESIDENCY (1973); Van Alstyne, "Congress, the President, and the Power to Declare War: A Requiem for Vietnam," 121 U. PA. L. REV. 1 (1972); Berger, "War-Making By The President," 121 U. PA. L. REV 29 (1972); Eagleton, "Congress and the War Powers," 37 MO. L. REV. (1972); Wormuth, "The Nixon Theory of the War Power: A Critique," 60 CALIF. L. REV. 648 (1972); Rehnquist, "The Constitutional Issues - Administration Position," 45 N.Y.U. L. REV. 628 (1970); Note, "Congress, the President, and the Power to Commit Forces to Combat,"

81 HARV. L. REV. 1771 (1968); F. WORMUTH, THE VIETNAM WAR: THE PRESIDENT VERSUS THE CONSTITUTION (1968); Moore, "International Law and the United States Role in Vietnam: A Reply," 76 YALE L. J. 1051 (1967); Dept. of State, Office of the Legal Adviser, "The Legality of United States Participation in the Defense of Viet Nam," 75 YALE L. J. 1085 (1966); Alford, "The Legality of American Involvement in Viet Nam: A Broader Perspective," 75 YALE L. J. 1109 (1966) (supporting arguments in favor of the legality of U.S. involvement in Vietnam); Falk, "International Law and the United States Role in the Viet Nam War," 75 YALE L. J. 1122, 1155 (1966) (criticizing the State Department position on the legality of U.S. involvement in Vietnam and expressing the remarkable position that the "President has the constitutional authority to commit our armed forces to the defense of South Viet Nam without a declaration of war *provided* that such 'a commitment' is otherwise in accord with international law."); Wright, "Legal Aspects of the Viet-Nam Situation," 60 AM. J. INT'L L. 750 (1966); Meeker, "Memorandum on the Legality of American Participation in the Defense of South Vietnam," STATE DEPARTMENT BULLETIN 474 (March 4, 1966) (reprinted in J. MOORE, LAW AND THE INDO-CHINA WAR 603–632 (1972). For a vigorous debate on the question, *see* CONGRESS, THE PRESIDENT, & FOREIGN POLICY (ABA Standing Committee on Law and National Security) (1984) (S. Soper, ed.).

3. *Commonwealth of Mass. v. Laird*, 451 F.2d 26 (1st Cir. 1971); *DaCosta v. Laird*, 448 F.2d 1368 (2d Cir. 1971) *(per curiam)*, *cert. denied*, 405 U.S. 979 (1972); *Orlando v. Laird*, 443 F.2d 1039 (2d Cir. 1971); *Drinan v. Nixon*, 364 F. Supp. 854 (D. Mass. 1973); *Meyers v. Nixon*, 339 F. Supp. 1388, 1390 (S.D. N.Y. 1972). *Cf. also Simmons v. U.S.*, 406 F.2d 456, 460 (5th Cir.) (draft legislation is not unconstitutional), *cert. denied*, 395 U.S. 982 (1969); *U.S. v. Mitchell*, 264 F. Supp. 874, 898 (D. Conn. 1965). *See* Sugarman, "Judicial Decisions Concerning the Constitutionality of United States Military Activity in Indochina: A Bibliography of Judicial Decisions," 13 COLUM. J. TRANSNAT'L. L. 470 (1974).

4. P.L. 88-408, 78 Stat. 384 (August 10, 1964). For background information on the Tonkin Gulf Resolution, *see* A. SCHLESINGER, THE IMPERIAL PRESIDENCY 177–182 (1973); D. HALBERSTAM, THE BEST AND THE BRIGHTEST 411–422 (1972).

5. *See, e.g.*, J. MOORE, LAW AND THE INDO-CHINA WAR (1972); J. LEHMAN, THE EXECUTIVE, CONGRESS, AND FOREIGN POLICY: STUDIES OF THE NIXON ADMINISTRATION Ch. 3 (1976).

6. The Supreme Court has described "the appropriation by Congress of funds" as "confirmation and ratification of the action of the Chief Executive." *Fleming v. Mohawk Wrecking & Lumber Co.*, 331 U.S. 111, 116 (1947).

7. *See, e.g.*, Chayes, "Grenada was Illegally Invaded," *N.Y. Times*, Nov. 15, 1983, at 35; Schlesinger, "Grenada Again: Living Within the Law," *The Wall Street Journal*, Dec. 14, 1983, at 30.

8. *See, e.g.*, Rostow, "Law Is Not a Suicide Pact," *N.Y. Times*, Nov. 15, 1983, at 35; J. MOORE, LAW AND THE GRENADA MISSION (1984).

9. 50 U.S.C. §§ 1541–1548. *See, e.g.*, J. MOORE, F. TIPSON, AND R. TURNER, NATIONAL SECURITY LAW (1990); R. TURNER, THE WAR

POWERS RESOLUTION (1983); Comment, "Congressional Control of Presidential War-Making under the War Powers Act: The Status of a Legislative Veto After *Chadha*," 132 U. PA. L. REV. 1217 (1984); Carter, "The Constitutionality of the War Powers Resolution," 70 U. VA. L. REV. 101 (1984); Wald, "The Future of the War Powers Resolution," 36 STAN. L. REV. 1407 (1984).

10. "Harvard Decides Grenada," *The Wall Street Journal,* Nov. 2, 1983, at 30.

11. This sort of confusion has been exhibited by such respected figures as former Secretary of State Cyrus R. Vance. Vance, "Striking the Balance: Congress and the President Under the War Powers Resolution," 133 U. PA. L. REV. 79 (1984).

12. All facts presented are based on unclassified sources.

13. *See* H. KOH, THE NATIONAL SECURITY CONSTITUTION: SHARING POWER AFTER THE IRAN-CONTRA AFFAIR (1990).

PART ONE

A Clash of Wills:
The Constitutional Balance
of War Powers

1

The Intent of the Framers

The Articles of Confederation
and the Constitutional Convention

Following the declaration by the American colonies of independence from the British Crown, the Continental Congress enacted the Articles of Confederation in 1777. From their ratification in 1781 until 1787, the Articles served to guide Congress and the several states in the governance of the infant nation. In 1787, the Articles were replaced by the United States Constitution.[1]

The differences between the Articles of Confederation and the Constitution are, of course, numerous. The most fundamental difference is that, while the Articles allocated power among the states and between the federal government and the states, the Constitution allocated power among the three branches of the federal government, reserving unallocated powers to the states.

The Articles of Confederation, like the Constitution, provided for a congressional declaration of war.[2] The Articles of Confederation were a failure. The problems associated with the Articles related to the unstable division of power between Congress and the several states, exacerbated by the absence from the Articles of a provision for a federal executive. As a result, the infant nation's foreign affairs were chaotic. Congress had the exclusive power to enter into treaties but had no way of enforcing the exclusivity of this authority. As a result, Georgia, for example, signed three treaties with the Creek nation in defiance of Congress.[3] In another embarrassing episode, Congress discovered, after it entered into the Treaty of Hopewell, which returned land claimed by North Carolina to the Cherokee nation, that North Carolina had already sold the land to its citizens. Virginia concluded a treaty with France and closed a loan with Spain.[4]

Such chaos did little to enhance national security. The strategic position of the United States before 1787 was precarious. The entire western frontier was claimed by Indian nations. To the northwest, the British occupied garrisons along the Great Lakes. Even in the northeast, British sympathizers in Canada threatened to seize land in present-day Maine.[5] To the south, the Spanish claimed Florida as well as access to the Mississippi River.[6]

As a result of these persistent border threats, the years preceding the Constitution were violent and unstable. State militias routinely usurped the federal war-making power in unauthorized actions against the Indian nations. In 1786, for example, the Virginia militia marched against the Shawnee to enforce Virginia's claims to land on the Miami River.[7] In Kentucky, actions to enforce American claims to land claimed by Indians led to the deaths of approximately 1,500 Kentuckians between 1783 and 1790.[8] With British support, Joseph Brant, a Mohawk chieftain who was also a captain in the British Army, led Mohawk forces against American settlers in the Mohawk Valley and along the Pennsylvania–New York border.[9]

In an especially obnoxious example of a major power thumbing its nose at the infant United States, Great Britain continued to occupy forts in U.S. territory after the 1783 peace treaty. The British had agreed by the 1783 treaty to surrender occupied garrisons in the Great Lakes region. As the ostensible result of America's failure to pay pre-war debts as the treaty required, the British refused to abandon the garrisons.[10] The garrisons commanded choke-points throughout the Great Lakes region and were therefore of strategic importance in preserving Britain's monopoly on the fur trade.[11] Some have suggested that the British never intended to give up the garrisons, intending instead to establish a buffer state on the American northwestern frontier.[12] Whatever the intentions of the British were, the fledgling United States lacked the ability to preserve its own collective interests along the border.

The failure of the Articles of Confederation to serve the national interest induced delegates from the several states to travel to Philadelphia in 1787 to devise a superior plan for national unity. One major issue at the Constitutional Convention concerned the distribution of power from the states to the federal government. Therefore, any inquiry such as this into the distribution of war powers between the President and Congress is hampered by the fact that allocation of power among the branches of the federal government was not the only issue discussed at the Convention.

Furthermore, the meaning of the records of the Constitutional Convention in the war powers context is not always obvious. One commentator has suggested that the interpretation of the constitutional war powers requries the "skills of . . . the Oracle of Apollo at Delphi."[13] The reasons for the record's ambiguity are, of course, many.[14] Among them is the fact that the Framers did not come to the Convention with a unified vision of federal governance. Differences on the critical issue of executive power can be seen by examining the various plans introduced by the delegates during the summer of 1787. On May 29, 1787, just before the debate on executive power opened, Edmund Randolph proposed the Virginia Plan. The Virginia Plan did not address expressly the issue of war powers or their distribution between the executive and legislative branches. Indeed, the terms of the Virginia Plan were vague even on the most general issues of legislative and executive power. For example, the Virginia Plan described the legislature's power as follows: "National Legislature . . . ought to be empowered to enjoy the Legislative Rights vested in Congress by the Confederation."[15] This tautology does little to clarify the separation of powers. The Virginia Plan also provided for the election by Congress of a chief executive whose duty was to execute the laws and who was to be granted "executive rights vested in Congress by the Confederation."[16] The "executive rights" to be vested in Congress were not defined. Since the Virginia Plan failed to address executive war making and foreign affairs powers, it implicitly proposed a weak executive with only indirect authority in the area of foreign relations. The Virginia Plan did not attract much support. To the extent that the Virginia Plan was capable of establishing anything, it would not have established a central government capable of addressing some of the federal problems unsolved by the Articles of Confederation.

Competing with the Virginia Plan was the Pinckney Plan, presented by Charles Pinckney of South Carolina.[17] The Pinckney Plan was more concrete than the Virginia Plan in specifying the powers of the legislative and executive branches. It granted Congress the power to raise an army and the Senate the "sole and exclusive power to declare war and to make treaties and to appoint ambassadors. . . ."[18] The Pinckney Plan also vested the "Executive Power" in a single President, who was named "Commander in chief of the army and navy of the United States and of the militia of the several states. . . ."[19] This proposal was similar to the allocation of power ultimately adopted except that it granted the Senate, not Congress as a whole, the power to declare war and the Senate, not the President, the power to make, as distinct from the power to ratify, treaties.

The debate over the executive power issue commenced on June 1, 1787. The initial focus of discussion was the question of whether the executive should be a single individual or a council. Randolph, the sponsor of the Virginia Plan, vigorously opposed vesting executive power in a single person, who would become "the fetus of monarchy."[20] He proposed a council of three men.

This idea of a collective executive was not greeted enthusiastically by Elbridge Gerry of Massachusetts, who "was at a loss to discover the policy of three members of the executive." He continued, "It would be extremely inconvenient in many instances, particularly in military matters, whether relating to the militia, or army, or a navy. It would be a general with three heads."[21] James Wilson of Pennsylvania acknowledged the legitimacy of Randolph's fears, but asserted that a single executive could avoid the hazards of monarchy.[22]

Charles Pinckney preferred a single executive, but "was afraid the Executive powers . . . might extend to peace and war . . . which would render the Executive a monarchy, of the worst kind, to wit an elective one."[23] Wilson stated: "He did not consider the Prerogatives of the British Monarch as a proper guide in defining the Executive Powers. Some of these prerogatives were of a Legislative nature. Among others that of war & peace &c."[24] Thus was the general question of executive organization joined to the war powers issue.

James Madison considered the discussion of whether the executive power should be vested in a single person to be premature. He thought the most reasonable first step was to define the executive power. He suggested a compromise of a "single Executive of long duration with a council, with liberty to depart from their opinion at his peril."[25] Madison did note that, in any case, the executive's powers should not "include the rights of war and peace. . . ."[26]

A third proposal, the New Jersey Plan, was presented on June 15, 1787 by William Paterson. Like the Virginia and Pinckney Plans, the New Jersey Plan avoided addressing expressly the issue of executive war powers. The New Jersey Plan did propose a plural Executive, which was authorized collectively "to direct all military operations; provided that none of the persons composing the federal Executive shall on any occasion take command of any troops, so as personally to conduct any enterprise as General, or in any other capacity."[27] Paterson clearly feared a military dictatorship. Pinckney addressed this issue on August 20, when he declared, "The military shall always be subordinate to the Civil power. . . ."[28]

A fourth plan was proposed by Alexander Hamilton on June 18 and for the first time the war powers issue was raised at length. Article IV, Clause 10 of the Hamilton Plan provided:

> The President . . . shall take care that the laws be faithfully executed. He shall be the commander in chief of the Army and Navy of the United States and of the Militia within the several States, and shall have the direction of war when commenced, but he shall not take the actual command in the field of any army without the consent of the Senate and Assembly. All treaties, conventions and agreements with foreign nations shall be made by him, by and with the advice and consent of the Senate. He shall have the appointment of the principal or Chief officer of each of the departments

of War, Naval Affairs, Finance, and Foreign Affairs; and shall have the nomination; and by and with the Consent of the Senate, the appointment of all other officers to be appointed under the authority of the United States, except such for whom different provision is made by this Constitution; . . . [29]

Hamilton proposed a single executive, whom he called the "Governour," empowered to conduct "the direction of war when authorized or begun; [and] to have with the advice and approbation of the Senate the power of making all treaties. . . ."[30] The Senate was to be granted the "sole power of declaring war, [and] the power of advising and approving all treaties."[31] Thus, although Hamilton's Plan did address expressly the war powers question, it did not answer it: if the "Governour" has the power to "direct" a war already "begun," who has the power to begin it?

The sentiment against executive power was a significant presence at the Constitutional Convention. In 1788, Patrick Henry of Virginia expressed his fear of a single executive to the Virginia Convention:

Your President may easily become king. . . . Where are your checks in this government? . . . If your American chief be a man of ambition and abilities, how easy is it for him to render himself absolute! . . . Can he not, at the head of his army, beat down every opposition? Away with your President! we shall have a king: the army will salute him monarch: your militia will leave you, and assist in making him king, and fight against you: and what have you to oppose this force? What will then become of you and your rights? Will not absolute despotism ensue?[32]

On the other hand, fears of what Jefferson called "legislative despotism" were also brought to the Constitutional Convention. James Madison spoke to the Convention on July 17, 1787 on the subject of legislative omnipotence. "Experience," he said, "had proved a tendency in our [state] governments to throw all power into the Legislative vortex."[33] He feared that without an executive check to legislative power, "a revolution of some kind or other would be inevitable."[34] Madison wrote later in The Federalist:

In a government where numerous and extensive prerogatives are placed in the hands of an hereditary monarch, the executive department is very justly regarded as the source of danger, and watched with all the jealousy which a zeal for liberty ought to inspire. . . . But in a representative republic, where the executive magistracy is carefully limited, both in the extent and duration of its power, . . . it is against the enterprising ambition of [the legislature] that the people ought to indulge all their jealousy and exhaust all their precautions.[35]

Madison's concerns over legislative tyranny were shared by Gouverneur Morris, who spoke to the Convention the day after Madison did, on July 19, 1787:

> The Legislature will continually seek to aggrandize & perpetuate themselves; and will seize those critical moments produced by war, invasion or convulsion for that purpose. It is necessary then that the Executive Magistrate should be the guardian of the people, even of the lower classes, agst. Legislative tyranny, against the Great & the wealthy who in the course of things will necessarily compose—the Legislative body.[36]

Ultimately, on July 26, 1787, the Convention voted for a single executive empowered to execute the laws and a national legislature empowered to enact them. A Committee of Detail was named to fill in the numerous gaps left by the Convention, which then adjourned for two weeks. When the Convention reconvened on August 6, 1787, the Committee of Detail reported on its progress. The Committee recommended that the Senate be granted the "power to make treaties" and the legislature the power to "make war" and "repel invasions."[37] In addition, the Committee recommended that the legislature be empowered to "raise armies," to "build and equip fleets," to "call forth the aid of the militia in order to execute the laws of the Union," to "enforce treaties," and to "suppress insurrections."[38] The executive was to be the "commander in chief of the Army and the Navy of the United States, and of the militia of the several states."[39] In the final draft, the President's command over the state militia was restricted to periods when Congress had called the state militia into federal service.

The debate over the Committee of Detail's draft constitution turned on August 13 to the relationship between the war powers and the question of which house of Congress should be granted the revenue and appropriation powers. James Wilson argued that the Senate should be involved in fiscal decision-making because major issues such as war powers were inherently bound up with fiscal issues.[40]

> War, commerce, and revenue are the great objects of the general government. All of them are connected with money. The restriction in favor of the [House of Representatives] would exclude the Senate from originating any important bills whatever.[41]

Edmund Randolph suspected the Senate would be too elitist to be affected by popular concerns. Therefore, he argued in favor of the more populist House as the superior institution for the appropriation of money ("the means of war") and the declaration of war:

When the people behold in the Senate, the countenance of an aristocracy; and in the president, the form at least of a little monarch, will not their alarms be sufficiently raised without taking from their immediate representatives, a right which has been so long appropriated to them. . . . The declaration of war he conceived ought not to be in the Senate composed of 26 men only, but rather in the other House. In the other House ought to be placed the origination of the means of war. . . .[42]

Thus the Framers' debate showed that the spending power of Congress was viewed consciously as a check on executive war-making. Professor Abraham Sofaer has noted that the Framers "did convey a strong impression that a military appropriation, passed for a specific purpose, could constitute legislative approval for the use of the form authorized to accomplish the purpose contemplated."[43] Professor Sofaer finds himself in good company, supported by both Madison and Hamilton. Congress, Madison wrote,

alone can propose the supplies requisite for the support of government. They in a word hold the purse—that powerful instrument by which we behold . . . the people gradually enlarging the sphere of its activity and importance, and finally reducing, as far as it seems to have wished, all the overgrown prerogatives of the other branches of the government. This power over the purse may, in fact, be regarded as the most complete and effectual weapon with which any constitution can arm the immediate representatives of the people, for obtaining a redress of every grievance, and for carrying into effect every just salutary measure.[44]

Hamilton agreed, but emphasized the importance of setting some limit on legislative military appropriation powers.

[T]he whole power of raising armies was lodged in the legislature, not in the executive; . . . there was to be found in respect to this object an important qualification even of the legislative discretion on that clause which forbids the appropriation of money for the support of an army for any longer period than two years—a precaution which upon a nearer view of it will appear to be a great and real security against military establishments without evident necessity.[45]

Jefferson, who was not present at the 1787 debates, wrote to Madison in 1789:

We have already given, in example, one effectual check to the dog of war, by transferring the power of declaring war from the Executive to the Legislative body, from those who are to spend to those who are to pay.

The Framers consciously viewed the spending power of Congress as a check on executive war-making.

The most famous war powers debate occurred on August 17, when Pinckney objected to the idea, contained in the Committee of Detail's draft, of granting to Congress as a whole the power to "make" war. He believed the Senate the more efficient forum for war-making debates, the House being "too numerous for such deliberations."[46] At the time, the draft constitution provided for treaties to be made by the Senate, not the President, so Pinckney viewed the Senate as the federal body endowed with definitive expertise in the area of foreign affairs. Pierce Butler, also of South Carolina, took Pinckney's position one step further by arguing that if, as Pinckney had suggested, efficiency was the criterion, the war powers should be vested in the executive.[47] Elbridge Gerry of Massachusetts replied to Butler's suggestion that the President be granted war-making power: "Mr. Gerry never expected to hear in a republic a motion to empower the Executive alone to declare war."[48]

Following Butler's remarks, Madison, seconded by Gerry, "moved to insert 'declare' striking out 'make' war; leaving to the Executive the power to repel sudden attacks."[49] Rufus King of Massachusetts endorsed the change because without it the power of Congress to " 'make' war might be understood to 'conduct' it which was an executive function."[50] Roger Sherman of Connecticut objected to the amendment on the ground that the President already had the power to defend the nation against sudden invasion and that to narrow the congressional authority from "make" war to "declare" war seemed to suggest an augmentation of executive power. "The Executive should be able to repel and not to commence war," he said.[51] Sherman objected to the narrowing of Congress' power by means of the Madison motion.

Despite these criticisms, Madison's motion carried, and Congress was granted power to "declare" war, not to "make" it. George Mason of Virginia supported the change, but "was against giving the power of war to the Executive, because [he was] not to be trusted with it. . . . He was for clogging rather than facilitating war; but for facilitating peace."[52] The change was also supported by James Wilson, who said to the Pennsylvania Convention:

> This [new] system will not hurry us into war; it is calculated to guard against it. It will not be in the power of a single man, or a single body of men, to involve us in such distress; for the important power of declaring war is vested in the legislature at large: this declaration must be made with the concurrence of the House of Representatives: from this circumstance we may draw a certain conclusion that nothing but our national interest can draw us into a war.[53]

On the whole, the Madison amendment reflects the Framers' recognition that some measure of war-making, at least to "repel sudden attacks," was recognized as an executive function. The limitation on congressional power contained in the amendment is consistent with Madison's fear of legislative tyranny.[54] In this way, the power of Congress to "declare" war was created. In granting Congress this power, the Framers ceded emergency war-making power to the President. Moreover, Congress was not granted what might be seen as the complementary power to "declare" peace. The Convention expressly rejected such a proposal.[55]

Set against the legislative power to declare war was the President's power to act as Commander-in-Chief.[56] Remarkably, this clause passed the Convention on August 27, 1787, with no debate on the record. The absence of recorded debate seems to suggest an absence of dissent on the question of whether the President should have command of the armed forces. Such unanimity is surprising since, only months before, the Convention had struggled over whether a single (as opposed to plural) executive with the command of the armed forces would become a military dictator. On the other hand, the August 27 vote to name the President the Commander-in-Chief might be explained by the proximity of the August 17 debate about the congressional power to "declare" war. The Framers probably viewed the former as an obvious implication of the latter. This conclusion is supported by the dramatic defeat of South Carolina Representative Thomas Tucker's August 18, 1789 proposal in Congress that the Constitution be amended to delete the "commander-in-chief" language from Article II and substitute language granting the "power to direct (agreeable to law) the operations" of the armed forces.[57]

In any case, the Convention named the President as Commander-in-Chief, whose powers were described by Alexander Hamilton as follows:

> The President is to be Commander in Chief of the army and navy of the United States. In this respect his authority would be nominally the same with that of King of Great Britain, but in substance much inferior to it. It would amount to nothing more than the supreme command and direction of the military and naval forces, as first General and Admiral of the confederacy; while that of the British King extends to the *declaring* of war and to the *raising* and *regulating* of fleets and armies; all which by the Constitution under consideration would appertain to the Legislature.[58]

Hamilton distinguished between the President and the British King on the basis of the legislature's power to declare war. He also, however, held out the possibility of undeclared war-making by the President.

> [I]t is the peculiar and exclusive province of Congress, *when the nation is at peace* to change that state into a state of war; whether from calculations

of policy, or from provocations, or injuries received: in other words, it belongs to Congress only, *to go to War.* But when a foreign nation declares or openly and outwardly makes war upon the United States, they are then by the very fact *already at war,* and any declaration on the part of Congress is nugatory; it is at least unnecessary.[59]

Hamilton's characterization fits well with the outcome of the August 17, 1787 debate on whether Congress can "make" war. The Framers concluded that Congress should not "make" war, but should be empowered to "declare" it. The President was left with the power to "make" war to "repel sudden attacks." During such an emergency, as Hamilton pointed out, a declaration of war is unnecessary because the nation is "already at war." Such exigency presents precisely the circumstance under which the Framers intended and foresaw unilateral presidential war-making.

However, the Framers did not intend for the President's power to be unrestrained. In arguing to the people of New York for ratification of the Constitution, Hamilton emphasized the power of impeachment as a check against presidential abuses.

> The President of the United States would be liable to be impeached, tried, and upon conviction of treason, bribery, or other high crimes or misdemeanors, removed from office; and would afterwards be liable to prosecution and punishment in the ordinary course of law. The person of the King of Great-Britain is sacred and inviolable: There is no constitutional tribunal to which he is amenable; no punishment to which he can be subjected without involving the crisis of a national revolution.[60]

On the same occasion, Hamilton emphasized the limited power of the President to utilize the state militias, which could be called to national service only by Congress.[61]

These features of the Constitution can be viewed as a structural disincentive to sustained presidential war-making. To the same end, Hamilton emphasized the Constitution's grant of treaty ratification power to Congress.

> The President is to have power with the advice and consent of the Senate to make treaties; provided two thirds of the Senators present concur. The King of Great-Britain is the sole and absolute representative of the nation in all foreign transactions. He can of his own accord make treaties of peace, commerce, alliance, and of every other description. . . . In this respect therefore, there is no comparison between the intended power of the President, and the actual power of the British sovereign. The one can perform alone, what the other can only do with the concurrence of a branch of the Legislature.[62]

Of course, in the following issue of *The Federalist,* Hamilton was just as anxious to emphasize the importance of a potent executive. "Energy in the executive," he wrote, "is a leading character in the definition of good government. It is essential to the protection of the community against foreign attacks. . . ."[63] Hamilton's view fits with that of Locke who worried that the legislature "is not always in being and is usually too numerous, and . . . too slow for the dispatch requisite to execution. . . ."[64] Hamilton was anxious to explain both sides of the war powers equilibrium. Neither Congress nor the President is omnipotent, both are strong and neither is endowed with a dispositive endowment of powers.

In addition to granting Congress appropriation power and the power to declare war, the Constitution reserves in Congress several specific powers relating to military action: (1) the power to grant letters of marque and reprisal; (2) the power to set rules of "captures on land and water"; (3) the power to call forth the militia; and (4) the power to make "rules for the government and regulation of the land and naval forces."[65] Some have argued that the reservation of these rights in Congress suggests that the Framers intended to vest Congress with the exclusive power to wage limited war.[66] But this argument only succeeds by sweeping aside *indicia* of the Framers' intent such as the August 17 debate on Madison's amendment. By limiting Congress' power to declaring, as opposed to making war, the Framers expressly opened the door to executive war-making for defensive purposes. This decision by the Framers was explained by Supreme Court Justice Burton as follows:

> [The Constitution] was written by a generation fresh from war. The people established a more perfect union, in part, so that they might the better defend themselves from military attack. In doing so they centralized far more military power and responsibility in the Chief Executive than previously had been done.[67]

The argument that all war powers are vested in Congress by virtue of the power to declare war is inconsistent with the historical role of declaration of war. The Framers clearly were familiar with the idea of undeclared war.[68] Most eighteenth century wars were undeclared.[69]

Moreover, several limitations on congressional power were introduced by the Framers. These limitations were not intended necessarily to restrict executive authority, so much as to protect the states from federal domination. Among these limitations: restrictions of army (but not naval) appropriations to a maximum of two years;[70] and (2) restrictions on the justifications for calling the state militia into federal service.[71] The restriction on army appropriations was the result of a proposal on August 10, 1787, by Elbridge Gerry that the peacetime army be limited to a few thousand men. He declared his opposition to the absence of a "check . . . [against] standing armies in time of peace."[72] On August 20, Charles Pinckney proposed the language: "No troops shall be kept up in time of peace, but by consent of the Legislature," in addition to the restriction that "no grants of money shall be made by the Legislature for supporting military Land forces, for more than one year at a time."[73] This proposed prohibition of a standing army was rejected.

The standing army was a critical prerequisite of presidential war powers. Since the state militia was not under the command of the President until and unless called by Congress to federal service, the absence of a standing army would have undermined the recognition by the Framers of lawful unilateral presidential war-making. Thus, on December 21, 1787, Hamilton wrote in opposition to limitations on Congress' discretion to fund for the national defense: "[T]he United States would then exhibit the most extraordinary spectacle which the world has yet seen—that of a nation incapacitated by its Constitution to prepare for defense, before it was actually invaded."[74] Hamilton later noted that in balancing the benefits and risks of congressional discretion, "it is better to hazard the abuse of confidence than to embarrass the government and endanger the public safety by impolitic restrictions on the legislative authority."[75] Hamilton rejected the threat of war-making conspiracies between Congress and the President, which had been offered as one reason to prohibit standing armies.[76] Ultimately, the Constitution did not prohibit a standing army. This decision by the Framers left the President with the *de facto* ability to "make" war. In light of the Framers' August 17 vote to reserve in the President the power to "make" war in emergencies, the Framers' decision not to prohibit a standing army hardly could have been a surprise. A vote against a standing army would have taken away from the President with one hand that which was given with the other. The vote in favor of a standing army confirms the intention of the Framers, manifested on August 17, to grant the President emergency war-making powers.

Another source of congressional involvement in war-making is the necessary-and-proper clause, granting Congress power to "make all laws which shall be necessary and proper for carrying into execution the foregoing powers, and all other powers vested by this Constitution in the government of the United States, or in any department or officer thereof."[77] Gerry objected to the addition of the necessary-and-proper clause by the Committee of Detail, as did Mason who noted that the "state legislatures have no security for powers now presumed to remain to them, or the people for their rights."[78] Jefferson's view, as expressed in 1791, was quite different. The Constitution was, he said, "enacted to lace . . . up [Congress] straitly within the enumerated powers, and those without which, as means, these powers could not be carried into effect."[79]

The necessary-and-proper clause represented a major departure from the Articles of Confederation, which barred Congress from exercising any power not expressly granted. Professor Laurence Tribe states the following general rule of implied legislative powers flowing from the necessary-and-proper clause:

> The exercise by Congress of power ancillary to an enumerated source of authority is constitutionally valid, so long as the ancillary power does not conflict with external limitations such as those of the Bill of Rights and of federalism.[80]

The basis for this construction of the necessary-and-proper clause is found in the 1819 Supreme Court opinion in *McCullock v. Maryland*.[81] There, the Court, in an opinion written by Chief Justice Marshall, held:

> Let the end be legitimate, let it be within the scope of the Constitution, and all means which are appropriate, which are plainly adopted to that end, which are not prohibited, but consistent with the letter and spirit of the Constitution, are constitutional.[82]

Unlike Congress, the President was not granted the power to do that which is "necessary and proper" to carry out his constitutional powers. He was, however, granted an "executive power,"[83] and the authorization to "take care that the laws be faithfully executed."[84] These grants of executive power were not fully described by the Framers. The views of the Framers on the nature of executive power, however, can be inferred from their debate on whether the executive should be singular or plural. James Wilson, Chairman of the Committee of Detail, believed in a strong executive, "a single magistrate, as giving most energy, dispatch, and responsibility to the office."[85] His views were consistent with those of the Chairman of the Committee of Style, Gouverneur Morris, who explained why Congress should not elect the President as follows:

> Our Country is an extensive one. We must either then renounce the blessings of the Union, or provide an Executive with sufficient vigor to pervade every part of it. . . . The Legislature will continually seek to aggrandise & perpetuate themselves; and will seize those critical moments produced by war, invasion or convulsion for that purpose. It is necessary then that the Executive Magistrate should be the guardian of the people, even of the lower classes, agst Legislative tyranny, against the Great & the wealthy who in the course of things will necessarily compose the Legislative body. . . .[86]

The views of Wilson and Morris prevailed when the Convention voted for a single executive.

Madison did not interpret the executive powers so broadly. He considered the Constitution's grant of executive power to the President as nothing more than an authorization "that a national Executive . . . be instituted with power to carry into effect the national law."[87] To the contrary, Hamilton argued that the President's enumerated Article II powers were not a "complete and perfect specification" of his executive powers. Rather, only some powers are specified, "leaving the rest to flow from the general grant of that [executive] power. . . ."[88] Hamilton's broad interpretation of executive power was accepted in 1926 by the Supreme Court in *Myers v. United States*.[89] Hamilton believed, moreover, that this broad executive power applied directly to the field of foreign affairs.

> The President is the Constitutional EXECUTOR of the laws. Our treaties, and the laws of nations, form a part of the law of the land. He, who is to execute the laws, must first judge for himself of their meaning. In order to the observance of that conduct which the laws of nations, combined with our treaties, prescribed to this country, in reference to the present war in Europe, it was necessary for the President to judge for himself, whether there was anything in our treaties, incompatible with an adherence to neutrality.[90]

In summary, the Framers granted Congress numerous war powers: to grant letters of marque and reprisal, to set the rules of capture, to make rules governing the military, to call forth the militia, to make appropriations, and to declare war.[91] But the Framers expressly withdrew from Congress the power to "make" war, reserving that power implicitly to the President, named the President the Commander-in-Chief, granted the President the power to make treaties with the advice and consent of the Senate, and made the President responsible for executing federal law. The Framers designed this array to create a balance between the two branches. Each has enormous power; neither can long ignore the other. For this reason, extreme arguments in favor of either branch are doomed. The most easily supported conclusion is that neither branch is the war-making branch; each branch has a specific set of war-making functions. The balance favors the President in the short run and Congress in the long run. Contrary to the suggestion of some,[92] the Framers did not create spheres of "shared" constitutional power for the President and Congress. Each branch has its own powers, separate and distinct, which affect the legal authority to wage war.[93]

Early Examples of Presidential War-making

One way to tell what people mean when they say something is to see what they do after they say it. It is not, of course, the case that the President's exercise of power proves that he has been granted that power by the Constitution. However, a review of presidential war-making by the earliest presidents might shed some light on what war powers the early presidents thought they had and what power their contemporaries allowed them to exercise.[94]

President Washington

In 1790, President Washington faced a diplomatic crisis caused by the seizure by Spain of British vessels in Nootka Sound, Vancouver. The question of which side, if any, to favor was difficult. Although Washington wished to avoid war with powerful Great Britain, he also wished to appease Spain, which controlled New Orleans and the mouth of the Mississippi River. President Washington unilaterally decided to remain neutral but to communicate provisos to both sides. Through his emissaries, the President warned Spain that the U.S. would not remain neutral if Spain failed to "yield our right to the common use of the [Mississippi River]. . . ."[95] He warned Britain that U.S. neutrality would end if Britain pursued "conquests" of lands contiguous to the United States, particularly what is now Louisiana, Alabama, and Florida. President Washington undertook these steps pursuant to his foreign affairs powers, without congressional approval.

Later in the Washington presidency, on February 1, 1793, France declared war against Britain. In response, on April 22, 1793, President Washington declared peace. It will be recalled that the Constitutional Convention had considered but rejected the idea of granting Congress the power to declare peace.[96] However, the Convention did not expressly grant the President this power. Thus did President Washington's action cause a serious debate, memorialized by Hamilton and Madison in the exchange between "Pacificus" and "Helvidius," respectively.[97] President Washington's action precipitating this debate was his declaration that the United States would remain neutral in the war between France and Great Britain.[98] Ultimately, Congress endorsed the President's neutrality proclamation by the Neutrality Act passed June 5, 1794.[99]

The clearest example of unilateral war-making by President Washington occurred in August of 1794, when General "Mad" Anthony Wayne defeated a force of the Miami Indians in the Battle of Fallen Timbers. This military action was undertaken without express congressional authorization, such as a declaration of war. It is true that in 1792 Congress had authorized the President to muster "such number of cavalry as, in his judgment, may be necessary for the protection of the frontiers."[100] It is also true that on September 29, 1789, Congress had authorized the President to call forth the militia "for the purpose . . . of protecting the inhabitants of the frontiers . . . from the hostile incursions of the Indians. . . ."[101] Pursuant to this congressional authorization, President Washington had written, on October 6, 1789, to Governor Arthur St. Clair of the Northwest Territory, directing him to muster 1,500 Virginia and Pennsylvania militiamen:

> The said militia to act in conjunction with the federal troops, in such operations, offensive or defensive, as you, and the commanding officer of the troops, conjointly, shall judge necessary for the public service, and the protection of the inhabitants and the posts.[102]

But this presidential authorization to Governor St. Clair exceeded the grant of authority contained in the September 29, 1789 Act. The President expressly authorized "offensive" action, as Congress had not. On April 30, 1790, Congress stated that the President was authorized to utilize "such part of the militia of the States respectively as he may judge necessary" for "protecting the inhabitants of the frontiers of the United States. . . ."[103]

General Wayne's success at Fallen Timbers was the culmination of a long campaign to answer attacks by the Miami and Shawnee tribes, in particular, on settlements along the Ohio River in the western territories. The President and Congress had received accounts of atrocities such as the massacre of school children, the burning of settlers at the stake, and the enslavement of women.[104] One can imagine that these reports were read by the President and Congress with the sort of alarm expressed by modern federal authorities in response to reports of international terrorism. President Washington responded to the threat with his October 6, 1789 order to Governor St. Clair. Governor St. Clair's troops, under the command of Pennsylvania militia Brigadier General Josiah Harmar, marched in 1790 against the Miami, burning their corn harvest and villages. However, several detachments of the 1,500-man force were defeated, including one 400-man detachment that lost 183 men.[105]

Harmar's defeat prompted calls in Congress for a larger force, which was authorized. However, the second campaign in November of 1791, under St. Clair's command, was even more disastrous. Of an original force of 2,300 men, only 1,300 arrived at the Miami Valley with the main force, the remainder having deserted or been left behind on detached duty.[106] St. Clair had been warned by Washington to "Beware of Surprise," but was surprised nevertheless by the Miami.[107] St. Clair's force was ambushed; 632 Americans were killed, 264 wounded.[108] St. Clair reported that the "most disgraceful part of the business is that the greatest part of the men threw away their arms and accoutrements, even . . . after the pursuit . . . had ceased. . . ."[109]

The defeat of St. Clair led to further enhancements of the frontier force. President Washington was provoked not only by St. Clair's defeat but also by the establishment by the British, who were in league with the Miami, of Fort Miami, twenty miles inside the western territory of the United States. This was the most recent of such incursions, beginning with Great Britain's refusal (until the Jay Treaty of 1796) to abandon its forts along the southern shores of the Great Lakes, as promised in the Treaty of 1783.[110] President Washington wrote to Congress requesting assistance in establishing an "effectual preparation for an event, which, notwithstanding the endeavors . . . to avert it, may, by circumstances beyond our control, be forced upon us."[111] Congress authorized 5,000 regulars, of which 3,229 accompanied General Wayne to Fort Washington (now Cincinnati, Ohio).

Without consulting Congress, however, President Washington caused the following order to be issued by Secretary Knox to General Wayne: "If, therefore, in the course of your operations against the Indian enemy, it should become necessary to dislodge the [British] party at the [fort located at the] rapids of the Miami, you are hereby authorized, in the name of the President of the United States, to do it. . . ."[112] Although General Wayne was also cautioned to treat the British with "politeness,"[113] General Wayne led 1,000 of his troops against a force of 500 Miami at Fallen Timbers near Fort Miami on August 20, 1794. On August 21, he received from the British Commander, Major William Campbell, a message asking why he was approaching Fort Miami. General Wayne replied:

> [W]ere you entitled to an answer, the most full and satisfactory one was announced to you from the muzzles of my small arms, yesterday morning, in the action against the horde of savages in the vicinity of your post, which terminated gloriously to the American arms. . . . [Had the Indians been] driven under the influence of the post and guns you mention, they would not have much impeded the progress of the victorious army under my command, as no such post was established at the commencement of the present war between the Indians and the United States.[114]

General Wayne demanded that the British withdraw. They did not. General Wayne destroyed "everything within view of the fort," and the British did not retaliate.[115] Wayne's victory contributed to the August 1795 Treaty of Greenville.[116]

The action undertaken at Fallen Timbers was not expressly authorized by Congress. President Washington's order to General Wayne exceeded the bounds of the Act of September 29, 1789, granting the President authority to call forth the militia to protect frontier settlers from Indians.[117] Congress had, on September 29, 1789, authorized the President to undertake actions to protect settlers from "incursions of the Indians." Congress had authorized the President to take what action he thought necessary for this purpose. But Congress did not authorize President Washington to do what he did; namely, to authorize "operations, offensive or defensive."

President Washington's order to General Wayne, as an early example of unilateral presidential war-making, suggests that, while not endorsed unanimously, the idea of presidential war-making was a part of mainstream thought in the late eighteenth century. It is true that Congress approved defensive action against the Indians and financed the actions against the Miami and the British.[118] However, Congress never explicitly authorized the President's offensive military actions.

In the same year, President Washington put down the Whiskey Rebellion in the western counties of Pennsylvania.[119] Congress had imposed a national excise tax upon the production of whiskey in 1790. For three years, farmers in these counties had resisted the tax; when the President sought to bring them to justice in the courts in 1794, the marshal who attempted to serve process was kidnapped.

On September 15, 1794, President Washington, on the basis of his authority as national executive, issued a proclamation threatening the rebels.[120]

Whereas certain violent and unwarrantable proceedings have lately taken place tending to obstruct the operation of the laws of the United States for raising a revenue upon spirits distilled within the same, enacted pursuant to express authority delegated in the Constitution of the United States, which proceedings are subversive of good order, contrary to the duty that every citizen owes to his country and to the laws, and of a nature dangerous to the very being of a government; and

Whereas it is the particular duty of the Executive "to take care that the laws be faithfully executed," and not only that duty but the permanent interests and happiness of the people require that every legal and necessary step should be pursued as well to prevent such violent and unwarrantable proceedings as to bring to justice the infractors of the laws and secure obedience thereto:

Now, therefore, I, George Washington, President of the United States, do by these presents most earnestly admonish and exhort all persons whom it may concern to refrain and desist from all unlawful combinations and proceedings whatsoever having the object or tending to obstruct the operation of the laws aforesaid. . . .[121]

On September 30, President Washington left Philadelphia for Bedford, Pennsylvania to inspect the federal troops. On October 21, he left the Governor of Virginia, "Light Horse Harry" Lee, in command of the troops. Lee and the militia marched on the western counties and suppressed the insurrection.[122]

President Washington's Proclamation reads as a textbook description of enforcement by the chief executive of congressional acts. Congress having outlawed certain activity, the President sought to enforce the will of Congress. The means ultimately used by President Washington to end the Whiskey Rebellion was the state militia of Pennsylvania, New Jersey, Maryland, and Virginia, which were called out by an act of Congress.[123] Thus did the Washington presidency present examples of both Congress' and the President's exercise of power over the military.

President Adams

In 1796, France was at war with Great Britain. The United States had declared its neutrality in this war between the great naval powers. In that year, the French decided to seize any American vessel that failed to carry a list of crewmembers. Pursuant to this policy, many American ships were captured between July 1796 and June 1797.[124] Nevertheless, President Adams hoped to avoid war. He also expressed, in his inaugural address, that failing a return to "friendship" with France, his intention "to lay the facts before the Legislature, that they may consider what further measures [such as declaration of war] the honor and interest of the Government and its constituents demand. . . ."[125] Despite his interest in accommodating Congress, President Adams believed in a strong national executive, without which "there can be no peace, order, liberty, or Property in Society."[126]

President Adams lost some of his interest in a rapprochement with France when France expelled the U.S. Ambassador, Charles Pinckney. President Adams convened Congress in a special session to propose an increase in the size of the army, the arming of merchant vessels, and the construction of frigates to protect convoys. Congress refused to authorize any such steps, but did authorize the President to deploy three frigates to protect U.S. commerce.[127] On April 18, 1797, President Adams unilaterally authorized the arming of merchant vessels sailing to the East Indies, but not those sailing to Europe or the West Indies.[128]

On January 24, 1798, the President solicited the views of his Cabinet on the question of whether he should ask Congress to declare war.

Attorney General Charles Lee thought he should. However, Secretary of War James McHenry, who relied heavily on the advice of Alexander Hamilton, urged undeclared hostility.

> An express declaration of hostility . . . would . . . subject us to all the chances of evil which can accrue from the vengeance of a nation stimulated by . . . extraordinary success. . . . A mitigated hostility will be the most likely to fall in with the general feeling, while it leaves a door open for negotiation, and secures some chances to avoid some of the extremities of a formal war.[129]

While he considered McHenry's advice, President Adams manifested his belief in executive discretion in foreign affairs during his dispute with Congress over the "XYZ" affair. President Adams had sent U.S. envoys to France in the hope of avoiding war. On March 4, 1798, President Adams received confidential messages from these envoys indicating the failure of their mission and revealing that French Foreign Ministry agents had attempted to bribe them. These messages encouraged President Adams to redouble his efforts to prepare for war with France, and President Adams so advised Congress. Congress asked the President to release the envoys' dispatches for congressional review. Although such disclosure would have helped the President in his attempt to nudge Congress away from neutrality, the President refused, fearing reprisals against the U.S. envoys in France.[130] After much debate during March and April, the President submitted the messages to Congress with one change: the names of the French agents were deleted and replaced by the designations, X, Y, and Z. The disclosure of the messages did turn U.S. sentiment against France.

In March, during the debate about whether to disclose the XYZ messages, the President again solicited his Cabinet's views on the need for a declaration of war. Attorney General Lee again urged the President to seek such a declaration. Secretary of War McHenry again urged the opposite: a "qualified hostility," which "while it secures the objects essential and preparatory to a state of open war, involves in it the fewest evils. . . ."[131] The result was the so-called "quasi-war" with France.[132] Enraged by the XYZ dispatches, Congress appropriated funds for the construction of forts and authorized the President at his discretion to raise an army. Congress also appropriated funds for additional frigates for the protection of sea lines of communication.[133]

Subsequently, Adams ordered Captain Richard Dale, the commander of one of the newly purchased vessels, the U.S.S. *Ganges,* to protect U.S. jurisdiction at sea by patrolling the mid-Atlantic coast, but to recognize that his authority was not unlimited. Captain Dale's orders stated:

"Congress possesses exclusively the Power to declare War, grant letters of Marque and Reprisal, and make Rules concerning Captures on Land and Water, and as neither has yet been done, your Operations must accordingly be partial and limited."[134] Captain Dale was ordered:

[If you find an armed vessel] committing Depredation on our Coast or attacking or having taken . . . any vessel . . . , to make every Exertion to prevent the Execution of such unlawful Proceedings, and to defend or liberate or retake the Vessel pursued, attached or captured, and send in the offending Vessel, to some port of the United States, to be delt [sic] with according to Law. . . .[135]

Captain Dale was also ordered:

[If you are] attacked by any armed Vessel . . . , to defend yourself to the Utmost. If the Assailant strikes [her colors], examine her Papers, and if She has not a regular Commission, and then in force, bring her into some Port of the United States, to be tried as a Pirate.[136]

These presidential orders are circumspect, to say the least. However, the Act of April 27, 1798, authorizing the purchase of the frigates, including the *Ganges,* did not expressly authorize employment of these vessels, as had the Act of July 1, 1797, which authorized three frigates to be "manned and employed" at the President's discretion. Therefore, the President's orders to Captain Dale, despite their cautionary language about Congress' powers, exceeded the scope of direct congressional authorization.[137]

President Adams expressed his beliefs about his unilateral powers following the November 1798 arrest by a British squadron of the American sloop, U.S.S. *Baltimore,* under the command of Captain Isaac Phillips. The commander of the British squadron, Captain Loring, ordered the *Baltimore* searched and her fifty-five man crew removed. Fifty men were returned, but five were determined to be British subjects and were impressed into his Majesty's service.

President Adams relieved Captain Phillips of his command and ordered all naval vessels:

. . . [O]n no pretense whatever, [will] you permit the public Vessel of War under your command, to be detained, or searched. . . . If force should be exerted to compel your Submission, you are to resist that force to the utmost of your power—and when overpowered by superior force, you are to Strike your flag and thus yield your Vessel as well as your Men—but never your men without your Vessel.[138]

President Adams was cautious and self-conscious in his exercise of war-making powers. But he demonstrated a belief in a zone of permissible unilateral presidential war-making.

President Jefferson

Early in his presidency, Thomas Jefferson, who viewed the congressional power to declare war as an "effectual check to the Dog of war,"[139] ordered the Navy to defend American commercial vessels in the Mediterranean against the Barbary pirates[140] without congressional declaration of war. President Jefferson had received information indicating that Tripoli had attacked U.S. merchantmen in March of 1801. Consequently, the President sent a squadron of frigates to Gibraltar, under the command of Commodore Richard Dale. When Commodore Dale arrived at Gibraltar, he met two Tripolitan vessels. However, he did not know of Tripoli's declaration of war and so merely blockaded them. President Jefferson wrote to James Madison: "What a pity he did not know of the war, [so that] . . . he might have taken their admiral and his ship."[141] Commodore Dale had learned of the war by his arrival in July of 1801 at Tripoli. Commodore Dale ordered Lieutenant Andrew Sterret, commanding the twelve-gun tender U.S.S. *Enterprise,* to obtain water at Malta. Commodore Dale ordered Mr. Sterret to engage any Tripolitan vessel encountered and not to capture it but instead to "heave all his Guns Over board Cut away his Masts, and leave him In a situation, that he can Just make out to get into some Port."[142] The *Enterprise* did engage and capture a fourteen-gun corsair of the Bey of Tripoli. President Jefferson reported to Congress:

> I sent a small squadron of frigates into the Mediterranean, with assurances to that Power [the Bey of Tripoli] of our sincere desire to remain in peace, but with orders to protect our commerce against the threatened attack. . . . [But the] Bey had already declared war. His cruisers were out. Two had arrived at Gibraltar. Our commerce in the Mediterranean was blockaded and that of the Atlantic in peril. The arrival of our squadron dispelled the danger. One of the Tripolitan cruisers, having fallen in with and engaged the small schooner *Enterprise,* commanded by Lieutenant Sterret, which had gone as a tender to our larger vessels, was captured, after a heavy slaughter of her men, without the loss of a single one on our part. . . . Unauthorized by the Constitution, without the sanction of Congress, to go beyond the line of defense, the [Tripolitan] vessel, being disabled from committing further hostilities, was liberated with its crew. The Legislature will doubtless consider whether, by authorizing measures of offense also, they will place our force on an equal footing with that of its adversaries. I communicate all material information on this subject, that in the exercise of this important function confided by the Constitution to the legislature

exclusively their judgment may form itself on a knowledge and consideration of every circumstance of weight.[143]

This message suggests no doubt in President Jefferson's mind about his authority to commit naval forces to combat for defensive purposes in the face of *de facto* war without a congressional declaration of war. It also suggests that President Jefferson recognized a prohibition against offensive presidential war-making. This latter appearance, however, may be misleading. Without Congressional authorization, President Jefferson ordered the *Enterprise,* along with the squadron to which it was attached, to engage Barbary naval forces without confirming actual hostility. On President Jefferson's behalf, General Samuel Smith, Acting Secretary of the Navy, wrote to Commodore Richard Dale on May 30, 1801:

> Recent accounts received from the consul of the United States, employed near the regencies of Algiers, Tunis and Tripoli, give cause to fear, that they will attack our commerce, if unprotected, within the Mediterranean; but particularly, such apprehension is justified by absolute threats on the part of the Dey of Tripoli.
>
> Under such circumstances, it is thought probable, that a small squadron of well appointed frigates appearing before their ports, will have a tendency to prevent their breaking the peace which has been made, and which has subsisted for some years, between them and the United States. It is also thought, that such a squadron, commanded by some of our most gallant officers, known to be stationed in the Mediterranean, will give confidence to our merchants, and tend greatly to increase the commerce of the country within those seas.
>
> I am therefore instructed by the President to direct, that you proceed with all possible expedition, with the squadron under your command, to the Mediterranean. . . .
>
> On your arrival at Gibraltar, you will be able to ascertain whether all or any of the Barbary powers shall have declared war against the United States. . . .
>
> From thence proceed again to Algiers. If there should be no hostile appearance on the part of those powers, and you should be well assured that no danger is to be apprehended from either of them, you may on the 15th October, commence your return homeward; but if there should be any cause for apprehension from either of those powers, you must place your ships in a situation to chastise them, in case of their declaring war or committing hostilities, and not commence your return to the United States, until the first day of December. . . .
>
> But should you find on your arrival at Gibraltar, that all the Barbary powers have declared war against the United States, you will then distribute your force in such a manner, as your judgment shall direct, so as best to protect our commerce and chastise their insolence—by sinking, burning,

or destroying their ships and vessels wherever you shall find them. The better to enable you to form a just determination, you are herewith furnished with a correct state of the strength and situation of each of the Barbary powers. The principal strength you will see, is that of Algiers. The force of Tunis and Tripoli is contemptible, and might be crushed with any one of the frigates under your command.

Should Algiers alone have declared war against the United States, you will cruise off that port so as effectually to prevent anything from going in or coming out, and you will sink, burn, or otherwise destroy their ships and vessels wherever you find them.

Should the Dey of Tripoli have declared war, (as he has threatened) against the United States, you will then proceed direct to that port, where you will lay your ship in such a position as effectually to prevent any of their vessels from going in or out. The Essex and Enterprize by cruising well on towards Tunis, will have it in their power to intercept any vessels which they have captured. By disguising your ships, it will be some weeks before they will know that the squadron is cruising in the Mediterranean, and give you a fair chance of punishing them.

If Tunis alone, or in concert with Tripoli, should have declared war against the United States, you will chastise them in like manner—by cruising with the squadron, from the small island of Maratimo near the island of Sicily, to Cape Blanco on the Barbary shore, you may effectually prevent the corsairs of either from intercepting our commerce in the material part of the Mediterranean Sea, and may intercept any prizes they may have made.[144]

The operating order to Commodore Dale is so belligerent that it cannot be read in any way which denies President Jefferson's clear intention to wage war unilaterally at any provocation. The question of whether Jefferson's message to Congress about the need for congressional approval prior to "go beyond the line of defense" is cynical is for the historians.[145] For the purpose of legal analysis, it is enough to suggest that the operating order to Commodore Dale establishes that in practice Jefferson believed in unilateral presidential war-making. Jefferson was not a delegate to the Constitutional Convention, so his views are not as indicative as would be a former delegate's. But Jefferson's actions indicate by example, as do those of Washington and Adams,[146] that, under some circumstances, the idea of presidential war-making was acceptable to the Founding Fathers.

Conclusion

The Framers did not codify the war powers. Neither the language of the Constitution nor the records of the debate at the Constitutional Convention support sweeping or extreme conclusions about the balance of power between Congress and the President. Two narrow and uncontroversial conclusions, however, can be drawn. First, the President is empowered unilaterally to "repel sudden attacks." This power tends to endow the President with initiative in the war powers balance. This advantage was exercised to varying degrees by Presidents Washington, Adams, and Jefferson. Second, the Congress is empowered to appropriate the national treasure, and to undertake other actions, such as calling out the militia, which have a long-run impact on war-making, whether initiated by the President or by Congress. The next chapter examines how the courts have viewed presidential war-making.

Notes

1. *See generally* S. MORISON, SOURCES AND DOCUMENTS ILLUS-TRATING THE AMERICAN REVOLUTION 1764–1788 AND THE FOR-MATION OF THE FEDERAL CONSTITUTION 180–181 (2d ed. 1975).

2. Articles of Confederation, Article IX.

3. F. MARKS, INDEPENDENCE ON TRIAL: FOREIGN AFFAIRS AND THE MAKING OF THE CONSTITUTION 4 (2d ed., 1986) ("MARKS"). *See also* R. HORSMAN, EXPANSION AND AMERICAN INDIAN POLICY, 1783–1812 (1967).

4. *See generally* Van Tyne, "Sovereignty in the American Revolution: An Historic Study," 12 AM. HIST. REV. 529, 539–545 (1907). *See also* G. WASHINGTON, 9 WRITINGS OF GEORGE WASHINGTON 187–188 (J. Sparks, ed., 1858).

5. MARKS, 5–6, 10. *See also* F. PRUCHA, THE SWORD OF THE REPUBLIC: THE UNITED STATES ARMY ON THE FRONTIER (1969); S. BENNIS, PINCKNEY'S TREATY, AMERICA'S ADVANTAGE FROM EUROPE'S DIS-TRESSES, 1783, 1800 (1960); C. NETTELS, THE EMERGENCE OF A NATIONAL ECONOMY, 1775–1815, 53 (1962); S. BENNIS, JAY'S TREATY: A STUDY IN COMMERCE AND DIPLOMACY, 6 (1923).

6. *See, e.g.,* A. WHITAKER, THE SPANISH-AMERICAN FRONTIER, 1783–1795 (1927); BURNETT (ed.), LETTERS OF THE CONTINENTAL CON-GRESS VII, 623–624 (Hugh Williamson to Thomas Jefferson, December 11, 1784); I DIPLOMATIC CORRESPONDENCE, 1783–1789, 562 (John Jay to U.S. Commissioners, January 14, 1785).

7. MARKS at 17; W. FORD (ed.), LETTERS OF JOSEPH JONES OF VIRGINIA 152–153 (1889) (Joseph L. Jones to James Madison, June 7, 1787).

8. *Id.*

9. MARKS at 20; R. DOWNES, COUNCIL FIRES ON THE UPPER OHIO 282–283 (1940); W. FORD (ed.), XXXII JOURNALS 368 (Report of Secretary Knox to Congress, July 18, 1787), 368 and 478.

10. MARKS at 6; C. RITCHESON, AFTERMATH OF THE REVOLUTION: BRITISH POLICY TOWARD THE UNITED STATES, 1783–1795, 75–79 (1969).

11. MARKS at 9.

12. MARKS at 6, n.5; NETTLES at 52; BENNIS at 6. *See also* RITCHESON at 167 and A. BURT, THE UNITED STATES, GREAT BRITAIN AND BRITISH NORTH AMERICA FROM THE REVOLUTION TO THE ESTABLISHMENT OF PEACE AFTER THE WAR OF 1812, Ch. 6 (1940).

13. E. KEYNES, UNDECLARED WAR: TWILIGHT ZONE OF CONSTITUTIONAL POWER 31 (1982).

14. *See, e.g.,* Reveley, "Constitutional Allocation of the War Powers Between the President and Congress: 1787–1788," 15 VA. J. INT. L. 73, 76 (1974). *See also* W. REVELEY, WAR POWERS OF THE PRESIDENT AND CONGRESS (1981).

15. M. FARRAND, I RECORDS OF THE FEDERAL CONVENTION of 1787, 21 (1911) ("RECORDS").

16. I RECORDS at 21.

17. III RECORDS at 604.

18. I RECORDS at 22 and III RECORDS at 599.

19. *Id.*

20. I RECORDS at 66.

21. *Id.* at 97.

22. *Id.* at 66.

23. *Id.* at 64.

24. *Id.* at 64–65.

25. *Id.* at 70.

26. *Id.*

27. *Id.* at 244.

28. II RECORDS at 341.

29. III RECORDS at 622–625.

30. *Id.* at 292.

31. *Id.*

32. ELLIOT, III THE DEBATES IN THE SEVERAL STATE CONVENTIONS ON THE ADOPTION OF THE FEDERAL CONSTITUTION 58–60 (1836).

33. II RECORDS at 35.

34. *Id.*

35. J. MADISON, THE FEDERALIST, No. 48.

36. II RECORDS at 52–54.

37. II RECORDS at 181–183.

38. *Id.*

39. *Id.* at 185.

40. *See* E. HUZAR, THE PURSE AND THE SWORD: CONTROL OF THE ARMY BY CONGRESS THROUGH MILITARY APPROPRIATIONS (1950).

41. II RECORDS at 275.

42. *Id.* at 278–279.

43. A. SOFAER, WAR FOREIGN AFFAIRS AND CONSTITUTIONAL POWER: THE ORIGINS 4, 57 (1976).

44. J. MADISON, "Federalist No. 58," THE FEDERALIST PAPERS 359 (1961).

45. A. HAMILTON, "Federalist No. 24," THE FEDERALIST PAPERS 158 (1961) (emphasis original).

46. II RECORDS at 318.

47. *Id.* at 319.

48. *Id.*

49. *Id.* at 318.

50. *Id.*

51. *Id.*

52. II RECORDS at 319.

53. ELLIOT, 2 DEBATES IN THE STATE CONVENTIONS 528.

54. Rostow, "The Reinterpretation Debate and Constitutional Law," 137 U. PA. L. REV. 1451, 1458 (1989) (quoting Madison, THE FEDERALIST No. 47 and No. 48 (B. Wright, ed., 1961)).

55. II RECORDS at 319.

56. *See* May, "The President Shall be Commander-in-Chief" (1787-1789), in THE ULTIMATE DECISION: THE PRESIDENT AS COMMANDER-IN-CHIEF 3-19 (E. May, ed., 1960).

57. A. SOFAER, FOREIGN AFFAIRS AND CONSTITUTIONAL POWER: THE ORIGINS 117 (1976).

58. A. HAMILTON, THE FEDERALIST, No. 69 (March 15, 1788) (emphasis original).

59. 7 WORKS OF ALEXANDER HAMILTON 746-747 (J. Hamilton, ed., 1857) (emphasis original).

60. A. HAMILTON, THE FEDERALIST NO. 69 (March 15, 1788). *Cf.* *U.S. v. Stuart,* _____ U.S. _____, 109 S.Ct. 1183, 1196 (1989) (Scalia, J., concurring).

61. A. HAMILTON, THE FEDERALIST NO. 69 (March 15, 1788).

62. *Id.*

63. A. HAMILTON, THE FEDERALIST NO. 70 (March 15, 1788).

64. J. LOCKE, THE SECOND TREATISE OF GOVERNMENT 92 (1952). *See also* J. JAY, THE FEDERALIST NO. 64, 392-393 (C. Rossiter, ed., 1961) (emphasis original).

65. U.S. CONST., Art. I, Sec. 8, Cl. 11. *See also* Lobel, "Covert War and Congressional Authority: Hidden War and Forgotten Power," 134 U. PA. L. REV. 1035 (1986); U.S. CONST., Art. I, Sec. 8, Cl. 15; U.S. CONST., Art. I, Sec. 8, Cl. 14.

66. *See, e.g.,* E. KEYNES, UNDECLARED WAR 37 (1982); M. PUSEY, THE WAY WE GO TO WAR 53 (1969).

67. *Duncan v. Kahanamoku,* 327 U.S. 304, 342 (1946) (Burton, J., dissenting).

68. J. MAURICE, HOSTILITIES WITHOUT DECLARATION OF WAR 1700-1870, 12-26 (1883); DE CONDE, THE QUASI-WAR: THE POLITICS AND DIPLOMACY OF THE UNDECLARED WAR WITH FRANCE 1797-1801 (1966).

69. E. CARSTEN, THE PRESENT LAW OF WAR AND NEUTRALITY 96 (1954) ("Between 1700 and 1870, declarations of war prior to hostilities only occurred in one case out of ten. . . ."); CONGRESS, THE PRESIDENT, AND THE WAR POWERS: HEARINGS BEFORE THE SUBCOMM. ON NATIONAL SECURITY POLICY AND SCIENTIFIC DEVELOPMENTS OF THE HOUSE COMM. ON FOREIGN AFFAIRS, 91st Cong., 2d Sess., 135–167, 137 (1970) (Testimony of Professor Abram Chayes). *See also Bas v. Tingy,* 4 U.S. (4 Dall.) 37, 45 (1800); *Talbot v. Seeman,* 4 U.S. (4 Dall.) 34 (1800).

70. U.S. CONST., Art. I, Sec. 8, Cl. 12.

71. U.S. CONST., Art. I, Sec. 8, Cl. 15.

72. II RECORDS at 329.

73. *Id.* at 341. *See also* ELLIOTT, I THE DEBATES IN THE SEVERAL STATE CONVENTIONS ON THE ADOPTION OF THE FEDERAL CONSTITUTION 370-371 (1836). 74. A. HAMILTON, THE FEDERALIST No. 25.

75. A. HAMILTON, THE FEDERALIST No. 26 at 159.

76. A. HAMILTON, THE FEDERALIST No. 25.

77. U.S. CONST., Art. II, Sec. 8, Cl. 18. *See* Van Alstyne, "The Role of Congress in Determining Incidental Powers of the President and the Federal Courts: A Comment on the Horizontal Effect of the Sweeping Clause," 40 LAW & CONTEMP. PROBS. 102; C. WARREN, THE MAKING OF THE CONSTITUTION 486–488 (1937).

78. II RECORDS at 633.

79. III RECORDS at 363.

80. L. TRIBE, AMERICAN CONSTITUTIONAL LAW 227 (1978).

81. 17 U.S. (4 Wheat.) 316 (1819). *See also Missouri v. Holland,* 252 U.S. 416 (1920).

82. 17 U.S. at 421.

83. U.S. CONST., Art. II, Sec. 1.

84. U.S. CONST., Art. II, Sec. 3.

85. I RECORDS at 65.

86. II RECORDS at 52–54.

87. I RECORDS at 67.

88. "Pacificus," No. 1 (June 29, 1793), 15 THE PAPERS OF ALEXANDER HAMILTON 39 (H. Syrett, ed., 1969).

89. 272 U.S. 52, 118 (1926). *See also* Rostow, "War, Foreign Affairs, and the Constitution," ENCYCLOPEDIA OF THE AMERICAN CONSTITUTION 2007, 2009 (L. Levy, K. Karst, and D. Mahoney, eds., 1986) ("Hamilton's view of the Presidency dominates the judicial opinions, the pattern of practice, the writings of scholars, and the pronouncements of senators and representatives.").

90. "Pacificus" as quoted in E. CORWIN, THE PRESIDENT: OFFICE AND POWERS 1787–1957 at 195 (1957).

91. The Supreme Court has recognized broad congressional war powers. *See, e.g., Lichter v. U.S.,* 334 U.S. 742 (1948) (excess profits tax); *Woods v. Cloyd W. Miller Co.,* 333 U.S. 138 (1948) (post-war rent control); *Bowles v. Willingham,* 321 U.S. 503 (1944) (rent control); *Yakus v. U.S.,* 321 U.S. 414 (1944) (price

controls); *Korematsu v. U.S.*, 323 U.S. 214 (1944) (detention and relocation of ethnic Japanese); *Hirabayashi v. U.S.*, 320 U.S. 81 (1943) (curfew on ethnic Japanese); *Debs v. U.S.*, 249 U.S. 211 (1919) (seditious speech).

92. *E.g.*, Koplow, "Constitutional Bait and Switch: Executive Reinterpretation of Arms Control Treaties," 137 U. PA. L. REV. 1353 (1989).

93. *See* Block, Casey, & Rivkin, "The Senate's Pie-In-The-Sky Treaty Interpretation Power and the Quest for Legislative Supremacy," 137 U. PA. L. REV. 1481, 1482 (1989).

94. It is worth emphasizing as a caveat that anecdotal examples of presidential war-making do not dispositively prove anything about the legality of presidential war-making. They are worth mentioning, however, to provide an indication of where the holders of war powers, who were contemporaries of the convention delegates, saw the limits of their powers.

95. A. SOFAER, WAR, FOREIGN RELATIONS AND CONSTITUTIONAL POWER: THE ORIGINS 102 (1976) ("SOFAER") (quoting May 29, 1790 letter from Gouverneur Morris to Thomas Jefferson).

96. II RECORDS at 319.

97. 4 THE WORKS OF ALEXANDER HAMILTON 437–444 (H. Lodge, ed., 1906); 6 THE WRITINGS OF JAMES MADISON 138–188 (G. Hunt, ed., 1906).

98. April 22, 1793 Proclamation, 1 AMERICAN STATE PAPERS: FOREIGN RELATIONS 140 (W. Lawrie and M. Clark, eds., 1833).

99. *See* Rostow, "War, Foreign Affairs, and the Constitution," ENCYCLOPEDIA OF THE AMERICAN CONSTITUTION 2007, 2010 (L. Levy, K. Karst, and D. Mahoney, eds., 1986).

100. Act of March 5, 1792, Sec. 2, 1 Stat. 241.

101. Act of September 29, 1789, Sec. 5, 1 Stat. 95, 96.

102. SOFAER at 120.

103. SOFAER at 120–121 (quoting Act of April 30, 1790, Sections 1, 16, 1 Stat. 119, 121).

104. E. HOYT, AMERICA'S WARS & MILITARY EXCURSIONS 96–98 (1987) ("HOYT").

105. W. HASSLER, THE PRESIDENT AS COMMANDER IN CHIEF 22–23 (1971) ("HASSLER"). *See also* HOYT at 97; Adams, "The Harmar Expedition of 1790," 50 OHIO ARCH. AND HIST. Q. (1941); Peckham, "Josiah Harmar and His Indian Expedition," 55 OHIO ARCH. AND HIST. Q. (1946).

106. HASSLER at 25.

107. HOYT at 97.

108. HASSLER at 25; HOYT at 98 (900 deaths).

109. HASSLER at 25. *See also* F. WILSON, ARTHUR ST.CLAIR (1944).

110. SOFAER at 124.

111. SOFAER at 125 (quoting Message of May 21, 1794).

112. C. BERDAHL, WAR POWERS OF THE EXECUTIVE IN THE UNITED STATES 62–63 (1921) (quoting FISH, AMERICAN DIPLOMACY 83–84).

113. SOFAER at 125.

114. SOFAER at 125–126.

115. SOFAER at 126.

116. HASSLER at 27–28.

117. Act of September 29, 1789, Ch. 25, 1 Stat. 95, 96.

118. *See, e.g.,* SOFAER at 126–127.

119. *See* L. BALDWIN, WHISKEY REBELS (1939); Cooke, "The Whiskey Insurrection: A Re-Evaluation," 30 PENN. HIST. (1963); Rich, "Washington and the Whiskey Insurrection," 65 PENN. MAG. OF HIST. AND BIO. (1941); President Washington's Sixth Annual Message to Congress, J. RICHARDSON, I MESSAGES AND PAPERS OF THE PRESIDENTS 1789–1897 at 154–156 (1899) ("RICHARDSON"); HASSLER at 28.

120. *See contra* HASSLER at 29 (authority as Commander-in-Chief).

121. Proclamation of September 15, 1794, RICHARDSON at 116–117.

122. HASSLER at 29–30.

123. "An Act To Provide For Calling Forth the Militia to Execute the Laws of the Union, Suppress Insurrections, and Repel Invasions," Act of May 2, 1792, Ch. 28, 1 Stat. 264. See Proclamations of August 7, 1794 and September 25, 1794, RICHARDSON at 150–154.

124. SOFAER at 139.

125. SOFAER at 140.

126. SOFAER at 132.

127. SOFAER at 140–141.

128. SOFAER at 140.

129. SOFAER at 142.

130. SOFAER at 134.

131. SOFAER at 142.

132. *See, e.g.,* Sofaer, "The Presidency, War and Foreign Affairs: Practice Under the Framers," 40 L. AND CONT. PROB. 12, 19–20 (1976); G. ALLEN, OUR NAVAL WAR WITH FRANCE (1967); DeCONDE, THE QUASI-WAR: THE POLITICS AND DIPLOMACY OF THE UNDECLARED WAR WITH FRANCE 1797–1801 (1966); J. MAURICE, HOSTILITIES WITHOUT DECLARATION OF WAR 1700–1870 at 12–26 (1883).

133. SOFAER at 147–154 (Act of April 27, 1798).

134. SOFAER at 156.

135. SOFAER at 156.

136. SOFAER at 156.

137. *Compare* SOFAER at 156–157.

138. SOFAER at 159.

139. Letter to James Madison, September 6, 1789, 15 THE PAPERS OF THOMAS JEFFERSON, 392, 397 (J. Boyd, ed., 1958).

140. *See* G. ALLEN, OUR NAVY AND THE BARBARY CORSAIRS (1965); H. NASH, THE FORGOTTEN WARS, 1798–1805, 287–289 (1961); S. BLYTH, HISTORY OF THE WAR BETWEEN THE UNITED STATES AND TRIPOLI AND OTHER BARBARY POWERS, 115–125 (1806).

141. SOFAER at 210.

142. SOFAER at 212.

143. RICHARDSON at 326–327. *See* 2 Stat. 129 (1802).

144. W. GOLDSMITH, I GROWTH OF PRESIDENTIAL POWER: A DOCUMENTARY HISTORY 373–376 (1974) (citing I STATE PAPERS AND DOCUMENTS OF THE UNITED STATES 75–78 (1814)) (reprinted with permission of Professor Goldsmith); 1 NAVAL DOCUMENTS RELATED TO THE UNITED STATES WARS WITH THE BARBARY POWERS, 465–467 (1939); Sofaer, "The Presidency, War and Foreign Affairs: Practice Under the Framers," 40 L. & CONT. PROB. 12 (1976).

145. *See* SOFAER at 212–213. The President was later granted broad authorization to make war against Tripoli. SOFAER at 215–216.

146. James Madison, a delegate to the Constitutional Convention, acted as Commander-in-Chief during the War of 1812. However, the War of 1812 was a war declared by Congress. President Madison's actions were not, therefore, unilateral.

2

Judicial Interpretation

[I]t is impossible to foresee or define the extent and variety of national exigencies, or the correspondent extent and variety of the means which may be necessary to satisfy them. The circumstances that endanger the safety of nations are infinite, and for this reason no constitutional shackles can wisely be imposed on the powers to which the care of it is committed.[1]

The Constitution's Framers wanted a President, not a King.[2] Indeed, the Articles of Confederation, ratified just six years before the Constitutional Convention of 1787, did not provide for a national executive at all. Even when the Constitution did create an executive, it limited executive discretion by granting to Congress the power to declare war and to ratify treaties, thus inviting a "struggle for power" in the area of foreign relations.[3] Just as the Framers did not mean to render the President omnipotent, however, they did not mean for the President to be an impotent, titular executive. The Framers did designate the President the primary agent for the conduct of foreign affairs, name him Commander-in-Chief, and grant him the executive powers.[4] Each of these three grants empowers the President under certain circumstances to use the military without congressional preauthorization.

The Foreign Affairs Power

Article II of the Constitution contains the President's enumerated powers. Among them is the "power, by and with the advice and consent of the Senate, to make treaties, provided two thirds of the Senators present concur. . . ."[5] By making treaties, the President sets the nation's foreign policy, which the Senate can bless or not after the fact. Complementing this treaty-making power are the powers to appoint and "receive" ambassadors.[6] Professor Louis Henkin has noted that the "power" to receive ambassadors appears to be more a mere "function" than a full-blown power, more suited to a figurehead than a head of

41

state.[7] Indeed, Alexander Hamilton characterized the power as "more a matter of dignity than of authority."[8] The same might be said of the power to appoint ambassadors. On the other hand, the President's power to recognize foreign ambassadors and appoint his own is significant in that it enables the President to name the diplomatic "players" on the basis of their substantive points of view. One commentator has found "immense authority latent in . . . [the President's] power of recognition."[9] This aspect of the President's foreign affairs power was exercised early on by President Washington when he expelled Minister Genet of France for violating the principles of U.S. neutrality in the war between France and Great Britain.[10] President Jefferson replied to a subsequent official communication from Genet addressed to the "Congress of the United States," as follows:

> As the President is the only channel of communication between the United States and foreign nations, it is from him alone that foreign nations or their agents are to learn what is or has been the will of the nation, and whatever he communicates as such they have a right and are bound to consider as the expression of the nation, and no foreign agent can be allowed to question it.[11]

In modern times, the issue of whether to recognize "Red" China was one of the critical issues in post-war foreign policy. So, the appointment and recognition powers cannot be easily dismissed.

Of course, the President's foreign affairs powers are not limited to appointing and receiving ambassadors. The President's power to direct foreign relations was placed at issue in *United States v. Curtiss-Wright Export Corp.,*[12] where the Supreme Court summarized the President's foreign affairs powers as follows:

> In this vast external realm [of foreign affairs], with its important, complicated, delicate and manifold problems, the President alone has the power to speak or listen as a representative of the nation. He *makes* treaties with the advice and consent of the Senate; but he alone negotiates. Into the field of negotiation the Senate cannot intrude; and Congress itself is powerless to invade it. As Marshall said in his great argument of March 7, 1800, in the House of Representatives, "The President is the sole organ of the nation in its external relations, and its sole representative with foreign nations." Annals, 6th Cong., col. 613.[13]

By this broad chacterization of the President's treaty-making power, the *Curtiss-Wright* Court established a line of demarcation between the President and the Senate: the President speaks for the nation in the international arena and the Senate does not. If the Senate becomes aware of representations made by the President in diplomatic circles that the Senate cannot abide, it can make its displeasure known to the President by a number of methods. Ultimately, the Senate can refuse to ratify the President's treaty. But even under circumstances where the Senate knows before the fact that the President is negotiating a treaty that will not be ratified, the Senate cannot prohibit the treaty negotiations themselves.[14]

Of course, the Senate can preauthorize the President to undertake representations in the field of international relations. Such congressional preauthorization was the predicate giving rise to the *Curtiss-Wright* case. The Curtiss-Wright Corporation was indicted for selling arms to Bolivia in violation of a presidential proclamation issued pursuant to a congressional resolution forbidding such sales. Curtiss-Wright challenged the indictment, contending that it was based on a proclamation founded on an unconstitutional delegation to the President of legislative power. The Court held that even if such a delegation would have been unconstitutional with respect to domestic affairs, it was not unconstitutional with respect to international affairs. The basis for this conclusion was the finding that the determination of appropriate action in the international arena is within the scope of discretionary presidential foreign affairs power. Thus, Congress "delegated" to the President power he already had.

The *Curtiss-Wright* Court clearly stated that the President may exert foreign affairs powers by means not only of legislative authority but also of "the very delicate, plenary and exclusive power of the President as the sole organ of the federal government in the field of international relations—a power which does not require as a basis for its exercise an act of Congress. . . ."[15] The Court continued:

> It is quite apparent that if, in the maintenance of our international relations, embarrassment—perhaps serious embarrassment—is to be avoided and success for our aims achieved, congressional legislation which is to be made effective through negotiation and inquiry within the international field must often accord to the President a degree of discretion and freedom from statutory restriction which would not be admissible were domestic affairs alone involved. Moreover, he, not Congress, has the better opportunity of knowing the conditions which prevail in foreign countries, and especially is this true in time of war. He has his confidential sources of information. He has his agents in the form of diplomatic, consular and other officials. Secrecy in respect of information gathered by them may be highly necessary, and the premature disclosure of it productive of harmful results.

The Court endorsed the idea of congressional participation in foreign relations by means of legislation authorizing presidential action in the international arena. But the Court was equally clear that, while Congress may outline its foreign policy preferences by means of legislation, the President is the nation's sole agent in negotiation and fact-finding. This view is consistent with that of Thomas Jefferson who, at least prior to becoming President, was suspicious of presidential power:

> The transaction of business with foreign nations is executive altogether; it belongs, then, to the head of that department, except as to such portions of it as are specifically submitted to the Senate.[16]

The President's failure to obtain a foreign objective desired by both the President and Congress, therefore, is not subject to second-guessing in any constitutional sense. This is not, of course, to say that the President's failure would not be subject to political consequences; in the political arena, Congress can punish the President to its collective heart's content. But Congress may not limit the President's authority in the diplomatic process itself.

> Indeed, so clearly is this true that the first President refused to accede to a request to lay before the House of Representatives the instructions, correspondence and documents relating to the negotiation of the Jay Treaty— a refusal the wisdom of which was recognized by the House itself and has never since been doubted. In his reply to the request, President Washington said:
> "The nature of foreign negotiations requires caution, and their success must often depend on secrecy; and even when brought to a conclusion a full disclosure of all the measures, demands, or eventual concessions which may have been proposed or contemplated would be extremely impolitic; for this might have a pernicious influence on future negotiations, or produce immediate inconveniences, perhaps danger and mischief, in relation to other powers. The necessity of such caution and secrecy was one cogent reason for vesting the power of making treaties in the President, with the advice and consent of the Senate, the principle on which that body was formed confining it to a small number of members. To admit, then, a right in the House of Representatives to demand and to have as a matter of course all the papers respecting a negotiation with a foreign power would be to establish a dangerous precedent." 1 Messages and Papers of the Presidents, p. 194.[17]

Ultimately, treaties negotiated by the President are subject to scrutiny by the Senate. This procedure provides the Senate with an effective means to induce voluntary presidential disclosure of pertinent facts relating to the treaty. Professor Corwin summarizes Congress' power in foreign affairs in terms of "post-hoc" scrutiny of presidential action, the appropriations power, and the power of impeachment.[18] These are profound powers that no President wisely would ignore. But the Senate ratification procedure itself does not necessarily provide the Senate with any formal means to check the many actions taken in the international arena, whether in the form of diplomatic agreement or not, that do not qualify as treaties subject to Senate ratification.[19] Professor Henkin[20] offers an impressive list of important international agreements never ratified by the Senate as treaties:

- The 1817 agreement with Great Britain disarming the Great Lakes;
- The 1897 agreement of President McKinley to provide troops during the Boxer Rebellion in China;
- The 1905 agreement to place the bankrupt customs houses of Santo Domingo under U.S. control to prevent seizure by European creditors;
- The 1907 agreement with Japan limiting immigration into the United States;
- The 1940 lend-lease agreement with Great Britain;
- The 1945 Yalta and Potsdam agreements.

President Roosevelt provided many examples of unilateral presidential activity in foreign relations in 1941 prior to the formal entry of the United States in World War II. The presidential steps preceding declared belligerency included the March 30, 1941 seizure of sixty-five Axis-controlled ships in American ports, the May 27, 1941 presidential proclamation of an "unlimited emergency" and order to the Navy to "sink on sight" any foreign submarine discovered in U.S. "defensive waters," the presidential authorization to U.S. naval forces to use "depth charges in self-defense against Axis submarines," the September 11, 1941 presidential announcement that "henceforth American patrols would defend the freedom of the seas by striking first at all Axis raiders operating within American defensive areas," and the October 8, 1941 presidential order to United States warships in the Atlantic to destroy any German or Italian sea or air forces encountered.[21]

Political and diplomatic considerations might compel the President to submit his diplomatic actions to Senate review. Foreign sovereigns might require Senate ratification as a precondition to their compliance with diplomatic agreements. But the Constitution itself does not require Senate ratification of all executive diplomatic agreements.

The ability of the President, through the Department of State, unilaterally to undertake a foreign policy not involving a treaty was recognized by the Supreme Court in *Ex parte Republic of Peru*.[22] The *Ex parte Peru* Court considered the question of whether the Republic of Peru, as the owner of a steamship sued in libel for failure to deliver cargo, was immune from suit in the U.S. courts on the basis of a grant of such immunity from the Department of State. This question was answered in the affirmative. The principle at stake, said the Court, was "that Courts may not exercise their jurisdiction, by seizure and detention of the property of a friendly sovereign, as to embarrass the executive arm of the government in conducting foreign relations."[23] The President's view on the matter was given dispositive effect by the Court.

> The certification and the request [by the State Department] that the vessel be declared immune must be accepted by the courts as a conclusive determination by the political arm of the Government that the continued retention of the vessel interferes with the proper conduct of our foreign relations. Upon the submission of this certification to the district court, it became the court's duty, in conformity to established principles, to release the vessel and to proceed no further in the cause.[24]

The Supreme Court went a step further in *Republic of Mexico v. Hoffman*,[25] when it considered whether the courts could recognize a foreign sovereign's claim to immunity from suit in the absence of guidance from the President. The facts were similar to the *Ex parte Peru* case; a vessel had been seized and a foreign sovereign, this time Mexico, claimed ownership and immunity from suit. However, the State Department had not granted immunity to Mexico, as it had to Peru. The "guiding principle" followed by the *Hoffman* Court was that "the courts should not so act as to embarrass the executive arm in its conduct of foreign affairs."[26] The Court noted that one way to embarrass the government would be to nullify a grant of immunity by the President, a step avoided in *Ex parte Peru*.

> But recognition by the courts of an immunity upon principles which the political department of government has not sanctioned may be equally embarrassing to it in securing the protection of our national interests and their recognition by other nations.[27]

Thus, the *Hoffman* Court found even the President's silence determinative of Mexico's request for immunity.

> We can only conclude that it is the national policy not to extend the immunity in the manner now suggested, and that it is the duty of the courts, in a matter so intimately associated with our foreign policy and which may profoundly affect it, not to enlarge an immunity to an extent which the government, though often asked, has not seen fit to recognize.[28]

The rule emerging from the *Ex parte Peru* and *Hoffman* cases is that the courts will treat as conclusive the President's preferences on the treatment to be accorded foreign sovereigns. It is important to note that congressional legislation was not at issue in either of the cases, so neither necessarily stands for the proposition that the President's power to determine the legal status of foreign sovereigns is exclusive of congressional oversight. However, both establish that the President's foreign affairs powers are plenary and do not require congressional sanctification, either before or after the fact, at least when they do not result in treaties.

In *United States v. Belmont*,[29] the Supreme Court confirmed expressly that the President has constitutional authority to make international agreements without congressional assent or ratification. The *Belmont* Court considered the validity of the Litvinov Agreement, by which the President unilaterally recognized the Soviet Union. The *Belmont* Court held that recognition to be within the scope of the President's power to conduct foreign relations and that it did not result in a treaty requiring Senate ratification.

> The recognition, establishment of diplomatic relations, the assignment, and agreement with respect thereto, were all parts of one transaction, resulting in an international compact between the two governments. That the negotiations, acceptance of the assignment and agreements and understandings in respect thereof were within the competence of the President may not be doubted. . . . And in respect of what was done here, the Executive had authority to speak as the sole organ of that government. The assignment and the agreements in connection therewith did not, as in the case of treaties, as that term is used in the treaty making clause of the Constitution (Article II, § 2), require the advice and consent of the Senate.

Having approved the President's role as the "sole organ" of the nation in foreign affairs, the *Belmont* Court offered a distinction between presidential undertakings in foreign affairs that require Senate approval and those that do not.

> A treaty signifies "a compact made between two or more independent nations with a view to the public welfare." . . . But an international compact, as this was, is not always a treaty which requires the participation of the Senate. There are many such compacts, of which a protocol, a modus vivendi, a postal convention, and agreements like that now under consideration are illustrations. . . . [30]

The *Belmont* rule was reaffirmed in another case considering the Litvinov Agreement, *United States v. Pink*.[31] The *Pink* Court, like the *Belmont* Court, granted presidential agreements status equal to treaties as the supreme law of the land. Consistent with *Pink,* the Supreme Court held in *First National City Bank v. Banco Nacional de Cuba:*

[W]here the Executive Branch, charged as it is with the primary responsibility for the conduct of foreign affairs, expressly represents to the Court that application of . . . [a] doctrine would not advance the interests of American foreign policy, that doctrine should not be applied by the courts.[32]

The *Pink* principle continues to be cited with approval. In *Dames & Moore*,[33] the Supreme Court cited *Pink* for the proposition that "the President does have some measure of power to enter into executive agreements without obtaining the advice and consent of the Senate."[34] The *Dames & Moore* Court upheld a series of Executive Orders by Presidents Carter and Reagan suspending claims in American courts against Iranian assets in favor of a tribunal created by agreement between the President and Iran for disposition of Iranian assets "frozen" during the Iran hostage crisis. Since the *Dames & Moore* Court found no conflict between Congress and the President on the question of the propriety of the Executive Orders,[35] the constitutional issue of whether presidential action in foreign affairs could trump the will of Congress was not presented.[36] Thus *Dames & Moore* did not push the frontier of constitutional law but did accomplish the continuation of the *Pink* principle. In summary:

"Executive agreements," whether fashioned by the Executive alone, pursuant to a prior treaty, or with the approval of the Congress, have essentially the same status under both international and domestic law as treaties. Even though their constitutional basis is different, the two types of documents have become almost interchangeable.[37]

Executive agreements have become more numerous than treaties. On January 1, 1972, 947 treaties and 4,359 executive agreements were in force.[38]

Even in foreign affairs, however, the President's power is not absolute. The Supreme Court has limited the President's foreign affairs powers by, for example, preventing the President from unilaterally surrendering a U.S. citizen to a foreign sovereign pursuant to an extradition request.[39]

[T]he Constitution creates no executive prerogative to dispose of the liberty of the individual. . . . There is no executive discretion to surrender him to a foreign government, unless that discretion is granted by law. It necessarily follows that as the legal authority does not exist save as it is given by act of Congress or by the terms of a treaty, it is not enough that statute or treaty does not deny the power to surrender.[40]

One reading of this limitation is that it restricts the President in the substantive conduct of foreign affairs by denying him the ability to grant an extradition request from a foreign power. But such a reading is overly broad, since it ignores that fact that the seizure by the President of a citizen without domestic authorization, such as a warrant from a court, not only is not specified as an executive power under the Constitution, but also is contrary to the Fourth Amendment. The conclusion that the President's power to conduct foreign affairs is limited by the Bill of Rights is not likely to cause surprise, given that such limitation is the role of the Bill of Rights in general.[41]

The President's plenary power to conduct foreign relations enables him to determine unilaterally how to manage relations with foreign states, even though such relationships might lead, either indirectly or directly, to war. A benign executive agreement of recognition of a particular nation might lead the U.S. into a hostile relationship with that nation's adversaries, thus risking war in an indirect way. War might be risked more directly by an executive agreement to supplement the security of a foreign nation whose enemies have threatened but not commenced hostilities. Such an agreement might be designed to avoid war, but nevertheless might subject U.S. forces to the possibility of military involvement. In neither case does the President commit U.S. forces to an existing conflict. In both cases, the President enters into an agreement that carries an inherent potential for war. The courts have not held that the validity of a presidential agreement is undermined by the fact that war is a possible outcome of the agreement.

The Power of the Commander-in-Chief[42]

The Constitution names the President as the "Commander-in-Chief of the Army and Navy of the United States, and of the militia of the several states. . . ."[43] This grant of power to the President is undoubtedly one of the most significant in the Constitution. Nevertheless, the record of the Convention reflects no debate on this critical clause. For this reason, among others, Supreme Court Justice Jackson noted in 1952:

> Just what our forefathers did envision, or would have envisioned had they foreseen modern conditions, must be derived from materials almost as enigmatic as the dreams Joseph was called upon to interpret for Pharaoh. A century and a half of partisan debate and scholarly speculation yields no net result but only supplies more or less apt quotations from respected sources on each side of any question. They largely cancel each other.[44]

The "enigmatic" record of the constitutional debate is consistent with the collective ambivalence expressed by the Framers about the war powers in general: the President, on the one hand, should not have unfettered war-making power and, on the other, should be able to respond to crises affecting national security. The tension in the Framers' ambivalent view is reflected in the views of James Madison and Alexander Hamilton.[45] James Madison, who worried about excessive executive power, emphasized the distinction between the President's power "to conduct a war" and Congress' power to decide "whether a war ought to be commenced, continued, or concluded."[46] Hamilton, on the other hand, favored strong executive war powers.

> [W]hen a foreign nation declares or openly and outwardly makes war upon the United States, they are then by the very fact *already at war,* and any declaration on the part of Congress is nugatory; it is at least unnecessary.[47]

But even Madison moved the Constitutional Convention to delete language in the draft Constitution empowering Congress to "make" war and to replace it with language granting Congress the power to "declare" war. Such a change, said Madison, would leave "to the executive the power to repel sudden attacks."[48] Madison's motion carried, indicating that even in withholding from the President the royal prerogative to declare war, the Framers implicitly granted the President some measure of power to defend the national security without a congressional declaration of war.[49]

Nothing in the record of the constitutional debates indicates that the Framers intended a congressional declaration of war to precede every use of the military by the Commander-in-Chief. Undeclared war was well known to the Framers.[50] Only one in ten military actions between 1700 and 1870 was preceded by a declaration of war.[51] In 1798, for example, President Adams embraced the suggestion of Secretary of War James McHenry not to seek a congressional declaration of war and instead to engage France in a "qualified hostility," which "while it secures the objects essential and preparatory to a state of open war, involves in it the fewest evils. . . ."[52]

This so-called "quasi-war" with France provided the courts with an early opportunity to confirm the lawfulness of undeclared war.[53] On March 31, 1799, the ship *Eliza* and her cargo, belonging to U.S. citizens, was captured by a French privateer on the high seas. The *Eliza* was recaptured on April 21, 1799 by the U.S.S. *Ganges.* The captain of the *Ganges* sought salvage on behalf of himself and his officers and crew pursuant to two acts of Congress, one of which provided that if a "public armed vessel of the United States" recaptured a vessel owned by a U.S. citizen, then the "recaptors" would be entitled to salvage equal to one-eighth the value of the ship and her cargo.[54] The second act of Congress also provided for salvage of one-eighth value for ships recaptured from "the enemy" within twenty-four hours. For ships recaptured after 96 hours, however, the second act provided for a salvage value of one-half.[55]

Thus the crew of the *Ganges* was entitled to salvage by statute. The question presented to the Supreme Court in *Bas v. Tingby* was whether the value was one-eighth or one-half. Since the *Ganges* had recaptured the *Eliza* after 96 hours, the pivotal issue was whether France was an "enemy" within the meaning of the second act, providing for one-half salvage. The argument against viewing France as an enemy was that Congress had not declared war against France. Since the purpose of a declaration of war is to activate all legal provisions pertaining to dealings with enemies of state, the absence of a declaration, it was argued, implied the absence of an enemy.

This argument was rejected and the Supreme Court ruled that the *Ganges* was entitled to one-half salvage because France was an "enemy" within the meaning of the second act. Justice Washington reasoned that war can be either "perfect" or "imperfect" in a legal sense and that an "imperfect" war is still a war.

> It may, I believe, be safely laid down, that every contention by force, between two nations, in external matters, under the authority of their respective governments, is not only war, but public war. If it be declared in form, it is called solemn, and is of the perfect kind; because one whole nation is at war with another whole nation; and all the members of the nation declaring war are authorized to commit hostilities against all the members of the other, in every place and under every circumstance. In such a war, all the members act under a general authority, and all the rights and consequences of war attach to their condition.
>
> But hostilities may subsist between two nations, more confined in its nature and extent; being limited as to places, persons and things; and this is more properly termed imperfect war; because not solemn, and because those who are authorized to commit hostilities act under special authority, and can go no further than to the extent of their commission. Still, however, it is public war, because it is an external contention by force, between some of the members of the two nations, authorized by the legitimate powers.
>
> It is a war between the two nations, though all the members are not authorized to commit hostilities, such as in a solemn war, where the government restrain the general power.[56]

The view of Justice Washington was amplified by Justice Chase.[57]

The *Bas* Court enunciated the principle that the legality of a war does not depend on the existence of a declaration by Congress. This is not to say that the *Bas* Court held congressional declarations to be superfluous. To the contrary, the Court viewed a declaration as a necessary predicate to "general" or "perfect" war. But the absence of a declaration does not, according to the *Bas* Court, deprive a military action of legal legitimacy. The *Bas* Court did not have occasion to reach the constitutional issue of whether undeclared war is lawful because the case involved a military action congressionally authorized by statute.

The following term, the Supreme Court visited a similar question in *Talbot v. Seeman.*[58] The difference between the *Bas* and *Talbot* cases was that the former involved a U.S. ship recaptured from France while the latter involved a neutral ship recaptured from France by the U.S. The ship *Amelia,* owned by a citizen of Hamburg (the modern state of Germany not yet existing), was captured on the high seas by the French corvette *La Diligente.* The *Amelia* was recaptured about a week later by the U.S.S. *Constitution,* commanded by Captain Silas Talbot, who brought an action in federal court seeking salvage pursuant to statute.

The *Talbot* Court ruled that the seizure of the *Amelia* was lawful and therefore authorized a salvage payment. The Court noted that no act of Congress authorized the capture of neutral ships but found that since the *Amelia,* although owned by a neutral party, was manned by a French crew, she was "considered *quo ad hoc* as a French vessel,"[59] and therefore an enemy vessel.

The *Talbot* Court then considered the argument against salvage, raised by the *Amelia's* owner, that while Captain Talbot might have made an excusable mistake in capturing the neutral *Amelia,* he could not claim salvage of a ship that turned out not to be, in fact, French. Chief Justice Marshall answered this objection in broad terms:

> The opinion of the court is, that had the character of the Amelia been completely ascertained by Captain Talbot, yet, as she was an armed vessel, under French authority, and in a condition to annoy the American Commerce, it was his duty to render her incapable of mischief.[60]

Thus the *Talbot* Court found the capture of both French and neutral shipping during the quasi-war with France to be lawful in spite of the absence of a declaration of war by Congress. The *Talbot* Court went one step further than the *Bas* Court: *Talbot* held lawful a military operation (that is, the capture of a neutral ship) beyond the scope of express statutory authorization. It even characterized the action of the military commander in terms of a "duty" to protect American commerce, thus laying the foundation for future cases exploring the Commander-in-Chief's duty to defend. The implications flowing from Chief Justice Marshall's opinion are limited, however, by the fact that the *Talbot* Court, like the *Bas* Court, did not expressly address the constitutional question of the powers of the Commander-in-Chief. Any conclusions about presidential war powers flowing from the *Talbot* decision are therefore implicit only.

Chief Justice Marshall considered the lawfulness of another seizure of a merchant vessel in *Little v. Barreme*.[61] Captain Little, the skipper of the frigate U.S.S. *Boston*, had seized the *Flying Fish*, a Danish merchantman, on the high seas en route *from* a French port. The seizure was undertaken pursuant to an act of Congress providing for the seizure of vessels on the high seas en route *to* French ports.[62] Congress had not authorized seizures of vessels en route *from* French ports. Captain Little seized the *Flying Fish* on the basis of operating orders from the Secretary of the Navy, incorporating the text of Congress' act.[63] However, the operating orders authorized seizures of vessels *from* French ports, thereby exceeding the terms of the congressional act. Justice Marshall explained that the construction of the Secretary of the Navy actually gave greater effect to Congress' goal of restricting trade with France.

> It was so obvious, that if only vessels sailing to a *French* port could be seized on the high seas, that the law would be very often evaded, that this act of congress appears to have received a different construction from the executive of the *United States;* a construction much better calculated to give it effect.[64]

Although the operating orders effectuated this congressional will as to U.S. policy toward France, they exceeded the bounds of statutory authority. Therefore, as to the private party harmed by the seizure, the seizure was unlawful. Captain Little was ordered to pay damages.

Chief Justice Marshall noted that in the absence of an act of Congress, the President might have been able to seize the *Flying Fish* in his capacity as national chief executive or as Commander-in-Chief.

> It is by no means clear that the president of the United States whose high duty it is to "take care that the laws be faithfully executed," and who is commander in chief of the armies and navies of the United States, might not, without any special authority for that purpose, in the then existing state of things, have empowered the officers commanding the armed vessels of the United States, to seize and send into port for adjudication, American vessels which were forfeited by being engaged in this illicit commerce.[65]

But the President, through the Secretary of the Navy, did not purport to issue the operating orders on the basis of any authority other than the statute. The President misconstrued the statute, and so the seizure was unlawful. Apparently, the parties to the litigation did not raise the issue of the President's constitutional authority. The *Little* Court did not, therefore, have occasion to reach the broader question of whether a seizure undertaken pursuant to the President's constitutional war powers, as distinct from statutory powers granted by Congress, would have been lawful.

The question of whether the President as Commander-in-Chief is entitled to wage war in the absence of any congressional authorization was addressed by subsequent courts. The rule emerging from these cases is that, regardless of whether the President can engage in offensive,[66] sustained war, he may act unilaterally to defend the security of the United States without congressional approval.[67] Although this power to defend[68] was not conferred on the President by the express language of the Constitution, it has been recognized by the Supreme Court. In *The Prize Cases,*[69] for example, the Supreme Court was asked to provide relief to the owners of ships captured and claimed as prizes pursuant to the blockade President Lincoln imposed on southern ports in April of 1861. The threshold question was whether the capture of the ships was justified by a state of war. The Court first found that a civil war is a war like any other war: two parties claiming mutually exclusive sovereignty prosecute their rights by force.[70] The absence of a declaration of war did not trouble the Court: "A civil war is never solemnly declared; it becomes such by its accidents. . . ."[71] Therefore, the Court concluded, a civil war may be conducted "on the same footing as if those opposing the Government were foreign enemies invading the land."[72]

Having erased any distinction between civil and non-civil war, the Court addressed the question of whether President Lincoln's conduct of the war was lawful. The Court noted that even as Commander-in-Chief and the national chief executive, he "has no power to initiate or declare a war. . . ."[73] Nevertheless, the Court characterized the President's power to defend as follows:

> If a war be made by invasion of a foreign nation, the President is not only authorized but bound to resist force by force. He does not initiate the war, but is bound to accept the challenge without waiting for any special legislative authority.[74]

The Court went on to find that the President was authorized to conduct the war without congressional approval regardless of the type of threat faced; the President is free to respond to the threat presented, regardless of form.

> However long may have been its previous conception, it nevertheless sprung forth suddenly from the parent brain, a Minerva in the full panoply of war. The President was bound to meet it in the shape it presented itself,

without waiting for Congress to baptize it with a name; and no name given to it by him or them could change the fact.[75]

The implication flowing from this remark is that the President's power to defend is not dependent upon the threat taking any particular form, such as the traditional threat of a foreign enemy wading ashore intending to march on our cities. The threat need not be so limited. Professor Henkin has concluded:

Without a Congressional declaration of war, the power of the President to use the troops and do anything else necessary to repel invasion is beyond question. Wilson even claimed the right to strike deep in Mexico. The President has power not merely to take measures to meet the invasion, but to wage in full the war imposed upon the United States.[76]

The conclusions of *The Prize Cases* Court are consistent with Hamilton's broad view of the President's war-making power. It is now axiomatic that the initiation of hostilities against the United States by another nation justifies unilateral presidential defensive war-making under the Constitution.[77] As a corollary, the President is constitutionally authorized to determine whether or not the United States is involved in a situation justifying the use of force for defensive purposes.[78]

Presidents came very early to be recognized as having power to employ the armed forces in defense of the person and property of Americans situated abroad against attack or imminent danger of it; and this recognition received judicial ratification even prior to the Civil War.[79]

The rationale for the rule that the President may wage defensive war without congressional approval is that the exigency[80] of circumstances justifies the President's action. In *Martin v. Mott*,[81] the Supreme Court stated:

We are all of opinion, that the authority to decide whether the exigency has arisen, belongs exclusively to the president, and that his decision is conclusive upon all other persons. We think that this construction necessarily results from the nature of the power itself. . . . The [military] power itself is to be exercised upon sudden emergencies, upon great occasions of state, and under circumstances which may be vital to the existence of the Union. A prompt and unhesitating obedience to orders is indispensable to the complete attainment of the object. The service is a military service, and the command of a military nature; and in such cases, every delay, and every obstacle to an efficient and immediate compliance, necessarily tend to jeopardize the public interests.[82]

The *Martin v. Mott* case arose from the War of 1812 between the U.S. and Great Britain. In 1795, Congress had passed the Militia Act, authorizing the President to call out the militia "whenever the United States shall be invaded, or be in imminent danger of invasion from any foreign nation or Indian tribe. . . ."[83] Jacob E. Mott was called upon to serve in the New York State Militia, but did not appear for induction. Mott was called before a general court-martial, convicted, and fined. Before this sanction could be approved by the President, a treaty of peace between the U.S. and Great Britain was concluded. Nevertheless, the fine was imposed, and when Mott could not pay it, he was sentenced to twelve months' imprisonment.

Mott challenged the authority of the court-martial and the President to punish him for his failure to report to duty. The *Mott* Court had no difficulty in finding the President authorized to call Mott to the nation's service and to punish Mott for his failure to appear. This authority was clearly granted by Congress in the Militia Act of 1795. Thus, the Court's assertion that the "authority to decide whether the exigency has arisen, belongs exclusively to the president," can be read to apply only to situations where Congress has authorized the President to act. Under this interpretation, the President's power is not exclusive of Congress but of subordinates in the military chain of command. There can be no doubt that the *Mott* Court did mean to find the President congressionally authorized and to prevent the President's subordinates from second-guessing him.

> While subordinate officers or soldiers are pausing to consider whether they ought to obey, or are scrupulously weighing the evidence of the facts upon which the commander-in-chief exercises the right to demand their services, the hostile enterprise may be accomplished, without the means of resistance.[84]

However, the *Mott* Court also found that the President as Chief Executive and Commander-in-Chief "is necessarily constituted the judge of the existence of the exigency, in the first instance, and is bound to act according to his belief of the facts." The most natural interpretation of the Court's opinion is that the President is so empowered under both the Militia Act of 1795 and the Constitution. The Supreme Court stated the constitutional rule more clearly in *The Prize Cases:*

> Whether the President in fulfilling his duties, as Commander-in-Chief, in suppressing an insurrection, has met with such armed hostile resistance, and a civil war of such alarming proportions as will compel him to accord to them the character of belligerents, is a question to be decided *by him*. . . .[85]

Thus the President is constitutionally authorized not only to defend against an imminent threat to the lives or property of U.S. citizens but also to determine whether a threat is sufficiently imminent to justify the use of force without a congressional declaration of war.[86]

This rule was recognized during the Vietnam War by the U.S. District Court in *U.S. v. Mitchell*.[87] The *Mitchell* Court was faced with a challenge to the constitutionality of the Universal Military Training and Service Act.[88] Mr. Mitchell had refused to report for induction and challenged the draft law on the ground that it was not constitutionally authorized by a congressional declaration of war. The *Mitchell* Court dismissed this argument by noting congressional authorization for the war other than a declaration of war, including various appropriations acts. The *Mitchell* Court asserted, "Unquestionably, the President can start the gun at home or abroad to meet force with force; he is not only authorized but bound to do so."[89]

The Executive Powers

Article II of the Constitution states: "The executive Power shall be vested in a President of the United States."[90] Article II also charges the President with the duty to "take care that the laws be faithfully executed."[91] These powers are known collectively as the executive powers, and can be characterized as an authorization for the President to do what is necessary to uphold the law. Such a characterization would be consistent with the views of John Locke, whose Theory of Prerogative provided for broad executive "discretion for the public good."[92] If Locke was the Framers' guide in the area of executive power, then the executive power includes the "power to act according to discretion for the public good, without the prescription of law and sometimes against it."[93]

Although the Supreme Court has not adopted this broad conception of presidential authority, it has acknowledged the generality of the President's grant of executive power. In *Myers v. United States*, the Court stated:

> The difference between the grant of legislative power under Article I to Congress, which is limited to powers therein enumerated, and the more general grant of the executive power to the President under Article II, is significant. The fact that the executive power is given in general terms strengthened by specific terms where emphasis is appropriate, and limited by direct expressions where limitation is needed . . . is a convincing indication that none was intended.[94]

Therefore, unlike Congress' powers, the President's executive powers are not all enumerated.[95] The view of the *Myers* Court is consistent with that of Alexander Hamilton, who wrote:

> The enumeration ought therefore to be considered, as intended merely to specify the principal articles implied in the definition of executive power; leaving the rest to flow from the general grant of that power, interpreted in conformity with other parts of the Constitution, and with the principles of free government.
>
> The general doctrine of our Constitution then is, that the *executive power* of the nation is vested in the President; subject only to the *exceptions* and *qualifications,* which are expressed in the instrument.[96]

However, proponents of executive power should not be carried away by the broadest implications of Locke, Hamilton, or *Myers.* Executive power is not unlimited, as Justice Jackson explained:

> The example of such unlimited executive power that must have most impressed the forefathers was the prerogative exercised by George III, and the description of its evils in the Declaration of Independence leads me to doubt that they were creating their new Executive in his image. Continental European examples were no more appealing. And if we seek instruction from our own times, we can match it only from the executive powers in those governments we disparagingly describe as totalitarian. I cannot accept the view that this [executive] clause is a grant in bulk of all conceivable executive power but regard it as an allocation to the presidential office of the generic powers thereafter stated.[97]

Indeed, one distinguished commentator has protested the growth of executive power with the admonition: "The records of the Constitutional Convention make it clear that the purposes of this clause [Art. II, Sec. 1] were simply to settle the question whether the executive branch should be plural or single and to give the executive a title."[98]

Thus it is clear that the President is not King. Nevertheless, the President, as national chief executive, is empowered to ensure national security. In particular, he is authorized to protect U.S. nationals from threats abroad. This rule was recognized by the federal district court in *Durand v. Hollins*[99] and later, in *dictum,* by the Supreme Court in *In re Neagle.*[100] The *Durand* Court considered the legality of President Pierce's ordering in 1854 of the naval bombardment of Greytown, Nicaragua by the U.S.S. *Cyane.* This bombardment was undertaken in response to the refusal of the revolutionary government to make reparations to the United States for an attack on the U.S. Consul in Greytown. The

Court approved the President's actions on the basis of his executive powers, broadly construed.

> As the executive head of the nation, the president is made the only legitimate organ of the general government, to open and carry on correspondence or negotiations with foreign nations, in matters concerning the interests of the country or of its citizens. It is to him, also, the citizens abroad must look for protection of person and of property, and for the faithful execution of the laws existing and intended for their protection. For this purpose, the whole executive power of the country is placed in his hands, under the constitution, and the laws passed in pursuance thereof; and different departments of government have been organized, through which this power may be most conveniently executed, whether by negotiation or by force—a department of state and a department of the navy.
>
> Now, as respects the interposition of the executive abroad, for the protection of the lives or property of the citizen, the duty must, of necessity, rest in the discretion of the president. Acts of lawless violence, or of threatened violence to the citizen or his property, cannot be anticipated and provided for; and the protection, to be effectual or of any avail, may, not unfrequently, require the most prompt and decided action. Under our system of government, the citizen abroad is as much entitled to protection as the citizen at home. The great object and duty of government is the protection of the lives, liberty, and property of the people composing it, whether abroad or at home; and any government failing in the accomplishment of the object, or the performance of the duty, is not worth preserving.[101]

As to the bombardment itself, the *Durand* Court held:

> The question whether it was the duty of the president to interpose for the protection of the citizens at Greytown against an irresponsible and marauding community that had established itself there, was a public political question, in which the government, as well as the citizens whose interests were involved, was concerned, and which belonged to the executive to determine; and his decision is final and conclusive, and justified the defendant in the execution of his orders given through the secretary of the navy.[102]

The *Neagle* decision arose out of a remarkable factual context, one that did not involve the war powers. A federal district court in California in 1886 rendered a decree finding that Sarah Althea Hill had forged a marriage certificate between herself and one William Sharon. The decree ordered her to cancel and return the forged documents. When she did not do so, she and her true husband, David S. Terry, were brought before a three-judge panel including a Supreme Court Justice, the Honorable Stephen Johnson Field, riding circuit. This panel rendered its decision against Hill and Terry. The opinion was being delivered in open court by Justice Field when Hill disrupted the proceedings by demanding to know of the Justice "the price he had sold himself for."[103] A federal marshal sought to restrain Hill and was assaulted, with the loss of a tooth, by Terry.

Hill and Terry were sentenced to jail for contempt. While imprisoned, Hill and Terry repeatedly threatened the life of Justice Field. As a result, David Neagle, as deputy federal marshal, was assigned to accompany Justice Field as he rode circuit in California. On August 14, 1889, Hill and Terry, having been freed from jail, boarded a train on which Justice Field and Marshal Neagle were riding. When the train stopped for breakfast at a station along the way, Terry walked behind Justice Field and struck him twice in the head. As Terry raised his fist for a third blow, Marshal Neagle shot and killed Terry.

Marshal Neagle was arrested and held under a charge of murder. Marshal Neagle was held because no act of Congress expressly authorized federal marshals to act as bodyguards for Supreme Court Justices. The Circuit Court freed Marshal Neagle on a writ of *habeas corpus*. The Supreme Court affirmed, rejecting the argument that Marshal Neagle's actions in defense of Justice Field were not undertaken pursuant to any law of the United States. The *Neagle* Court decided that Marshal Neagle could not be imprisoned for the performance of his duty[104] and that his duty was not defined by any act of Congress but by the executive power of the President.

The *Neagle* Court found that the President's power to "take care that the laws be faithfully executed" does not limit the power of the President to the enforcement only of the express terms of acts of Congress, but extends to the enforcement of "rights, duties and obligations growing out of the Constitution itself, international relations, and all the protection implied by the nature of the government under the Constitution. . . ."[105] Indeed, the President's authority to prosecute a criminal matter is exclusive and discretionary.[106]

The reach of this incompletely defined inherent executive power is subject to serious question. The issue was joined in the writings of two former presidents, Theodore Roosevelt and William Howard Taft. President Theodore Roosevelt described his "stewardship" theory of presidential prerogative in terms of his own actions for the public good.

I did not usurp power, but I did greatly broaden the use of executive power. In other words, I acted for the public welfare, I acted for the common well-being of all our people, whenever and in whatever manner was necessary, unless prevented by direct constitutional or legislative prohibition. I did not care a rap for the mere form and show of power; I cared immensely for the use that could be made of the substance.[107]

President Taft criticized this point of view, offering instead the theory of enumerated presidential power.

The true view of the executive functions is, as I conceive it, that the President can exercise no power which cannot be fairly and reasonably traced to some specific grant of power or justly implied and included within such express grant as proper and necessary.[108]

It is interesting to note that not even President Theodore Roosevelt would go as far as Locke, who viewed executive prerogative as extending even to the violation of law.

This debate continues. The proponents of executive power are on the firmest ground in the context of war powers. The *Neagle* Court related with approval the following incident:

One of the most remarkable episodes in the history of our foreign relations, and which has become an attractive historical incident, is the case of Martin Koszta, a native of Hungary, who, though not fully a naturalized citizen of the United States, had in due form of law made his declaration of intention to become a citizen. While in Smyrna he was seized by command of the Austrian consul general at that place, and carried on board the Hussar, an Austrian vessel, where he was held in close confinement. Captain Ingraham, in command of the American sloop of war St. Louis, arriving in port at that critical period, and ascertaining that Koszta had with him his naturalization papers, demanded his surrender to him, and was compelled to train his guns upon the Austrian vessel before his demands were complied with. It was, however, to prevent bloodshed, agreed that Koszta should be placed in the hands of the French consul subject to the result of diplomatic negotiations between Austria and the United States. The celebrated correspondence between Mr. Marcy, Secretary of State and Chevalier Hulsemann, the Austrian minister at Washington, which arose out of this affair and resulted in the release and restoration to liberty of Koszta, attracted a great deal of public attention, and the position assumed by Mr. Marcy met the approval of the country and of Congress, who voted a gold medal to Captain Ingraham for his conduct in the affair. Upon what act of Congress then existing can any one lay his finger in support of the action of our government in this matter?[109]

By this example, the *Neagle* Court expressed the principle, albeit in *dictum,* that the President is constitutionally authorized as the national executive to take military action on behalf of a citizen not fully naturalized and, *a fortiori,* a full citizen. The Court took the analysis one step further by indicating that the President could take preemptive action to defend against a threat to U.S. property.[110] The principle vindicated by the *Neagle* Court is that the chief executive need not await express congressional authorization before undertaking an action to prevent unlawful activity directed against the United States. Thus, the executive power can be seen in terms parallel to the power of the Commander-in-Chief to defend the national security and the power of the chief diplomat to identify threats to national security.

The Steel Seizure Case: A War Powers Limit

On June 24, 1950, North Korea invaded the Republic of (South) Korea. Following this attack, the President sought from Congress the powers to requisition and allocate goods, set prices and wages, and otherwise determine productive capacity and priorities among goods.[111] On September 8, 1950, Congress granted these powers. On December 16, 1950, President Truman proclaimed a national emergency. On October 10, 1951, Congress passed the Mutual Security Act of 1951 to authorize "military, economical and technical assistance to friendly countries," including the Republic of Korea.[112] Between June 1950 and June 1952, Congress appropriated $130 billion of defense and military assistance to allies, including the Republic of Korea.[113] Congress never declared war against North Korea.

In 1951, about a year after the North Korean invasion, a dispute arose between the United Steelworkers of America and a multitude of steel companies. Collective bargaining failed to achieve a resolution of their differences, and, on December 18, 1951, the union notified the steel companies of its intention to strike beginning December 31, 1951. Both the Federal Mediation and Conciliation Service and the Federal Wage Stabilization Board intervened in order to effect a settlement. Neither agency succeeded and, on April 4, 1952, the union called a nationwide strike for April 19, 1952.

President Truman determined that in light of the existence of a state of emergency and the fact that "American fighting men . . . are now engaged in deadly combat with the forces of aggression in Korea,"[114] the national security required a continuation of steel production. In order to "assure the continued availability of steel . . . during the existing emergency," the President authorized the Secretary of Commerce to seize and operate the steel mills.[115] President Truman forbade the union from interfering with the operation of the plants. The federal government thereby became a steel conglomerate.[116]

The steel companies sued Secretary of Commerce Sawyer, asking the federal district court to enjoin the execution of the Executive Order authorizing the seizure. The Secretary of Commerce argued that the Executive Order sought to avoid a strike in order to protect the national security during a time of war. The district court agreed with the steel companies and issued an order invalidating the Executive Order and directing the Secretary of Commerce to disregard the Executive Order.[117] The same day, the district court's order was stayed by the Court of Appeals.[118] The Supreme Court agreed to hear argument on an emergency basis and affirmed the judgment of the district court.

The Supreme Court determined that the President did not have statutory authorization from Congress to seize the steel mills. Therefore, "if the President had authority to issue the order he did, it must be found in some provision of the Constitution."[119] Secretary Sawyer did not argue that the Constitution granted the President such power by its express language. Rather, Secretary Sawyer urged that the grant of presidential power was implied in the Constitution.

One such source of implied presidential power was the command-in-chief of the armed forces. The Supreme Court rejected this argument out of hand. The Court noted that the powers of the Commander-in-Chief affect the President's ability to control the military, not private industry. The determination of whether steel production was sufficiently important to justify the prohibition of a strike was a "job for the Nation's Lawmakers, not for its military authorities."[120]

The Supreme Court was equally clear in rejecting the argument that the Constitution contains an implicit authorization of presidential seizures of private industry in the name of national security. The executive power authorizes the President to execute and enforce the laws of Congress, said the Court, not to make law. The Executive Order was, the Court concluded, essentially a piece of legislation enacted by the President, not Congress. Law-making is a congressional function in "both good and bad times."[121] Absent congressional authorization, the Executive Order could not, and did not, stand.

The sweeping opinion of the Court obscured differences of opinion among the Justices on the question of the precise reason why the President's actions were unauthorized. Justice Frankfurter's concurring opinion placed emphasis on the fact that the Labor Management Relations Act of 1947[122] ("LMRA") did not authorize presidential seizure of industry. The LMRA was written to deal with the problems caused by failures in collective bargaining. Congress specifically addressed the issue of how best to address a "national emergency" caused by a strike. Congress considered granting the President power to seize industries when strikes gave rise to emergency conditions. On the balance of considerations, Congress chose not to lodge this power in the President.[123] Justice Frankfurter interpreted this congressional rejection of presidential seizure power in the LMRA as a message to the President: "You may not seize. Please report to us and ask us for seizure power if you think it is needed in a specific situation."[124] This, of course, President Truman did not do.

Justice Frankfurter also rejected the contention that the Defense Production Act of 1950[125] implicitly granted the President seizure power. Under Title V of the Defense Production Act, the President was authorized to "initiate voluntary conferences between management [and] labor."[126] Justice Frankfurter found that this grant of authority did not imply power to seize plants in the event that the expressly authorized "voluntary conferences" failed to stabilize the labor situation in a strategic industry. Justice Frankfurter stated:

> It is one thing to draw an intention of Congress from general language and to say that Congress would have explicitly written what is inferred, where Congress has not addressed itself to a specific situation. It is quite impossible, however, when Congress did specifically address itself to a problem, as Congress did to that of seizure, to find secreted in the interstices of legislation the very grant of power which Congress consciously withheld. To find authority so explicitly withheld is not merely to disregard in a particular instance the clear will of Congress. It is to disrespect the whole legislative process and the constitutional division of authority between President and Congress.[127]

Both Justice Frankfurter and Justice Douglas emphasized that the Court's task was not to determine which branch of government would "most expeditiously" deal with the steel crisis.[128] Each quoted the dissent of Justice Brandeis in *Myers v. U.S.:*

> The doctrine of separation of powers was adopted by the Convention of 1787 not to promote efficiency but to preclude the exercise of arbitrary power. The purpose was, not to avoid friction, but, by means of the inevitable friction incident to the distribution of governmental powers among three departments, to save the people from autocracy.[129]

Justice Douglas noted the convenience of allowing the President to seize the steel industry, but rebelled "at the thought that the grant [to the President as Commander-in-Chief] . . . carries with it authority over civilian affairs."[130]

Justice Jackson's famous concurring opinion commenced by noting the "poverty of really useful and unambiguous authority applicable to concrete problems of executive power. . . ."[131] Although the Steel Seizure case presented one of the most serious challenges to presidential power ever lodged, the Supreme Court could find little guidance in either case law or the history of the Constitutional Convention of 1787. Operating within these constraints, Justice Jackson described three categories of executive authority. The first was express congressional authorization. When Congress has granted the President power, reasoned Justice Jackson, the President's claim to power is the most sure because the two branches are in agreement. It might be that in such a situation the President would consider the congressional authorization unnecessary; but where Congress already has extended authorization, the question of constitutional power is not presented.

An example of Justice Jackson's first category of presidential action is found in the case of *U.S. v. Curtiss-Wright Corp.*[132] In *Curtiss-Wright,* the Court considered the problem of whether a congressional resolution delegating to the President the authority to determine whether to activate the terms of the resolution was an unconstitutional delegation of law-making power from Congress to the President.

On May 28, 1934, Congress issued a joint resolution of both houses stating that "if the President finds that the prohibition of the sale of arms and munitions of war in the United States to those countries [Bolivia and Paraguay] now engaged in armed conflict in the Chaco may contribute to the reestablishment of peace between these countries . . . ," then such arms sales shall be unlawful.[133] On the same date, President Roosevelt issued the required finding by means of a Proclamation.[134] However, on November 14, 1935, President Roosevelt revoked his proclamation of May 28, 1934, and issued a finding that the prohibition of arms sales to Bolivia and Paraguay would no longer be necessary as a contribution to the reestablishment of peace.[135]

The central question before the *Curtiss-Wright* Court was whether Congress unconstitutionally had granted law-making power to the President. The argument for finding the grant unconstitutional was based on the fact that the congressional resolution could be activated to prohibit arms sales only by presidential proclamation. Such a mechanism was equivalent, the argument continued, to a grant of legislative power to the executive. Since the Constitution forbids one branch of government from exercising the powers of another, the argument concluded, such a delegation would be unconstitutional.

The Court disagreed. The Court decided that the delegation of powers relating to domestic affairs should be judged by a standard different from that relating to foreign affairs. In other words, the possibility that the delegation to the President of legislative powers over domestic issues might be unconstitutional had no bearing on whether the delegation of powers relating to foreign affairs would be unconstitutional.

The Court found that in foreign affairs, "with its important, complicated delicate and manifold problems, the President alone has the power to speak or listen as a representative of the nation. He *makes* treaties with the advice and consent of the Senate; but he alone negotiates."[136] The Court concluded that since the President's power to conduct foreign relations was "plenary and exclusive," the President need not rely on an act of Congress as the "basis for its exercise."[137] Among the bases for this conclusion was the finding that the President knows better than Congress the "conditions which prevail in foreign countries."[138] Therefore, legislation such as that at issue in *Curtiss-Wright,* that becomes effective only upon a presidential finding regarding the conditions prevailing in a foreign region, seemed to the Court to have a reasonable basis. Furthermore, the effectiveness of foreign policy depends, said the Court, on the President's flexibility. The President must be free to adopt delicate responses to sensitive situations. He must, for example, avoid the disclosure of confidential sources of information. He must also, as President Washington had pointed out, be sure to avoid "full disclosure of all the measures, demands, or eventual concessions which may have proposed or contemplated . . . for this might have a pernicious influence on future negotiations, or produce immediate inconveniences, perhaps danger and mischief, in relation to their powers."[139]

The *Curtiss-Wright* opinion thus provides an example of Justice Jackson's first category of Presidential authority: an express grant of power to the President by Congress. The second category defined by Justice Jackson is that of express delegation of power directly from the Constitution to the President. Although this seems a straightforward categorical definition, Justice Jackson pointed out the existence of a "zone of twilight" along the boundary of congressional and presidential power granted directly by the Constitution.[140] He cited as an example President Lincoln's suspension of the writ of *habeas corpus* during the Civil War. The Constitution implies that the writ of *habeas corpus* may be suspended in time of emergency,[141] but does not say by what branch of government. President Lincoln claimed that the power was executive, not legislative, but the issue became moot when Congress ratified President Lincoln's actions[142] by the Habeas Corpus Act of 1863.[143]

Within Justice Jackson's second category, the balance of power is determined by the "imperatives of events" rather than "abstract theories of law."[144] Justice Jackson concluded: "Therefore, congressional inertia, indifference or quiescence may sometimes, at least as a practical matter, enable, if not invite, measures on independent presidential responsibility."[145] But the Steel Seizure Case did not fall into this second category.

Justice Jackson offered a third category into which he fit the Steel Seizure Case: a presidential undertaking contrary to the will of Congress based solely on the President's view of his own constitutional powers. Presidential action in this third category is subject to the most severe judicial scrutiny, according to Justice Jackson.

The Solicitor General, on behalf of the President, had argued that the seizure of a strategic industry in time of *de facto* war was an implied constitutional power of the President. The Solicitor General's reasoning went like this: if the President, as Commander-in-Chief and in the name of national security, undertakes a military action, he must be free under the Constitution to do everything necessary to prevail, including seizing private industry. This position reflected the argument raised by the government in the district court below.[146]

Justice Jackson rejected the Solicitor General's position because it proved too much. Justice Jackson recharacterized the Solicitor General's argument as follows: the President unilaterally and without consent of Congress undertakes a military operation and then seeks to take further steps to support the undertaking. The President thereby creates a situation that necessitates unlimited growth in the power of the Commander-in-Chief, extending to control over civilian assets.[147] Justice Jackson concluded that even in time of war, the Commander in Chief of the military is not "Commander-in-Chief of the country."[148]

> That seems to be the logic of an argument tendered at our bar—that the President having, on his own responsibility, sent American troops abroad derives from that act "affirmative power" to seize the means of producing a supply of steel for them. . . .
>
> I cannot foresee all that it might entail if the Court should endorse this argument. Nothing in our Constitution is plainer than that declaration of a war is entrusted only to Congress. Of course, a state of war may in fact exist without a formal declaration. But no doctrine that the Court could promulgate would seem to me more sinister and alarming than that a President whose conduct of foreign affairs is so largely uncontrolled, and often even is unknown, can vastly enlarge his mastery over the internal affairs of the country by his own commitment of the Nation's armed forces to some foreign venture. I do not, however, find it necessary or appropriate to consider the legal status of the Korean enterprise to discountenance argument based on it.[149]

Moreover, Justice Jackson emphasized that the seizure of the steel mills appeared to fall into the realm of supplying revenue to the war effort, a legislative function.

> Assuming that we are in a war *de facto,* whether it is or is not a war *de jure,* does that empower the Commander in Chief to seize industries he thinks necessary to supply our army? The Constitution expressly places in Congress power "to raise and *support* Armies" and "to *provide* and *maintain* a Navy." [Emphasis supplied.] This certainly lays upon Congress primary responsibility for supplying the armed forces. Congress alone controls the

raising of revenues and their appropriation and may determine in what manner and by what means they shall be spent for military and naval procurement. I suppose no one would doubt that Congress can take over war supply as a Government enterprise.[150]

Justice Jackson concurred in the majority opinion that the President had exceeded his constitutional grant of authority when he seized the steel industry. He also cited with approval President Wilson's decision to approach Congress for permission to allow merchant ships to deploy defensive weapons, before U.S. involvement in World War I.[151]

Justice Jackson did not write the opinion of the Steel Seizure Court. His concurrence is notable for its clarity and for his willingness to focus on the war powers issue, as distinct from the numerous other issues raised in the case. What the Court held was that the President's constitutional powers as Commander-in-Chief, however extensive in the conduct of military operations *per se,* do not extend to domestic, non-military operations, such as steel making. In other words, the President cannot enlarge his domestic powers, as Justice Jackson explained, merely by sweeping reference to a military requirement. Thus did the Steel Seizure Court discover and mark an outside limit to the President's war powers.

Conclusion

The recognition of broad presidential war powers necessarily raises the question of whether such powers will be exercised wisely. This question is especially compelling in the era of nuclear deterrence. One commentator has remarked, "Technology [specifically, nuclear weaponry] has modified the Constitution: the President, perforce, becomes the only man in the system capable of exercising judgment under the extraordinary limits now imposed by secrecy, complexity, and time."[152] If the President himself is empowered to determine whether he is constitutionally authorized to exercise his war powers, is not the temptation to act guilefully too overwhelming to resist?

The *Martin v. Mott* Court answered as follows:

It is no answer, that such a power may be abused, for there is no power which is not susceptible of abuse. The remedy for this, as well as for all other official misconduct, if it should occur, is to be found in the constitution itself. In a free government, the danger must be remote, since, in addition to the high qualities which the executive must be presumed to possess, of public virtue, and honest devotion to the public interests, the frequency of elections, and the watchfulness of the representatives of the nation, carry with them all the checks which can be useful to guard against usurpation or wanton tyranny.[153]

In short, the *Mott* Court was not willing to assume an abuse of power, by virtue of the existence of the power. To the contrary, the Court ruled that the presumption worked in the President's favor.

When the president exercises an authority confided to him by law, the presumption is, that it is exercised in pursuance of law. Every public officer is presumed to act in obedience to his duty, until the contrary is shown; and, *a fortiori,* this presumption ought to be favorably applied to the chief magistrate of the Union. It is not necessary to aver, that the act which he might rightfully do, was so done. If the fact of the existence of the exigency were averred, it would be traversable, and, of course, might be passed upon by a jury; and thus the legality of the orders of the president would depend, not on his own judgment of the facts, but upon the finding of those facts, upon the proofs submitted to a jury [a result expressly disfavored in *Vanderheyden v. Young,* 11 Johns. 150].[154]

The risk of abuse of the President's power does not, therefore, resolve the question of what power is allocated to the President. The President's actions will be presumed by the courts to be in good faith, absent some factual indication to the contrary. In any case, the President's power to wage defensive war unilaterally is not without limit. Since Congress has the power of appropriation, Congress can refuse to fund disapproved military activity undertaken by the President.[155] Congress undertook such steps during the Vietnam War.[156] Alexander Hamilton articulated the general rule "that the purpose the limit and the fund of every expenditure should be ascertained by a previous law."[157] The President may not act unilaterally to appropriate; he requires the authority of Congress. Although Congress "usually feels legally, politically, or morally obligated to appropriate funds to maintain the President's foreign affairs establishment and to implement his treaties and other foreign undertakings, Congress can readily refuse to appropriate when it believes the President has exceeded his powers."[158]

Congress also possesses the ultimate weapon: impeachment of the President for "high crimes and misdemeanors."[159] It takes little imagination to conceive the possibility of an atrocity committed in the exercise of presidential war-making that could lead to impeachment. In addition to this power, Congress possesses the power to declare war.[160] The power to declare war is enormous in scope. As Eugene Rostow has written:

A declaration of war has far-reaching consequences, including: the authorization of unlimited hostilities, the possible internment of enemy aliens, the sequestration of enemy property, and the imposition of regulations, such as censorship, that would be unthinkable in peacetime.[161]

On the other hand, the power to declare war is not a power to veto presidential war-making. Although a few commentators have read Congress' power to declare war to incorporate a power to "declare *against* a war,"[162] no authoritative source supports such a conclusion. Indeed, the Framers unanimously rejected a proposal to grant Congress the power to declare war "and peace."[163] It is clear that once a military operation has been commenced, Congress may not interfere with the command decisions of the President. The Supreme Court has stated:

> Congress has the power not only to raise and support and govern armies, but to declare war. It has, therefore, the power to provide by law for carrying on war. This power necessarily extends to all legislation essential to the prosecution of war with vigor and success, except such as interfere with the command of the forces and the conduct of campaigns. That power and duty belong to the President as Commander-in-Chief.[164]

The Supreme Court laid down a limit on presidential war powers in *Youngstown Sheet & Tube Co. v. Sawyer.*[165] There, the Court disapproved presidential "bootstrapping" of war-making powers into domestic powers reserved to Congress. On the other hand, Justice Jackson was careful to establish that his disapproval of presidential "bootstrapping" did not suggest a limitation on the President's authority as Commander-in-Chief to address threats to national security originating abroad. He stated:

> We should not use this occasion to circumscribe, much less to contract, the lawful role of the President as Commander in Chief. I should indulge the widest latitude of interpretation to sustain his exclusive function to command the instruments of national force, at least when turned against the outside world for the security of our society.[166]

The Supreme Court has also rejected the contention that the President's war powers are themselves sufficient to justify the prior restraint of publication of documents embarrassing to the federal government, namely, the "Pentagon Papers."[167] The *New York Times* Court held that the First Amendment prohibited the President from restraining publication of documents, when Congress had not prohibited such publication.[168] Thus the *New York Times* opinion, like the Steel Seizure opinion, prevents presidential bootstrapping. However, because it deals only with ancillary powers, the *New York Times* opinion is not a restriction on presidential war-making *per se.*[169]

This balance of power is not altogether satisfying to those concerned about the practical effectiveness of congressional checks on the President. Professor Louis Henkin has remarked:

> No one can disentangle the war powers of the two branches, including their powers to act towards the enemy. . . . [But such an arrangement of] power often begets a race for initiative and the President will usually "get there first."[170]

A guileful President, for example, would experience little difficulty identifying or even creating a threatening incident abroad sufficiently provocative to justify the use of force. Similarly, a cynical President might find it expedient to undertake an offensive military campaign and simply label it a defensive, preemptive action. Although Congress might have the power under such circumstances to bar the use of federal funds for combat, it might lack the political will to do so. The President's power to commit forces to combat in the name of national defense thus would present Congress with a *fait accompli*, a war to be terminated by a congressional vote for withdrawal short of victory.[171] War would become in such a situation, as Madison feared, "the true nurse of executive aggrandizement."[172]

The Constitution, however, was not designed to predetermine a politically satisfying balance of power. Rather, the constitutional allocation was meant to establish the legal limits within which the political process might produce such an equilibrium. This is to say that the Constitution sets boundaries beyond which the President and Congress may not stray during a political clash over the use of force. The political questions raised by a President's unilateral decision to use military force include whether the decision is morally sound, whether it enjoys domestic popular support, and whether it serves the strategic interests of the United States. The constitutional issue is much more narrow: whether the President acted within the bounds of his authority to make war unilaterally, a question that can be answered without reference to whether the President's actions were politic or wise.[173] The next chapter emphasizes the difference between legal and political war-making issues by examining the doctrine of nonjusticiability.

Notes

1. A. HAMILTON, THE FEDERALIST NO. 23 at 200 (B. Wright, ed., 1961) (emphasis deleted).

2. "Fear of a return of Executive authority like that exercised by the Royal Governors or by the King had been ever present in the States from the beginning

of the Revolution." C. WARREN, THE MAKING OF THE CONSTITUTION 173 (1928). *But see* Rostow, "War, Foreign Affairs, and the Constitution," ENCYCLOPEDIA OF THE AMERICAN CONSTITUTION 2007, 2008 (L. Levy, K. Karst, and D. Mahoney, eds., 1986) ("The President is effectively both king and prime minister. . . .").

3. E. CORWIN, THE PRESIDENT: OFFICE AND POWERS 1787–1984, 255 (1984). *See also,* J. LEHMAN, THE EXECUTIVE, CONGRESS, AND FOREIGN POLICY: STUDIES OF THE NIXON ADMINISTRATION, Ch. 2 (1976).

4. *See generally* L. HENKIN, FOREIGN AFFAIRS AND THE CONSTI-TUTION (1972).

5. U.S. CONST., Art. II, Sec. 2, Cl. 2. *See* A QUESTION OF BALANCE: THE PRESIDENT, THE CONGRESS, AND FOREIGN POLICY (T. Mann, ed. 1990); C. CRABB and P. HOLT, INVITATION TO STRUGGLE: CON-GRESS, THE PRESIDENT, AND FOREIGN POLICY (1989); T. FRANCK & E. WEISBAND, FOREIGN POLICY BY CONGRESS (1979); J. LEHMAN, THE EXECUTIVE, CONGRESS, AND FOREIGN POLICY: STUDIES OF THE NIXON ADMINISTRATION, Ch. 4 (1976) (case study of executive agreement for U.S. use of bases of Spain); E. CORWIN, THE PRESIDENT'S CONTROL OF FOREIGN RELATIONS (1917); "Symposium: Foreign Affairs and the Constitution: The Roles of Congress, the President, and the Courts," 43 U. MIAMI L. REV. 1 (1988).

6. U.S. CONST., Art. II, Sec. 2, Cl. 2; Sec. 3.

7. L. HENKIN, FOREIGN AFFAIRS AND THE CONSTITUTION 41 (1972).

8. A. HAMILTON, THE FEDERALIST NO. 69.

9. LASKI, THE AMERICAN PRESIDENCY 174–175 (1940).

10. L. HENKIN, FOREIGN AFFAIRS AND THE CONSTITUTION 47 (1972); E. CORWIN, THE PRESIDENT: OFFICE AND POWERS 1787–1957 at 182 (1957); S. BEMIS, A DIPLOMATIC HISTORY OF THE UNITED STATES 98 (1955).

11. E. CORWIN, THE PRESIDENT: OFFICE AND POWERS 1787–1957 at 178 (1957) (quoting November 22, 1793 letter from Jefferson to Genet, 9 WRITINGS OF THOMAS JEFFERSON 256 (Mem. ed.)).

12. 299 U.S. 304 (1936). *See* Lofgren, *"United States v. Curtiss-Wright Export Corporation:* An Historical Reassessment," 83 YALE L. J. 1 (1973).

13. 299 U.S. at 319 (emphasis original).

14. *E.g.,* E. CORWIN, THE PRESIDENT: OFFICE AND POWERS, 1787–1984, 207–208 (1984). *See contra* Fisher, "Congressional Participation in the Treaty Process," 137 U. PA. L. REV. 1511, 1512 (1989).

15. 299 U.S. at 320. *See also Chicago & S. Air Lines, Inc. v. Waterman S.S. Corp.,* 333 U.S. 103, 109 (1948) (President is "the Nation's organ in foreign affairs").

16. 5 WRITINGS OF THOMAS JEFFERSON 161 (Ford, ed., 1895).

17. 299 U.S. at 320–321.

18. E. CORWIN, THE PRESIDENT'S CONTROL OF FOREIGN RELA-TIONS 36 (1917).

19. *See, e.g.,* L. HENKIN, FOREIGN AFFAIRS AND THE CONSTITUTION 48 (1972); Matthews, "The Constitutional Power of the President to Conclude International Agreements," 64 YALE L. J. 345 (1955); McDougal & Lans, "Treaties and Agreements: Interchangeable Instruments of National Policy," 54 YALE L. J. 181 (1945).

20. L. HENKIN, FOREIGN AFFAIRS AND THE CONSTITUTION 179–180 (1972).

21. E. CORWIN, THE PRESIDENT: OFFICE AND POWERS 1787–1957 at 202–204 (1957) (quoting *Total War and the Constitution* at 29–31). *Cf. also* N. GRUNDSTEIN, PRESIDENTIAL DELEGATION OF AUTHORITY IN WARTIME (1961).

22. 318 U.S. 578 (1943).

23. 318 U.S. at 588.

24. 318 U.S. at 589.

25. 324 U.S. 30 (1945).

26. 324 U.S. at 35.

27. 324 U.S. at 36.

28. 324 U.S. at 38.

29. 301 U.S. 324 (1937). *See also* Berger, "The Presidential Monopoly of Foreign Relations," 71 MICH. L. REV. 1 (1972); Mathews, "The Constitutional Power of the President to Conclude International Agreements," 64 YALE L. J. 345 (1955); Wright, "The United States and International Agreements," 38 AM. J. INT'L. L. 341 (1944).

30. 301 U.S. at 330–331. *See also* B. Altman & Co. v. U.S., 224 U.S. 583, 600–601 (1912).

31. 315 U.S. 203 (1942).

32. 406 U.S. 759, 768 (1972). *See also Banco Nacional de Cuba v. Sabbatino,* 376 U.S. 398 (1964).

33. *Dames & Moore v. Regan,* 453 U.S. 654, 682 (1981).

34. *Id.*

35. 453 U.S. at 680. In the same year, the Supreme Court held that in the context of foreign affairs, congressional acquiescence may be found in the failure of Congress to object to long-standing practices of the President. *Haig v. Agee,* 453 U.S. 280, 300 (1981). *See also Zemel v. Rusk,* 381 U.S. 1, 11–12 (1965).

36. For a much more dramatic reading of the *Dames & Moore* opinion, *see* Koh, "Why the President (Almost) Always Wins in Foreign Affairs: Lessons of the Iran-Contra Affair," 97 YALE L. J. 1255, 1310 (1988).

37. Koplow, "Constitutional Bait and Switch: Executive Reinterpretation of Arms Control Treaties," 137 U. PA. L. REV. 1353, 1391 (1989).

38. Rehm, "Making Foreign Policy through International Agreement," in THE CONSTITUTION AND THE CONDUCT OF FOREIGN POLICY 126, 127 (F. Wilcox and R. Frank, eds., 1976) (also characterizing 97% of the executive agreements as "congressional-executive"). *See also* C. ROSSITER AND R. LONGAKER, THE SUPREME COURT AND THE COMMANDER IN CHIEF 153 (1976).

39. *Valentine v. United States ex rel. Neidecker,* 299 U.S. 5 (1936).

40. 299 U.S. at 9.

41. *See also New York Times Co. v. United States,* 403 U.S. 713 (1971) (First Amendment); *Kent v. Dulles,* 357 U.S. 116 (1958) (Fifth Amendment); *Reid v. Covert,* 354 U.S. 1 (1957).

42. *See generally* Hall, "The Constitution and Presidential War-Making Against Libya," 42 NAVAL WAR COLLEGE REV. 30 (Summer 1989).

43. U.S. CONST., Art. II, Sec. 2, Cl. 1.

44. *Youngstown Sheet & Tube Co. v. Sawyer,* 343 U.S. 579, 634 (1952) (Jackson, J., concurring).

45. *See* Lofgren, "War-Making Under the Constitution: The Original Understanding," 81 YALE L. J. 672, 680 (1972).

46. "Helvidius" Number 1 (24 August 1793), 15 THE PAPERS OF JAMES MADISON 71 (T. Mason, R. Rutland, and J. Sisson, eds., 1985).

47. 7 WORKS OF ALEXANDER HAMILTON 746–747 (J. Hamilton, ed., 1857) (emphasis original).

48. II RECORDS at 318.

49. *See* Chapter 1.

50. *See, e.g.,* J. MAURICE, HOSTILITIES WITHOUT DECLARATION OF WAR 1700–1870, 12–26 (1883). *See also* DeCONDE, THE QUASI-WAR: THE POLITICS AND DIPLOMACY OF THE UNDECLARED WAR WITH FRANCE 1797–1801 (1966).

51. E. CARSTEN, THE PRESENT LAW OF WAR AND NEUTRALITY 96 (1954) (as quoted in R. TURNER, THE WAR POWERS RESOLUTION: ITS IMPLEMENTATION IN THEORY AND PRACTICE 38 n.45 (1983)).

52. ADAMS PAPERS, Massachusetts Historical Society microfilm (as quoted in Sofaer, "The Presidency, War and Foreign Affairs: Practice Under the Framers," 40 L. & CONT. PROB. 12, 19–20 (1976)). *See also* A. SOFAER, WAR, FOREIGN AFFAIRS, AND CONSTITUTIONAL POWER: THE ORIGINS 139–161 (1976).

53. *Bas v. Tinghy,* 4 U.S. (4 Dall.) 36 (1800).

54. 1 Stat. 574, § 2 (1798).

55. 1 Stat. 716, §§ 7 and 9 (1799).

56. 4 U.S. at 39–40.

57. 4 U.S. at 44.

58. 5 U.S. (1 Cr.) 1 (1801).

59. 5 U.S. at 31.

60. *Id.*

61. 6 U.S. (2 Cr.) 170 (1804).

62. *Id.* at 177.

63. *Id.* at 178 (emphasis original).

64. *Id.* at 178 (emphasis original).

65. *Id.* at 177 (emphasis removed).

66. *See* E. KEYNES, UNDECLARED WAR: TWILIGHT ZONE OF CONSTITUTIONAL POWER (1982). *See also* Testimony of John Norton Moore, "Congress, the President, and the War Powers: Hearing Before the Committee on Foreign Affairs, House of Representatives," 91st Cong., 2d Sess. (June 25,

1970); Moore, "The National Executive and the Use of the Armed Forces Abroad," 21 NAVAL WAR COLLEGE REV. 28 (1969).

67. *See, e.g.,* Emerson, "The War Powers Resolution Tested: The President's Independent Defense Power," 51 NOTRE DAME LAWYER 187, 192 (1975).

68. See *generally* C. BERDAHL, WAR POWERS OF THE EXECUTIVE IN THE UNITED STATES 58-77 (1921).

69. 67 U.S. 635 (1863).

70. 67 U.S. at 666.

71. *Id.*

72. 67 U.S. at 668.

73. *Id.*

74. *Id. See also U.S. v. Curtiss-Wright Corp.,* 299 U.S. 304 (1936); *Myers v. U.S.,* 272 U.S. 52 (1926).

75. 67 U.S. at 669.

76. L. HENKIN, FOREIGN AFFAIRS AND THE CONSTITUTION 52 (1972).

77. *E.g.,* C. ROSSITER AND R. LONGAKER, THE SUPREME COURT AND COMMANDER IN CHIEF 138 (1976).

78. 67 U.S. at 670.

79. E. CORWIN, THE CONSTITUTION AND WHAT IT MEANS TODAY 60 (8th ed., 1946).

80. The Constitution expressly grants the individual states an analogous power to act militarily under exigent circumstances. U.S. CONST., Art. I, Sec. 10, Cl. 3 ("No state shall without the consent of Congress . . . engage in war, unless actually invaded, or in such imminent danger as will not admit of delay."). *See also* Articles of Confederation, Art. VI ("No state shall engage in any war without the consent of . . . Congress . . . , unless such state be actually invaded by enemies, or shall have received advice of a resolution being formed by some nation of Indians to invade such state, and the danger is so imminent as not to admit of a delay till the . . . Congress . . . can be consulted. . . .").

81. 25 U.S. (12 Wheat.) 19 (1827)

82. 25 U.S. at 30. *See also Arver v. U.S.,* 245 U.S. 366 (1918).

83. 25 U.S. at 29.

84. 25 U.S. at 30-31.

85. *The Prize Cases,* 67 U.S. 635, 670 (1863) (emphasis original).

86. *Id.* (President has the power to recognize the existence of a state of *de facto* war).

87. 246 F. Supp. 874, 898 (D. Conn. 1965).

88. 50 U.S.C. § 462.

89. 246 F. Supp. 874, 898 (D. Conn. 1965).

90. U.S. CONST., Art. II, Sec. 1.

91. U.S. CONST., Art. II, Sec. 3.

92. J. LOCKE, "Second Treatise of Civil Government," in THE SECOND TREATISE OF GOVERNMENT AND A LETTER CONCERNING TOLERATION 81-82 (1966) (Bk. II, Ch. 14, para. 160).

93. Berns, "Constitutional Power and the Defense of Free Government: The Case of Abraham Lincoln," in TERRORISM: HOW THE WEST CAN WIN 151 (B. Netanyahu, ed., 1986) (quoting Locke).

94. *Myers v. United States,* 272 U.S. 52, 128 (1926).

95. L. TRIBE, AMERICAN CONSTITUTIONAL LAW 159 (1978). *See also* Note, "A Defense of the War Powers Resolution," 93 YALE L. J. 1330, 1337 (1984).

96. A. HAMILTON, 7 WORKS OF ALEXANDER HAMILTON 76, 81 (1851) (emphasis original).

97. *Youngstown Co. v. Sawyer,* 343 U.S. 579, 641 (1952).

98. Corwin, "The Steel Seizure Case: A Judicial Brick Without Straw," 53 COLUM. L. REV. 53 (1953).

99. *Durand v. Hollins,* 4 Blatch. 451, 8 F. Cas. 111 (No. 4186) (C.C.S.D. N.Y. 1860) (Nelson, J.).

100. 135 U.S. 1, 64 (1890). *See also The Slaughterhouse Cases,* 83 U.S. (16 Wall.) 36, 79 (1873); *Martin v. Mott,* 25 U.S. (12 Wheat.) 19 (1827).

101. 8 F. Cas. at 112.

102. *Id.*

103. 135 U.S. at 45.

104. 135 U.S. at 58.

105. 135 U.S. at 64.

106. *The Confiscation Cases,* 74 U.S. (7 Wall.) 454 (1869); *U.S. v. Cox,* 342 F.2d 167, 171 (5th Cir.), *cert. denied sub nom., Cox v. Hauberg,* 381 U.S. 935 (1965). *Cf. also U.S. v. Nixon,* 418 U.S. 683, 693 (1974).

107. T. ROOSEVELT, AN AUTOBIOGRAPHY (1913).

108. W. TAFT, OUR CHIEF MAGISTRATE AND HIS POWERS (1916).

109. 135 U.S. at 64.

110. 135 U.S. at 65. *See also* C. ROSSITER AND L. LONGAKER, THE SUPREME COURT AND THE COMMANDER IN CHIEF 143 (1976); Eagleton, "The August 15 Compromise and the War Powers of Congress," 18 ST.LOUIS U. L. REV. 1 (1973).

111. Defense Production Act of 1950, 50 U.S.C. § 2061, 64 Stat. 798 (1950), amended, 65 Stat. 131 (1951).

112. Mutual Security Act of 1957, 65 Stat. 373 (1951).

113. *Youngstown Sheet & Tube Co. v. Sawyer,* 343 U.S. 579, 670 (1952) (Vinson, C.J., dissenting).

114. Executive Order 10340 (April 8, 1952), 17 FED. REG. 3139 (1952).

115. *Id.*

116. *See generally* MARCUS, TRUMAN AND THE STEEL SEIZURE CASE (1977). *See also* E. CORWIN, PRESIDENTIAL POWER AND THE CON- STITUTION 121–140 (1976); Corwin, "The Steel Seizure Case: A Judicial Brick Without Straw," 53 COLUM. L. REV. 53 (1953); Schubert, "The Steel Seizure Case: Presidential Responsibility and Judicial Irresponsibility," 6 WESTERN POLITICAL QUARTERLY 61 (1953); Kauper, "The Steel Seizure Case: Congress, the President, and the Supreme Court," 51 MICH. L. REV. 141 (1952); Freund, "The Supreme Court, 1951 Term, Foreward: The Year of the Steel Case," 66 HARV. L. REV. 89–95 (1952).

117. 103 F. Supp. 569 (1952).

118. 197 F.2d 937 (1952).

119. 343 U.S. at 587.

120. 343 U.S. at 587.

121. 343 U.S. at 589.

122. 50 U.S.C. § 1503.

123. 343 U.S. at 601.

124. 343 U.S. at 603.

125. 64 Stat. 798 (1950), amended, 65 Stat. 131 (1951).

126. *Id.* at 812. (Title V, Sec. 502).

127. 343 U.S. at 609.

128. *Id.* at 630.

129. 272 U.S. 52, 293 (1926).

130. 343 U.S. at 632.

131. 343 U.S. at 634.

132. 299 U.S. 304 (1936).

133. 48 Stat. 811 (1934).

134. 48 Stat. 1744 (1934).

135. 49 Stat. 3480 (1935).

136. 299 U.S. at 319.

137. 299 U.S. at 320.

138. *Id.*

139. 299 U.S. at 320–321 (quoting RICHARDSON, I MESSAGES AND PAPERS OF THE PRESIDENTS 194).

140. 343 U.S. at 637.

141. U.S. CONST., Art. I, Sec. 9, Cl. 2.

142. 343 U.S. at 637 n.3 (citing *Ex parte Merryman,* 17 Fed. Cases 144; *Ex parte Milligan,* 71 U.S. 3 (1866)).

143. 12 Stat. 755 (1863).

144. 343 U.S. at 637.

145. *Id.*

146. C. ROSSITER AND R. LONGAKER, THE SUPREME COURT AND THE COMMANDER IN CHIEF, xix–xx (1976) (quoting Oral Argument Transcript 371–372, House of Representatives, 82d Cong., 2d Sess., H. Doc. No. 534, Part I (1950)).

147. 343 U.S. at 642.

148. 343 U.S. at 644.

149. 343 U.S. at 642–643.

150. 343 U.S. at 643.

151. *Id.* at 647 n.16 (quoting RICHARDSON, XVII MESSAGES AND PAPERS OF THE PRESIDENTS 8211).

152. R. NEUSTADT, PRESIDENTIAL POWER: THE POLITICS OF LEADERSHIP 212 (1968). *See also* Goldstein, "The Failure of Constitutional Control Over War Powers in the Nuclear Age: The Argument for a Constitutional Amendment," 40 STAN. L. REV. 1543 (1988).

153. 25 U.S. at 32–33. *See also Luther v. Borden,* 48 U.S. (7 How.) 1, 44 (1849) ("It is said that this power in the President is dangerous to liberty, and may be abused. All power may be abused if placed in unworthy hands. But it would be difficult, we think, to point out any other hands in which this power would be more safe, and at the same time equally effectual.").

154. 25 U.S. at 32–33. For a similar presumption in Congress' favor, *see Fleming v. Page,* 50 U.S. (9 How.) 603, 614 (1850) ("A war, therefore, declared by Congress, can never be presumed to be waged for the purpose of conquest or the acquisition of territory. . . .").

155. U.S. CONST., Art. I, Sec. 8. *See, e.g., Helvering v. Davis,* 301 U.S. 619 (1937); *Steward Machine Co. v. Davis,* 301 U.S. 548 (1937); *United States v. Butler,* 297 U.S. 1, 66 (1936). *See also* L. TRIBE, AMERICAN CONSTITU-TIONAL LAW 247–249 (1978); C. ROSSITER AND R. LONGAKER, THE SUPREME COURT AND THE COMMANDER IN CHIEF 161–167 (1976) (impoundment by the President of appropriated funds); J. LEHMAN, THE EXECUTIVE, CONGRESS, AND FOREIGN POLICY: STUDIES OF THE NIXON ADMINISTRATION Ch. 6 (1976); L. FISHER, PRESIDENTIAL SPENDING POWER 107–118, 252–256 (1975) ("FISHER").

156. *See, e.g.,* Supplemental Appropriations Act, 87 Stat. 134 (1973); Supplemental Foreign Aid Authorization Act, P.L. 91-652, 84 Stat. 1942 (1971); Foreign Military Sales Act Extension, P.L. 91-672, 84 Stat. 2053 (1970); Defense Procurement Act, P.L. 91-441, 84 Stat. 905 (1970); Defense Procurement Authorization Act, P.L. 91-121, 83 Stat. 204 (1969); Defense Appropriations Act, P.L. 91-171, 83 Stat. 469 (1969). *See* J. LEHMAN, THE EXECUTIVE, CONGRESS, AND FOREIGN POLICY: STUDIES OF THE NIXON ADMINISTRATION Ch. 3 (1976).

157. FISHER at 257.

158. FISHER at 254–255 (quoting L. HENKIN, FOREIGN AFFAIRS AND THE CONSTITUTION 79 (1972)).

159. U.S. CONST., Art. II, Sec. 4.

160. U.S. CONST., Art. I, Sec. 8.

161. Rostow, "War, Foreign Affairs, and the Constitution," ENCYCLOPEDIA OF THE AMERICAN CONSTITUTION 2007, 2010 (L. Levy, K. Karst, and D. Mahoney, eds., 1986).

162. Van Alstyne, "Congress, the President, and the Power to Declare War: A Requiem for Vietnam," 121 U. PA. L. REV. 1, 5 (1972); L. HENKIN, FOREIGN AFFAIRS AND THE CONSTITUTION 81 (1972).

163. II RECORDS at 319.

164. *Ex parte Milligan,* 71 U.S. (4 Wall.) 139 (1866). *See also Swaim v. U.S.,* 28 Court of Claims 173, *aff'd,* 165 U.S. 553 (1897).

165. 343 U.S. 579 (1952).

166. 343 U.S. at 643.

167. *New York Times Co. v. United States,* 403 U.S. 713 (1971) *(per curiam).*

168. 403 U.S. at 732.

169. Only Justice Douglas suggested the possibility that the prior restraint was unlawful because it arose from an undeclared war. 403 U.S. at 722.

170. L. HENKIN, FOREIGN AFFAIRS AND THE CONSTITUTION 105 (1972).

171. This is the problem the War Powers Resolution was intended to solve. However, the War Powers Resolution's only pre-conflict requirement on the President is "consultation" with Congress. *See* Hall, "War Powers By The Clock," 113 U.S. Naval Institute PROCEEDINGS 36 (1987).

172. Letters of Helvidius (1793), 6 THE WRITINGS OF JAMES MADISON 138, 174 (G. Hunt, ed., 1906).

173. *Cf.* Lobel, "Covert War and Congressional Authority: Hidden War and Forgotten Power," 134 U. PA. L. REV. 1035, 1071 (1986); Wright, "The Power of the Executive to Use Military Forces Abroad," 10 VA. J. INT'L. L. 1, 49 (1969).

3

Nonjusticiability

The judiciary has visited only rarely the question of the President's power to wage war unilaterally. As Chapter 2 shows, the courts, with few exceptions, have upheld the President on those rare visitations. The courts' reluctance to examine the President's decisions to use the military was summarized in 1849 by the Supreme Court in *Luther v. Borden*.

After the President has acted and called out the militia, is a Circuit Court of the United States authorized to inquire whether his decision was right? . . . If it could, then it would become the duty of the court (provided that it came to the conclusion that the President had decided incorrectly) to discharge those who were arrested or detained by the troops in the service of the United States. . . . If the judicial power extends so far, the guarantee contained in the Constitution of the United States is a guarantee of anarchy, and not of order. Yet if this right does not reside in the courts when the conflict is raging, if the judicial power is at that time bound to follow the decision of the political, it must be equally bound when the contest is over.

It is said that this power in the President is dangerous to liberty, and may be abused. All power may be abused if placed in unworthy hands. But it would be difficult, we think, to point out any other hands in which this power would be more safe, and at the same time equally effectual. When citizens of the same State are in arms against each other, and the constituted authorities unable to execute the laws, the interposition of the United States must be prompt, or it is of little value. The ordinary course of proceedings in courts of justice would be utterly unfit for the crisis. And the elevated office of the President, chosen as he is by the people of the United States, and the high responsibility he could not fail to feel when acting in a case of so much moment, appear to furnish as strong safeguards against a wilful abuse of power as human prudence and foresight could well provide. At all events, it is conferred upon him by the Constitution and laws of the United States, and must therefore be respected and enforced in its judicial tribunals.[1]

In *Luther,* the Supreme Court viewed the President's decision to use force as "political" and therefore beyond the scope of judicial review. To understand this reluctance to intrude, which continues today, the "political question doctrine" must be examined.

The Political Question Doctrine

Article III of the U.S. Constitution creates the power of the federal courts to resolve certain disputes. The Constitution's grant of jurisdiction limits the power of the courts to the determination of "cases" or "controversies."[2] These two limiting words have become terms of art, around which has developed the doctrine of justiciability.

The justiciability doctrine limits the federal courts to "questions presented in an adversary context" and to issues not more properly decided by the other two branches of government.[3] In other words, by the doctrine of justiciability, the court itself decides where the limits on its own actions should lie. In the exercise of this discretion, the courts follow the rule of Chief Justice Marshall: "It is most true that this Court will not take jurisdiction if it should not; but it is equally true, that it must take jurisdiction if it should."[4] This remark appears in the late twentieth century to be a truism, but was hardly obvious in the early nineteenth. The Chief Justice's *dictum* was written little more than a decade after the Supreme Court first enunciated and exercised its power to determine whether an act of Congress was "repugnant" to the Constitution and therefore invalid.[5] As commonplace as it seems today, the Supreme Court's power to determine the constitutionality of legislative acts is not granted by the plain language of the Constitution.[6] All the language of Article III does is establish the "judicial power" to all "cases . . . arising under this Constitution" and federal statutory law as well as to all "controversies" either involving the United States as a party or involving parties of diverse citizenship.[7] Article III defines the Supreme Court's original jurisdiction; that is, its power to be the first federal forum to consider a question. Article III neither expressly defines the limits of the courts' "judicial power" nor expressly identifies what branch of the government should determine its scope.

The Supreme Court exercised the power to determine the scope of its own "judicial power" in 1803 when it held in *Marbury v. Madison* that an act of Congress purporting to empower the Supreme Court to issue original writs of mandamus exceeded the bounds of Article III of the Constitution.[8] The question before the *Marbury* Court was whether the Judiciary Act of 1789, which was in conflict with Article III, could be invalidated by the Supreme Court.[9] This question placed the Supreme Court in an awkward position: the Supreme Court was being asked to rule as the final authority on the Constitution's grant of power to the Supreme Court. Thus the Court found itself facing a conceptual conflict of interests.

The *Marbury* case raised at a time of significant political change an issue of profound political consequences. In 1800, Thomas Jefferson was elected President. Emboldened by his own victory and that of his Republican Party in controlling Congress, Jefferson sought to restrict the power of judges appointed by the Federalist who preceded him, John Adams.[10] Against this background, William Marbury asked the Supreme Court to issue a writ of mandamus directing James Madison, President Jefferson's Secretary of State, to deliver a commission appointing Marbury a justice of the peace for the District of Columbia. Marbury had been one of President Adams' "Midnight Judges," appointed in the final hours of the Adams presidency. The commission had not been delivered to Marbury before the end of Adams' presidency, and Secretary of State Madison, on Jefferson's orders, refused to deliver it. It is interesting to note that Madison's immediate predecessor as Secretary of State was Chief Justice John Marshall, who wrote the opinion in *Marbury v. Madison* and that Chief Justice Marshall was appointed in 1801, just before Jefferson became President.

The *Marbury* Court held that, although Marbury was entitled to the commission, the Supreme Court was not the proper federal forum to hear his petition for the issuance of a writ of mandamus. By holding that the Supreme Court could not issue the writ of mandamus as an original (versus appellate) forum, the *Marbury* Court was "in the delightful position . . . of rejecting and assuming power in a single breath."[11] That is, the *Marbury* Court determined that it lacked the original jurisdiction to order the Secretary of State to deliver the commission, but it also determined that It enjoyed the power to make such determinations of the scope of its own power.

The *Marbury* Court decided that it was empowered to protect the separation of powers between the branches of the government by ensuring that no branch exceeds its constitutional authority. In doing so, the *Marbury* Court set the judiciary's "watch dog" agenda, as Professor Haskins explains:

> What is especially important about the latter part of the [*Marbury*] opinion . . . is [Chief Justice] Marshall's attempt to differentiate "law" from "politics," and in doing so, to insist on the vitality of the "rule of law" as an unfailing mechanism for making this distinction, as well as reinforcing the constitutional doctrine of separation of powers.[12]

Among the mechanisms to be honored in protecting the separation of powers is the prohibition against judicial resolution of political questions.

The judiciary has retained to the present this power to invalidate acts of Congress and the President on the basis of unconstitutionality. In exercising this power, the Supreme Court has respected it, recognizing that a failure of restraint could lead to judicial adventurism. The Court monitors carefully its drift into areas where it "should not" venture. The Supreme Court summarized these restrictions in *Flast v. Cohen:*

> Justiciability is itself a concept of uncertain meaning and scope. Its reach is illustrated by the various grounds upon which questions sought to be adjudicated in federal courts have been held not to be justiciable. Thus, no justiciable controversy is presented when the parties seek adjudication of only a political question, when the parties are asking for an advisory opinion, when the question sought to be adjudicated has been mooted by subsequent developments, and when there is no standing to maintain the action. Yet it remains true that "[j]usticiability is . . . not a legal concept with a fixed content or susceptible of scientific verification. Its utilization is the resultant of many subtle pressures. . . ."[13]

As the *Flast* Court indicated, one self-imposed restriction on the judicial power is the "political question" doctrine.[14] The political question doctrine is a subset of the justiciability doctrine, restraining courts from venturing beyond the mandate to decide "cases" or "controversies" into the realm of political disputes. The courts do not wish to make determinations of policy reserved to elected officials, because they do not view themselves a "bevy of Platonic Guardians."[15] To the contrary, the existence of the political question doctrine illustrates the courts' conception of their own limitations. Some cases raise "issues that bring into question the very capacity of judicial judgment."[16] These are the cases to which the political question doctrine applies.

The political question doctrine has been applied to strike a balance between competing democratic values: popular sovereignty and constitutional imperatives.[17] The judiciary does not question the wisdom of legislative acts, for example, because the legislature's acts are deemed to reflect the will of the people; but the courts will intervene if Congress acts in contravention of the Constitution.[18]

A plain example of this balance is found in the context of voting rights. In *Colegrove v. Green,*[19] a group of voters brought suit to complain that they were denied equal protection of the laws because of malapportionment of voting power. These voters lived in Illinois, where congressional districts had been determined in 1901 on the basis of the 1900 census. Several decades later, when the suit was brought, the population of Illinois had not only grown, but had also been redistributed within the state from rural to urban areas. Because the boundaries of congressional districts remained fixed during this period, the votes in the high growth areas were debased. That is, votes from high growth areas were worth less than votes from low growth areas, so each voter in the high growth area had a smaller effect on the outcome of a congressional election.[20]

Although voters in high growth areas were harmed by the action, the *Colegrove* Court would not resolve the issue. The voters sought an injunction to prevent Illinois officials from holding another election until they cured the malapportionment problem. Despite the critically important democratic value at stake, namely, the equivalence of every citizen's vote, the opinion of the *Colegrove* Court was that the issue was "of a peculiarly political nature and therefore not . . . for judicial determination."[21] Justice Frankfurter summarized:

> To sustain this action would cut very deep into the very being of Congress. Courts ought not to enter this political thicket. The remedy for unfairness in districting is to secure State legislatures that will apportion properly, or to invoke the ample powers of Congress.[22]

The *Colegrove* opinion's apparently *per se* prohibition against judicial inquiry into the question of whether malapportionment violates the equal protection clause was lifted by a subsequent apportionment case, *Baker v. Carr*.[23] In *Baker*, voters sued on the same basis as the voters in *Colegrove*. Their claim was dismissed by the trial court. The Supreme Court ordered a new trial to consider the merits of the voters' complaint. The *Baker* Court set forth a multi-part test to determine whether a case or controversy involves a nonjusticiable political question. An issue is a nonjusticiable political question when it involves

> a textually demonstrable constitutional commitment of the issue to a coordinate political department; or a lack of judicially discoverable and manageable standards for resolving it; or the impossibility of deciding without an initial policy determination of a kind clearly for nonjudicial discretion; or the impossibility of a court's undertaking independent res- olution without expressing lack of the respect due coordinate branches of government; or an unusual need for unquestioning adherence to a political decision already made; or the potentiality of embarrassment from multi- farious pronouncements by various departments on one question.[24]

Although *Baker* has been found by some to "repudiate" *Colegrove*,[25] its effect is not quite so dramatic.[26] The *Baker* Court did not order the trial court to enter the "political thicket" to review legislative policy. Rather, it ruled that the trial court may determine whether the reason for the malapportionment was mere inertia, that is, whether the "discrimination reflects *no* policy, but simply arbitrary and capricious action."[27]

Regardless of the effect of *Baker* on apportionment cases, the political question doctrine remains in full force. Even in stating its limits, the *Baker* Court reaffirmed the vitality of the political question doctrine.

> The doctrine of which we treat is one of "political questions," not one of "political cases." The courts cannot reject as "no lawsuit" a bona fide controversy as to whether some action denominated "political" exceeds constitutional authority.[28]

The point is that there exists an area of inquiry into which the judiciary will not venture for fear of interfering with the political will of the people. The question is how the courts know the location of this domain, as Professor Laurence Tribe explains:

> To make such a determination [of political question], a court must first of all construe the relevant constitutional text, and seek to identify the purposes the particular provision serves within the constitutional scheme as a whole. At this stage of the analysis, the court would find particularly relevant the fact that the constitutional provision by its terms grants authority to another branch of government; if the provision recognizes such authority, the court will have to consider the possibility of conflicting conclusions, and the actual necessity for parallel judicial and political remedies. But ultimately, the political question inquiry turns as much on the court's conception of judicial competence as on the constitutional text. Thus the political question doctrine, like other justiciability doctrines, at bottom reflects the mixture of constitutional interpretation and judicial discretion which is an inevitable by-product of the efforts of federal courts to define their own limitations.[29]

In *Chicago & S. Air Lines v. Waterman S.S. Corp.*,[30] the Supreme Court was asked to review executive branch determinations regarding international air routes. The Court declined to do so, stating:

> [T]he very nature of executive decisions as to foreign policy is political, not judicial. Such decisions . . . are delicate, complex, and involve large elements of prophecy. . . . They are decisions of a kind for which the Judiciary has neither aptitude, facilities nor responsibility. . . . [31]

The *Waterman* Court's prohibition, while sweeping, is not absolute. The *Baker* Court stated in *dictum* that "it is error to suppose that every case or controversy which touches foreign relations lies beyond judicial cognizance."[32] The *Baker* Court's remark refers implicitly to the following rule of thumb: "while the Executive is immune from judicial oversight while engaged in the negotiation of treaties," the courts may construe and assess the validity of treaties when they adversely affect the constitutional rights of individuals.[33]

In performing this balancing act with respect to political questions, the courts most recently have followed a "functional" approach.[34] The essential characteristic of this approach is that the courts will not venture beyond the limits of their expertise in reaching constitutional issues. Courts are particularly hesitant to intrude into international affairs[35] because they "know" so little of such matters. Of course, this reasoning is tautological because the reason courts lack such knowledge is that they decline opportunities to learn about foreign affairs through litigation. It cannot be that foreign affairs is a field too complex, in an absolute sense, for the court to enter, after all, the courts routinely consider complex cases in other areas such as antitrust law and international commercial transactions.[36] Nevertheless, the judiciary considers itself relatively incompetent (compared to the President and Congress) to enter the field of foreign affairs.

The Supreme Court has applied the political question doctrine to find nonjusticiable a case concerning the training of the Ohio National Guard, thereby demonstrating its lack of interest in participating in the command of the military. In *Gilligan v. Morgan*,[37] plaintiffs sought to obtain review under the Fourteenth Amendment's Due Process Clause of the adequacy of Guard training. The plaintiffs alleged that poor training and leadership of the Guard had caused the deaths of several Kent State University students and injury to others during a protest demonstration in May of 1970. Plaintiffs sought injunctive relief based upon a "judicial evaluation of the appropriateness of the 'training, weaponry and orders' of the Ohio National Guard," specifically requiring that the Court "establish standards for the training, kind of weapons and scope and kind of orders to control the actions of the National Guard."[38] The Court declined to reach the merits on the ground that the questions involved powers delegated by the Constitution expressly to Congress and the President.

> It would be difficult to think of a clearer example of the type of governmental action that was intended by the Constitution to be left to the political branches directly responsible—as the Judicial Branch is not—to the electoral process. Moreover, it is difficult to conceive of an area of governmental activity in which the courts have less competence. The complex, subtle, and professional decisions as to the composition, training, equipping, and

control of a military force are essentially professional military judgments, subject *always* to civilian control of the Legislative and Executive Branches.[39]

In contrast to the supervisory task plaintiffs in *Gilligan* requested of the courts, the judicial function the courts were asked to undertake in *U.S. v. Nixon*[40] was familiar, even routine. In *U.S. v. Nixon,* the Court was asked to quash a subpoena, a request frequently made of the courts. However, in the *Nixon* case, the motion was by the President and the subpoena was from the Special Prosecutor. The President argued that the Court lacked jurisdiction to issue a subpoena because the President's dispute with the Special Prosecutor (a member of the executive branch) was an "intra-branch dispute" and therefore a nonjusticiable political question.[41] The Supreme Court rejected the contention that all intra-branch disputes involve nonjusticiable political questions. The Court found that the conflict between the President and the Special Prosecutor involved an issue "traditionally" resolved by the courts: "the production or nonproduction of specified evidence deemed by the Special Prosecutor to be relevant and admissible in a pending criminal case."[42] The Court held that "[w]hatever the correct answer on the merits, these issues are 'of a type which are traditionally justiciable.'"[43] Thus the Court was assured that it would not stray from its traditional areas of expertise.

Despite the many hints and implications left by the Supreme Court over the years, the application of the political question doctrine to the field of foreign affairs is not well-settled. This was demonstrated in 1979 in *Goldwater v. Carter,*[44] where the Supreme Court ordered the dismissal of a lawsuit by congressmen seeking to prevent President Carter from terminating unilaterally a mutual defense treaty with Taiwan. The congressmen claimed that, since the President cannot enact treaties unilaterally, he cannot terminate them unilaterally. The Court refused to address the issue, but was unable to produce a majority opinion on why the lawsuit should be dismissed.

The *Goldwater* Court found a majority on the result (which was to remand for dismissal), but not on the rationale. Justice Rehnquist, writing for a plurality, found the issue to be a "political question" and therefore nonjusticiable. Justice Rehnquist, relying on *Coleman v. Miller,*[45] found:

> [T]he instant dispute is a nonjusticiable political dispute that should be left for resolution by the Executive and Legislative Branches of the Government. Here, while the Constitution is express as to the manner in which the Senate shall participate in the ratification of a treaty, it is silent as to that body's participation in the abrogation of a treaty.[46]

Justice Rehnquist found the argument for finding the matter a political question especially "compelling" because it involved "foreign relations—

specifically a treaty commitment to use military force in the defense of a foreign government if attacked."[47] Justice Rehnquist concluded by urging that the lower court's order be vacated so that it would not "spawn any legal consequences."[48]

Justice Powell concurred in the majority's decision to remand the case with instructions to dismiss the matter and vacate the judgment. However, he disagreed strongly with the plurality's view that the matter was a nonjusticiable political question. Justice Powell specifically disagreed with Justice Rehnquist's argument that the foreign affairs context of the lawsuit emphasized the political nature of the controversy. Justice Powell noted that, although challenging, the constitutional inquiry would not involve either a "review of the President's activities as Commander in Chief" or an "impermissible interference in the field of foreign affairs."[49] Justice Powell viewed the case as only touching on the field of foreign affairs,[50] but focusing on the sort of question the Supreme Court was meant to address: the "division of power between Congress and the President."[51] For Justice Powell, the case did not present a political question but was nevertheless not properly before the Court because it was not "ripe":

> Prudential considerations persuade me that a dispute between Congress and the President is not ready for judicial review unless and until each branch has taken action asserting its constitutional authority.[52]

Since Congress had not voted to reject the President's claim of constitutional authority, the case was not ripe and was therefore not justiciable.

Justice Brennan also disagreed with the plurality's view. He stated that the political question doctrine "does not pertain when a court is faced with the *antecedent* question whether a particular branch has been constitutionally designated as the repository of political decision-making power . . . The issue of decision-making authority must be resolved as a matter of constitutional law, not political discretion; accordingly, it falls within the competence of the courts."[53] Justice Brennan went on to state that the Court would have no trouble resolving the constitutional issue. The President's decision to repudiate the mutual defense treaty with Taiwan grows from the President's unilateral power to recognize foreign nations. "Our cases firmly establish that the Constitution commits to the President alone the power to recognize, and withdraw recognition from, foreign regimes."[54] Therefore, given the opportunity to reach the merits, Justice Brennan would have endorsed the President's position.

The *Goldwater* plurality opinion, as broad as it is in its implications, should not be read as barring lawsuits against the President altogether. Although the Supreme Court has been very careful about allowing such suits, it has expressly permitted them. In *Nixon v. Fitzgerald*,[55] the Court did not address the political question doctrine itself but did find: "It is settled law that the separation-of-powers doctrine does not bar every exercise of jurisdiction over the President of the United States."[56]

Despite the Supreme Court's willingness to exercise jurisdiction over the President and the inability of the *Goldwater* Court to muster a majority as to the rationale, one federal court recently dismissed a lawsuit brought under the War Powers Resolution ("WPR")[57] on the ground that it raised a nonjusticiable political question.[58] In *Lowry v. Reagan,* the plaintiff congressmen sought to obtain from the court an order requiring the President to submit a WPR Section 4(a)(1) report regarding the presence of U.S. forces in the Persian Gulf. The filing of such a report would have marked the beginning of a sixty-day period after which the President would have been required to withdraw U.S. forces from the Persian Gulf, in the absence of an authorizing vote from Congress.[59] The *Lowry* Court held that because resolution of the dispute involved a judicial inquiry into matters intimately related to the President's conduct of foreign affairs, the Court would decline review. The Court explained:

> Having analyzed the question in this case, the Court concludes that plaintiffs' request for declaratory relief presents a nonjusticiable political question. If the Court were to grant or deny declaratory relief, and decide whether United States Armed Forces stationed in the Persian Gulf are engaged in "hostilities or . . . [in] situations where imminent involvement in hostilities is clearly indicated by the circumstances," the Court would risk "the potentiality of embarrassment [that would result] from multifarious pronouncements by various departments on one question." Indeed, such a declaration necessarily would contradict legislative pronouncements on one side or the other of this issue. Moreover, a declaration of "hostilities" by this Court could impact on statements by the Executive that the United States is neutral in the Iran-Iraq war and, moreover, might create doubts in the international community regarding the resolve of the United States to adhere to this position. Because this Court concludes that the volatile situation in the Persian Gulf demands, in the words of *Baker v. Carr,* a "single-voiced view," the Court refrains from joining the debate on the question of whether "hostilities" exist in that region.[60]

The *Lowry* Court noted in *dictum* that these presidential considerations would not have been relevant had Congress passed a resolution demanding a WPR Section 4(a)(1) report from the President.[61] In such a circumstance, the Court reasoned, it would have been presented with "an issue ripe for judicial review."[62] This is a confusing remark since it appears to merge the ripeness and political question doctrines. Any such merger by the Court was erroneous: a "ripe" controversy might nevertheless be inappropriate for judicial review on political question grounds. Indeed, this is the issue on which Justice Powell departed from Justice Rehnquist's plurality opinion in *Goldwater*. The presentation to the court of a future WPR controversy that is ripe will not necessarily be justiciable.[63]

Vietnam Cases: The Courts Are Silent

Between 1965 and 1973, many challenges to the constitutionality of the Vietnam War were brought to the courts.[64] Most were dismissed on political question grounds. Of the courts that did not feel constrained by the political question doctrine, one district court ruled that the war in Vietnam was not authorized by Congress and was therefore unlawful. That ruling was overturned on appeal.[65] It is not possible to know whether the courts that did reach the merits would have done so if they had intended to declare the war unlawful. Such a ruling on the merits would have produced serious political consequences, thereby encouraging the invocation of the political question doctrine. But such second-guessing yields little insight; the best course is to take the courts at their word.

The "word" of most of the courts considering legal challenges to the war in Vietnam was that the issue was a political question beyond the scope of judicial review.[66] In *Sarnoff v. Connally*,[67] the Court considered a challenge to congressional appropriations[68] for the Vietnam War. The basis of this challenge was the contention that any appropriation for war unsupported by a congressional declaration of war was an invalid delegation of war-making power by the Congress to the President. The Court found that since the power to conduct foreign affairs is not vested in the judiciary, the question was political and therefore nonjusticiable.

The *Sarnoff* Court's statement of the political question doctrine was not entirely accurate.[69] Courts refuse to consider political questions not because they lack the power to do so but because they lack the expertise. The courts, for example, routinely review the constitutionality of statutes which the judiciary has no power to enact. Therefore, although the Court has no power to conduct foreign affairs, it does have the power, strictly speaking, to review the constitutionality of foreign affairs legislation. Under the political question doctrine, courts refuse to exercise this power as a matter of discretion. The *Sarnoff* Court declined to exercise its power of review.

Another court, in *Berk v. Laird*,[70] reached a similar result on the basis of the political question doctrine. The *Berk* Court heard the appeal of Private Berk, who sought a declaratory judgment voiding his orders to report for duty in Vietnam. The *Berk* Court refused to issue such a declaration, holding that the issue raised might be a political question. Since Congress had passed the Tonkin Gulf Resolution, the Court reasoned, the issue was not whether the President could execute a war-fighting policy without a word of authorization by Congress. Rather, the question was whether the Tonkin Gulf Resolution was adequate authorization given Congress' power to declare war. The *Berk* Court could not imagine a set of "judicially discoverable and manageable standards"[71] for answering this question, but remanded Private Berk's cause to the district court for consideration of whether the political question doctrine precluded judicial action. Thus was Private Berk given an opportunity to present facts sufficient to remove the case from the limits of the political question doctrine.

Unlike the *Sarnoff* Court, the *Berk* Court recognized that it had the "power" to address Private Berk's complaint. The *Berk* Court declined the exercise of its power in order to avoid a political question. The *Berk* Court found that since it has power to address the issue, the matter was justiciable, but declined to address the issue on political question grounds. A more precise statement of the *Berk* Court's decision is this: the *Berk* Court had the power to review the constitutionality of Private Berk's orders, thanks to *Marbury v. Madison,* but the matter was not justiciable because it involved a political question.

In another challenge to the constitutionality of the Vietnam War, similar to that in *Berk,* the United States Court of Appeals for the District of Columbia Circuit refused to consider the request of an Army private to invalidate his orders to report for duty in Vietnam. In *Luftig v. McNamara,*[72] Private Luftig sought a declaration that his orders to Vietnam were invalid because the President lacked the authority to send him to war without a congressional declaration of war. The *Luftig* Court invoked the political question doctrine. The Court noted: "It is difficult to think of an area less suited for judicial action than that into which . . . [Private Luftig] would have us intrude."[73] The Court found that judges are precluded from "overseeing the conduct of foreign policy or the use and disposition of military power."[74] These matters, the Court concluded, are within the exclusive domain of Congress and the President.[75] The *Luftig* Court issued its opinion for the sole purpose of making "it clear to others comparably situated and similarly inclined that resort to the courts is futile, in addition to being wasteful of judicial time, for which there are urgent legitimate demands."[76]

Contrasting the short treatment of the issue given by the *Luftig* Court is the lengthy opinion in *Atlee v. Laird.*[77] The *Atlee* Court reviewed in considerable detail the background and origins of the political question doctrine. Having identified the principle to be protected, the Court ruled that plaintiffs' claim that the Vietnam War was unconstitutional was a political question not properly resolved by the Court.

The *Atlee* Court found that to address the constitutionality of the Vietnam War, it would have been required to determine three factors:

(1) whether the Vietnam War was a "war"; (2) whether Congress had authorized the "war"; and (3) whether the President may wage an undeclared war. The *Atlee* Court concluded that each of these questions was political. On the issue of whether the Vietnam War was a war, the Court felt that sufficient data could be found to support such a determination. But the Court would not make this determination because it felt unable to measure the consequences of its decision. The Court was especially worried that its determination that a war was being waged in Vietnam would activate a complex array of treaty obligations, placing both the President and U.S. allies abroad in the "untenable" position of evaluating the effect of the Vietnam War on their duties under various treaties.

More broad still was the *Atlee* Court's concern that courts could not develop standards to determine when the nation is at war. This concern appears at first to be absurd. After all, no one who has ever fought in a war has doubted that what he was doing was fighting in a war. However, the execution of an act of war does not necessarily determine whether a nation is in a state of war. For example, the use of air power to destroy ground targets in Libya was an act of war. In the days and weeks following the air strike, many wondered whether the United States and Libya were in a state of war. But once the fervor had dissipated, few considered the United States and Libya to be at war. A measurement of the intensity necessary for a series of hostile acts to be equated with a state of war is, therefore, a more delicate operation than it might at first appear to be. It is not, therefore, surprising that the *Atlee* Court wished to avoid the issue entirely. This sort of discretionary issue avoidance is characteristic of the political question doctrine.

The *Atlee* Court also refused to consider whether Congress had authorized the war in Vietnam. The Court felt that to determine whether or not acts of appropriation and conscription by Congress amounted to authorization would require the "interrogation" of congressmen in order to divine their true intentions. This, the Court felt, would amount to an undue intrusion into congressional prerogatives. This rationale is a bit difficult to understand, however, in light of the fact that the central task of a court conducting the routine operation of statutory interpretation is to determine the intention of Congress.

Finally, the *Atlee* Court refused to consider whether the President may conduct a war without a congressional declaration. The Court noted that the President is empowered to defend the nation and that when the President perceives a threat, he has "extraordinary war-making powers." For this proposition, the *Atlee* Court cited *The Prize Cases*,[78] where the Supreme Court found President Lincoln justified in ordering a blockade

of southern ports in 1861, during a *de facto* civil war but in the absence
of a declaration of war.[79]

The *Atlee* Court, then, recognized that to void the actions of the
President, it would have to find an absence of a sufficient threat to the
national security to justify unilateral presidential war-making. The Court,
noting the difference of opinion on this question among reasonable people,
could not find the President's view wholly unreasonable. The Court also
considered itself incompetent to review all the geopolitical data necessary
to evaluate the significance of the threat perceived by the President.
Finally, the Court found that even if it could evaluate the threat to
national security, it would, by establishing rigid standards for the President
in conducting national security policy, arbitrarily limit the President's
options during a future threat. Accordingly, the *Atlee* Court invoked the
political question doctrine.

Another court, in *Davi v. Laird*,[80] considered the claim of citizens
seeking an injunction against the use of their taxes to conduct the Vietnam
War. The plaintiffs argued that no action by Congress short of a formal
declaration of war could justify military involvement by the United States
in Vietnam. The plaintiffs thus sought to avoid the difficult question of
whether Congress authorized the war when it appropriated funds for use
by the military in Vietnam and enacted the Selective Service Act in order
to meet the military's manpower needs by means of a draft.

The *Davi* Court rejected the all-or-nothing approach of the plaintiffs.
To the *Davi* Court, the salient issue raised by the case was whether
congressional actions short of declaration of war served to authorize the
Commander-in-Chief to wage war. But, while recognizing that the adequacy of congressional authorization was the central issue presented, the
Court refused to resolve the issue, basing its refusal on the political
question doctrine.

> It is crystal clear that if there is one political question in the fabric of
> government of the Republic, it is whether or not to maintain a war, and
> if so, whether to maintain it as an imperfect or declared war. Into this
> seamless web of national and international politics, the courts should not
> intrude.[81]

The *Davi* Court believed that the power to wage war is shared by
Congress and the President. It characterized the structure of this ar-
rangement as a "'delicate fabric' of checks and balances."[82] The Court
found that the judiciary was not a part of this "fabric" and could not
therefore exercise a supervisory role in determining the adequacy of
congressional actions. The circumstances that prevent the courts' participation are exactly those that make the "fabric" so delicate to begin with.

The *Davi* Court noted that the Supreme Court had long recognized the state of "imperfect," undeclared war.[83] Thus, the delicate constitutional fabric is capable of doing more than clothing a state of war with a formal declaration or withholding such approval. Its weave contains not only black and white, but shades of gray. The *Davi* Court noted that Congress might, for a "myriad of conceivable reasons," elect not to declare war when a state of war was approved. Among these reasons is the fear of activating the treaty obligations of the United States and its allies. In such a situation, Congress would be able, as indeed it was during the Vietnam War, to approve the war by means of appropriation. If Congress' sentiment changed and it wished to end the war, it could vote to do so. Any interference by the judiciary, the *Davi* Court held, would unacceptably limit the options of Congress and disrupt the Constitution's balance of power.[84]

Vietnam Cases: The Courts Speak

On some occasions during the Vietnam War, the courts did address the substantive issue of the constitutionality of the war. The first court to do so was faced, in *U.S. v. Mitchell*,[85] with a challenge to the constitutionality of the Universal Military Training and Service Act.[86] Mr. Mitchell had refused to report for induction and challenged the draft law on the ground that it was not constitutionally authorized by a congressional declaration of war. The *Mitchell* Court dismissed this argument by noting the existence of congressional authorization for the war other than a declaration of war, including various appropriations acts.[87] Whether or nor Congress intended a war, it intended a draft. Since Congress has the constitutional power to raise and support armies,[88] it need not seek additional authorization. Indeed, the Court viewed Mitchell's argument as a claim that Congress could not enact a peacetime draft, a proposition for which the Court had no patience.

Other courts overcame the political question obstacle to hold the war in Vietnam to be constitutionally authorized. In *Berk v. Laird*,[89] discussed previously, the appellate court refused, on the basis of the political question doctrine, to issue an injunction preventing the Army from sending Private Berk to Vietnam. The *Berk* Court concluded, however, that if the parties could produce evidence at trial to establish whether or not Congress had authorized the war, then the Court might not be restrained by the political question doctrine. The *Berk* Court noted that it could not foresee how such evidence could show the sufficiency of any congressional authorization.

At trial on remand, Private Berk sought to make the showing required by the appellate court.[90] The trial court held that the sufficiency of congressional authorization of the Vietnam War was a political question. Private Berk appealed a second time, and his appeal was joined by that of a brother at arms, Private Orlando, who sought the same sort of injunction.[91] Private Orlando's request for an injunction had been denied not on political question grounds but on the basis of congressional authorization by means of appropriations measures and the draft law passed by Congress. In other words, Orlando's claim was rejected on the merits, unlike Private Berk's claim, which was denied on political question grounds.

The appeals of Berk and Orlando were considered together by the appellate court in *Orlando v. Laird*.[92] The *Orlando* Court seemed to depart somewhat from its previous ruling in *Berk*. The *Berk* Court had denied Private Berk the relief requested on political question grounds. However, the Court had remanded to give Private Berk an opportunity to present his evidence at trial to show that the issue of the sufficiency of congressional authorization was manageable enough to escape the limits of the political question doctrine.

But the *Orlando* Court interpreted its previous ruling in *Berk* as implying that the political question doctrine did not foreclose judicial inquiry into the question of whether Congress had issued *some* authorization for the Vietnam War. The *Berk* Court really had not so limited the remand, leaving it to the district court to determine the effect of any new evidence on the applicability of the political question doctrine. In any case, the *Orlando* Court held that the political question doctrine did not prevent a court from asking whether Congress had been, at some level, a joint participant in the war-making decision. Further, the *Orlando* Court held that Congress had participated with the President in the making of war in Vietnam. It cited as examples the broad authorization to the President contained in the Tonkin Gulf Resolution. The Court also characterized the congressional appropriations as ratifications of the President's "initiatives."[93] To show the intention of Congress to help the President wage war, the *Orlando* Court cited congressional declarations of purpose in appropriations measures: the 1967 Appropriations Act, for example, stated Congress' "firm intention to provide all necessary support for members of the Armed Forces of the United States fighting in Vietnam."[94] Finally, the Court cited Congress' continuation of the Military Selective Service Act as evidence of congressional participation in war-making in Vietnam.

However, having found that Congress participated in the making of war in Vietnam, the *Orlando* Court declined to answer the question of whether Congress' participation was sufficient to satisfy the constitutional war-making standard. This question was held to be foreclosed by the political question doctrine.

The choice, for example, between an explicit declaration on the one hand and a resolution and war-implementing legislation, on the other, as the medium for expression of congressional consent . . . involves the political question doctrine.[95]

The *Orlando* Court determined that Congress' decision to not declare war but to authorize spending for war might reflect concern over disturbing the relationship between the United States and other nations. The Court considered the realm of international relations to be off limits to the courts: "The making of a policy decision . . . [regarding diplomacy, foreign policy, and military strategy] is clearly within the constitutional domain of those two branches [Congress and the President] and is just as clearly not within the competency of power of the judiciary."[96] So, although the *Orlando* Court was free to inquire into whether Congress had had *some* say in the war-making decision, it was not free to ask about the adequacy of the method of its approval.

The same appellate court visited the political question issue for a third time in *DaCosta v. Laird.*[97] The *DaCosta* Court was asked to reconsider its conclusion in *Orlando* that Congress was a participant in war-making in Vietnam in light of the fact that the Tonkin Gulf Resolution had been repealed. The *DaCosta* Court held that *Orlando* was not based solely on the Tonkin Gulf Resolution.

In other words, there was sufficient legislative action in extending the Selective Service Act and in appropriating billions of dollars to carry on military and naval operations in Vietnam to ratify and approve the measures taken by the Executive, even in the absence of the Gulf of Tonkin Resolutions.[98]

The *DaCosta* Court also found that the legislative history of the Tonkin Gulf Resolution's repeal did not establish a congressional intent to "undeclare" the war.[99] The Court cited the failure of both the Senate and the House to pass an "amendment to the draft extension bill to prevent the use of funds for the deployment or maintenance of United States Armed Forces in Indochina after specified dates."[100] In fact, as the Court noted, within days of the defeat of this amendment, Congress voted to extend the Selective Service Act.[101] Although this extension carried with it a sense of Congress that United States forces be withdrawn in a prompt and orderly fashion, it did not set any deadlines or "quarrel with the fact that troops were in Indochina."[102] The *DaCosta* Court reached the merits in the sense that it found congressional participation in the war, but did not go beyond this finding to disturb *Orlando*. Therefore, *Orlando* stands as a example of the effect of the political

question doctrine in allowing one inquiry (whether Congress has authorized war) and preventing another (whether such authorization is sufficient).

Conclusion

The judiciary, having discovered in *Marbury v. Madison,* its constitutional authority to determine the limits of its own authority, has been
circumspect in its self-monitoring task. One manifestation of this cir-
cumspection is the concept of nonjusticiability and its subset, the political
question doctrine. Generally, the courts have viewed direct challenges
to the President's war-making authority to be nonjusticiable political
questions, although both the *Lowry* opinion and Justice Brennan's concurrence in *Goldwater* suggest possible exceptions to the general rule.
This feature of war powers jurisprudence explains the relative paucity of
judicial authority on war powers questions.[103] It also suggests that,
wherever the war powers equilibrium lies, it is not likely to be located
and fully described by the courts.

The courts' reluctance to examine war-making issues does not necessarily imply anything about the courts' views on presidential war-
making. The political question doctrine would raise obstacles to members
of Congress seeking judicial restraint of presidential war-making that is
beyond the scope of the President's constitutional authority. But difficulty
in enforcement does not render lawful that which is unlawful. An unlawful
act by the President that is unreviewable is nevertheless unlawful. Whether
a particular instance of presidential war-making is lawful or not, the
issue is not likely to be resolved by the courts.

Notes

1. 48 U.S. (7 How.) 1 (1849).
2. U.S. CONST., Art. III, Sec. 2.
3. *Flast v. Cohen,* 392 U.S. 83, 94–95 (1968). *See also* L. TRIBE, CON-
STITUTIONAL LAW ("TRIBE") 53 (1978); E. KEYNES, UNDECLARED
WAR: TWILIGHT ZONE OF CONSTITUTIONAL POWER 60 (1982).
4. *Cohens v. Virginia,* 19 U.S. (6 Wheat.) 264, 403 (1821).
5. *Marbury v. Madison,* 5 U.S. (1 Cr.) 137 (1803). *See also Fletcher v. Peck,*
10 U.S. (6 Cr.) 87 (1810).
6. *See* A. BICKEL, THE LEAST DANGEROUS BRANCH ("BICKEL") 11
(1962). *See contra* Wechsler, "Toward Neutral Principles of Constitutional Law,"
73 HARV. L. REV. 1 (1959).
7. U.S. CONST., Art. III, Sec. 2.
8. 5 U.S. (1 Cr.) 137 (1803).
9. Professor Bickel argues that Chief Justice Marshall "begged the question-
in-chief, which was not whether an act repugnant to the Constitution could

stand, but who should be empowered to decide that the Act is repugnant." BICKEL at 3. The *Marbury* Court could have decided, for example, that Congress can determine the constitutionality of its own laws, along the lines followed in the British Parliament.

10. G. Haskins, "Foundations of Power: John Marshall," 2 HISTORY OF THE SUPREME COURT OF THE UNITED STATES, PART I, Ch. 5, 7 (1981).

11. R. McCLOSKEY, THE AMERICAN SUPREME COURT 42 (1960).

12. Haskins, "Man Versus Political Power: A Crisis in American Constitutional Law," in L'INDIVIDU FACE AU POUVOIR, 50 RECUEILS DE LA SOCIETE JEAN BODIN POUR L'HISTOIRE COMPARATIVE DES INSTITUTIONS 435, 437 (Paris 1988). *See also* Haskins, "Law Versus Politics in the Early Years of the Marshall Court," 130 U. PA. L. REV. 1–11 (1981).

13. *Flast v. Cohen*, 392 U.S. 83, 95 (1968) (quoting *Poe v. Ullman*, 367 U.S. 497, 508 (1961)). *See also Warth v. Seldin*, 422 U.S. 490, 500–501 (1975); *Schlesinger v. Reservists to Stop the War*, 418 U.S. 208, 215 and n.5 (1974) (standing); *Powell v. McCormack*, 395 U.S. 486, 549 (1969) (policital question doctrine not a bar); Note, "Congressional Access to the Federal Courts," 90 HARV. L. REV. 1632 (1977).

14. *See, e.g., Baker v. Carr*, 369 U.S. 186, 210 (1962); *Colegrove v. Green*, 328 U.S. 549, 552 (1946); *Pacific States Tel. & Tel. Co. v. Oregon*, 223 U.S. 118 (1912); *Luther v. Borden*, 48 U.S. (7 How.) 1 (1849); *Stuart v. Laird*, U.S. (1 Cr.) 308, 309 (1803); *Hollingsworth v. Virginia*, 3 U.S. (3 Dal.) 378, 382 (1798); *Hylton v. U.S.*, 3 U.S. (3 Dal.) 171, 175 (1796). *See also* Finkelstein, "Judicial Self-Limitation," 37 HARV. L. REV. 338 (1924); Finkelstein, "Some Further Notes on Judicial Self- Limitation," 39 HARV. L. REV. 221 (1926); Weston, "Political Questions," 38 HARV. L. REV. 296 (1925); Frankfurter, "John Marshall and the Judicial Function," 69 HARV. L. REV. 217, 227 (1955); Scharpf, "Judicial Review and the Political Question: A Functional Analysis," 75 YALE L. J. 517, 536 (1966); Henkin, "Is There a 'Political Question' Doctrine?" 85 YALE L. J. 597, 601 (1976).

15. L. HAND, THE BILL OF RIGHTS 73 (1958).

16. BICKEL at 184.

17. *See, e.g.,* Choper, "The Supreme Court and the Political Branches: Democratic Theory and Practice," 122 U. PA. L. Rev. 810, 816 (1974); Rostow, "The Democratic Character of Judicial Review," 66 HARV. L. REV. 193, 194 (1952).

18. *See, e.g.,* Choper, 122 U. PA. L. REV. at 810; Bishin, "Judicial Review in Democratic Theory," 50 S. CAL. L. REV. 1099, 1102 (1977).

19. *Colegrove v. Green*, 328 U.S. 549 (1946).

20. BICKEL at 190.

21. 328 U.S. at 552. The courts have intervened in cases where malapportionment abridges the right to vote "on account of race, color, or previous condition of servitude," as prohibited by the Fifteenth Amendment. *See, e.g., Gomillion v. Lightfoot*, 364 U.S. 339 (1960); *Terry v. Adams*, 345 U.S. 461 (1953).

22. 328 U.S. at 556.

23. 369 U.S. 186 (1962). *See also Reynolds v. Sims*, 377 U.S. 533 (1964).

24. 369 U.S. at 217.

25. *E.g.*, TRIBE at 75.

26. *E.g.*, BICKEL at 195.

27. 369 U.S. at 226. *See* BICKEL at 195–197.

28. 369 U.S. at 217.

29. TRIBE at 79.

30. 333 U.S. 103 (1948).

31. 333 U.S. at 111.

32. 369 U.S. at 211. *See Japan Whaling Ass'n v. American Cetacean Soc.*, 478 U.S. 221, 229–230 (1986).

33. TRIBE at 77 n.35. *See also* L. HENKIN, FOREIGN AFFAIRS AND THE CONSTITUTION 210–216 (1972).

34. The Supreme Court's approach to the political question doctrine has been described alternatively as "classical," "prudential," and "functional." *See* TRIBE at 71, n.1; Wechsler, 73 HARV. L. REV. at 9 ("classical" view); BICKEL at 23, 69 ("prudential" view); Scharpf, 75 YALE L. J. at 566 ("functional" view). The classical view is expressed in *Marbury v. Madison:* a question cannot be resolved by the court unless the text of the Constitution brings the question within the court's jurisdiction. The "prudential" view is that the court ought not enter areas where it risks losing its credibility and hence its authority. The "functional" view is that the court should avoid inquiring into matters where it is not suited, relative to other branches of the government, to gather the necessary information.

35. *See, e.g.*, Tigar, "Judicial Power, the 'Political Question' Doctrine, and Foreign Relations," 17 U.C.L.A. L. REV. 1135 (1970).

36. *See, e.g.*, Carter, "The Constitutionality of the War Powers Resolution," 70 VA. L. REV. 101 (1984).

37. 413 U.S. 1 (1973). *See also Laird v. Tatum*, 408 U.S. 1, 15–16 (1972); *Duncan v. Kahanamoku*, 327 U.S. 304 (1946); *Sterling v. Constantin*, 287 U.S. 378 (1932).

38. 413 U.S. at 5–6.

39. 413 U.S. at 10 (emphasis in original).

40. 418 U.S. 683 (1974).

41. 418 U.S. at 692–693.

42. 418 U.S. at 696–697.

43. 418 U.S. at 697 (quoting *U.S. v. ICC*, 337 U.S. 426, 430 (1949) (justiciable controversy even though United States is, in effect, suing itself)).

44. 444 U.S. 996 (1979).

45. 307 U.S. 433 (1939).

46. 444 U.S. at 1003.

47. 444 U.S. at 1003–1004.

48. 444 U.S. at 1005.

49. 444 U.S. at 999.

50. *Baker*, 369 U.S. at 211-214 (summarizing cases).

51. 444 U.S. at 999. *See also Buckley v. Valeo,* 424 U.S. 1, 138 (1976) *(per curiam); U.S. v. Nixon,* 418 U.S. 683, 707 (1974); *The Pocket Veto Case,* 279 U.S. 655, 676 (1929); *Myers v. U.S.,* 272 U.S. 52 (1926).

52. 444 U.S. at 997. *See also Buckley v. Valeo,* 424 U.S. 1, 113–118 (1976); *Regional Rail Reorganization Act Cases,* 419 U.S. 102, 140 (1974); *Socialist Labor Party v. Gilligan,* 406 U.S. 583, 588 (1972).

53. 444 U.S. 1007 (emphasis original). *Cf. also Powell v. McCormack,* 395 U.S. 486, 548 (1969) ("textual commitment" prong of *Baker* test does not bar judicial review of Adam Clayton Powell's claim that he was unlawfully prevented from taking his seat in the House of Representatives).

54. 444 U.S. at 1007 (citing *Banco Nacional de Cuba v. Sabbatino,* 376 U.S. 398, 410 (1964); *Baker v. Carr,* 369 U.S. 186, 212 (1962); *U.S. v. Pink,* 315 U.S. 203, 228–230 (1942)).

55. 457 U.S. 731 (1982). *See also Weinberger v. Catholic Action of Hawaii/ Peace Education Project,* 454 U.S. 139, 146–147 (1981) (relying on *Totten v. U.S.,* 92 U.S. 105, 107 (1876), in concluding that issues involving disclosure of military secrets are "beyond judicial scrutiny").

56. 457 U.S. at 753–754 (citations omitted).

57. 50 U.S.C. §§ 1541, *et seq.*

58. *Lowry v. Reagan,* 676 F. Supp. 333, 339 (D.D.C. 1987). *See also Ange v. Bush,* No. 90-2792 slip op. (D.D.C. December 13, 1990) (dismissing suit against President Bush regarding Operation Desert Shield on political question and ripeness grounds). *But see Dellums v. Bush,* No. 90-2866 slip op. (D.D.C. December 13, 1990) (suit against President Bush regarding Operation Desert Shield barred not by political question doctrine but by doctrine of ripeness).

59. *See* Chapter 4.

60. 676 F. Supp. at 340 (footnotes omitted).

61. 676 F. Supp. at 341 (quoting *Goldwater,* 444 U.S. at 1000–1001).

62. 676 F. Supp. at 341.

63. *See also Crockett v. Reagan,* 558 F. Supp. 893 (D.D.C. 1982), *aff'd per curiam,* 720 F.2d 1355 (D.C. Cir. 1983), *cert. denied,* 467 U.S. 1251 (1984) (WPR issue nonjusticiable because fact-finding is beyond court's expertise). *Crockett* is examined more fully in Chapter 4.

64. *Mitchell v. Laird,,* 488 F.2d 611 (D.C. Cir. 1973); *Mottola v. Nixon,* 464 F.2d 178 (9th Cir. 1972) (suit dismissed on standing grounds); *Commonwealth of Mass. v. Laird,* 451 F.2d 26 (1st Cir. 1971); *DaCosta v. Laird,* 448 F.2d 1368 (2d Cir. 1971) *(per curiam), cert. denied,* 405 U.S. 979 (1972); *Orlando v. Laird,* 443 F.2d 1039 (2d Cir. 1971); *Sarnoff v. Connally,* 457 F.2d 809 (9th Cir.) *(per curiam), cert. denied sub nom. Sarnoff v. Schultz,* 409 U.S. 929 (1972); *Berk v. Laird,* 429 F.2d 302 (2d Cir. 1970), *cert. denied,* 404 U.S. 869 (1971); *Velvel v. Nixon,* 415 F.2d 236 (10th Cir.), *cert. denied,* 396 U.S. 1042 1970); *Luftig v. McNamara,* 373 F.2d 664 (D.C. Cir.) *(per curiam), cert. denied,* 387 U.S. 945 (1967); *Mora v. McNamara,* 387 F.2d 862 (D.C. Cir.), *cert. denied,* 389 U.S. 934 (1967); *Drinan v. Nixon,* 364 F. Supp. 854 (D. Mass. 1973); *Atlee v. Laird,* 347 F. Supp. 689 (E.D. Pa. 1972), *aff'd.,* 411 U.S. 911 (1973); *Meyers v. Nixon,* 339 F. Supp. 1388, 1390 (S.D. N.Y. 1972); *Davi v. Laird,* 318

F. Supp. 478 (W.D. Va. 1970); *Switkes v. Laird,* 316 F. Supp. 358 (S.D. N.Y. 1970); *U.S. v. Sisson,* 294 F. Supp. 511, 515 (D. Mass. 1968), *appeal dismissed,* 399 U.S. 267 (1970). *Cf. also Simmons v. U.S.,* 406 F.2d 456, 460 (5th Cir.) (draft legislation is not unconstitutional), *cert. denied,* 395 U.S. 982 (1969); *U.S. v. Mitchell,* 264 F. Supp. 874, 874, 898 (D. Conn. 1965). *See also* Sugarman, "Judicial Decisions Concerning the Constitutionality of the United States Military in Indo-China: A Bibliography of Court Decisions," 13 COLUM. J. TRANSNAT'L. L. 470 (1974); C. ROSSITER and R. LONGAKER, THE SUPREME COURT AND THE COMMANDER IN CHIEF 146–149 (1976).

65. *Holtzman v. Schlesinger,* 361 F. Supp. 553 (E.D. N.Y.), *rev'd,* 484 F.2d 1307 (2d Cir.), *cert. denied,* 416 U.S. 936 (1973).

66. *See* C. ROSSITER and R. LONGAKER, THE SUPREME COURT AND THE COMMANDER IN CHIEF 145–148 (1976).

67. 457 F.2d 809 (9th Cir.) *(per curiam), cert. denied sub nom., Sarnoff v. Schultz,* 409 U.S. 929 (1972).

68. The Foreign Assistance Act of 1961, 22 U.S.C. §§ 2318, 2360, 2364.

69. The same mistake was made by the court in *Velvel v. Johnson,* 287 F. Supp. 846 (D. Kan. 1968). The *Velvel* Court, like the *Sarnoff* Court, ultimately held the matter of the constitutionality of the Vietnam War to be a political question. *See* Velvel, "The Vietnam War: Unconstitutional, Justiciable and Jurisdictionally Attackable," 16 KAN. L. REV. 449 (1968).

70. 429 F.2d 302 (2d Cir. 1970). *See also Switkes v. Laird,* 316 F. Supp. 358 (S.D. N.Y. 1970) (following *Berk*).

71. 429 F.2d at 305, *quoting Baker v. Carr,* 369 U.S. 186, 217 (1962).

72. 373 F.2d 664 (D.C. Cir.) *(per curiam), cert. denied,* 387 U.S. 945 (1967).

73. *Id.* at 665.

74. *Id.* at 666.

75. *Id., citing Johnson v. Eisentrager,* 339 U.S. 763 (1950); *Chicago & Southern Air Lines, Inc. v. Waterman S.S. Corp.,* 333 U.S. 103, 111 (1948); *Eminente v. Johnson,* 124 U.S. App. D.C. 56, 361 F.2d 73, *cert. denied,* 385 U.S. 929, (1966); *Pauling v. McNamara,* 118 U.S. App. D.C. 50, 331 F.2d 796 (1963), *cert. denied,* 377 U.S. 933, (1964); *Pauling v. McElroy,* 107 U.S. App. D.C. 372, 278 F.2d 252, *cert. denied,* 364 U.S. 835 (1960).

76. 373 F.2d at 665.

77. 347 F. Supp. 689 (E.D. Pa. 1972).

78. 67 U.S. 635 (1862).

79. *See* Chapter 2.

80. 318 F. Supp. 478 (W.D. Va. 1970).

81. *Id.* at 484.

82. *Id.* at 480.

83. *See, e.g., Bas v. Tingy,* 4 U.S. (4 Dall.) 37, 45 (1800).

84. This is essentially the position taken by a court in two cases involving the same defendant, indicted for refusing to report for induction into the armed forces. *U.S. v. Sisson,* 294 F. Supp. 515 (1968); *U.S. v. Sisson,* 294 F. Supp. 511 (1968).

85. 246 F. Supp 874, 898 (D. Conn. 1965).

86. 50 U.S.C. § 462.

87. 246 F. Supp. at 898.

88. U.S. CONST., Art. I, Sec. 8, Cl. 12.

89. 429 F.2d 302 (2d Cir. 1970).

90. 317 F. Supp. 715 (E.D. N.Y. 1970).

91. *Orlando v. Laird,* 317 F. Supp. 1013, 1019 (E.D. N.Y. 1970).

92. 443 F.2d 1039 (2d Cir. 1971).

93. 443 F.2d at 1042.

94. *Id.,* n.2.

95. *Id.* at 1043.

96. *Id.*

97. 448 F.2d 1368 (2d Cir. 1971) *(per curiam).*

98. *Id.* at 1369.

99. *Id.* (citing Cong. Rep. No. 1805, 91st Cong., 2d Sess., U.S. Code Cong. and Ad. News at 6069 (1970)).

100. *Id.* at 1370 (citing 117 Cong. Rec. Serv. 9275, 9279 (June 16, 1971) (Chiles Amendment and McGovern-Hatfield Amendment) and 117 Cong. Rec. Serv. 5410 (June 17, 1971)).

101. *Id.* at 1370.

102. *Id.*

103. It is not a coincidence that so many of the early cases discussing war powers involved libel against merchant ships. *The Prize Cases,* 67 U.S. 635 (1862); *Little v. Barreme,* 6 U.S. (2 Cr.) 170 (1804); *Talbot v. Seeman,* 5 U.S. (1 Cr.) 1 (1801); *Bas v. Tinghy,* 4 U.S. (4 Dall.) 36 (1800). These cases did not involve direct challenges to the President's war powers *per se.* Rather, they involved property rights jeopardized by the seizure of merchant vessels. Thus, the courts did not inquire into the question of whether discretion required the courts to decline review.

4

The War Powers Resolution

Bad laws are the worst sort of tyranny.[1]

Summary of the War Powers Resolution

Congress passed the War Powers Resolution ("WPR")[2] in 1973 over President Nixon's veto. Since then, the WPR has been the subject of great controversy.[3] The stated purpose of the WPR was to induce greater congressional participation in presidential war-making decisions.[4] The WPR's preamble states that the WPR's purpose is to "insure that the collective judgment of both the Congress and the President will apply" to the use of armed force.[5] The preamble also states that the WPR is "necessary and proper"[6] to ensure that the President's authority as Commander-in-Chief is limited to three situations: "(1) a declaration of war [by Congress], (2) specific statutory authorization [by Congress], or (3) a national emergency created by attack upon the United States, its territories or possessions, or its armed forces."[7]

Pursuant to this statement of purpose, the WPR imposes four limitations upon the President's power to order U.S. forces into hostile situations. First, the President "in every possible instance shall consult with Congress before introducing United States Armed Forces into hostilities or into situations where imminent involvement in hostilities is clearly indicated by the circumstances."[8] This consultation clause is the only pre-hostilities requirement of the WPR and plainly stops short of requiring congressional pre-authorization.

The second requirement of the WPR directs the President to report to Congress in writing within 48 hours of introducing U.S. forces into "hostilities or into situations where imminent involvement in hostilities is clearly indicated by the circumstances," or into the "territory, airspace, or waters of a foreign nation, while equipped for combat," or into a foreign nation to "substantially enlarge" the U.S. military presence there.[9]

If the President reports to Congress under this provision, he must continue reporting at least every six months if U.S. forces remain committed to the situation inducing the original report.[10]

The third limitation on the President's war-making authority is the automatic termination provision of the WPR. Under this provision, the President must "terminate the use" of the armed forces within sixty days of a "hostilities" report to Congress, unless Congress expressly authorizes their continued use.[11] The President can obtain an additional thirty days to withdraw the armed forces if he certifies to Congress in writing that such an extension is necessary to provide for a safe withdrawal. The apparent effect of the automatic termination provision is to free Congress of the need to vote against the disapproved use of force sixty days after the President has reported; Congress must vote only if it wishes to endorse the President's use of force.[12]

Although the WPR's automatic termination provision grants the President a sixty-day license to use military force, it does not grant him a sixty-day *carte blanche*. Notwithstanding the sixty-day provision, Congress may direct the President to remove U.S. armed forces from unauthorized hostilities by means of a concurrent resolution.[13] This legislative veto[14] provision is unconstitutional.[15]

Consultation and Reporting

The threshold issue raised by the WPR's consultation and reporting requirements is the definition of the circumstances that activate them. The WPR requires consultation before "introducing United States Armed Forces into hostilities or into situations where imminent involvement in hostilities is clearly indicated by the circumstances. . . ." The ambiguity latent in the WPR's "hostilities" standard was illustrated by President Reagan's deployment of the Middle East Force to the Persian Gulf. In the Persian Gulf, U.S. forces were not intentionally "introduced" by the President into hostilities until the September 21, 1987 attack on the *Iran Ajr*, five months after Kuwait agreed to accept U.S. protection in the Persian Gulf.[16] Prior to September 21, U.S. forces arguably were involved in "hostilities" when the U.S.S. *Stark* was accidentally attacked by an Iraqi aircraft on May 17. However, even if the attack on the *Stark* qualified as an instance of "hostilities," it did not activate the WPR because the President did not introduce the *Stark* into hostilities in the sense of intentionally placing the ship in a military conflict with Iraq. The attack was an accident. After September 21, 1987, further hostilities were neither "imminent" nor "clearly indicated." The President did not order U.S. naval vessels to undertake any further military action against Iranian targets. The Navy, by sailing in harm's way, was still vulnerable to hostile acts, but was not expected to be subjected to or to commit any. So even if the September 21 attack on the *Iran Ajr* started the sixty-day "clock," the "clock" stopped because the hostile U.S. operation ended.

Some uses of the military clearly have involved U.S. forces in actual hostilities. One of these was the 1986 air strike against Libya.[17] Some members of Congress, including House Republican Leader Robert Michel, objected to the 1986 air strike against Libya on the ground that the President had failed to comply with the WPR's consultation provision. The President had advised congressional leaders of the strike three hours before it commenced, an amount of notice Representative Michel considered insufficient for meaningful consultation. This objection was also raised after Operation Urgent Fury in Grenada, even though the President advised congressional leaders of the mission the night before its commencement. Similar objections have been made following instances of presidential war-making such as the recapture of the S.S. *Mayaguez* in May of 1975.[18]

These objections raise the question of how early discussion must commence to qualify as consultation. If the President had convened congressional leaders during the April 14 air strike against Libya, he obviously would not have satisfied the statutory requirement of pre-conflict consultation. But would one hour of notice have been enough? If not, then how many hours are required? The WPR does not state a minimum threshold of notice, undoubtedly because such linedrawing is inherently incoherent. The most reasonable standard lies in the position expressed by the President in 1986: since the President was able to call off the air strikes against Libya at the time of his meeting with congressional leaders and since the meeting fulfilled the WPR objective of pre-hostilities communication between the President and Congress, the consultation requirement was satisfied. The same can be said of the President's consultation with Congress before Operation Urgent Fury in Grenada: while the consultation did not provide Congress with sufficient notice to determine whether it would take the actions chosen by the President, it was not meant to. The President had the power and the responsibility to determine the appropriate response under emergency conditions.[19] By consulting with Congress, he was not inviting congressional participation in the command of the armed forces but soliciting Congress' point of view before the fact.

Indeed, lengthy consultation would demand that the President divert resources from the military crisis itself to the satisfaction of an ambiguous legal provision. As President Ford said in 1977, "When a crisis breaks, it is impossible to draw the Congress into the decision-making process in an effective way."[20] He continued, "There is absolutely no way American foreign policy can be conducted or military operations commanded by 535 members of Congress even if they all happen to be on Capital Hill when they are needed."[21] The President is empowered by the Constitution unilaterally to use the military in emergencies. The WPR cannot limit this constitutional entitlement. If consultation became too cumbersome, it would not be required as a matter of law. The lack of a legal requirement to consult, however, does not inform the separate question of whether the President would be wise to do so. Surely, it would be desirable for the President to consult with Congress and even to have Congress' approval prior to undertaking military operations.

Senator Jacob Javits, one of the co-sponsors and original authors of the WPR, would not agree with former President Ford. His position was this:

> [The WPR] is an effort to learn from the lessons of the last tragic decade of war in Vietnam which has cost our nation so heavily in blood, treasure, and morale. The War Powers Act would assure that any future decision to commit the United States to any warmaking must be shared in by the Congress to be lawful.[22]

Although Senator Javits expressed his view of the purpose of the WPR with great clarity, his primary goal, that of sharing the President's warmaking power, was not achieved in the final version of the WPR. The WPR does not require congressional permission to use force or congressional involvement in the operational planning process. Were such specific congressional activities contemplated, the WPR would have identified them. But the WPR did not do so, probably as the result of Congress' recognition that it lacks the constitutional authority to require such participation. The Constitution confers on the President both the ultimate command of the armed forces and foreign affairs powers.[23] The power to respond to emergencies with military force is in the hands of the President,[24] a legal rule directly at odds with Senator Javits' view. If the WPR required the President to obtain congressional permission before employing military force, it would be unconstitutional.

There are also practical (as distinct from theoretical constitutional) problems with the consultation requirement. One is the fact that when Congress is out of session, the President may experience great difficulty in locating even the congressional leadership. President Ford explained the difficulty in locating congressional leaders at the time of the evacuation of Da Nang, South Vietnam in 1975.

> Not a single leader of either party remained in the capital. Three of them were in Greece, two in the People's Republic of China, two in Mexico, one in Europe, and another in the Middle East. The rest were in twelve widely scattered locations in the United States. Obviously, the "consultation"

called for by the act was impossible. Although we went to incredible lengths to reach them and explain the situation, we did not succeed. There was simply no way that I could have drawn Congress into the decision-making process when the crisis was at hand, and I was not about to withhold the help of our forces in a humanitarian evacuation.[25]

President Ford experienced the same sort of difficulty in 1976 during the evacuation of Lebanon.

On June 18, 1976, we began the first evacuation of American citizens from the civil war in Lebanon. The Congress was not in recess, but had adjourned for the day.

As telephone calls were made, we discovered, among other things, that one member of Congress had an unlisted number which his press secretary refused to divulge. After trying and failing to reach another member of Congress, we were told by his assistant that the congressman did not need to be reached.

We tried so hard to reach a third member of Congress that our resourceful White House operators had the local police leave a note on the congressman's beach cottage door: "Please call the White House."[26]

Following consultation, the President must report to Congress within 48 hours of introducing U.S. forces into imminent or actual hostilities under WPR Section 4(a)(1). This requirement is of consequence primarily because the submission of such a report starts the WPR's sixty-day "clock."[27] This reporting requirement, on its face, does not necessarily restrict the President's ability to use force in emergencies because the use of force in emergencies does not necessarily correspond to a strategy of attrition. Rather, by definition, the President's emergency powers apply to current exigencies, the long-term implications of which are left for consideration at the end of the emergency. The air strike against Libya offers an especially clear example: because the April 14 tactical air strike did not necessarily contemplate a second strike, the sixty-day clock stopped running when the aircraft returned to their respective bases. Of course, it is possible that a long cycle of tactical strikes and withdrawals might encourage Congress to take some action to keep the sixty-day clock running. But the length of such a tactical cycle is legally indeterminate; political pressure, and not the legal force of the WPR, would be the ultimate cause of any such congressional action.

The deployment of Marines to Lebanon provides a counterexample. When the President sent the Marines to Lebanon on September 29, 1982, he did not promise an early withdrawal. In fact, they stayed for a year and a half. As a result, some members of Congress thought the WPR required a presidential report to Congress, activating the sixty-day clock.[28] Although the President did submit a report, it did not limit the Marines to a sixty-day mission. Since the President was constitutionally authorized to send the Marines to Lebanon without prior congressional approval, Congress lacked the constitutional power to require the withdrawal of forces after sixty days.[29]

Unlike the 1982 deployment of Marines to Lebanon, the 1986 air strikes against Libya rather unambiguously involved "hostilities." The WPR, on its face, required a report from the President on the Libya air strikes. Indeed, one was provided within the WPR's 48-hour period.[30] Had the President taken the position that he was constitutionally entitled never to report to Congress on the air strikes, he would have occupied unstable legal ground. The President enjoys no absolute right to withhold information from Congress.[31] Undoubtedly, Congress enjoys the right to demand information from the President in order to exercise its constitutional powers, most notably those of appropriations.[32] So, there is a legitimate basis for congressional demands for information on military operations. Where the WPR might exceed the limit of permissible congressional access to presidential information is in the requirement that such information be supplied within 48 hours of the first use of force. It takes little ingenuity to imagine that the President might be occupied during the first 48 hours of hostilities with his responsibilities as Commander-in-Chief, into which zone of responsibility Congress may not intrude. For example, in 1975, President Ford used military force to free the crew of the S.S. *Mayaguez*. The seizure of the ship occurred on May 12, 1975 and the withdrawal of U.S. forces took place on May 15, over 48 hours later. In spite of his busy schedule during the operation, President Ford managed to report within 48 hours.[33] To the extent that the reporting requirement would have interfered in President Ford's command of the armed forces, President Ford was not required to comply. Eventually President Ford could have been required to inform Congress of the operation, but not necessarily within 48 hours. Despite the lack of a compelling legal requirement to do so, however, presidents might and, judging from President Reagan's practice of reporting, probably will feel inclined to report for reasons other than legal compulsion.

The Sixty-Day "Clock"

In the aftermath of each introduction of military elements into hostile situations since 1973, critics of the use of limited force have protested the failure of the President to comply with the WPR. The presidential response uniformly has been a rejection of the constitutionality of the WPR. Indeed, the constitutionality of the WPR has been denied by every President since 1973. In spite of this serious challenge to the very existence of the WPR, the sixty-day limitation is widely viewed as a strong restriction on the President's war-making power.

The sixty-day "clock" was intended to strike a balance between the war-making functions of the President and Congress. By not requiring congressional approval before employing military force, Congress effectively conceded that the President has some flexibility under the law to respond to emergencies. The WPR, however, did impose a time-limit to prevent the President from unilaterally committing U.S. forces to an extended conflict.

The WPR was drafted using the Vietnam War as a model for future hostilities.[34] Senator Javits explained:

> The approach taken in the War Powers Bill reverses the situation by placing the burden on the Executive to come to Congress for specific authority. The sponsors of the Bill believe that this [sixty-day limitation] provision will provide an important national safeguard against creeping involvement in future Vietnam style wars.[35]

The WPR did not contemplate an "era of violent peace,"[36] where numerous violent or potentially violent crises blur into one long emergency.[37] One consequence of this imperfect congressional foresight is ambiguity in the determination of the beginning and end of the sixty-day period.

When President Reagan sent the Marines to Lebanon in September of 1982, the President told Congress that he did not expect the Marines to engage in hostilities. Only in June of 1983, following an attack on a Marine position and the car-bombing of the U.S. embassy, did Congress act to prevent the President from expanding the size of the U.S. force in Lebanon.[38] Following the deaths in combat of four Marines during August and September of 1983, pressure in Congress mounted to invoke the WPR's sixty-day limit in order to induce the withdrawal of the Marines. The President compromised with Congress by exchanging a promise that "the American Force will not engage in combat," except for self-defense, for a congressional authorization of an 18-month extension of the Marine deployment.[39] Less than a month later, 241 servicemen were killed by a suicide bomber, and in February of 1984 the remaining troops were reembarked aboard amphibious ships under protection of air cover and naval gunfire.

In March of 1984, the President declared that U.S. participation in the multinational force had ended. At no point in the period of direct U.S. military involvement in Lebanon was the WPR invoked to force the withdrawal of U.S. forces. The only WPR invocation was contained in the Multinational Force in Lebanon Resolution, which expressly authorized the presence of U.S. forces in Lebanon. Furthermore, the Multinational

Force in Lebanon Resolution was enacted only after U.S. forces had been in Lebanon for almost a year. The President sent the U.S. Marines to a forward position in one of the world's most unstable locations, but the sixty-day limitation was not activated.

The Lebanon experience suggests that in spite of the WPR's apparently automatic timing provision, Congress must expressly invoke the WPR in order to restrain the President if he does not issue a WPR report. Such a conclusion is supported by the decision of a federal court in *Crockett v. Reagan.*[40]

Nonjusticiability

If a dispute arises between the President and Congress over the WPR, it might be resolved in two forums: the courts and the political arena. One such dispute could arise over the definition of "hostilities" under the WPR. Some circumstances present themselves in a form all can agree involve actual or imminent hostilities. The air strikes against Libya and Operation Urgent Fury in Grenada are two examples. But in other cases, "hostilities" are in the eye of the beholder: some thought the deployment of the Middle East Force to the Persian Gulf meant that U.S. forces were facing imminent hostilities, while others did not.

The task of defining the term "hostilities" fell to a federal district court in *Crockett v. Reagan.*[41] The *Crockett* Court was asked to determine whether U.S. troops in El Salvador were facing imminent "hostilities," but found itself incompetent to resolve the issue. In *Crockett*, a group of congressmen challenged the presence of U.S. forces in El Salvador. The congressmen sought from the Court an order requiring the President to remove U.S. forces from El Salvador, where they had been deployed for more than 60 days without express congressional authorization. The congressmen characterized the mission of the U.S. military forces as combat oriented and likely to lead to U.S. casualties. They asserted that 56 military personnel were assigned to combat areas. They argued that U.S. military personnel were therefore in danger, citing two armed attacks on positions occupied by U.S. personnel.[42] In addition, the congressmen asserted that U.S. forces were "fighting side by side" with Salvadoran government forces. This allegation was based on a newspaper article. They also referred to a second newspaper article reporting that U.S. forces in El Salvador were drawing "hostile fire pay."[43]

The President, on the other hand, stated that the mission of U.S. forces in El Salvador was only to provide training and not to provide assistance in combat or otherwise to participate in the planning or execution of combat operations.[44] The congressmen argued that the mission of U.S. military personnel in El Salvador was sufficiently dangerous as to involve imminent hostilities within the meaning of the WPR. The President responded that U.S. forces were not serving in combat roles, so even if future casualties could be imagined, U.S. forces were not involved in hostilities, actual or imminent. The Court found itself unable to resolve the factual dispute of how imminent hostilities involving U.S. forces in El Salvador might be.

> [T]he question presented does require judicial inquiry into sensitive military matters. Even if the plaintiffs could introduce admissible evidence concerning the state of hostilities in various geographical areas in El Salvador where U.S. forces are stationed and the exact nature of U.S. participation in the conflict (and this information may well be unavailable except through inadmissible newspaper articles), the Court no doubt would be presented conflicting evidence on those issues by defendants. The Court lacks the resources and expertise (which are accessible to the Congress) to resolve disputed questions of fact concerning the military situation in El Salvador.[45]

Accordingly, the Court considered the WPR controversy "nonjusticiable."[46] The Court did point out that it had not declined to adjudicate the issues presented on the ground that they involved the "apportionment of power between the executive and legislative branches." As the Court stated, "The duty of courts to decide such questions has been repeatedly reaffirmed by the Supreme Court."[47] The Court, having satisfied itself that it was not ducking the constitutional issue of the allocation of war powers, concluded:

> [T]he factfinding that would be necessary to determine whether U.S. forces have been introduced into hostilities or imminent hostilities in El Salvador renders this case in its current posture nonjusticiable. The questions as to the nature and extent of the United States' presence in El Salvador and whether a report under the WPR is mandated because our forces have been subject to hostile fire or are taking part in the war effort are appropriate for congressional, not judicial, investigation and determination.[48]

As a result of the *Crockett* Court's holding, the issue of how the term "hostilities" would be interpreted went, and continues to go, unresolved.[49] The Court did say that "a case could arise with facts less elusive than these" and that in such a case the Court would be able to determine the existence of hostilities. It cited as an example a case about the seven-year Vietnam War, in which "hostilities had resulted in one million deaths, including those of 50,000 Americans, and for which the United States had spent at least one hundred billion dollars."[50] Lacking such a dramatic factual record, however, the Court declined the opportunity to become involved in the fact-finding necessary to resolve the WPR issues.

The significance of this application of the justiciability doctrine is that no court has determined when the sixty-day clock should start. A court is not likely even to reach the question of whether the President needs congressional approval to undertake a military activity abroad. This judicial finding supports two conclusions.

First, if a court cannot determine the meaning of the statutory term "hostilities," then it will not order the withdrawal of U.S. forces when the President has not reported to Congress under the WPR and Congress has not acted to order such a withdrawal. Congress must take some action to activate the sixty-day limitation when the President has not reported. The *Crockett* Court found:

> [T]he legislative scheme [of the WPR] did not contemplate court-ordered withdrawal [of military forces] when no report has been filed, but rather, it leaves open the possibility for a court to order that a report be filed or, alternatively, withdrawal 60 days after a report was filed or required to be filed by a court or Congress. . . . [W]hile the involvement will automatically terminate after 60 days if either house fails to act or if the two houses are unable to reach an agreement, this can only occur after open and formal consideration of the question by both full houses, provided that at least one member of either house introduces a bill or resolution. In contrast, when no report has been submitted, there will not necessarily be any debate or floor consideration of the issue at all. If plaintiffs' position is correct, total congressional inaction (which perhaps could signify general agreement with the President's appraisal that no report is required) could result in mandatory withdrawal of U.S. forces if a court adjudged that they had been introduced into hostilities more than 60 days previously. In all of the extensive debate on the mandatory withdrawal provision, this possibility was never entertained.[51]

The Court recognized that congressional silence could actually mean congressional approval of the President's actions and worried that to order withdrawal before a report had been submitted "could thwart the will of the majority of Congress."[52] Requiring the filing of a report, on the other hand, cannot thwart the will of Congress, the Court reasoned. The Court did not address the issue of whether requiring the filing of a report itself could thwart the will of the President. Thus did the *Crockett* Court hold open the possibility that a court could, at some date in the future, order the President to submit a WPR report.

The second conclusion flowing from the *Crockett* opinion is that even if Congress does activate the sixty-day limitation on the ground of existing or imminent hostilities involving U.S. forces, the courts will hesitate before ordering the President to withdraw after sixty days. Although the *Crockett* Court indicated that it would consider ordering a withdrawal of U.S. forces sixty days after a congressional resolution requiring a WPR report, it is difficult to see how it could actually do so, consistent with its opinion. If Congress had required a report on the situation in El Salvador, and if U.S. forces had remained in El Salvador for more than sixty days following the imposition of the reporting requirement, congressional plaintiffs could have requested that the Court order the withdrawal of troops. But the Court would have faced precisely the question it declined to answer: whether "hostilities" exist or are clearly imminent. There simply is no way to avoid this issue in considering the enforcement of the WPR because the WPR's sixty-day withdrawal provision, by its own terms, only applies to actual or clearly imminent hostilities. It is unlikely that this stalemate between the President and Congress would be judicially resolved.

The practical result of *Crockett* is clear: when the President has not reported to Congress, Congress must act to invoke the WPR. Such congressional action is not automatic and may be slow in coming, as the Lebanon experience shows.[53] Furthermore, any dispute between the legislative and executive branches will not necessarily be mediated by the courts, as *Crockett* indicates. The more likely forum for resolution is the political arena.

As a result of the *Crockett* decision, a disagreement between the President and Congress on the use of force, at least in a factual context less extreme than that of the Vietnam War, is likely to be resolved not by the courts, but by the political process. That is, the issue will be resolved not by reference to a legal standard such as the WPR but by reference to the political standard of whether the use of military force is supported by popular endorsement. In effect, the American people decide. Some might argue that this populist approach to war-making has been discredited by the history of American involvement in the Vietnam War and that the existence of the WPR itself is evidence of the failure of non-statutory war-making. This argument, however, fails to answer the question of what Vietnam era problems were solved by the WPR. Congress was certainly aware of the existence of hostilities as it financed the Vietnam War year after year; the enactment of the WPR ten years earlier would not have affected either Congress' notice of a state of war or its constitutional appropriations power.[54]

The War Powers Resolution
and the President's Power to Defend

The constitutionality of the WPR has been the subject of vigorous debate[55] since its enactment in 1973. Proponents of the WPR argue that since Congress exclusively is empowered to declare war,[56] Congress can delegate a portion of its war-making authority to the President, allowing him to respond to emergencies, while retaining the power to determine whether to authorize a continuation of the President's war-making beyond a limited period. Opponents[57] of the WPR claim that the WPR is not constitutional because it seeks to limit the war-making power vested in the President by means of his authority as Commander-in-Chief[58] to defend the national security.[59]

An application of the WPR which seeks to restrain the President from exercising his constitutional authority to defend the national security is unconstitutional. The question is, when is the President authorized under the Constitution to make war? There is little doubt that the President's power to defend is activated upon the invasion by hostile forces of the United States or its territory or possessions, an attack against U.S. forces stationed abroad, or an attack against United States citizens or property abroad.[60] Indeed, the preamble to the WPR demonstrates a congressional recognition that the President is constitutionally authorized to make war during "a national emergency created by attack upon the United States, its territories or possessions, or its armed forces."[61]

The source for such a conclusion about presidential war powers is the Supreme Court, which recognized at an early date that the legality of a war did not necessarily depend on the existence of a congressional declaration of war.[62] The Supreme Court also has identified the right of the President to act unilaterally to defend the United States against invasion.

> If a war be made by invasion of a foreign nation, the President is not only authorized but bound to resist force by force. He does not initiate war, but is bound to accept the challenge without waiting for any special legislative authority.[63]

The Supreme Court has gone at least one step further than Congress did in the WPR preamble by recognizing the President's authority to defend U.S. citizens abroad.[64]

The reason for the Supreme Court's deference to the President's power to defend is its recognition of the necessity for speed in responding to threats against national security. This judicial recognition is supported by the records, such as they are, of the Constitutional Convention in 1787. Of course, the collective intention of the Framers on the question of war powers is difficult to determine. Supreme Court Justice Jackson called the record of the constitutional debates "enigmatic."[65] Nevertheless, the records do indicate that the Framers intended for the President to have the power to defend the national security without congressional authorization.[66] Even James Madison, who feared that war would become "the true nurse of executive aggrandizement,"[67] offered a motion to delete draft language granting Congress the constitutional power to "make" war and substitute the now familiar language granting Congress the power to "declare" war. The reason Madison wanted this change was to grant to the President "the power to repel sudden attacks."[68] Madison's motion carried.

The Supreme Court has based its rulings on the President's defensive power on this change in language at the Constitutional Convention, among other factors. The Supreme Court not only has ratified the President's constitutional authority to defend under exigent circumstances but also has held that the President is the competent authority to decide whether a threat justifies the exercise of his defensive war-making power: "We are all of opinion, that the authority to decide whether the exigency has arisen, belongs exclusively to the president, and that his decision is conclusive upon all other persons."[69] This conclusion was confirmed by *The Prize Cases* Court, which held that the issue of whether a threat to national security justifies a military response by the President "is a question to be decided *by him*. . . ."[70]

Thus emerge both the axiom that the President is constitutionally empowered to defend the national security unilaterally and the corollary that the President may decide whether the circumstances warrant the exercise of this power.[71] These rules, of course, beg the question of when presidential war-making is offensive rather than defensive. The boundary is blurred by the fact that a defensive strategy can yield ostensibly offensive tactics. The U.S. Maritime Strategy,[72] for example, is designed to defend U.S. allies and interests from Soviet aggression, but may involve apparently offensive tactics such as carrier-based air strikes. By the terms of the Maritime Strategy, the United States intends to employ its maritime forces in forward areas in order to "take the fight to the enemy." Although the Maritime Strategy is not limited to war in the European theater, a war between NATO and Soviet forces provides an obvious example of the effect of the Maritime Strategy. If Soviet forces invaded a NATO country, the United States would take military action to defend that NATO country. In order to do so, the United States would convoy men and materiel to Europe by sea. The Soviet Union would seek to disrupt these sea lines of communication, thus commencing a battle for the Atlantic. Under the Maritime Strategy, U.S. forces will not wait for Soviet forces to reach the sea lines of communication, but will attack Soviet forces before they are under way, hoping to preempt a Soviet attack. Such military operations, despite their originally defensive purpose, might appear, in isolation, to be offensive. The solution of this puzzle is not self-evident because it depends on the President's purpose rather than his choice of tactics.

This difficulty in measurement, however, does not preclude analysis of the constitutionality of the WPR as applied. There exist scenarios involving offensive presidential war-making that could be easily disguised as defensive. But there also exist scenarios of presidential war-making irrefutably defensive in nature. The existence of such truly defensive scenarios is the factor most suggestive of the WPR's doubtful constitutionality in application. This proposition may be tested by a hypothetical example.

Suppose that a group of ten American civilian tourists are kidnapped by Libyan terrorists during a visit to the Mediterranean. The hostages are spirited to Tripoli and imprisoned in the military side of the Tripoli airport. The President orders a rescue mission. U.S. forces land at Tripoli airport and engage the terrorists. Simultaneously, naval aircraft from a task force in the Mediterranean bomb military targets around Tripoli to prevent Libyan military support for the terrorists.

Unfortunately, the one-day operation is only partially successful: five of the ten hostages are recovered and U.S. forces are withdrawn. The other five are unharmed but remain in captivity at a new, unknown location. Due to the mixed success of the operation, public support is uneven. The President's opponents in Congress demand that the President report to Congress pursuant to the WPR, thereby starting the sixty-day clock. Their objective is to prevent the President from ordering a second rescue mission after sixty days from the date of the report. In order to appease these opponents, the President complies. Sixty-five days later, the CIA advises the President that it has located the remaining five hostages in a Libyan coastal town, accessible by amphibious forces. The President wants to order a second rescue operation. Would such a mission be lawful?

A statutory argument for the lawfulness of such an operation is that, although the sixty-day clock started running when the President reported under the WPR, the sixty-day limitation does not apply because the President did not continue involving U.S. forces in actual or imminent hostilities during that period. Thus, since the clock stopped when hostilities ended at the end of the one-day operation, the automatic termination provision is not activated.

Even if this statutory argument failed, however, the second rescue mission would not be unlawful. The constitutional argument in favor of the lawfulness of the second mission is that even if the terms of the WPR appear to bar the President from continuing hostilities against the Libyan terrorists, the bar is unconstitutional because it seeks to prevent the President from doing that which he is constitutionally empowered to do. The President has the constitutional authority to use military force defensively. The Supreme Court has found that the President may exercise that authority to rescue American citizens abroad.[73] The second mission against the Libyan terrorists would fall within that constitutional authorization, so the employment of the automatic termination provision to prevent the President's exercise of his lawful authority would be unconstitutional.

It might be, of course, that Congress' position is more wise than the President's. The CIA, for example, might be incorrect about the location of the hostages, who may be endangered by the mission. Thus, the automatic termination might be in the hostages' best interest. But the Congress' superior wisdom would not trump the Constitution's authorization to the President. In this application,[74] and any like it, the sixty-day automatic termination provision would be unconstitutional.

The Unconstitutionality of the Congressional Termination Provision

The WPR allows Congress to direct the President to withdraw U.S. forces at any time by means of a concurrent resolution. Thus, the WPR provides for the "legislative veto" of the President's actions within the scope of the WPR. But in *Immigration and Naturalization Service v. Chadha*,[75] the United States Supreme Court held that, when Congress is constitutionally empowered to set policy in an area and delegates this power to the executive branch, the Constitution does not permit Congress to retain the right to veto by legislation the actions of the executive branch undertaken pursuant to this delegation. Therefore, the WPR's legislative veto provision is unconstitutional.

The *Chadha* Court considered the constitutionality of a legislative veto contained in the Immigration and Naturalization Act ("INA"),[76] by which Congress granted authority to the Department of Justice to set immigration policy. Under the INA, the Immigration and Naturalization Service ("INS") was authorized to conduct hearings and order individuals deported. Mr. Chadha was such an individual. Mr. Chadha was an East Indian student whose student visa had expired, but whose deportation had been suspended by an immigration judge seeking to prevent hardship to Chadha. However, under the INA, Congress had reserved the power to disapprove by legislative veto any such action by the INS and exercised its power in the case of Mr. Chadha. Mr. Chadha then brought an action challenging the authority of Congress to so veto the immigration judge's suspension of his deportation.

Mr. Chadha won. The Supreme Court disapproved the INA's legislative veto for two reasons. First, the legislative veto provision violated the Constitution's presentment clauses,[77] under which legislation must be presented to the President in order to become law.[78] Second, the INA's

legislative veto provision violated the Constitution's bicameral requirement,[79] which prevents a bill from becoming effective without the approval
of both houses of Congress. The only four exceptions to this general
rule are explicitly stated in the text of the Constitution: the Senate's
power to ratify treaties, the Senate's power to approve or disapprove
presidential appointments, the House of Representatives' power to initiate
an impeachment, and the Senate's power to conduct an impeachment
trial.[80]

The INA violated both of these constitutional standards because the
legislative veto took effect without the President's involvement and with
the concurrence of only one house. Since the *Chadha* Court found these
provisions of the Constitution to be "integral parts of the constitutional
design for the separation of powers,"[81] it held that the INA's legislative
veto was unconstitutional. The Court reasoned:

> The bicameral requirement, the Presentment Clauses, the President's veto,
> and the Congress' power to override a veto were intended to erect enduring
> checks on each Branch and to protect the people from the improvident
> exercise of power by mandating certain prescribed steps. To preserve those
> checks, and maintain the separation of powers, the carefully defined limits
> on the power of each Branch must not be eroded. To accomplish what
> has been attempted by one House of Congress in this case requires action
> in conformity with the express procedures of the Constitution's prescription
> for legislative action: passage by a majority of both Houses and presentment
> to the President.[82]

One difference between the WPR's legislative veto and the INA's is
that the WPR's legislative veto is bicameral; that is, no one house of the
two houses of Congress is empowered by the WPR to veto presidential
war-making. It has been argued that this distinction saves the WPR's
legislative veto from constitutional invalidation.[83] But this difference does
not provide a meaningful distinction between the WPR's legislative veto
and that of the INA.[84] Both the current WPR and the INA feature a
legislative veto provision that bypasses the constitutional requirement
that legislation be presented to the President. This characteristic is
indisputably offensive to the concept of separation of powers, under
which Congress and the President exercise separate and necessary law-
making powers.

> The records of the Constitutional Convention reveal that the requirement
> that all legislation be presented to the President and the Presidential veto
> were considered so imperative that the draftsmen took special pains to
> assure that these requirements could not be circumvented. . . . The decision
> to provide the President with a limited and qualified power to nullify

proposed legislation by veto was based on the profound conviction of the Framers that the powers conferred on Congress were the powers to be most carefully circumscribed.[85]

The structure of checks and balances depends on the bicameral requirement as well as the presentment requirement. Therefore, under the central principle of *Chadha,* that of separation of powers, the current WPR's legislative veto is unconstitutional.

The reason that *Chadha* is fatal to the WPR's congressional termination provision is the similarity between the WPR provision and the legislative veto struck down in *Chadha.*[86] Assuming, for the moment, that Congress has the exclusive constitutional power to decide when a war will be waged, *Chadha* establishes that once Congress has delegated this power to the President, it cannot retain the power to veto the President's actions. This means that Congress, having delegated limited war-making power to the President, cannot veto the actions of the President ordered pursuant to this congressional delegation of power.

Of course, the assumption that Congress has the original and exclusive constitutional power to make war is false. Although Congress has the power to declare war, to raise an army, and to maintain a navy,[87] the President is the Commander-in-Chief and the chief diplomat.[88] At the very least, all the powers necessary to wage war were not vested in Congress. Furthermore, the President exercises the power to wage war unilaterally in emergencies.[89] Therefore, it is not clear that Congress possessed the power it delegated to the President by means of the WPR. If the WPR is read as a delegation of the power to declare war, then it clearly involves a power within the constitutional province of Congress. In this event, the WPR's legislative veto is similar to that of the INA in that it involves a delegation of congressional authority to the President. However, if the WPR is read to delegate the power to make war during a sixty-day emergency, it delegates to the President a power already vested by the Constitution and which Congress has no power to abridge. Under this latter interpretation, the legislative veto in the WPR is invalid not only under *Chadha* but also under the constitutional war powers. What *Chadha* implies is that, even if Congress did have the power it delegated by means of the WPR, its attempt to limit that delegation is without effect. Either way, the congressional limitation provision of the WPR is unconstitutional.

The War Powers Resolution Amended

Senator George J. Mitchell (D., ME) has characterized the WPR's legacy as a fifteen-year procedural debate that has obscured substantive issues. He says, "We have spent countless hours proposing, filibustering and debating measures to invoke a law [the WPR]—rather than assessing the wisdom of the policy that prompted the deployment of forces."[90] Senator Sam Nunn (D., GA) has pointed out that the WPR's provision requiring automatic withdrawal of U.S. forces after sixty days "gives foreign governments and terrorist groups a lever for influencing U.S. policy debate."[91] He concludes, "It means they can jerk us around."[92]

On May 19, 1988, Senators Nunn and Mitchell, along with Senators Robert C. Byrd (D., WV) and John W. Warner (R., VA), introduced legislation in the Senate to amend the WPR.[93] The proposed amendment would improve the WPR by eliminating the WPR's unconstitutional legislative veto and the vexing sixty-day automatic termination provision and by changing the constitutional basis of the WPR's limitations on presidential war-making.[94]

Summary of the Amended WPR

The proposed amendments to the WPR[95] would cause several changes. First, the amended WPR would repeal the preamble to the WPR, which states incorrectly that the Constitution limits the President's unilateral war-making power to emergencies created by an attack upon the United States, its territories or possessions, or its armed forces.[96] This change might be read as an acknowledgement that the President's war-making power under the Constitution is not quite so limited. At the very least, it appears to reflect a recognition of the inadequacy of such restrictive statements in defining the scope of presidential war powers; if the President is empowered only to respond to an attack upon the United States, does that mean that he may not use force to preempt an attack upon the United States? Of course, the answer is "no," but the preamble to the WPR does not say so.

Second, the amended WPR would redefine the consultation requirement.[97] One of the ambiguities in the current WPR concerns the meaning of consultation. Is it enough for the President to inform congressional leaders of his intention to use the military? With whom must the President consult? Is it enough to consult with the House and Senate leadership?

These questions are not answered by the current WPR, but are answered by the amended WPR. The amended WPR would require the President to consult with the Speaker of the House, the President Pro Tempore of the Senate, and the majority and minority leadership of both the House and the Senate.[98] In addition, the amended WPR would provide that these individuals meet with the President on a regular basis to discuss national security issues. The amended WPR would also create a "permanent consultative group"[99] ("PERMCOG") consisting of the following individuals: the Speaker of the House, the President Pro Tempore of the Senate, the majority and minority leaders of each house, the chairman and ranking minority members of the House Committee on Foreign Affairs, the Senate Committee on Foreign Relations, the House and Senate Committees on Armed Services, the House Permanent Select Committee on Intelligence, and the Senate Select Committee on Intelligence. The President, under the amended WPR, would meet with PERMCOG upon the request of a majority of its members. The President would be able to decline the demand of PERMCOG to meet only under "extraordinary circumstances affecting the most vital security interests" of the U.S.[100] So the amended WPR creates two groups, the first of which the President must consult "in every possible instance" before introducing U.S. forces into actual or imminent hostilities. The second group, PERMCOG, may demand meetings with the President upon a majority vote.

The most obvious problem with the consultation provision of the amended WPR is the long list of individuals in Congress who must be consulted. Presumably, this requirement is based on the overlapping jurisdictions of many House and Senate committees. But, as President Ford discovered during the Da Nang and Lebanon evacuations,[101] reaching even a relatively small number of congressmen on short notice can be difficult. The procedure created by the amended WPR is at least as cumbersome as that of the WPR, thus creating an incentive for the President to bypass its stated requirements.

The third and most significant change brought by the amended WPR would be the elimination of the sixty-day clock. The entire concept of automatic termination of hostilities is eliminated by the amended WPR.[102] In its place would be inserted a procedure under which Congress can either approve or condemn the President's use of force. This procedure works as follows: in every instance where the President is required to issue Congress a report on his use of the military, PERMCOG members vote on whether to approve the President's use of force. PERMCOG may decide to introduce a joint resolution either requiring the President to withdraw forces or approving the President's continued use of U.S. forces. In addition, any member of either house may introduce such a joint resolution or bill. The consequences of a vote under the amended WPR ordering the President to withdraw would be that no previously appropriated funds could be spent by the President in such a way as to violate the provisions of the resolution.[103] Thus the amended WPR seeks to use Congress' constitutional appropriation power as a blunt cudgel.

Hostilities

The amended WPR does not provide a definition of "hostilities" or otherwise clarify the meaning of this critical term. It does, however, reduce the effect of the ambiguity by eliminating the sixty-day clock. Under the amended WPR, the debate over whether a particular situation involves hostilities will remain intensive, but the consequence will not lead to the activation of any mechanism to cause the automatic withdrawal of U.S. forces. As a result, a foreign adversary facing the insertion of U.S. forces into critical proximity would no longer have the option of simply waiting sixty days to see whether the WPR causes a withdrawal. The amended WPR, by removing the sixty-day clock, renders this tactic less viable.

The Effect of the Proposed WPR Amendment on the President's Power to Defend

The amended WPR eliminates the automatic termination provision and replaces it with a mechanism by which Congress can vote a resolution demanding the withdrawal of U.S. forces. The amended WPR would thereby obliterate the sixty-day clock, the feature of the WPR most offensive to the Constitution's authorization of presidential war-making. Under the amended WPR, the constitutional war powers issue would arise only if Congress expressly disapproved a specific instance of presidential war-making and ordered a withdrawal of U.S. forces pursuant to the amended WPR. At that point, the question would be whether such an application of the amended WPR would be constitutional. The withdrawal provisions of the amended WPR would find their constitutional basis in Congress' appropriation power,[104] rather than on the restrictive interpretation of the President's war-making power contained in the current WPR's preamble. As a result, the amended WPR would be based upon a more promising constitutional premise than is the current WPR and would provide a mechanism for Congress to consider military operational appropriations on a case-by-case basis.[105]

Although this change would improve the WPR's constitutional legitimacy, it would not cure all of the WPR's constitutional war powers defects. In the hostage rescue scenario, the President would be required by the terms of both the current and the amended WPR to consult with and report to Congress on the military operation. However, the President's authority to use force to rescue Americans abroad is unilateral. If the purpose of the consultation and reporting requirements is to give Congress the opportunity to participate in the President's constitutionally authorized actions as Commander-in-Chief, the requirements would overreach Congress' authority. If the purpose of a presidential report is to enable

Congress to appropriate, however, the congressional demand stands on a more legitimate footing. Of course, the legal debate over whether the President is compelled to report or consult does nothing to inform the question of whether consultation or reporting would be politic or wise. Most agree that communication between the President and Congress on matters of war and peace is a political ideal. The point is that Congress is not empowered by the Constitution to pursue this political ideal by sharing in the President's command decisions.

Legislative Veto

The separation of powers problem in the current WPR is corrected by the elimination of the legislative veto altogether. The amended WPR might raise presentment clause problems depending on the wording of previous appropriations bills and the joint resolution demanding the withdrawal of U.S. forces. If such a joint resolution revoked the President's previously enacted authority to spend money for military operations, then it might be invalid as an unconstitutional legislative veto.

Conclusion

The WPR requires the President to report to Congress upon introducing U.S. forces into actual or imminent hostilities. As the history of the Lebanon Emergency Assistance Act makes clear, however, the President and Congress may disagree on the definition of "hostilities." Furthermore, as the *Crockett* case shows, this disagreement is not likely to be judicially resolved, because the courts perceive themselves incapable of deciding, as a matter of fact, whether or not hostilities exist or are clearly imminent. So the WPR's requirement of a report by the President is not necessarily restrictive.

Moreover, even when the President does report to Congress, he does not limit significantly his flexibility. In the context of military emergencies, such as the tactical air strikes against Libya, the sixty-day clock is likely to stop so soon after starting that it may as well not even exist. If Congress disagrees with this conclusion, the dispute may become a political, not a legal, battle, as *Crockett* implies.

The WPR and its ostensibly plain language establishing a sixty-day clock encourage the division of operations into two categories: those that can be accomplished within sixty days and those that cannot. But an operationally meaningful division along such arbitrary lines is virtually impossible to accomplish. Military operations are not exempt from Murphy's Law: the best presumption is that anything that can go wrong, will. This ensures that even the least ambitious operations may encounter difficulties that can be overcome only by sustained and determined effort. A "low intensity" sequence of violent exchanges can easily consume sixty days.

The fact that an operation does not achieve its objective within sixty days of the first use of force does not mean that it must end, even under the terms of the WPR. Because the WPR is not activated automatically, either the President or Congress must act to invoke its provisions. Only after such action does the sixty-day clock start "ticking." As congressional action relating to U.S. forces in Lebanon illustrates, invocation of the WPR may not be forthcoming.

Even if Congress does act to restrain the President, the WPR may not be an effective restrictive mechanism. If the form of congressional action is a legislative veto, it has no force because it is unconstitutional. If the form of congressional action is a resolution starting the sixty-day clock and if the President disagrees with the congressional finding of the existence of hostilities, the WPR will not necessarily provide a framework for resolution. Rather, the issue is likely to be resolved outside the statutory framework, in the unregulated political arena. The courts are unlikely to mediate because they are unwilling to second-guess the President on the question of whether hostilities exist or are clearly imminent.

This leaves the balance of war-making power about where it would be without the WPR. The President is limited by political pressure and, significantly, by Congress' power of the purse. The legal force of the WPR adds little in the way of further restricting the exercise of the President's war powers.

The amended WPR would create a more definite consultation procedure than that contained in the current WPR and would eliminate the sixty-day clock. As a result of the latter change, the unconstitutional legislative veto would be removed along with the automatic termination provision, the constitutionality of which is also subject to doubt. In addition, the amended WPR would bring Congress closer to the spirit of the Framers' intention that Congress express its opposition to war by means of a vote. The current WPR ostensibly enables Congress to force the withdrawal of U.S. forces without actually stating that it favors such a withdrawal. This automatic termination provision is not in keeping with the Framers' belief in the vigorous debate in Congress of great issues. By contrast, the amended WPR encourages members of Congress to take a public stand on critical issues of war and peace. By eliminating the automatic termination provision, the amended WPR would require Congress to focus on the substantive question of the wisdom of the President's use of force rather than on the procedural question of whether the sixty-day clock has started. The amended WPR, as imperfect as it would be, would enable Congress to play a more productive role in the war-making process.[106]

The amended WPR, however, would contain two major constitutional flaws. First, it would continue to require reports from and consultations with the President. To the extent that Congress seeks thereby to interfere with the President's constitutionally authorized command decisions, these requirements lack a constitutional basis. Second, the amended WPR provides a mechanism to cut off funding of disfavored military activities without presenting such legislation to the President for his signature. Such a procedure might be inconsistent with the Constitution's presentment clauses, depending on the language of the applicable acts.

A war powers resolution, amended or not, is not a necessary prerequisite for Congress to be involved in the war-making process. Congress' legal authority to affect presidential war-making is determined by the Constitution, not its own resolutions. But Congress apparently wishes to retain on the books some form of resolution regarding the war powers. Given that congressional preference, the amended WPR, while not constitutionally flawless, would represent an improvement over the current WPR regime. Perhaps more than anything, the amended WPR illustrates the difficulty of *a priori* codification of a procedure for balancing congressional and presidential war powers. Congress might more effectively deal with war powers issues on an *ad hoc* basis, without a war powers resolution. Thus might Congress address substantive issues of war and peace without procedural distractions.

Notes

1. Edmund Burke, Speech at Bristol Previous to the Election (1780).

2. 50 U.S.C. §§ 1541–1548. Much of this chapter is based on Hall, "War Powers by the Clock," 113 U.S. Naval Institute PROCEEDINGS 36 (1987), with the permission of the United States Naval Institute.

3. *See, e.g.,* Part I, THE FETTERED PRESIDENCY: LEGAL CONSTRAINTS ON THE EXECUTIVE BRANCH (L. Crovitz and J. Rabkin, eds., 1989); Rostow, "Once More Into the Breach: The War Powers Resolution Revisited," 21 VAL. U. L. REV. 1 (1986); Rushkoff, "A Defense of the War Powers Resolution," 93 YALE L. REV. 1331 (1984); Tower, "Congress v. the President: The Formulation and Implementation of American Foreign Policy," FOREIGN AFFAIRS 238 (Winter 1981–1982); King and Leavens, "Curbing the Dog of War: The War Powers Resolution," 18 HARV. INT'L. L. J. 55 (1977); Allison, "Making War: The President and Congress," 40 L. AND CONT. PROB. 86 (1976) (benefit of WPR is that it gives opponents of force basis for opposition that is not perceived as "soft"); Reveley, "The Power to Make War," in THE CONSTITUTION AND THE CONDUCT OF FOREIGN POLICY 83 (F. Wilcox and R. Frank, eds., 1976); Ehrlich, "The Legal Process in Foreign Affairs: Military

Intervention—A Testing Case," 27 STAN. L. REV. 648 (1975) (benefit of WPR is that lawyers will be involved in decision to use force); Spong, "The War Powers Resolution Revisited: Historic Accomplishment or Surrender?" 16 WILL. & MARY L. REV. 823 (1975); Rostow, "Great Cases Make Bad Law: The War Powers Act," 50 TEX. L. REV. 833 (1972); Kelly, "Proposed Legislation Curbing the War Powers of the President," 76 DICK. L. REV. 411 (1972).

4. Committee on Foreign Affairs, THE WAR POWERS RESOLUTION (1982); Hearings on War Powers: A Test of Compliance Before the Subcommittee on International Security and Scientific Affairs of the House Committee on International Relations, 94th Cong., 1st Sess. 93 (1975). *See also* R. TURNER, THE WAR POWERS RESOLUTION: ITS IMPLEMENTATION IN THEORY AND PRACTICE (Foreign Policy Research Institute 1983) ("TURNER"); Jenkins, "The War Powers Resolution: Statutory Limitation on the Commander-in-Chief," HARV. J. ON LEG. 181 (1974). *Cf. also* Fuller, "The National Emergency Dilemma: Balancing the Executive's Crisis Powers with the Need for Account-ability," 52 SO. CAL. L. REV. 1453 (1979).

5. 50 U.S.C. § 1541(a).

6. 50 U.S.C. § 1541(b), citing U.S. CONST., Art. I, Sec. 8.

7. 50 U.S.C. § 1541(c).

8. 50 U.S.C. § 1542. The meaning of "hostilities" is not self-evident. *See Crockett v. Reagan,* 558 F. Supp. 893 (D.D.C.), *aff'd,* 720 F.2d 1355 (D.C. Cir.), *cert. denied,* 467 U.S. 1251 (1982). *See also* Note, "Realism, Liberalism, and the War Powers Resolution," 102 HARV. L. REV. 637 (1988); Cruden, "The War-Making Process," 68 MIL. L. REV. 35, 100 (1975).

9. 50 U.S.C. § 1543(a).

10. 50 U.S.C. § 1543(c).

11. 50 U.S.C. § 1544(b).

12. *But see Crockett v. Reagan,* 558 F. Supp. 893 (D.D.C. 1982) (holding that if the President has not reported, Congress must require a report before the sixty-day automatic termination provision can take effect), *aff'd,* 720 F.2d 1355 (D.C. Cir. 1983), *cert. denied,* 467 U.S. 1251 (1984).

13. 50 U.S.C. § 1544(c). *See also* 50 U.S.C. §§ 1545–1546.

14. *See INS v. Chadha,* 462 U.S. 919 (1983) (unicameral legislative veto violates separation of powers).

15. *See, e.g.,* Comment, "Resolving Challenges to Statutes Containing Un-constitutional Legislative Veto Provisions," 85 COL. L. REV. 1808 (1985); Comment, "Congressional Control of Presidential War-Making Under the War Powers Act: The Status of a Legislative Veto After *Chadha,*" 132 U. PA. L. REV. 1217 (1984); Comment, "Applying *Chadha:* The Fate of the War Powers Resolution," 24 SANTA CLARA L. REV. 697 (1984). *But see* Buchanan, "In Defense of the War Powers Resolution: *Chadha* Does Not Apply," 22 HOUSTON L. REV. 1155 (1985).

16. *See* Chapter 8.

17. *See* Chapter 7.

18. *See, e.g.,* Zutz, "The Recapture of the S.S. *Mayaguez:* Failure of the Consultation Clause of the War Powers Resolution," 8 N.Y.U. J. OF INT'L. L.

AND POL. 457 (1976); Cruden, "The War-Making Process," 69 MIL. L. REV. 35, 128 (1975).

19. *See* Chapter 2.

20. *N. Y. Times,* Apr. 12, 1977 at 14 (April 11, 1977 speech at University of Kentucky).

21. *Id.*

22. 119 Cong. Rec. 1394 (1973).

23. U.S. CONST., Art. II, Sec. 2, Cls. 1 and 2.

24. *See* Chapter 2.

25. TURNER at 53 (reprinted with permission of the Foreign Policy Research Institute).

26. *Id.* at 65 (reprinted with permission of the Foreign Policy Research Institute).

27. A report under Section 4(a)(2), required upon deployment of troops "equipped for combat," does not start the sixty-day clock.

28. Senators Percy and Pell called for a Section 4(a)(1) report on September 24, 1982. TURNER at 83.

29. *See* Chapter 5.

30. *See* Chapter 7.

31. *Nixon v. Administrator of General Services,* 433 U.S. 425 (1977); *United States v. Nixon,* 418 U.S. 683 (1974); *United States v. Poindexter,* 1990 U.S. Dist. LEXIS 2881 (March 21, 1990).

32. L. TRIBE, AMERICAN CONSTITUTIONAL LAW 247–249 (1978).

33. TURNER at 63.

34. *See, e.g.,* Franck, "After the Fall: The New Procedural Framework for Congressional Control Over The War Power," 71 AM. J. INT'L. L. 605 (1977).

35. 119 Cong. Rec. 1400 (1973). *See also* J. JAVITS, WHO MAKES WAR (1973); Javits, "War Powers Reconsidered," FOREIGN AFFAIRS 130, 133 (1985); Javits, "The War Powers Crisis," 8 NEW ENG. L. REV. 157 (1973).

36. Chief of Naval Operations Admiral James D. Watkins, "The Maritime Strategy," U.S. Naval Institute PROCEEDINGS Supplement, January 1986.

37. *See* Ratner, "The Coordinated Warmaking Power—Legislative, Executive, and Judicial Roles," 44 SO. CAL. L. REV. 461, 469 (1971) ("[T]he President may sometimes conclude that offense is the best defense.").

38. Lebanon Emergency Assistance Act of 1983, Public Law 98–43 (June 27, 1983).

39. Multinational Force in Lebanon Resolution, Public Law 98–119 (October 12, 1983).

40. 558 F. Supp. 893 (D.D.C. 1982), *aff'd,* 720 F.2d 1355 (D.C. Cir. 1983), *cert. denied,* 467 U.S. 1251 (1984). *See generally* Carter, "The Constitutionality of the War Powers Resolution," 70 U. VA. L. REV. 101 (1984) and Wald, "The Future of the War Powers Resolution," 36 STAN. L. REV. 1407 (1984).

41. 558 F. Supp. 893 (D.D.C. 1982), *aff'd,* 720 F.2d 1355 (D.C. Cir. 1983), *cert. denied,* 467 U.S. 1251 (1984).

42. 558 F. Supp. at 897.

43. *Id.*

44. 558 F. Supp. at 897.

45. 558 F. Supp. at 898 (citing *Atlee v. Laird,* 347 F. Supp. 689 (E.D. Pa. 1972), *aff'd,* 411 U.S. 921 (1973); *Holtzman v. Schlesinger,* 484 F.2d 1307 (2d Cir. 1973), *cert. denied,* 416 U.S. 936 (1974)).

46. *See* Chapter 3.

47. 558 F. Supp. at 898 (citing *Nixon v. Fitzgerald,* 457 U.S. 731 (1982); *U.S. v. Nixon,* 418 U.S. 683 (1974); *Buckley v. Valeo,* 424 U.S. 1 (1976)).

48. 558 F. Supp. at 898.

49. *Lowry v. Reagan,* 676 F. Supp. 333 (D.D.C. 1987) (dismissing action to require application of WPR to Persian Gulf situation).

50. 558 F. Supp. at 898 (citing *Mitchell v. Laird,* 488 F.2d 611 (D.C. Cir. 1973)).

51. 558 F. Supp. at 901.

52. *Id.*

53. The House of Representatives did pass a resolution to start the sixty-day clock after the Grenada operation. 129 CONG. REC. H8933 (November 1, 1983). Although the Senate had attempted to add a similar resolution as an amendment to a bill raising the national debt ceiling, the Senate neither passed the debt ceiling bill containing the WPR amendment nor voted on the House resolution.

54. *See, e.g.,* Turner, "Congress and the Commitment to Vietnam," CONGRESS, THE PRESIDENT, AND FOREIGN POLICY (ABA Standing Committee on Law and National Security) 75–87 (1984).

55. *See, e.g.,* TURNER; American Enterprise Institute Forum, "War Powers and the Constitution" (1983); Vance, "Striking the Balance: Congress and the President Under the War Powers Resolution," 133 U. PA. L. REV. 79 (1984); Carter, "The Constitutionality of the War Powers Resolution," 70 U. VA. L. REV. 101 (1984); Wald, "The Future of the War Powers Resolution," 36 STAN. L. REV. 1407 (1984); Note, "A Defense of the War Powers Resolution," 93 YALE L. J. 1330 (1984). *See also,* Torricelli, "The War Powers Resolution After the Libya Crisis," 7 PACE L. REV. 661 (1987).

56. U.S. CONST., Art. I, Sec. 8, Cl. 11.

57. *See, e.g.,* Emerson, "The War Powers Resolution Tested: The President's Independent Defense Power," 51 NOTRE DAME LAWYER 187, 192 (1975); Rostow, "Great Cases Make Bad Law: The War Powers Act," 50 TEX. L. REV. 833 (1972). *See also* Goldwater, "The President's Ability to Protect Americans' Freedoms—The Warmaking Power," 1971 L. AND SOC. ORDER 423 (1971).

58. U.S. CONST., Art. II, Sec. 2, Cl. 1.

59. *In re Neagle,* 135 U.S. 1 (1890); *The Slaughterhouse Cases,* 83 U.S. (16 Wall.) 36, 79 (1873); *The Prize Cases,* 67 U.S. 635, 670 (1863); *Martin v. Mott,* 25 U.S. (12 Wheat.) 19, 30–31 (1827); *Durand v. Hollins,* 8 F. Cas. 111 (No. 4186) (C.C.S.D. N.Y. 1860) (Nelson, J., on circuit from the Supreme Ct.).

60. *See* Chapter 2.

61. 50 U.S.C. § 1541(c)(3).

62. *Talbot v. Seeman,* 5 U.S. (1 Cr.) 1 (1801); *Bas v. Tinghy,* 4 U.S. (9 Dall.) 37 (1800).

63. *The Prize Cases,* 67 U.S. 635, 668 (1863) (upholding President Lincoln's blockade of Confederate ports). *See also U.S. v. Curtiss-Wright Corp.,* 299 U.S. 304 (1936); *Myers v. U.S.,* 272 U.S. 52 (1926).

64. *In re Neagle,* 135 U.S. 1, 64 (1890). *See also The Slaughterhouse Cases,* 83 U.S. (16 Wall.) 36, 79 (1873); *Durand v. Hollins,* 8 F. Cas. 111 (No. 4186) (C.C.S.D.N.Y. 1860) (Nelson, J., on circuit from the Supreme Court). *See also* E. CORWIN, THE CONSTITUTION AND WHAT IT MEANS TODAY 60 (8th ed. 1946) ("Presidents came very early to be recognized as having the power to employ the armed forces in defense of the person and property of Americans situated abroad against attack or imminent danger of it; and this recognition received judicial ratification even prior to the Civil War.").

65. *Youngstown Sheet & Tube Co. v. Sawyer,* 343 U.S. 579, 634 (1952) (Jackson, J., concurring).

66. *See* Chapter 1.

67. Letters of Helvidius (1793), 6 THE WRITINGS OF JAMES MADISON 138, 174 (G. Hunt, ed., 1906).

68. M. FARRAND, 2 RECORDS OF THE CONSTITUTIONAL CON VENTION 318.

69. *Martin v. Mott,* 25 U.S. (12 Wheat.) 19, 30 (1827).

70. *The Prize Cases,* 67 U.S. 635, 670 (1863) (emphasis original).

71. *See* Chapter 2.

72. Chief of Naval Operations, Admiral James D. Watkins, "The Maritime Strategy," U.S. Naval Institute PROCEEDINGS Supplement (January 1986).

73. *See* Chapter 2.

74. It is possible to imagine an application of the WPR that would be constitutional. For example, if the President attacked Mexico militarily for reasons unrelated to national defense, the application of the WPR to force a withdrawal would survive constitutional scrutiny.

75. 462 U.S. 919 (1983).

76. 8 U.S.C. § 1101, *et seq.*

77. U.S. CONST., Art. I, Sec. 7, Cls. 2 and 3.

78. The *Chadha* Court did identify as an exception to the presentment clause the procedure for amending the Constitution, which does not include presentment to the President. 462 U.S. at 955 n.21 (citing *Hollingsworth v. Virginia,* 3 Dall. 378 (1798)).

79. U.S. CONST., Art. I, Secs. 1, 7.

80. 462 U.S. at 955.

81. 462 U.S. at 946.

82. 462 U.S. at 958–959.

83. Buchanan, "In Defense of the War Powers Resolution: *Chadha* Does Not Apply," 22 HOUSTON L. REV. 1155 (1985); Note, "A Defense of the War Powers Resolution," 93 YALE L. REV. 1330, 1349–1350 (1984). *See also* Berdes and Huber, "Making the War Powers Resolution Work: The View From the Trench (A Response to Professor Glennon)," 17 LOY. L. A. L. REV. 671 (1984); Ides, "Congress, Constitutional Responsibility and the War Power," 17 LOY. L. A. L. REV. 599 (1984); Zablocki, "War Power Resolution: Its Past Record and Future Promise," 17 LOY. L. A. L. REV. 579 (1984).

84. *See, e.g.,* Glennon, "The War Powers Resolution: Sad Record, Dismal Promise," 17 LOY. L. A. L. REV. 657 (1984); Glennon, "The War Powers Resolution Ten Years Later: More Politics Than Law," 78 AM. J. INT'L. L. 571, 577–578 (1984). Comment, "Resolving Challenges to Statutes Containing Unconstitutional Legislative Veto Provisions," 85 COL. L. REV. 1808 (1985); Comment, "Congressional Control of Presidential War-Making Under the War Powers Act: The Status of a Legislative Veto After *Chadha,*" 132 U. PA. L. REV. 1217 (1984); Comment, "Applying *Chadha:* The Fate of the War Powers Resolution," 24 SANTA CLARA L. REV. 697 (1984).

85. 462 U.S. at 946–947.

86. *See, e.g.,* Gauvin, "Comment: Congressional Control of Presidential War-Making Under the War Powers Act: The Status of a Legislative Veto After *Chadha,*" 132 U. PA. L. REV. 1217 (1984).

87. U.S. CONST., Art. I, Sec. 8, Cls. 11, 12, and 13.

88. U.S. CONST., Art. II, Sec. 2, Cls. 1 and 2.

89. *See* Chapter 2.

90. *N.Y. Times,* May 20, 1988, p.3, col.2.

91. *Id.*

92. *Navy Times,* Jun. 6, 1988, p.10, col.1.

93. S.J. Res. 323 (100th Cong., 2d Sess., May 19, 1988) (reintroduced as Senate Bill 2 in 101st Congress). For a criticism, *see* Ely, "Suppose Congress Wanted A War Powers Act That Worked," 88 COL. L. REV. 1379 (1988).

94. The amendment is not the first or only proposed change to the WPR.

95. S.J. Res. 323 (100th Cong., 2d Sess., May 19, 1988).

96. 50 U.S.C. § 1541(c).

97. 50 U.S.C. § 1542.

98. S.J. Res. 323, Section 3(2).

99. S.J. Res. 323, Section 3(2).

100. *Id.*

101. TURNER at 53.

102. Section 4(a).

103. Section 6(a).

104. U.S. CONST., Art. I, Sec. 8. *See* Glennon, "Strengthening the War Powers Resolution: The Case For Purse-Strings Restrictions," 60 MINN. L. REV. 1 (1975).

105. *But see* Glennon, "The War Powers Resolution Ten Years Later: More Politics Than Law," 78 AM. J. INT'L. L. 571 (1984) (congressional complacency).

106. *See* Rostow, "War, Foreign Affairs, and the Constitution," ENCYCLOPEDIA OF THE AMERICAN CONSTITUTION 2007, 2012 (L. Levy, K. Karst, D. Mahoney, eds., 1986) (The WPR converts "almost every serious foreign policy problem into a debate between Congress and the President about constitutional power, making the conduct of foreign relations even more cumbersome and contentious than is the case already.").

PART TWO

The Reagan Wars: 1980–1988

Lebanon

- —— International boundary
- – – – Armistice Line, 1949
- ——— Province boundary
- ★ National capital
- ⊙ Province capital
- —— Road
- +—+— Railroad

0 5 10 15 Kilometers
0 5 10   15 Miles

35°30'
36°00'
36°30'

Al Ḩamīdīyah
S Y R I A
Nahr an Nahr
Tall Kalakh
An Nahr al Kabīr
Baḩrat Ḩimṣ
Al Qubayyāt
Ḩalbā
Al Qusayr
34°30'

Al Mīnāʼ
⊙ Tripoli
Nahr al Mūsá
Al Ḩirmil

ASH SHAMĀL
Shikkā
Amyūn
Al Qāʻ
Al Batrūn
Bsharrī
Dūmā
Nahr al Jawz
Nahr al ʻĀṣī

Jubayl
Nahr Ibrāhīm
Nahr al Līṭānī
AL BIQĀʻ

34°00'
Jūniyah
Baʻlabakk
34°00'

Bikfayyā

★ Beirut
BAYRŪT
Zaḩlah
B'abdā
JABAL LUBNĀN
Rīyāq
Mediterranean Sea
ʻAlayh
Shtawrah

Ad Dāmūr
Bayt ad Dīn
Al Quṭayfah

Barjā
S Y R I A
Jubb Jannīn
Nahr Baradá
Sidon
Nahr al Awwalī
Ad Dimās
Dūmā
Jazzīn
Al Qirʻawn
Damascus
Buḩayrat al ʻUtaybah
Az Zahrānī
Rāshayyā
33°30'

Qaṭanā

An Nabaṭīyah at Taḩtā
Nahr al Ḩāṣbānī
Nahr al Aʻwaj
Marjiʻyūn

Tyre
Nahr al Līṭānī
AL JANŪB
UNDOF Zone

Bāniyās
An Nāqūrah
Bint Jubayl
GOLAN HEIGHTS (Israeli occupied)
Aṣ Ṣanamayn
Rumaysh
Al Qunayṭirah

Gadaf
Jordan River
Aṣ Ṣūrah aṣ Ṣughrá
Nahariyya
I S R A E L
35°30'
36°00'
Boundary representation is not necessarily authoritative 36°30'
33°00'

U.S. Government Publication

5

Lebanon, 1982–1984

The Multi-National Force in Lebanon

Lebanon became independent of France in 1943. The ethnic composition of Lebanon is complex, to say the least. It is a country of three million people and seventeen officially recognized religious groups, including Maronite Christians, Orthodox Christians, Sunni Muslims, Shi'ite Muslims, and members of the Druze sect.[1] Factional divisions among these groups have weakened the Lebanese government, as has the involvement of Israel, Syria, Iraq, Iran, Jordan, and the Palestine Liberation Organization ("PLO") in Lebanese affairs. The various subsets of the Lebanese population governed themselves after 1943 by a "National Pact," which provided for proportionate representation of each group in the national government. In addition, Christians promised not to seek the intervention of Western powers and Sunni Muslims promised not to invite Syrian intervention.[2] The fragile ethnic balance of the new nation was threatened in 1948, when about 100,000 Palestinian Arabs departed the newly created nation of Israel.[3] In 1958, Maronite Christians and Muslims fought a civil war that resulted in U.S. intervention.[4] On July 15, 1958, at the request of President Chamoun of Lebanon, President Eisenhower ordered 5,000 Marines to Beirut.[5] The U.S. force was increased to 14,000 in the weeks that followed. U.S. troops were withdrawn in October of 1958.[6] The 1958 civil war was a manifestation of the continuing inability of Lebanese factions to discover a political equilibrium. Adding to Lebanon's instability was its inability to settle on a role for the disenfranchised Palestinians, who formed the PLO in 1968, dedicated to the destruction and substitution of Israel for a Palestinian homeland. In 1971, 150,000 additional Palestinians arrived in Lebanon, having been expelled from Jordan by King Hussein.[7]

Lebanon suffered another civil war in 1975 and 1976, resulting in 80,000 deaths. The fighting began on April 13, 1975, when the PLO attacked a church where the family of Maronite Christian Pierre Gemayel, founder of the Phalange Party, had gathered. In January, 1976, PLO forces massacred about 10,000 Christians in Damour, south of Beirut.[8] Christian militias retaliated against the Tel Zaatar refugee camp in October, reportedly equalling the PLO's savagery.[9] The PLO aligned with Muslim and Druze forces, causing the Christians to seek Israeli support. Thus ended the National Pact under which solicitation of foreign intervention was foresworn. Meetings between the Christians and the Israelis were held off the Lebanese coast aboard Israeli missile boats in the Spring of 1976.[10] The result was Israeli military aid to the Christian militias. Even more remarkable was Syria's 1976 switch from supporting the PLO. In July of 1976, Syria entered Lebanon to support the Christians against the PLO.[11] At the outbreak of the civil war, Syrian forces had been made available to serve with the PLO. Apparently, however, with its increasing success, the PLO cooperated less and less with Syria in planning a future for Lebanon along lines dictated by Syria. In July of 1976, the Syrians sent 40,000 troops as part of an Arab Deterrent Force. However, unlike the troops from Saudi Arabia, Yemen, Libya, and the Sudan, Syrian troops were not withdrawn by the end of 1976. Instead, Syrians remained in control of Beirut and the Beka'a Valley to the east.[12]

Israeli aid to the Christians was increased following the 1977 election of Menachem Begin as Prime Minister. In 1978, Israeli forces attacked PLO positions in southern Lebanon in Operation "Litani." By 1981, the tide had turned and Christian forces were firing on Syrians.[13] The Syrians responded by laying siege to Zahle, a Christian Orthodox city. The Israelis shot down a Syrian helicopter near Zahle, causing the Syrians to install fourteen SA-6 surface-to-air missile ("SAM") batteries in the Beka'a Valley.[14] Tensions increased in June and July of 1981 as Israel conducted air strikes against the PLO, and PLO artillery and rockets in southern Lebanon struck targets in Israel's northern Galilee.[15] U.S. Ambassador Philip Habib negotiated a ceasefire.[16]

However, on June 3, 1982, three gunmen attempted to assassinate Shlomo Argov, the Israeli Ambassador to Great Britain. One source reports that one member of the assassination team was a Syrian intelligence officer.[17] Former Secretary of Defense Caspar W. Weinberger reports that the attack was conducted by the anti-Arafat Abu Nidal terrorist organization.[18] Prime Minister Begin ordered a retaliatory air strike against PLO targets in southern Lebanon. The PLO answered with a rocket attack against northern Israel. On June 6, Israel commenced Operation "Peace for Galilee." The purpose of the operation was to move the PLO at least 40 kilometers north, beyond artillery and rocket range.[19] Israeli forces crossed the Lebanese border at 11:00 a.m. on June 6.[20] The city of Tyre in southern Lebanon was isolated by 8:00 p.m. On June 8, Israeli forces secured Sidon, north of Tyre on the Lebanese coast.[21] On June 9, Israeli forces attacked and destroyed seventeen of the nineteen

SAM batteries located in the Beka'a Valley. The Syrian commitment of airpower in defense of the batteries did not turn out well for Syria: the Syrians lost 41 aircraft; the Israelis lost none.[22] On June 10, Syrian and Israeli air forces tangled again with the loss of an additional 25 Syrian aircraft and no Israeli aircraft.[23] On June 11, Israeli forces surrounded Beirut and commenced bombarding the city. That day, a ceasefire between Israel and Syria went into effect, but not before 18 additional Syrian aircraft were shot down.[24] The total loss of Syrian aircraft over Lebanon was 91.[25] On June 12, a ceasefire between Israel and the PLO went into effect. By June 14, Israeli and Phalange Christian forces joined in East Beirut.[26] On July 1, Israel began a siege of Beirut, which contained at least 14,000 PLO troops, about half of whom had retreated to Beirut after being routed by Israel in southern Lebanon.[27]

U.S. concern about the escalating violence had led to the June 24 evacuation by the 32d U.S. Marine Amphibious Unit ("MAU") of U.S. citizens from the city of Juniyah, Lebanon, just north of Beirut. Following the imposition of the Israeli blockade on Beirut, the United States, in the person of Ambassador Philip Habib, negotiated an evacuation by sealift of PLO forces from Beirut.[28] Operation Peace for Galilee had by this time cost 368 Israeli dead, 1,500 PLO dead, and 1,200 Syrian dead.[29] The evacuation was conducted under the supervision of a multi-national force ("MNF") consisting of 800 U.S. Marines from the 32d MAU, and 400 French, 200 British, and 800 Italian troops. At the request of the government of Lebanon, U.S. forces joined the MNF on August 25.[30] Their mission was expected to last no more than 30 days.[31] The mission of the U.S. contingent to the MNF was to:

> Support Ambassador Habib and the MNF committee in their efforts to have PLO members evacuated from the Beirut area; occupy and secure the port of Beirut in conjunction with the Lebanese Armed Forces; maintain close and continuous contact with other MNF members; and be prepared to withdraw on order.[32]

During this initial deployment to Beirut, the Marines supervised the evacuation by civilian ships of 6,436 PLO members.[33] During the evacuation, the Marines' rules of engagement allowed them to carry unloaded weapons and reserved the right of the on-scene commander to determine if force was necessary for self-defense.[34] For the most part, Marine weapons remained unloaded. However, "[d]uring critical periods, selected marksmen had magazines inserted, rounds chambered, and were ready to engage any threat."[35] In addition, Cobra attack helicopters were kept on alert for air support. Despite the fact the PLO forces periodically discharged their weapons into the air as they were transported to ships, the evacuation was concluded without major incident. Following the completion of the evacuation, the U.S. contingent to the MNF was withdrawn on September 10, 1982.

The lull in hostilities was short lived, however. On September 14, 1982, Lebanese President-Elect Bashir Gemayel, who had been elected on August 23, was assassinated.[36] Bashir Gemayel was the son of Pierre Gemayel, founder of the Phalange Party of Maronite Christians. One source reported that the bombing was carried out by a Syrian agent named Habib Chartouny.[37] Following the assassination, Israeli forces entered and occupied West Beirut. On September 16 through 18, 1982, Lebanese Phalange militiamen massacred about 700 Palestinian and Lebanese civilians in the Sabara and Shatila refugee camps in retaliation for President-Elect Bashir Gemayel's death.[38] Lebanon appeared to be headed for anarchy. Israel, which had allowed Phalange forces to enter Sabara and Shatila, responded to international outrage by withdrawing from Beirut in favor of the Lebanese Army. The Lebanese government requested that U.S. forces return to Lebanon.[39] On September 26, the French and Italian forces returned to Beirut. On September 29, the 32d MAU landed in Beirut, joining 2,200 French and Italian troops as part of the MNF. Twelve hundred Marines took up positions near the Beirut International Airport. The Marines were located in this position to separate Israeli forces from the city of Beirut. The next day, one Marine was killed and three were wounded while clearing unexploded ordnance from the area of Beirut International Airport.[40]

The mission of the Marines, as expressed by the Joint Chiefs of Staff to the Commander-in-Chief Europe, the theater commander, was to "establish an environment that will permit the Lebanese armed forces to carry out their responsibilities in the Beirut area."[41] The operations of U.S. forces in Lebanon were described on September 24, 1982 by the Commander-in-Chief Europe as follows:

> Provide security posts at intersections of assigned section of line and major avenues of approach into city of Beirut from south/southeast *to deny passage of hostile armed elements* in order to provide an environment which will permit LAF to carry out their responsibilities in city of Beirut. . . . Commander U.S. Forces will provide air/naval gunfire support as required.[42]

The Long Commission later found that "perceptions of the basic mission varied at different levels of command."[43]

The 32d MAU was relieved by the 24th MAU on October 30. On November 1, the Secretary of Defense approved Marine participation in daylight patrols in east Beirut, Baabda, and Yarze. The first patrol was conducted on November 4. On December 13, the 24th MAU started training Lebanese Armed Forces ("LAF") soldiers in order to give the Lebanese government the ability to control events in Lebanon.[44] The Marines trained 75 Lebanese in general military skills, as well as amphibious and vertical assault operations.[45]

In January of 1983, Israeli forces conducted reconnaissance patrols near U.S. positions and made several attempts to penetrate U.S. Marine positions. On one occasion, stray Israeli rounds landed on U.S. positions, presumably from an Israeli patrol conducting reconnaissance by fire. These contacts were the subject of discussions between U.S. Marine and Israeli ground commanders. To achieve better communication between U.S. and Israeli forces, a radio link between U.S. and Israeli headquarters in Lebanon was established on January 29.[46] Tactical communication between the two forces did not, however, improve. On February 2, three Israeli tanks attempted to pass through the position of Marine Company L, under the command of Captain Charles B. Johnson. The tanks attempted to penetrate a section of fence where Company L had blocked an Israeli armored personnel carrier on January 20. Captain Johnson was concerned that Israeli penetration of his position would cause a firefight between Lebanese and Israeli forces. In such an event, U.S. forces would have supported the LAF. In order to prevent such a confrontation, Captain Johnson stood in the path of the tanks and ordered them to stop. The Israeli commander stopped the lead tank six inches from Captain Johnson and advised him that the Israelis would pass through. Captain Johnson, leaving little room for doubt about his point of view, said, "You will have to kill me first." He then drew his pistol and chambered a round. The lead tank pulled over, and Captain Johnson approached to continue his discussions with the Israeli commander. At that moment, however, the second tank advanced. Captain Johnson jumped on the second tank, grabbed the Israeli tank officer, and ordered the tank to stop. It did. The three tanks returned to the Israeli patrol area.[47]

The 22d MAU, redesignated from the 32d MAU, relieved the 24th MAU on February 15, 1983. The 22d MAU Marines were issued a wallet-sized "white card" summarizing the rules of engagement, as follows:

Guidelines of Rules of Engagement

1. When on the post, mobile or foot patrol, keep loaded magazine in weapon, bolt closed, weapon on safe, no round in the chamber.
2. Do not chamber a round unless told to do so by a commissioned officer unless you must act in immediate self-defense where deadly force is authorized.
3. Keep ammo for crew served weapons readily available but not loaded. Weapon is on safe.
4. Call local forces to assist in self-defense effort. Notify headquarters.

5. Use only minimum degree of force to accomplish any mission.

6. Stop use of force when it is no longer needed to accomplish the mission.

7. If you receive effective hostile fire, direct your fire at the source. If possible, use friendly snipers.

8. Respect civilian property; do not attack it unless absolutely necessary to protect friendly forces.

9. Protect innocent civilians from harm.

10. Respect and protect recognized medical agencies such as Red Cross, Red Crescent, etc.[48]

On February 21, 1983, the 22d MAU conducted relief operations in Quartaba and in the central mountains of Lebanon, an area suffering from the effects of a severe blizzard. On March 16, five Marines were wounded by a hand grenade thrown at a Marine patrol in Ouzai, north of the Beirut International Airport. A Lebanese who supported the Amal was later arrested, convicted of throwing the grenade, and sentenced to death. On April 17, a sniper fired on a Marine sentry. The bullet passed through the pocket of the sentry's utility trousers, but missed his leg. For the first time, Marines returned fire.

On April 18, 1983, the U.S. Embassy in Beirut was bombed. Seventeen U.S. citizens and more than 40 other people were killed and over 100 were injured. Among the casualties were one Marine killed and eight Marines wounded.[49] The bombing was undertaken by a terrorist driving a van carrying 2,000 pounds of explosives. One source reports that the bombing had been "traced . . . right to Syrian intelligence."[50] Following the bombing of the U.S. Embassy, the MAU was ordered to provide security for the British and American embassies. Accordingly, the rules of engagement were amended to allow MAU embassy security forces to fire when a "hostile act" had been committed. A hostile act was defined as "rounds fired at the embassy, embassy personnel, embassy vehicle, or Marine sentries."[51] Thus did the 22d MAU come to operate under two sets of rules of engagement, one for embassy duty and the other for duty elsewhere.

On May 5, a U.S. Marine helicopter was hit with ground fire while performing reconnaissance of an artillery exchange between Druze and Christian forces. Nevertheless, prospects for peace brightened on May 17, 1983, when the U.S., Israel, and Lebanon signed an agreement providing for the withdrawal of Israeli forces from southern Lebanon and new security procedures for the region. This agreement was premised upon the withdrawal of Syrian and PLO forces from Beirut. Unfortunately, neither Syria nor the PLO was a signatory to the agreement, and each refused to withdraw its forces prior to an Israeli withdrawal.[52] Former

Secretary of Defense Weinberger has argued that it was a mistake to leave U.S. forces in Lebanon after it became apparent that PLO, Israeli, and Syrian forces would not withdraw.[53]

On May 30, 1983, the 24th MAU relieved the 22d MAU and conducted patrols with the LAF on June 25. In July, fighting between LAF and the Druze militia escalated. On July 22, Marine positions at the Beirut International Airport were shelled by Druze 102mm mortar and 122mm rocket fire. Two Marines and one sailor were wounded, and the airport was closed. On August 10 and 11, approximately 35 mortar and rocket rounds fired by Druze militia landed on Marine positions at Beirut International Airport, wounding one Marine. On August 10, three Lebanese Cabinet ministers were kidnapped by Druze forces.

On August 28, 1983, the LAF and the Druze militia engaged in heavy fighting which spilled into the Marine compound. U.S. Marine positions were hit with rocket-propelled grenades and semiautomatic rifle fire. U.S. Marines returned fire, using rifles and machine guns.[54] On August 29, two Marines were killed and fourteen were wounded in Druze rocket, artillery, and mortar attacks.[55] The Marines fired illumination rounds over a Druze rocket battery to dissuade the militiamen from continuing the attack. In addition, the guided-missile cruiser U.S.S. *Belknap* fired illumination rounds from its five-inch guns. These warnings had no noticeable effect on the Druze batteries. Accordingly, the Marines fired six 155mm Howitzer rounds, silencing a Druze position and reportedly killing three and wounding fifteen militiamen.[56] Later in the day, an armored personnel carrier fired on a joint Marine-LAF checkpoint. In response, two Marine Cobra attack helicopters launched a search for the armored personnel carrier. One of the Cobras was hit with machine gun fire, and the other launched a five-inch Zuni rocket at the machine gun, destroying it. On August 31, Moslem forces shelled the U.S. Ambassador's residence and the Marines replied with 155mm artillery. On September 6, 1983, Marine positions were shelled again, killing two Marines and wounding two others.[57]

Sporadic fighting took place throughout September. Between August 28 and September 6, four Marines were killed and 28 were wounded in action.[58] On September 8, the frigate U.S.S. *Bowen* fired its five-inch guns, destroying a Druze militia artillery battery that had been shelling the Marines. On September 16, the destroyer U.S.S. *John Rodgers* and the *Bowen* fired five-inch guns at Syrian controlled Lebanon in response to shelling of the U.S. Ambassador's residence.

On September 19, the *John Rodgers,* the destroyer U.S.S. *Arthur Radford,* the *Bowen,* and the cruiser U.S.S. *Virginia* fired 360 five-inch rounds in direct support of LAF positions in Suq-al-Gharb, just south of Beirut in the Shuf mountains. Suq-al-Gharb was held by the LAF but was surrounded by Druze militia forces. The LAF, under heavy artillery barrage, had requested U.S. help to prevent the fall of Suq-al-Gharb.[59] The LAF reported that U.S. naval gunfire caused the Druze to retreat.[60] However, as a result of this direct support of the LAF, some anti-LAF forces viewed the U.S. as a declared belligerent, rather than a neutral "presence."[61]

On September 20, the *John Rodgers* and the *Virginia* fired their five-inch guns in response to the shelling of the U.S. Ambassador's residence. Also on September 20, unknown forces fired SA-7 SAMs on two U.S. Navy reconnaissance aircraft. On September 21, the *John Rodgers* and the *Arthur Radford* fired their guns in response to the continued shelling of Marines at Beirut International Airport. On September 23, the *Virginia* supported Marine 81mm mortar and 155mm artillery fire with her five-inch guns in response to an attack on Marine positions.

On September 24, the battleship U.S.S. *New Jersey* arrived off the Lebanon shore, the day before a negotiated ceasefire went into effect. The Soviet Union viewed the ceasefire as having "positive significance," but pressed for a withdrawal of U.S. forces. The U.S. Foreign Broadcast Information Service concluded: "Moscow's cautious backing for the cease-fire is in line with the position adopted by Syria and Syrian-supported factions in Lebanon."[62]

On October 8, 1983, President Reagan gave a radio address summarizing the situation in Lebanon:

> Lebanon, the site of refugee camps for a great many Palestinians, had been torn by strife for several years. There were factions, each with its own militia, fighting each other. Terrorists in Lebanon violated Israel's northern border, killing innocent civilians. Syrian forces occupied the eastern part of Lebanon. Israeli military finally invaded from the south to force the PLO attackers away from the border. There could be no implementation of our peace initiative until this situation was resolved.
>
> With our allies—England, France and Italy—we proposed a withdrawal of all foreign forces from Lebanon and formed a multinational force to help maintain order and stability in the Beirut area while a new Lebanese Government and army undertook to restore sovereignty throughout Lebanon. . . .
>
> The presence of our marines as part of the multinational force demonstrates that Lebanon does not stand alone. Peace for the Middle East and a fair settlement of the Palestinian problem is truly in our national interest.[63]

On the day of the President's speech, two Marines were wounded by sniper fire. The ceasefire deteriorated through the rest of October. On October 5, two Marine Cobra helicopters were hit by ground fire. On October 8, two Marines were wounded by snipers.[64] On October 13, one Marine was wounded in a grenade attack. On October 14, one Marine was killed and three were wounded by snipers. On October 15, Marine sharpshooters, responding to the October 14 attack, killed four snipers. The next day, another Marine was killed and five were wounded by sniper fire.[65] On October 19, four Marines were wounded by a remotely detonated car bomb along a convoy route. But the worst was yet to come.

At 6:22 A.M. (local) on Sunday, October 23, 1983, 241 servicemen were killed and 70 were wounded when the U.S. Marine Battalion Landing Team headquarters at Beirut International Airport was bombed.[66] More Marines died on October 23 than on "any single day since D-Day on Iwo Jima."[67] The bomb was delivered by a Mercedes-Benz stake bed truck driven by a single terrorist through the parking lot south of the headquarters building. The truck crashed through barbed wire and concertina before penetrating the central lobby of the building and exploding. The Long Commission Report summarizes the truck bombing as follows:

> Five eyewitnesses described a large, yellow Mercedes-Benz stake bed truck traveling at a speed reportedly in excess of 35 mph, moving from the public parking lot south of the BLT Headquarters building through the barbed wire and concertina fence, into the main entrance of the building, where it detonated at approximately 0622 Beirut time. . . . [The truck] was observed by the sentry on Post 6 accelerating westward and parallel to the wire barricade. The truck then abruptly turned north, ran over the wire barricade, and accelerated northward between Posts 6 and 7.
>
> The sentry on Post 7 heard the truck as it ran over the wire, then observed it and immediately suspected it was a vehicle bomb. He inserted a magazine in his M-16 rifle, chambered a round, shouldered the weapon, and took aim but did not fire because by that time the truck had already penetrated the building.
>
> Both sentries realized the truck was, in fact, a "car bomb" and therefore took cover within their respective bunkers. One sentry hid in the corner of his bunker and did not observe the detonation. The other sentry partially observed the detonation from behind the blast wall to the rear of the bunker. He saw the top of the building explode vertically in a V shape. He then took cover inside his bunker for protection from the falling debris.[68]

On November 22, Secretary of Defense Caspar Weinberger stated that the bombing of the Marine headquarters had been undertaken by Iranians with the "sponsorship, knowledge, and authority of the Syrian government."[69]

On October 31, 1983, the Commandant of the Marine Corps testified before the Senate Armed Services Committee:

It is of particular importance to note that the [on-scene] Commander's security was oriented toward the threat of the past several months, i.e., artillery, rockets, mortars, small arms and car bombs. In this context, his security efforts had been successful. Obviously, the Commander's security arrangements were inadequate to counter this form of "kamikaze" attack [with a five-ton truck]. But, we have yet to find any shred of intelligence which would have alerted a reasonable and prudent commander to this new and unique threat.[70]

It is noteworthy that on-scene commander Colonel Timothy Geraghty did not believe the rules of engagement would have allowed a sentry to fire on a vehicle forcibly entering the compound.[71] After studying reports of the bombing, President Reagan concluded on December 27, 1983:

I do not believe that the local commanders on the ground, men who have suffered quite enough, should be punished for not fully comprehending the nature of today's terrorist threat. . . . If there is to be blame, it properly rests here in this office and with this President.[72]

On October 28, an additional Marine rifle company was added to the U.S. contingent to the MNF. On November 4, 1983, the Israeli Military Governor's headquarters at Tyre was destroyed by a truck bomb, killing 29 soldiers and 32 prisoners. Israel conducted retaliatory air strikes. On November 9, all "non-essential" Marines were ordered to reembark aboard amphibious ships in order to reduce the number of Marines ashore. On November 19, the 24th MAU was relieved by the 22d. Throughout November, U.S. Marine positions at the Beirut International Airport were subjected to sniper attacks as well as mortar, artillery, and rocket attacks.

On December 3, the carrier U.S.S. *Kennedy* launched an F-14 fighter to perform a reconnaissance flight over Lebanon. During the flight, the crew detected a Soviet-made SA-7 heat-seeking anti-aircraft missile. The F-14 evaded the SAM and reported the attack. The President considered his response. Unfortunately, the President was advised incorrectly that the sixteen-inch guns of the *New Jersey* could not reach the targets under consideration. The President ordered a retaliatory air strike.[73] On the morning of December 4, the U.S.S. *Independence* launched eighteen attack aircraft and the *Kennedy* launched ten.[74] The attack aircraft bombed anti-aircraft sites in the Shuf and Metu mountains, northeast of Beirut.[75] The U.S. aircraft reported anti-aircraft fire and SA-7 and SA-9 missile launches. One ammunition dump and one anti-aircraft site were destroyed, and eleven other targets were hit.[76] Two of the A-7 light attack bombers from the *Independence* were hit as they returned to the carrier. One of these was recovered aboard the *Independence*. The other, flown by Commander Edward Andrews, the commander of the air wing ("CAG"), was not. Commander Andrews ejected and was rescued and returned to the *Independence*.[77]

The December 4 air strike involved another casualty. An A-6 bomber from the *Kennedy* was hit as it descended with its load of 1,000 pound bombs toward the target area. The two aviators, Lieutenant Mark Lange and Lieutenant Bobby Goodman, ejected. Lieutenant Lange's leg was severed and he bled to death on the ground. Lieutenant Goodman survived the ejection and was captured by the Syrians. Lieutenant Goodman was released on January 3, 1984 during a visit to Syria by Democratic presidential candidate Jesse Jackson. Former Secretary of the Navy John Lehman later recommended that a roll of quarters and Jesse Jackson's telephone number be added to aviators' survival vests.[78]

On December 4, the night of the air strike, Marines at Beirut International Airport were attacked by 122mm rockets launched from Syrian territory.[79] Eight Marines were killed and two were wounded. The Marines returned fire on December 6 and December 8.[80] The destroyer U.S.S. *Claude V. Ricketts* supported the Marines with naval gunfire.[81] On December 13, U.S. F-14s flying reconnaissance missions reported ground fire. The cruiser U.S.S. *Ticonderoga* and the destroyer U.S.S. *Tattnall* responded with fifteen and twenty-five-inch rounds, respectively.[82] On December 14, anti-aircraft sites in Syria-controlled Lebanon fired upon an F-14 photo reconnaissance flight. In retaliation, on December 14 and 15, the *New Jersey* fired its sixteen-inch and five-inch guns and the *Ticonderoga* and *Tattnall* fired their five-inch guns at anti-aircraft sites.[83] Six anti-aircraft sites were destroyed.[84]

During the month of January, 74 Navy Construction Battalion "Seabees" and 99 Marine combat engineers undertook a three-phase construction project to improve the physical security of the Marine compound. They emplaced 400 sea-land containers as underground bunkers, 192 prefabricated bunkers, 156 two-man foxholes, a perimeter ditch, and a wall of "Dragon's Teeth" to protect against vehicle assaults. The cost of this project totaled about six million dollars.[85]

On January 8, one Marine was killed exiting a helicopter in Beirut. On January 13, Marines at Beirut International Airport fought a thirty-minute small arms battle on the Marines' eastern perimeter. Two days later, Druze forces fired 23mm guns on Beirut International Airport. U.S. Marines returned fire, as did the *New Jersey* and the *Tattnall*. On January 30, two more Marines were killed and two more were wounded.[86] In February, heavy fighting culminated in increased control by Druze and Moslem militia forces of a large portion of Beirut. This trend was hastened by the February 4 shelling by the LAF of South Beirut and Khaldah, where many Muslim LAF soldiers lived. Within two days, all

Muslims had deserted the LAF.[87] The situation continued to deteriorate during February. One observer has concluded that during February, it became "evident that the Marine presence at Beirut International Airport was no longer contributing to the hoped-for process of national reconciliation."[88]

On February 7, President Reagan announced the reembarkation of Marines from Beirut International Airport to amphibious ships off the Lebanese coast. The same day, the Marines commenced evacuation of American Embassy employees and their dependents. On February 8, 1984, Syrian artillery batteries fired some 5,000 rounds into portions of West Beirut controlled by the Christian militia. The *New Jersey* fired 270 rounds and destroyed eight Syrian artillery batteries.[89] The same day, Major Alfred L. Butler, III, the Marine Liaison Officer to the LAF, died as a result of an accidental discharge. He was the last U.S. serviceman to die in Lebanon in 1984. During the deployment to Lebanon, 266 servicemen were killed.[90] The Marines withdrew during the period February 21–26, after successfully evacuating U.S. civilians and other foreign nationals by helicopter on February 10 and 11.

On February 26, the Marines formally passed control of Beirut International Airport to the LAF. After striking the colors, the Marines were asked by Colonel Fahim Qortabawi, the LAF Liaison Officer, "You are leaving?" The MAU Commander, Colonel Faulkner, answered, "Yes, we are really leaving. Our eastern positions have already been vacated, we're in pullback positions now . . . , and we are in the final throes of embarkation. Yes, Colonel Qortabawi, we are really leaving." Colonel Qortabawi, who was Christian, replied, "I have no way to go home. To go home, I have to go through Muslim checkpoints. You can get me to the Ministry of Defense by helo ride?" Colonel Faulkner replied, "Yes, we can do that."[91]

In March, the President declared the end of U.S. participation in the MNF.[92] A terrorist reportedly announced that the United States had been driven from Lebanon by two "martyrs": the one who drove a car bomb into the U.S. embassy and the other who drove a truck bomb into the U.S. Marine headquarters.[93]

The Multi-National Force in Lebanon and the U.S. Constitution

The U.S. military deployment to Lebanon was widely regarded as a failure, partly as a result of the 241 deaths in the truck bombing, but also as a result of the apparent absence of any positive and enduring geopolitical effect. Lebanon was at least as unstable after the Marine deployment as it had been before. The Long Commission, which had been convened to examine the causes of the October 23 tragedy, offered the following recommendation:

> The Commission recommends that the Secretary of Defense continues to urge that the National Security Council undertake a reexamination of alternative means of achieving U.S. objectives in Lebanon, to include a comprehensive assessment of the military options being developed by the chain of command and a more vigorous and demanding approach to pursuing diplomatic alternatives.[94]

The Long Commission's recommendation seems carefully worded to avoid the appearance that the Commission had exceeded the scope of its charter. Nevertheless, the Long Commission did suggest the possibility that the deployment of armed forces to Lebanon had been a mistake and that this mistake ultimately caused the deaths of 241 servicemen on October 23.

This is a stark assessment, one shared by many commentators, public officials, and private citizens.[95] Because the President's decision to deploy U.S. forces to Lebanon can be viewed as unpopular, unlike, for example, his decision to use force against Libya in 1986, it presents an interesting test for the lawfulness of such unilateral presidential decisions. The Lebanon case history serves to illustrate the point that the lawfulness of a presidential employment of military force does not depend on its popularity.

The President's original decision in August 1982 to join the MNF in Lebanon was unilateral. At the time of the August deployment, President Reagan advised Congress that he did not expect U.S. forces to engage in hostilities.[96] Unfortunately, this presidential expectation was not realized. By the end of May, 1983, five Marines had been wounded in action and seventeen Americans had been killed in the bombing of the American Embassy in Beirut. Nevertheless, Congress did not act formally on the issue of U.S. participation in the MNF until June of 1983, when it passed the Lebanon Emergency Assistance Act of 1983. When it did act, Congress did not require the withdrawal of any U.S. forces from Lebanon. The Act provided, "The President shall obtain statutory authorization from Congress with respect to any substantial *expansion* in the number or role in Lebanon of the United States Armed Forces. . . ."[97] When he signed the Act into law, President Reagan stated:

> Section 4(a) of the act confirms this administration's announced intention with respect to congressional authorization concerning any future substantial expansion in the number or role of U.S. forces in Lebanon. As indicated in its legislative history, that section does not prevent the initiation of such

actions, if circumstances require it, while Congress is considering a request
for statutory authorization; nor, of course, is it intended to infringe upon
the constitutional authority of the President as Commander in Chief,
particularly with respect to contingencies not expected in the context of
the multinational effort to strengthen the sovereignty and independence of
Lebanon.[98]

The President sought to have it both ways; on the one hand, he accepted
Congress' nominal involvement in the MNF issue and, on the other, he
reserved his right to act unilaterally.

Congress increased pressure on the President as Marine casualties
increased during the summer of 1983. The result was a compromise
manifested in October, 1983 by the Multi-National Force in Lebanon
Resolution.[99] The Multi-National Force in Lebanon Resolution contained
congressional authorization for an 18-month extension of the Marine
deployment. This authorization was based on the President's representation
that the "American Forces will not engage in combat," except for self-
defense. The self-defense exception was not further defined.[100]

The President's initial decision to send the Marines to Lebanon in
August of 1982 to assist in the evacuation of PLO forces from Beirut
was undertaken pursuant to his power to conduct foreign affairs. As the
United States' chief diplomatic agent, the President granted Lebanon's
request for troops to join the MNF. As Commander-in-Chief, the President
directed U.S. forces to deploy to Lebanon pursuant to international
agreement and to follow prescribed rules of engagement. He did not
purport to order U.S. troops to Lebanon under exigent circumstances
to defend the national security. As chief diplomat, the President acted
in a way that would not necessarily lead to the use of military force,
but might. He sent troops to Lebanon to "support Ambassador Habib,"
but not necessarily to fight. This "support" took the form of a "presence,"
through which U.S. military forces acted as a police force during the
evacuation. The risk of military involvement is present in many diplomatic
commitments made by the President in conducting foreign affairs; one
implication of the communion of friendship is common enemies.

In the context of the violent Lebanese conflict and the fact that
participation in the MNF led to the deaths of 266 servicemen over a
nineteen-month period, the distinction between the President's powers
as Commander-in-Chief and his powers as the primary diplomatic agent
for the conduct of foreign affairs is blurry. To maintain the distinction,
it is necessary to recall that in the summer of 1982 the President did
not have the benefit of perfect foresight. Furthermore, the President did
not deploy the Marines to Lebanon with the stated intention of employing
force against the many enemies of the government of Lebanon. This is

a critical factor that differentiates the Lebanon deployment from the air strikes against Libya and Operation Urgent Fury in Grenada. In this initial decision to provide U.S. troops to Lebanon, therefore, the President was not acting as "first General and Admiral."[101]

The question, then, is whether the foreign affairs powers of the President justify President Reagan's unilateral decision to grant Lebanon's request for U.S. participation in the MNF. The answer is that they do. The President is authorized under the Constitution to exercise the "plenary and exclusive power . . . as the sole organ of the federal government in the field of international relations. . . ."[102] This means that the President is the sole diplomatic agent of the nation, the sole recipient of the demands and requests of foreign states. When a foreign state, such as Lebanon, wishes to request military assistance from the United States, it must approach the President. If the President grants the request and an agreement is manifested in a treaty, the President must seek the Senate's advice and consent.[103] But not all international agreements require such Senate ratification. The President is constitutionally empowered to negotiate and act pursuant to executive agreements never ratified by the Senate.[104] In *United States v. Belmont,* the Supreme Court confirmed the President's power to establish unilaterally diplomatic relations with foreign states.[105] The *Belmont* Court expressly held that international compacts negotiated by the President are not necessarily treaties requiring Senate ratification.

The *Belmont* rule was reaffirmed in *First National City Bank v. Banco Nacional de Cuba,* where the Supreme Court held that since the President is "charged . . . with the primary responsibility for foreign affairs," the courts will consider his opinion as to what actions "advance the interests of American foreign policy" to be dispositive, at least in the absence of express congressional disapproval.[106] Since Congress never disapproved the deployment of troops to Lebanon and since under *Banco Nacional,* the President was constitutionally authorized to act, no clash of constitutional authority between the President and Congress arose over the Lebanon deployment. Indeed, the Lebanon Emergency Assistance Act of 1983 and the Multi-National Force in Lebanon Resolution authorized the presence of U.S. troops in Lebanon.

While executive agreements lack the political and legal benefits of Senate ratification, the lack of such benefits does not imply the necessity of ratification. Presidential commitments of military force are the prime examples of the sort of executive agreements not requiring Senate ratification.[107] The President's agreement with Lebanon was such an executive diplomatic agreement.[108] Diplomatic arrangements involving the military might, of course, involve appropriations, for which Congress is responsible. But the President is constitutionally empowered to undertake an agreement with a foreign state. President Reagan was authorized, under the conditions present in 1982, unilaterally to commit U.S. forces to the MNF.

Since the President's original decision to participate in the MNF was based primarily on his foreign affairs powers, it did not present initially the issue of whether exigent circumstances justified the unilateral use of force by the Commander-in-Chief. As U.S. participation in the MNF led to casualties, however, the question arose whether the President as Commander-in-Chief was empowered to order the use of force. As Druze militia and other forces claimed more Marines, combat casualties appeared to be interrelated. The President found it increasingly difficult to characterize the casualties as unfortunate accidents that did not imply direct U.S. involvement in the Lebanese war. The debate between those arguing that U.S. forces were not directly involved in the Lebanon civil war and those arguing that U.S. Marines were serving as an occupational combat force raged until the bombing of October 23, 1983.

It might be argued that Lebanon was such a dangerous place in August and September of 1982 that the President could have expected U.S. troops to become involved in armed conflict. This premise, in turn, might suggest that the President was deploying U.S. forces as Commander-in-Chief. If accurate, this characterization of the President's decision would imply the legal necessity for the President to identify exigent circumstances. But this characterization puts the cart before the horse. It is not the case that every time the President undertakes an obligation in the realm of foreign affairs that could have a military implication, he must be able to show exigent circumstances justifying the use of force. Again, the key fact is that the Marines were sent to Lebanon to deter rather than incite violence. If the Marines were sent to Lebanon to wage war, their orders did not say so: their mission was to "establish an environment" within which the LAF could carry out its "responsibilities." If the President meant to order the Marines to fight, he did it in a roundabout way.

The Marines were subjected to sporadic military threats in early 1983: the Israelis sought to penetrate U.S. positions in January and February, and, in March, five Marines were wounded in a terrorist attack. None of this changed the essential character of the deployment. The President had not ordered the Marines to use force, except in self-defense. The President clearly is allowed to order the military to use force in defense of its own positions.[109] The fact that tensions increased in April and May with the bombing of the U.S. Embassy and the May 5 attack on a Marine helicopter similarly did not affect the legal basis of the deployment. From the President's point of view, the legal basis of the deployment was established in September of 1982 when Lebanon requested U.S. military assistance. Subsequent violent events, even including the October 23, 1983 bombing, did not change the facts giving rise to U.S. participation in the MNF. It would be remarkable indeed if the enemies of the United States could undermine the legal legitimacy of U.S. military actions simply by attacking U.S. forces.

From Congress' point of view, however, the growing number of U.S. casualties in 1983 and the bombing of the American Embassy in Beirut rendered increasingly likely the prospect of Marine involvement in combat. Congress appeared to worry about the possibility of a *fait accompli;* that is, Congress expressed concern that the President, having placed U.S. forces in a hostile zone, would have the power to keep them there for defensive purposes once combat commenced. Thus the interaction between Congress and the President in mid-1983 might have been induced by a recognition by Congress that it was being squeezed out of any policy-making role by the interaction of two presidential powers, the power to conduct foreign affairs and the power to command the armed forces. Nevertheless, the Lebanon Emergency Assistance Act, enacted on June 27, 1983, did not purport to restrict the President's ability to keep the Marines in Lebanon. Rather, it authorized their presence. The effect of the bill was to involve Congress in the policy-making process in order to induce increasing involvement in the future.

In July and early August of 1983, Marine positions were subjected to Druze artillery, rocket, and mortar attacks. Three Marines and one sailor were injured. On August 28, 1983, the Marines fired on Druze positions. This date, since it corresponds to a major change in the Marines' operating posture, is a convenient point to mark the change in the President's constitutional power base from foreign affairs to command-in-chief of the armed forces. The authority to fire on the Druze militia came not from the chief diplomat, for diplomacy was apparently on the wane; it came from the Commander-in-Chief. When the Druze militia attacked, exigent circumstances were present to justify the use of force by U.S. forces without congressional authorization or even congressional knowledge.

Between August 28 and the September 25, 1983 ceasefire, U.S. forces, including surface naval vessels offshore, fired on hostile positions in support of the Marines at the Beirut International Airport, in support of the LAF, and in response to the August 31 shelling of the U.S. Ambassador's residence. On October 8 and October 14, one Marine was killed and six Marines were wounded in sniper attacks. The Marines responded in kind on October 15. These actions by U.S. forces were not undertaken as part of an offensive strategy; rather, they were responses to manifest military threats. As such, they were purely defensive. No one seriously doubts the President's power as Commander-in-Chief to undertake the defense of U.S. forces actually under attack. Therefore, the President's actions were constitutional.

This conclusion raises two questions. First, at what point does a series of seemingly unrelated attacks against U.S. forces deployed abroad amount to a single "war" being fought against the United States? This is a question that has no plain answer. But the answer does not matter because even if the conflict in Lebanon were to be labeled a "war," undeclared by Congress, the President would remain constitutionally empowered to protect U.S. forces under attack. Furthermore, even if the U.S. was involved in a "war" in Lebanon once some critical mass of casualties or hostile acts was reached, the fact remains that U.S. forces initially became involved in the situation leading to "war" as a result of the President's legitimate (if unsuccessful) actions as the chief diplomat. He did not send troops to Lebanon intending to fight a war, but to prevent one. His attempt failed, but his constitutional authority to undertake the original deployment remained intact.

The second question raised by the conclusion that the President's actions in Lebanon were lawful is this: if the President's actions as chief diplomat are ill-advised and result in attacks on U.S. forces, is he nevertheless able to exercise the full range of his defensive powers as Commander-in-Chief? The concern underlying this question is that the web of presidential powers appears to be seamless when the President undertakes some reckless act in the field of foreign relations and then enjoys broad powers over the military when his recklessness leads to attacks against U.S. interests. The answer to this question is that the war powers are not the source for punishment of the President for poor judgment. The penalty for the President's mistakes is not the loss of his powers to defend national security, including the tactical defense of U.S. troops. The troops are not required to pay for the President's mistakes. The penalty for poor judgment must be found elsewhere, most obviously in the political arena. The Constitution allows the President to be wrong in conducting foreign affairs, just as it allows him to be wrong in exercising his constitutional share of domestic powers. For example, the President, through the Attorney General, might prosecute a citizen for a crime he did not commit. In such a circumstance, the jury should find the defendant not guilty. It is not the case that each such not guilty verdict erodes the constitutional basis for the President's future acts to enforce the law.

Congress passed the Multi-National Force in Lebanon Resolution ("MNFILR") on October 12, 1983. The MNFILR authorized continued deployment of the Marines to Lebanon, as did the Lebanon Emergency Assistance Act, but limited the congressional authorization to eighteen months. As part of a compromise with Congress, the President signed the MNFILR. Regardless of the MNFILR's congressional authorization, the President was authorized by the Constitution to allow the Marines to defend themselves, whether for a period of eighteen months or longer. Nevertheless, the refusal of the President to withdraw troops within eighteen months might have led to a lawsuit by members of Congress against the President. The plaintiff congressmen would have said that the MNFILR should be enforced as written, that it means what it says and says what it means. The President would have responded that the MNFILR cannot bind him since it purports to limit by congressional action the President's constitutional authority to defend U.S. troops. The plaintiff congressmen would have replied that the President waived any such constitutional authority by agreeing to the MNFILR. The President would have denied that his accession to the MNFILR's compromise was a waiver of constitutional authority as Commander-in-Chief. He would have reminded the plaintiff congressmen that, in signing the MNFILR, he expressly denied any such waiver: "I believe it is, therefore, important for me to state, in signing this resolution, that I do not and cannot cede any of the authority vested in me under the Constitution as President and Commander-in-Chief of United States Armed Forces."[110]

It is likely that the court would refrain from hearing such a claim on political question grounds.[111] If the court agreed to reach the issue of the President's constitutional authority to exceed the limits of the MNFILR, it probably would rule for the President if he stated that the continued deployment was necessary for national security reasons such as the protection of U.S. troops. The citation to national security is not a magical incantation. Although the President is entitled under *Martin v. Mott* to a presumption of good faith, the plaintiff congressmen could introduce evidence of his bad faith. If the court was persuaded of the President's bad faith, it could require the President to offer actual proof of the threat to national security, which the court would consider along with any evidence offered by the plaintiff congressmen.

The President expressly denied any waiver of constitutional authority under the MNFILR.[112] Furthermore, whatever the President agreed to do under the MNFILR, he agreed to do only under the conditions existing at the time the MNFILR became law. Thus, any significant change of circumstances (such as the bombing of the Marine headquarters on October 23) could have nullified any concessions by the President. Even if the MNFILR could be read to contain the President's waiver, the MNFILR would not reduce his authority under the Constitution. The Constitution cannot be amended by means of legislation alone.

The October 23, 1983 destruction of the Marine headquarters at Beirut International Airport, and the consequential deaths of 241 servicemen, was a national tragedy. Despite this fact and the fact that many considered the incident to be the culmination of the sloppy execution of a poorly considered policy, it carried no constitutional implications.

As terrible as the attack was in human terms and as poor the policy might have been in political, strategic, and diplomatic terms, it did not affect the President's power to deploy the Marines to Lebanon, either retrospectively or prospectively. It simply is not the case that the enemy's success against U.S. forces reduces the President's authority to direct U.S. forces.

On December 4, the President ordered an air strike by naval forces against targets in Syrian-controlled Lebanon in retaliation for the launching of a SAM against an F-14 reconnaissance flight the day before. This air strike, which led to the loss of two attack aircraft and one pilot, and the imprisonment of a second pilot, has been the subject of intense criticism. Unlike the air strike against Libya, the air strike against Lebanon is not typically listed among the great moments of the Reagan presidency.[113] Some of the criticism is focused on the quality of the strike planning and the selection of air power rather than naval guns to deliver the attack. Some of the criticism is focused on the fact that the United States responded with force when a SAM was unsuccessfully launched at a U.S. fighter but did not retaliate immediately for the October 23 bombing of the Marine compound. Whatever the merit of these criticisms, they serve to illustrate that the success or popularity of a military action does not affect its constitutional basis. The President was empowered to order retaliation for an attack on U.S. forces. He was entitled to order the air strike if it was necessary, in his sole judgment, to deter future attacks or otherwise defend U.S. security interests. His decision might have been unwise, but it was not unlawful.

The Multi-National Force in Lebanon and the War Powers Resolution

The War Powers Resolution ("WPR") requires the President to consult with Congress before introducing U.S. forces into situations where hostilities are imminent.[114] At the time the President deployed the Marines to Lebanon to join the MNF, he had told Congress that he did not expect the Marines to become involved in hostilities. The Long Commission confirmed this view:

> It was contemplated from the outset that the USMNF would operate in a relatively benign environment. Syrian forces were not considered a significant threat to the MNF. The major threats were thought to be unexploded ordnance and possible sniper and small unit attacks from PLO and Leftist militias. It was anticipated that the USMNF would be perceived by the various factions as evenhanded and neutral and that this perception would hold through the expected 60 day duration of the operation.

> The environment into which the USMNF actually deployed in September 1982, while not necessarily benign was, for the most part, not hostile. The Marines were warmly welcomed and seemed genuinely to be appreciated by the majority of Lebanese.[115]

The President's statement was based on his optimism, in spite of the turbulent recent history of Lebanon, that the presence of the MNF would induce restraint on the part of the warring factions in Lebanon. In other words, the President believed that the U.S. presence in the MNF would decrease the likelihood of hostilities in Lebanon. It eventually developed, of course, that the President was wrong. Nevertheless, the President was entitled under the Constitution to be optimistic in the summer of 1982. Since the WPR requires that imminent hostilities be "clearly indicated by the circumstances," and since the President contended that hostilities were not imminent, no consultation was required by the terms of the WPR. The President, nevertheless, did consult with Congress during the summer of 1982.[116]

The conclusion that no consultation was required by the terms of the WPR raises the question of whether the President is empowered by the WPR unilaterally to decide whether hostilities are imminent. That is, if the President has decided that hostilities are not imminent, must he ask Congress to certify his decision or otherwise confirm his judgment? In the alternative, does the WPR provide that the obligation to consult is not activated where the President in his sole discretion does not find hostilities to be imminent? The statutory language does not provide a clear answer to these questions. The WPR's language refers to "imminent hostilities" as a condition existing in the state of nature, like, for example, the color green. But "imminent hostilities" is not an obvious natural condition. Identifying it is like determining whether turquoise is green or blue.

In light of the reluctance of the courts to mediate differences of opinion as to the presence of imminent hostilities,[117] no one of two reasonable interpretations of the same set of facts is likely to be approved by a neutral forum. A disagreement about the existence of imminent hostilities is liable to result in a legal, if not political, stalemate. Since Congress could have expressed its intention had it meant to require congressional certification of imminent hostilities, this ambiguity may mean that Congress did not intend to impose any such requirement. If so, Congress was on firm constitutional ground: since Congress has no power to require congressional approval when the Constitution grants the President the unilateral power to make war, language commanding congressional certification would be invalid.

Even as U.S. forces became involved in actual hostilities in Lebanon, the President was not required by law to consult. This is true for two reasons. First, although hindsight suggests that U.S. forces were involved in sustained hostilities in 1983, the President did not have the benefit of foresight at the beginning of any arguable period of hostilities. Since the involvement of U.S. forces in past hostilities does not clearly indicate future imminent hostilities, the President never was required to consult, even by the terms of the WPR itself. This conclusion serves to illustrate the flawed condition of the statutory language of the WPR. The consultation requirement requires that Congress and the President look into a crystal ball to determine whether hostilities are likely in the future. The WPR offers no assistance to Congress and the President as to the best means of identifying the most accurate prediction.

As a constitutional matter, the President is entitled to deference in his crystal ball gazing when it comes to foreign affairs. The President is the "sole organ" of the government in the field of foreign affairs, and enjoys a "degree of discretion and freedom from statutory restriction" that would be impermissible in domestic affairs.[118] Moreover, as Commander-in-Chief, the President's determination that defensive action is necessary to protect armed forces abroad is entitled to the "presumption" that his power is being "exercised in pursuance of law."[119] To the extent that the consultation requirement of the WPR conflicts with these constitutional principles, the consultation requirement is not binding. Therefore, although the WPR, by its terms, would have required the President to consult with Congress prior to inserting U.S. forces into imminent hostilities in Lebanon, it did not require him to consult prior to deploying U.S. forces into a situation where he, the President, did not consider hostilities to be imminent. As a matter of law, this presidential determination is presumptively final. As a matter of politics, it is only the beginning.

The WPR also requires, at Section 4(a)(2), a report whenever U.S. forces are introduced "into the territory . . . of a foreign nation, while equipped for combat. . . ."[120] The apparent force of this language is to avoid some of the ambiguities of the consultation requirement by requiring a report whenever combat-equipped troops are deployed into situations where hostilities are not imminent, under anyone's interpretation. It would be difficult to argue that the Marines sent to Lebanon were not "equipped for combat," even if they did not intend to become involved in combat. Thus the deployment of Marines to Lebanon in 1982 fit this statutory category.

When the President reported to Congress on August 24, 1982, he did so "consistent with" the WPR. The President's report focused on the "equipped for combat" language of WPR Section 4(a)(2), and disavowed involvement in hostilities.

> In accordance with my desire that the Congress be fully informed on this matter, and consistent with the War Powers Resolution, I am hereby providing a report on the deployment and mission of these members of the United States Armed Forces. . . . These troops are equipped with weapons consistent with their non-combat mission, including usual infantry weapons. . . . According to our agreement with the Government of Lebanon, the United States military personnel will be withdrawn from Lebanon within thirty days.
> I want to emphasize that there is no intention or expectation that U.S. Armed Forces will become involved in hostilities. . . . [I]n the event of a breakdown in its implementation, the multinational force will be withdrawn. Although we cannot rule out isolated acts of violence, all appropriate precautions have . . . been taken to assure the safety of U.S. military personnel during their brief assignment to Lebanon.
> This deployment . . . is being undertaken pursuant to the President's constitutional authority with respect to the conduct of foreign relations and as Commander-in-Chief of the United States Armed Forces.[121]

This communication qualifies as a WPR report, although the WPR is not clear on what sort of report is actually required. By submitting a report, the President did not start the sixty-day clock because he did not submit a report pursuant to Section 4(a)(1), pertaining to "hostilities" or "imminent hostilities." Rather, he reported under the "equipped for combat" provision, which does not start the sixty-day clock. Whether the clock started or not, the President was constitutionally authorized to send the Marines to Lebanon unilaterally. Therefore, since the WPR cannot trump the Constitution, the WPR's reporting requirement did not act to limit the President to sixty days.

The initial U.S. contingent to the MNF was withdrawn within sixty days, operating in Lebanon only between August 25 and September 10, 1982. U.S. troops returned on September 29, however, and the reporting question was raised anew. Again, the President submitted a report "consistent with" the WPR. The President's September 29, 1982 report stated:

> In accordance with my desire that the Congress be fully informed on this matter, and consistent with the War Powers Resolution, I am hereby providing a report on the deployment and mission of these members of the United States armed forces. . . . Their mission is to provide an interposition force at agreed locations. . . . In carrying out this mission, the American force will not engage in combat. It may, however, exercise

the right of self-defense and will be equipped accordingly. . . . Although
it is not possible at this time to predict the precise duration of the presence
of U.S. forces in Beirut, our agreement with the Government of Lebanon
makes clear that they will be needed only for a limited period. . . .[122]

If this report started the sixty-day clock on September 29, 1982, then
the deadline expired more than a year before the President withdrew
U.S. troops from Lebanon. But the report did not start the sixty-day
clock because it was not a report pursuant to Section 4(a)(1) regarding
"hostilities" and "imminent hostilities." The President stated, to the
contrary, that hostilities were not expected. The report appeared to be
a Section 4(a)(2) "equipped for combat" report, which does not start
the sixty-day clock. Apparently, the President's September 29, 1982 report
was intentionally vague on the distinction between Sections 4(a)(1) and
4(a)(2). In a memorandum to the President, the Secretary of State and
the Secretary of Defense wrote:

> The Secretary of State
> Washington
> September 25, 1982
>
> Memorandum For: The President
> From: George P. Shultz
>   Caspar W. Weinberger
> Subject: War Powers and Lebanon
>
> The reporting requirements of the War Powers Resolution necessitate a
> report to the Congress within 48 hours after the introduction of U.S.
> forces into Beirut. A draft report, similar to the one which you submitted
> prior to the introduction of U.S. forces on August 24, is attached for your
> approval.
>
> *Character of Report*
> The War Powers Resolution requires a report within 48 hours whenever
> U.S. forces "equipped for combat" are introduced into foreign territory.
> This provision is clearly applicable to the Beirut operation.
> The Resolution also requires consultation with Congress prior to the
> introduction of U.S. forces into hostilities or into situations in which
> "imminent involvement in hostilities is clearly indicated by the circum-
> stances," and a report within 48 hours after U.S. forces are so introduced.
> A controversial provision of the Resolution states that when forces are
> introduced into a hostile situation, they must be withdrawn within 60
> days absent an express Congressional authorization or immediately if the
> Congress so declares by concurrent resolution.
> The War Powers Resolution does not require that we stipulate on which
> basis the report is being submitted. Because we believe the U.S. force will
> not be involved in combat, we could specify that the report is being

submitted under the "equipped for combat" requirement. However, this might needlessly antagonize some members of Congress who may believe that the "imminent hostilities" standard is applicable. Your report on the first introduction of forces into Beirut in August did not indicate the basis for its submission and there was no adverse Congressional reaction. We believe that the same course should be followed in this case.

Timing

Although the report does not need to be submitted until 48 hours after the introduction of U.S. forces, we believe that, as in the case of the August report, it is preferable to submit an immediate report. This will avoid the risk that events in the intervening 48 hours may call into question the statement in the report of our intention and expectation that our forces will not be involved in hostilities.

Congressional Aspects

While the War Powers Resolution does not technically require advance consultation with Congress if U.S. forces are not introduced into actual or imminent hostilities, we have already, for policy reasons, consulted with key Members of Congress and expect to continue to do so as events develop.

Recommendation

That you approve the attached draft report and transmit it immediately following the initial deployment of U.S. forces into Lebanese territory.[123]

On August 28, 1983, U.S. Marines fired on Druze positions, thereby committing an unambiguously hostile act. Arguably, therefore, a report was required by the terms of the WPR. The significance of such a report would be the starting of the WPR's sixty-day clock. Of course, the Marines were acting in self-defense, an undertaking clearly within the scope of the President's authority. Thus, the WPR exerted no legal restrictive pressure on the President in this circumstance. Nevertheless, on August 30, 1983, the President did report to Congress on the August 28–29 actions, and did so "consistent with" with WPR.[124]

The *Crockett v. Reagan* Court determined that in order to start the sixty-day clock, Congress must undertake some action to manifest its belief that a WPR report is required.[125] Absent such congressional action, it is not clear that the President does not enjoy the full support of Congress. Congress did not take such action until October 12, 1983, when the MNFILR determined that the "requirements of Section 4(a)(1) of the War Powers Resolution became operative on August 29, 1983," the date when two Marines were killed and fourteen injured in an exchange of rocket, artillery, and mortar fire, following the use of force on August 28.

In addition to stating Congress' collective opinion that the WPR applied to the MNF in Lebanon, the MNFILR authorized the U.S. presence for a period of eighteen months. The President disagreed with the congressional assertion that the WPR had been activated by the actions on August 28–29, noting that "the initiation of isolated or infrequent acts of violence against United States Armed Forces does not necessarily constitute actual or imminent involvement in hostilities, even if casualties to those forces result."[126] He continued:

> I believe it is, therefore, important for me to state, in signing this resolution, that I do not and cannot cede any of the authority vested in me under the Constitution as President and as Commander in Chief of United States Armed Forces. Nor should my signing be viewed as any acknowledgement that the President's constitutional authority can be impermissibly infringed by statute, that congressional authorization would be required if and when the period specified in section 5(b) of the War Powers Resolution might be deemed to have been triggered and the period had expired, or that section 6 of the Multinational Force in Lebanon Resolution may be interpreted to revise the President's constitutional authority to deploy United States Armed Forces. Let me underscore, however, that any differences we may have over institutional prerogatives will in no way diminish my intention to proceed in the manner outlined in my letter of September 27, 1983, to achieve the important bipartisan goals reflected in this resolution.[127]

The President, in signing the MNFILR, accepted the eighteen-month authorization, but not the eighteen-month limitation. He noted, correctly, that his powers as Commander-in-Chief could not be limited by an act of Congress. This dispute never matured beyond an exchange of views, however, because the U.S. contingent to the MNF was withdrawn within eighteen months.

Notes

1. Report of the Department of Defense Commission on Beirut International Airport Terrorist Attack, October 23, 1983 at 24 (December 20, 1983) ("Long Commission Report"); S. KATZ and L. RUSSELL, ARMIES IN LEBANON, 1982–1984 at 1–3 (1985) ("KATZ and RUSSELL").

2. Long Commission Report at 25.

3. Long Commission Report at 27; KATZ and RUSSELL at 3 (400,000 refugees).

4. B. FRANK, U.S. MARINES IN LEBANON 1982–1984 at 6 (1987) ("FRANK").

5. Historical Studies Div., Bureau of Public Affairs, Dept. of State, "Armed Actions By the United States Without a Declaration of War, 1789–1967," at 11–12 (Research Project No. 806A August 1967).

6. *Id.*

7. KATZ and RUSSELL at 3–4; Long Commission Report at 27.

8. KATZ and RUSSELL at 5.

9. KATZ and RUSSELL at 5.

10. KATZ and RUSSELL at 7.

11. C. WEINBERGER, FIGHTING FOR PEACE 139 (1990).

12. KATZ and RUSSELL at 8–9.

13. KATZ and RUSSELL at 8–9.

14. C. WEINBERGER, FIGHTING FOR PEACE 140 (1990); KATZ and RUSSELL at 9 (two helicopters shot down).

15. KATZ and RUSSELL at 10–11; C. WEINBERGER, FIGHTING FOR PEACE 140 (1990).

16. C. WEINBERGER, FIGHTING FOR PEACE 140 (1990).

17. KATZ and RUSSELL at 11.

18. C. WEINBERGER, FIGHTING FOR PEACE 141–142 (1990).

19. KATZ and RUSSELL at 18.

20. KATZ and RUSSELL at 12; Long Commission Report at 27–28.

21. KATZ and RUSSELL at 17.

22. KATZ and RUSSELL at 19.

23. KATZ and RUSSELL at 20.

24. KATZ and RUSSELL at 21.

25. KATZ and RUSSELL at 19. *See also* C. WEINBERGER, FIGHTING FOR PEACE 142 (1990) (over 70 Syrian aircraft destroyed in a few hours).

26. Long Commission Report at 29; Evans, "Navy-Marine Corps Team in Lebanon," 110 U.S. Naval Institute PROCEEDINGS 133 (1984) ("Evans").

27. KATZ and RUSSELL at 22–23.

28. KATZ and RUSSELL at 24; Long Commission Report at 29.

29. KATZ and RUSSELL at 24.

30. Letter to the Speaker of the House and the President Pro Tempore of the Senate on the Deployment of United States Forces in Beirut, Lebanon, August 24, 1982, II PUBLIC PAPERS OF THE PRESIDENTS OF THE UNITED STATES: RONALD REAGAN, 1982 at 1078 (1983). *But see* C. WEINBERGER, FIGHTING FOR PEACE 144 (1990) (Marines deployed in July 1982).

31. Letter to the Speaker of the House and the President Pro Tempore of the Senate on the Deployment of United States Forces in Beirut, Lebanon, August 24, 1982, II PUBLIC PAPERS OF THE PRESIDENTS OF THE UNITED STATES: RONALD REAGAN, 1982 at 1078 (1983).

32. FRANK at 12.

33. FRANK at 15.

34. FRANK at 17.

35. FRANK at 21 (quoting report of Lt.Col. Johnston, USMC, commanding the Beirut port area).

36. *See* B. WOODWARD, VEIL: THE SECRET WARS OF THE CIA 1981–1987 (1987) ("WOODWARD") at 217–219 (describing Bashir Gemayel as a paid CIA man).

37. *Id.* at 219.

38. *Id.* at 219; C. WEINBERGER, FIGHTING FOR PEACE 151 (1990).

39. Long Commission Report at 39; FRANK at 22; Letter to the Speaker of the House and the President Pro Tempore of the Senate Reporting on United States Participation in the Multinational Force in Lebanon, II PUBLIC PAPERS OF THE PRESIDENTS OF THE UNITED STATES: RONALD REAGAN, 1982 at 1238 (1983).

40. Ferrante and Miller, "Chronology: Marines in Lebanon," 110 U.S. Naval Institute PROCEEDINGS 298, 300 (May 1984) ("Ferrante & Miller").

41. Long Commission Report at 35. *See also* Long Commission Report at 29–34.

42. Long Commission Report at 36 (emphasis added by Long Commission).

43. Long Commission Report at 38. *See also* C. WEINBERGER, FIGHTING FOR PEACE 152 (1990).

44. Evans at 134; FRANK at 149.

45. FRANK at 149; Ferrante & Miller at 300.

46. Ferrante & Miller at 310.

47. FRANK at 45–47.

48. FRANK at 50.

49. Wright, "U.S. Naval Operations in 1983," 110 U.S. Naval Institute PROCEEDINGS 52, 59 (1984) ("Wright").

50. WOODWARD at 286.

51. FRANK at 64.

52. C. WEINBERGER, FIGHTING FOR PEACE 155 (1990).

53. *Id.* at 160.

54. Ferrante & Miller at 300.

55. Wright at 59; Letter to the Speaker of the House and the President Pro Tempore of the Senate on the United States Participation in the Multinational Force in Lebanon, II PUBLIC PAPERS OF THE PRESIDENTS OF THE UNITED STATES: RONALD REAGAN, 1983 at 1216 (1985).

56. FRANK at 78.

57. Wright at 59.

58. FRANK at 150.

59. Evans at 136–137.

60. FRANK at 88.

61. Evans at 137.

62. Foreign Broadcast Information Service, "Trends in Communist Media," September 28, 1983 at 11 (approved for release December 1, 1987).

63. 19 WEEKLY COMPILATION OF PRESIDENTIAL DOCUMENTS, October 8, 1983 at 1417.

64. Ferrante & Miller at 303.

65. FRANK at 150–151.

66. On the same morning, the headquarters of the French contingent to the MNF was also bombed, killing 58 French paratroops. On November 4, Israeli headquarters in Tyre was destroyed by a truck bomb, leaving 23 Israelis dead. KATZ and RUSSELL at 35.

67. J. MOSKIN, THE U.S. MARINE CORPS STORY (2d ed. 1987) ("MOS-KIN") at 729.

68. Long Commission Report at 83–84.

69. FRANK at 151; Ferrante & Miller at 303.

70. FRANK at 168–169.

71. Long Commission Report at 50–51.

72. Long Commission Report at 11.

73. J. LEHMAN, COMMAND OF THE SEAS: A PERSONAL STORY (1988) ("LEHMAN") at 326–327; C. WEINBERGER, FIGHTING FOR PEACE 166 (1990) (two U.S. aircraft fired upon). For criticism of the air strike, *see* E. LUTTWAK, THE PENTAGON AND THE ART OF WAR 58–60 (1984).

74. Wright at 59.

75. Wright at 59–60.

76. Wright at 61.

77. G. WILSON, SUPER CARRIER: AN INSIDE ACCOUNT OF LIFE ABOARD THE WORLD'S MOST POWERFUL SHIP, THE U.S.S. JOHN F. KENNEDY 142 (1986).

78. LEHMAN at 332.

79. MOSKIN at 743; FRANK at 152.

80. MOSKIN at 743.

81. Wright at 61.

82. Wright at 61.

83. Wright at 21.

84. LEHMAN at 334.

85. FRANK at 129.

86. MOSKIN at 744.

87. FRANK at 132.

88. Evans at 139.

89. LEHMAN at 334.

90. MOSKIN at 745.

91. FRANK at 137.

92. FRANK at 152–153.

93. MOSKIN at 745.

94. Long Commission Report at 8.

95. *See, e.g.,* C. WEINBERGER, FIGHTING FOR PEACE 154–174 (1990).

96. 18 WEEKLY COMPILATION OF PRESIDENTIAL DOCUMENTS, August 30, 1982, at 1065–1066.

97. Public Law 98-43 (June 27, 1983) (emphasis supplied).

98. 19 WEEKLY COMPILATION OF PRESIDENTIAL DOCUMENTS, June 27, 1983, at 931.

99. Public Law 98-119 (October 12, 1983).

100. *See supra* the MNF Rules of Engagement.

101. A. HAMILTON, THE FEDERALIST, NO. 69 (March 15, 1788).

102. *United States v. Curtiss-Wright Export Corp.,* 299 U.S. 304, 320 (1936). *See also United States v. Belmont,* 301 U.S. 324 (1937); *Myers v. United States,* 272 U.S. 52, 118 (1926).

103. U.S. CONST. Art. II, Sec. 2, Cl. 2.

104. *See* Chapter 2; *Republic of Mexico v. Hoffman,* 324 U.S. 30 (1945); *Ex parte Peru,* 318 U.S. 578 (1943). *See also* Mathews, "The Constitutional Power of the President to Conclude International Agreements," 64 YALE L. J. 345 (1955).

105. *United States v. Belmont,* 301 U.S. 324, 330–331 (1937).

106. 406 U.S. 759, 768 (1972). *See also Dames & Moore v. Regan,* 453 U.S. 654, 682 (1982); *United States v. Pink,* 315 U.S. 203 (1942).

107. L. TRIBE, AMERICAN CONSTITUTIONAL LAW 170–171 (1978) ("At the very least, the President is empowered to employ executive agreements within the penumbras of enumerated presidential powers as, for example, when invoking the Commander in Chief power to justify an armistice agreement."); L. HENKIN, FOREIGN AFFAIRS AND THE CONSTITUTION 177 (1972). *See also* Chapter 8.

108. *See generally* Chapter 2. *See also, e.g., Republic of Mexico v. Hoffman,* 324 U.S. 30 (1945); *ex parte Peru,* 318 U.S. 578 (1943); *United States v. Belmont,* 301 U.S. 324 (1937).

109. *See* Chapter 2.

110. 19 WEEKLY COMPILATION OF PRESIDENTIAL DOCUMENTS, October 12, 1983, at 1422.

111. *See, e.g., Lowry v. Reagan,* 676 F. Supp. 333 (D.D.C. 1987); *Crockett v. Reagan,* 558 F. Supp. 893 (D.D.C.), *aff'd,* 720 F.2d 1355 (D.C. Cir.), *cert. denied,* 467 U.S. 1251 (1982).

112. 19 WEEKLY COMPILATION OF PRESIDENTIAL DOCUMENTS, October 12, 1983, at 1422.

113. *See, e.g.,* former Secretary of the Navy Lehman's remarks in J. LEHMAN, COMMAND OF THE SEAS (1988).

114. 50 U.S.C. § 1542.

115. Long Commission Report at 39.

116. TURNER at 81. *See also* Javits, "War Powers Reconsidered," FOREIGN AFFAIRS 130, 135 (1985).

117. *See, e.g., Lowry v. Reagan,* 676 F. Supp. 333 (D.D.C. 1987); *Crockett v. Reagan,* 558 F. Supp. 893 (D.D.C.), *aff'd,* 720 F.2d 1355 (D.C. Cir.), *cert. denied,* 467 U.S. 1251 (1982).

118. *Curtiss-Wright,* 299 U.S. at 320.

119. *Martin v. Mott,* 25 U.S. (12 Wheat.) 19, 32–33 (1827).

120. 50 U.S.C. § 1543.

121. Letter to the Speaker of the House and the President Pro Tempore of the Senate on the Deployment of United States Forces in Beirut, Lebanon, August 24, 1982, II PUBLIC PAPERS OF THE PRESIDENTS OF THE UNITED STATES: RONALD REAGAN, 1982 at 1078–1079 (1983). *See also* TURNER at 82.

122. Letter to the Speaker of the House and the President Pro Tempore of the Senate Reporting on United States Participation in the Multinational Force in Lebanon, September 29, 1982, II PUBLIC PAPERS OF THE PRESIDENTS OF THE UNITED STATES: RONALD REAGAN, 1982 at 1238 (1983). *See also* TURNER at 84.

123. Obtained from Department of State by Freedom of Information Act Request.

124. Letter to the Speaker of the House and the President Pro Tempore of the Senate Reporting on United States Participation in the Multinational Force in Lebanon, August 30, 1983, II PUBLIC PAPERS OF THE PRESIDENTS OF THE UNITED STATES: RONALD REAGAN, 1983 at 1216 (1985).

125. *Crockett v. Reagan,* 558 F. Supp. 893 (D.D.C.), *aff'd,* 720 F.2d 1355 (D.C. Cir.), *cert. denied,* 467 U.S. 1251 (1982).

126. 19 WEEKLY COMPILATION OF PRESIDENTIAL DOCUMENTS, October 12, 1983, at 1422.

127. *Id.* at 1422–1423.

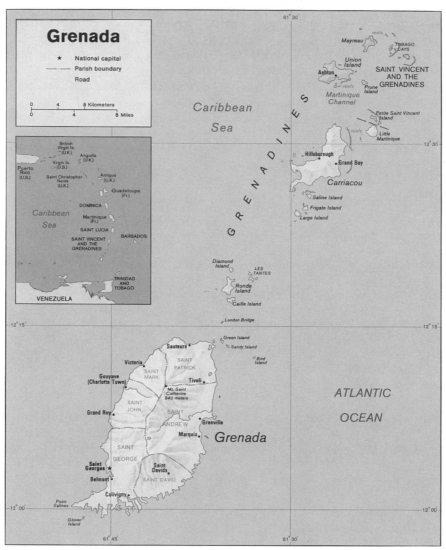

Grenada

★   National capital

-----   Parish boundary

Road

0   4   8 Kilometers

0   4   8 Miles

Caribbean Sea

Mayreau

Union Island

Ashton

TOBAGO CAYS

SAINT VINCENT AND THE GRENADINES

reefs

Prune Island

Martinique Channel

Petite Saint Vincent Island

reefs

Little Martinique

12° 30'

Hillsborough

Grand Bay

Carriacou

Saline Island

Frigate Island

Large Island

G R E N A D I N E S

61° 30'

British Virgin Is. (U.K.)

Virgin Is. (U.S.)

Anguilla (U.K.)

Puerto Rico (U.S.)

Saint Christopher Nevis (U.K.)

Antigua (U.K.)

Guadeloupe (Fr.)

DOMINICA

Caribbean Sea

Martinique (Fr.)

SAINT LUCIA

BARBADOS

SAINT VINCENT AND THE GRENADINES

TRINIDAD AND TOBAGO

VENEZUELA

Diamond Island

LES TANTES

Ronde Island

Caille Island

London Bridge

12° 15'

12° 15'

Green Island

Sandy Island

Sauteurs

Bird Island

Victoria

SAINT PATRICK

SAINT MARK

Tivoli

Gouyave (Charlotte Town)

Mt. Saint Catherine 840 meters

SAINT JOHN

SAINT ANDREW

SAINT

Grand Roy

Grenville

Marquis

Grenada

SAINT GEORGE

Saint Georges ★

Saint Davids

SAINT DAVID

Belmont

Calivigny

Point Salines

12° 00'

12° 00'

Glover Island

ATLANTIC OCEAN

61° 45'

61° 30'

U.S. Government Publication

6

Grenada, 1983

Operation Urgent Fury

Grenada is the southernmost of the Windward Islands, part of the Antilles Archipelago, separating the Caribbean Sea from the Atlantic Ocean. It has been described by an unknown commentator as, "Just south of paradise, just north of frustration."[1] Grenada's location is strategically significant. In a war in Europe, Africa, or Asia, approximately eighty-five percent of the tonnage to be shipped to support U.S. military action would pass from ports on the Gulf of Mexico, through either the sixty-mile wide Straits of Florida or the ninety-mile wide Yucatan Channel.[2] Grenada, unlike Cuba, does not sit astride these choke points. However, Grenada is closer to these choke points than is the Soviet Union.

On October 25, 1983, U.S. Army and Marine Corps troops landed on Grenada to seize control of the island from Grenadian and Cuban forces.[3] They did so pursuant to presidential direction without a declaration of war or other congressional authorization. They were supported by U.S. naval forces and the U.S. Air Force. Accompanying the U.S. forces were 300 troops from member nations of the Organization of Eastern Caribbean States ("OECS"), as well as Jamaica and Barbados. The OECS member nations are Antigua-and-Barbuda, Dominica, Montserrat, St. Kitts-Nevis, St. Lucia, St. Vincent, and Grenada. Within five days of the initial landing, U.S. and allied forces controlled the island. "Operation Urgent Fury," as the operation was called, presents unambiguously an example of unilateral war-making by the President.

Grenada became independent of Great Britain on February 7, 1974, under the leadership of its eccentric Prime Minister, Sir Eric Gairy.[4] From the start of his tenure as independent Grenada's first Prime Minister, Sir Eric faced opposition by the New Jewel Movement, a leftist party formed in March of 1973.[5] Sir Eric sought to intimidate the opposition with a paramilitary squad known as the Mongoose Gang, which responded to protests with batons and guns.[6] Sir Eric stated his point of view as follows: "He who opposes me opposes God."[7] On March 13, 1979, while Sir Eric visited the United Nations to discuss the relationship between voodoo and unidentified flying objects,[8] the New Jewel Movement seized control of the government by a nearly bloodless *coup d'etat*. Maurice Bishop became the Prime Minister of what was called the People's Revolutionary Government. The new government was soon recognized by the U.S. on the basis of Bishop's promises that elections would be held soon.[9] Some have said that Bishop was sufficiently popular that he would have won a general election, had he called one.[10] Bishop was a barrister who had earned a law degree in Great Britain, returning to Grenada in 1970. In 1972, he co-founded the "Movement for Assemblies of the People" to oppose Prime Minister Gairy.[11] Bishop's party aligned in 1973 with Unison Whiteman's Joint Endeavor for Welfare, Education, and Liberation ("JEWEL") party, forming the New Jewel Movement.[12]

On March 25, 1979, Bishop announced the suspension of the 1974 Constitution.[13] However, Bishop retained membership in the British Commonwealth and did not eliminate the position of Governor-General, an office empowered under the 1974 Constitution to exercise the "executive authority of Grenada."[14] Bishop sought from the start to lead a Marxist-Leninist revolution.[15] He stated a goal of government domination of all Grenadian institutions:

> That the state sector must be built to be the dominant sector, . . . [w]e must assume to take control over all financial institutions over a period of time. . . . We must assume total control of all foreign trade, and also of some aspects of internal trade. . . . We must assume total control of all public utilities—electricity, telephone, water, transport.[16]

Bishop issued new laws by proclamation and sought thereby to exert control over all aspects of island life.[17]

In October, 1979, Bishop announced, "We think our revolution contributes to the acceleration of the process of decolonization in our area, where there are still enclaves under British, French, and—in the case of Puerto Rico—U.S. domination, and that our revolution is part, together with the Sandinista triumph in Nicaragua, of the revolutionary advances in Latin America."[18] In 1982, Bishop expressed his fear that "if we are not careful, capitalism rather than socialism will be the end product. . . ."[19] He concluded, "[O]ur primary task must be to sink the ideas of Marxism/Leninism amongst the working people so that their own ideological level can advance."[20]

Bishop moved quickly to align himself with the Soviet Union and Cuba, executing numerous trade and military assistance agreements with the Soviet bloc. Indeed, on the very day the U.S. recognized his government, Bishop announced his intention to seek arms and military agreements with Cuba.[21] During 1979, Grenada received its first arms shipments from Cuba, including 100 pistols, 200 machine guns, 3,400 rifles (Soviet AK-47, U.S. M-16, and British .303), 100 rocket launchers, twelve 82mm mortars, and twelve 12.7mm antiaircraft machine guns.[22] Over the next four years, Bishop obtained over $33 million in aid from Cuba.[23] By mid-1983, 400–600 Cuban workers and technicians were present on the island, many participating in Cuba's construction of a 9,000–10,000 foot runway at Point Salines Airport in Grenada. The Reagan administration viewed this runway as unnecessary for Grenada's relatively small tourist industry and therefore a manifestation of Cuban-Soviet military expansionism in the Caribbean Basin.[24] In particular, the United States viewed the airport as a potential staging location for Cuban logistical flights to Angola and Soviet logistical flights to Nicaragua.[25] The diary of Liam James, a New Jewel Movement Central Committee member, was captured after Operation Urgent Fury and stated: "Airport will be used for Cubans and Soviets [sic] military."[26] As Ludlow Flower, the U.S. chargé d'affaires in Barbados, put it:

> It isn't the airport per se that bothers us. Lots of islands around here have airports of comparable size. It is that the airport in Grenada was primarily financed and built by the Cubans, who tend not to do these things out of a sense of Christian charity. . . . With the completion of the Point Salines airport next year, and the additional military development in the Calivigny and Egmont harbor areas, there will exist a complex that would make deployment of Cuban and other hostile forces to Latin American and African points easier.
> Indeed the complex could be thought of as a stationary aircraft carrier.[27]

In June of 1983, the CIA reported the growth of Soviet efforts to "undermine U.S. power and authority" in the Caribbean Basin.[28] In addition, the CIA viewed Soviet activity in Grenada, among other Caribbean nations, as an attempt to increase "Moscow's own military role."[29] The CIA pointed to the development of Grenadian ports and the Port Salines Airport as examples of Soviet expansionist activities in the region.

> The Soviets are now reportedly surveying port development—for civilian purposes—in two places, at Grenville in Grenada and at San Juan del Sur on the Pacific Coast of Nicaragua. Both are small and relatively isolated ports that could eventually provide some limited support for Soviet naval forces.
> The completion of the Point Salines airfield in Grenada will make it possible for the kind of TU-95 Soviet naval reconnaissance planes that now operate periodically from Cuba to expand their coverage further into the

South Atlantic. New airfields now being built in Nicaragua and other improvements there would also enable the USSR to show the flag and extend its military reach by regular military flights over the eastern Pacific. Moscow, however, has little military need for such activity.[30]

A CIA message summarized the strategic significance of Cuban involvement in Grenada.

With the Cubans diligently working on the airport, completion of the new airport could realistically occur in 1984. The strategic value of the island will: 1) enable Cuban aircraft to use the airport for resupply flights to Africa specifically to Angola if Cape Verde stopover is refused; 2) as a secure staging area for clandestine uses; 3) enable Cubans to fly directly to Libya and visa [sic] versa. The Calivigny military facility, which is virtually completed, which will house approximately 800 personnel, will probably be used as a Cuban military training area for neighboring islands' radicals as well as a headquarters for the Cuban advisory force. Calivigny, with its coastal location, is an ideal place for mounting seaborne operations. There is no indication that the Cubans intend to use Egmont Harbor for military purposes but the potential for such usage is available.[31]

The CIA determined that the Soviets had promised to provide Grenada with $26.5 million in military aid between 1980 and 1985 in the form of armored personnel carriers, AK-47 rifles, and munitions.[32] This aid was manifested by three agreements between Grenada and the Soviet Union. The first, dated October 27, 1980, provided: "The USSR shall ensure in 1980–81, free of charge, the delivery to the Government of Grenada of special and other equipment . . . in the amount of 4.4 [U.S. $5.85 million] million rubles," specifically: twelve 82mm mortars, 24 RPG-7s, 1,054 machine and submachine guns, eighteen 23mm ZU antiaircraft guns, 1,500 carbines, and 28 Gaz trucks.[33] A second agreement, dated February 9, 1981, provided for eight BTR-60PB armored personnel carriers, two BRDM-2 armored cars, 47 other vehicles, 1,000 submachine guns, 1,000 grenades, 60 radios, 12,600 uniforms, and other equipment, for a total value of $6.65 million.[34] The third agreement, dated July 27, 1982, provided for the shipment during the period 1983–1985 of additional military equipment worth $13.3 million, including 50 BTR-152VI armored personnel carriers, thirty 76mm guns, thirty 57mm antitank guns, fifty GRAD-P portable launchers, sixty 82mm mortars, and 2,000 AK-47 rifles.[35] The total quantity of equipment to be shipped to Grenada would have been sufficient to supply an army of 10,000 or twenty-five percent of the adult population of Grenada, according to one commentator.[36] By way of contrast, the Peoples Revolutionary Army in

1983 was composed of between 700 and 1,200 regulars and several thousand militia.[37] North Korea promised $12 million in military aid.[38]

By mid-November 1983, following Operation Urgent Fury, over 580 tons of military equipment had been confiscated in Grenada.[39] The intelligence community expressed ambivalence about the meaning of this large volume of military equipment. On the one hand, an interagency assessment concluded: "We believe the large numbers of weapons seized in Grenada were intended primarily for use by Grenadians in their own defense. . . ."[40] On the other hand, the interagency assessment found: "We believe that some of the weapons from the stockpile in Grenada . . . could be shipped to other countries in the region, but there is no known documentary support of this."[41]

Grenada's alignment with Cuba became complete by August of 1983 when the *New York Times* reported Cubans present "at every level and in virtually every meeting of the Grenadian government."[42] In addition to the runway at Point Salines, Cuba had provided, by August 1983, agricultural, literacy, and medical services experts, fishing and transportation advisors, a 75-kilowatt transmitter and a 400-foot transmitting antenna for Radio Free Grenada.[43] The CIA found: "The extent of Cuban support for Radio Free Grenada suggests that Havana, in addition to using the station to consolidate Bishop's revolution, looked upon it as a Cuban propaganda surrogate in the eastern Caribbean. . . ."[44] Total Cuban annual aid was estimated at about $66 million, $33 million of which was for the airport project.[45] In return, Grenada toed the Soviet-Cuban line in international affairs: 92% of Grenada's votes in the United Nations General Assembly were the same as those of the Soviet bloc, including Grenada's vote against sanctioning the Soviet Union for its invasion of Afghanistan.[46] As Bishop wrote to Fidel Castro, "In whatever ways and at whatever price the heroic internationalist people of Cuba can always count on [the] total solidarity, support and cooperation of the Grenada revolution."[47]

Bishop's moves to the left were not quick enough, however, for Deputy Prime Minister Coard, a firm Leninist and Bishop's major rival for power. Adding to the perception that Bishop's support of the Marxist-Leninist program was "soft" was Bishop's June 1983 trip to the United States, where he met with William Clark, President Reagan's national security advisor, and others.[48] But Bishop's political difficulties started before June of 1983. Under attack from Coard and the extreme left, the Bishop Government had experienced a slow disintegration of its authority since 1982.[49] During its July 13–19, 1983 meeting, the First Plenary Session of the New Jewel Movement Central Committee stated: "[O]ur Party has demonstrated many weaknesses—ideologically, politically and organizationally."[50] The Session concluded that the New Jewel Movement had failed "to transform itself ideologically and organizationally and to exercise firm leadership along a Leninist path."[51] During an August 26, 1983 meeting of the Central Committee, Minister of Mobilization Selwyn Strachan stated, "Sections of the party have begun to rebel against the higher organs of the party. . . . This silent rebellion will turn into open rebellion if we do not address it now. . . ."[52] When the Central Committee met a third time on September 14 through 16, Phyllis Coard, wife of the Deputy Prime Minister, stated:

> All programmes of the Revolution are in a very weak condition, while propaganda work is still very bad. . . . If this is allowed to continue the party will disintegrate in a matter of five to six months. . . . [T]he Comrade Leader [Bishop] has not taken responsibility, not given the necessary guidance, . . . is disorganized very often, avoids responsibilities for critical areas of work. . . .[53]

As a result of the leftist Coard faction's dissatisfaction with Bishop, the party organization was restructured to provide more power to Bernard Coard, who was granted control of the Politburo and the organizing committee of the New Jewel Movement, as well as the armed forces.[54] Bishop remained as Prime Minister, at least in name. Bishop was not actually removed from office because, despite the declining economy and increasing involvement of Cuba and the Soviet Union in Grenadian affairs, Bishop remained popular with the public.[55] Bishop was, after all, the man who deposed the mad Sir Eric Gairy after suffering beatings at the hands of Gairy's Mongoose Gang and the loss of his father, shot dead by Gairy's police during a protest march.[56] Rather than remove Bishop, the Politburo elected to have the best of both worlds, removing control of Grenadian institutions from Bishop while refraining from removing him from his highly visible role as titular leader. On September 25, 1983, the Politburo met to criticize Bishop and invite him to accept joint leadership with Coard. Bishop, sensing the turn of events in Coard's favor, accepted and publicly embraced Coard.[57] Bishop announced, "I sincerely accept the criticism and will fulfill the decision in practice."[58]

In an apparent effort to gain support from Grenada's foreign uncles, Bishop traveled on September 27 to Czechoslovakia, Hungary, East Berlin, the Soviet Union, and Cuba.[59] Bishop had met "in the spirit of friendship and complete mutual understanding" with Soviet Foreign Minister Andrey Gromyko on April 15, 1983.[60] He returned on October 8, having experienced a change of heart on the question of joint leadership. He expressed his doubts on October 11 to his ally Vincent Noel and reported that he had heard talk of an "Afghanistan solution,"[61] in apparent reference to the assassination of the prime minister of Afghanistan by the political opposition. At the Central Committee meeting on October 12, Bishop challenged the reallocation of power to Coard.[62] On October 13, Bishop was placed under house arrest. On October 14, Radio Free Grenada announced that Bishop had been expelled from the Party. The Minister of Mobilization Selwyn Strachan announced in a public square in St. George's that Coard had succeeded Bishop as Prime Minister. He was shouted down and chased from the scene.[63] In response to public objection, Coard retreated to his home.[64] In response to these developments, the U.S. Joint Chiefs of Staff directed the Commander-in-Chief of the Atlantic Fleet to prepare plans to evacuate U.S. citizens from Grenada.[65] General Hudson Austin, the Minister of Defense, made the following statement on October 17:

> Sisters and brothers, over the past four-and-a-half years, the Central Committee has struggled very hard to win Comrade Bishop to a position of collective leadership. Comrade Bishop was hoping to use the masses' love for him and violate the principled stand by the Central Committee of the party . . . even with all the love and admiration which exist within our party for Comrade Maurice [Bishop], the entire membership, except for a tiny minority, fully support the position of the Central Committee. . . . Comrade Bishop is at home and he is quite safe.[66]

The result of this political intrigue was chaos and murder. On October 18, five ministers loyal to Prime Minister Bishop resigned: Minister of Education Jacqueline Creft, Minister of Housing Norris Bain, Minister of Agriculture George Louison, Minister of Tourism Lyden Rhamdhanny, and Foreign (External) Affairs Minister Unison Whiteman.[67] On October 18, two to three thousand demonstrators took to the streets of Grenville, chanting, "We want Maurice Bishop," "We don't want Communism," and "We want Democracy."[68] On October 19, now known as "Bloody Wednesday," a crowd of 3,000, apparently led by former Minister of Foreign (External) Affairs Unison Whiteman, marched on Bishop's home, freeing him as well as Jacqueline Creft, who was not only the former Minister of Education but also Bishop's paramour.[69] The crowd left Bishop's home at about 10:00 a.m. and marched on Fort Rupert, which they occupied without significant resistance at about 11:00 a.m. At 1:00 p.m., the People's Revolutionary Army attacked the fort, firing on the unarmed crowd with a heavy caliber machine gun. Over fifty civilians, including women and children, were killed or wounded.[70] Bishop reportedly exclaimed, "Oh God, Oh God, they've turned their guns on the masses."[71] Bishop, Whiteman, Creft, former Minister of Housing Norris Bain, Fitzroy Bain, Evelyn Bullen, Evelyn Maitland, and Keith Hailing were marched into the fort's interior courtyard and executed at about 2:00 p.m.[72] The execution was not accomplished according to plan. Coard had desired Bishop's passing to look accidental, but events conspired against Coard.[73] Since Bishop and his party survived the attack on Fort Rupert, the military personnel holding them in the courtyard had to request orders from Coard. This left Coard with the choice of executing them or not, but removed the option of "accidental" death. Coard chose execution. They heard the following death sentence: "Comrades, turn around. This is an order from the Central Committee, that you shall be executed by fire. It is not my order, it is the Central Committee's."[74] Then they were shot.[75] The bodies were burned.[76]

After the execution, the Central Committee, which had assembled at Fort Frederick overlooking Fort Rupert, observed a flare fired from Fort Rupert. General Austin exclaimed, "Mission accomplished."[77] A Central Committee communique stated on October 19:

> Today our People's Revolutionary Army has gained victory over the right opportunists and reactionary forces which attacked the Headquarters of our Ministry of Defence. These anti-worker elements using the working people as a shield entered Fort Rupert.
> Our patriotic men, loving the masses and rather than killing them since we understood that they were being used, we held our fire. . . .
> Comrades, today Wednesday 19th October, history was made again. All patriots and revolutionaries will never forget this day when counter-revolution, the friends of imperialism, were crushed. This victory today will ensure that our glorious Party the NJM will live on and grow from strength to strength leading and guiding the Armed Forces and the Revolution. . . .[78]

Chaos followed. Coard remained hidden at Fort Frederick. In his apparent absence, Radio Free Grenada announced on October 19 the formation of a Revolutionary Military Council under the direction of General Hudson Austin. On October 20, General Austin declared: "The Revolutionary Armed Forces were forced to storm the Fort [Rupert], and in the process Maurice Bishop, Unison Whiteman, Vincent Noel, Norris Bain, Fitzroy Bain, and Jacqueline Creft were killed. . . . Maurice Bishop had declared his intentions to wipe out the entire leadership of the party, and the army. . . . The Revolution itself would have been wiped out."[79] Of course, four or five of the six casualties named by Austin had been executed at the order of Coard and the Central Committee.[80] Austin also announced a 24-hour shoot-on-sight curfew to quell the rioting and looting. "Let it be clearly understood that the Revolutionary Military Council will govern with absolute strictness.

Anyone who seeks to demonstrate or disturb the peace will be shot. . . . Anyone violating this curfew will be shot on sight."[81]

In response to news of the coup on October 19, the U.S. Joint Chiefs of Staff sent a warning order to Commander-in-Chief Atlantic to prepare to evacuate noncombatants from Grenada.[82] In the days following the coup, no one was sure which individuals or groups ran the government. On October 19, Ambassador Milan Bish advised Washington from Barbados:

> There appears to be imminent danger to U.S. citizens resident on Grenada due to the current deteriorating situation, which includes reports of rioting, personnel casualties (possibly deaths), automatic weapons being discharged, Soviet-built armored personnel carriers in the Grenadian streets and some loss of water and electricity on the island. . . . AmEmbassy Bridgetown recommends that the United States should now be prepared to conduct an emergency evacuation of U.S. citizens residing in Grenada.[83]

On October 19, two foreign service officers attempted to fly to Grenada from Barbados but were denied permission to land.[84] The U.S. Embassy in Barbados could not obtain assurances from Grenadian authorities that U.S. citizens were not in danger.[85]

The governments of the OECS and other Caribbean nations publicly broke with the new regime in Grenada. Antiqua and Barbuda refused to recognize the new regime. Barbados, St. Lucia, Montserrat, and St. Kitts-Nevis condemned the ruling Revolutionary Military Council. Prime Minister Tom Adams of Barbados described his sense of "horror at these brutal and vicious murders." He said, "I do not think it will be possible to accommodate so wide a range of governments within the Caribbean. It goes far beyond ideological pluralism. This is the difference between barbarians and [civilized] human beings."[86] Prime Minister Edward Seaga of Jamaica said, "The government of Jamaica, while not in sympathy with the ideology of the Bishop government, is repulsed by the tragic death of Mr. Bishop and his colleagues under the new regime of Cuban-trained Army generals and other Marxist [ideologues]. . . ."[87] Michael Manley, the former Prime Minister of Jamaica and supporter of the New Jewel Movement, described Bloody Wednesday as a "squalid betrayal of the hopes of the ordinary people of our region."[88] Dominica announced that it would not recognize an illegal regime. Jamaica broke diplomatic relations, and Trinidad and Tobago imposed trade sanctions against Grenada.[89]

On October 20, even Cuba condemned the killing of Bishop and his cabinet ministers, by means of a letter from Castro to the Revolutionary Military Council:

No doctrine, principle, or position proclaimed as revolutionary, nor any internal division can justify such brutal procedures as the physical elimination of Bishop and the prominent group of honest and worthy leaders who died yesterday.

The death of Bishop and his comrades must be clarified; and had they been executed in cold blood, those responsible for it deserve exemplary punishment. . . . [O]ur political relations with the new Grenadian leadership must be subjected to a serious and profound analysis.[90]

When asked for military assistance to repel any amphibious assault on Grenada, Castro refused. He stated:

If the US intervenes, we must vigorously defend ourselves as if we were in Cuba, in our camp sites, in our workplaces close by, but only if we are directly attacked. I repeat: only if we are directly attacked. We would thus be defending ourselves, not the Government [of Grenada] or its deeds. If the Yankees land on the runway section near the University or on its surroundings to evacuate their citizens, fully refrain from interfering. . . .[91]

Castro did order Cubans on Grenada to act defensively if necessary.

The Grenadian revolutionaries should try to win over the people for the defense of the country. . . . If Grenada is invaded by the US, the Cuban personnel will defend their positions in their camps and working areas with all their energy and courage. . . . It is impossible to assign them any other mission.[92]

Castro's passions ran both ways: on the one hand, he was disinclined to lend support to a regime that had just murdered his ally Bishop; on the other hand, he resisted the idea of allowing U.S. forces to land on Grenada unopposed. In comparison to Castro, the reaction of TASS was subdued: "A tense situation has formed in the country [of Grenada] following sharp differences and a split in the leadership of the New Jewel Movement."[93]

On October 21, the threat of regional instability induced President Reagan to divert to the Caribbean the U.S.S. *Independence* and her battle group, which was en route to relieve U.S. naval forces in Lebanon.[94] Taking note of this diversion, Fidel Castro advised the U.S. that Cuba would not interfere, but sent Colonel Pedro Tortolo Comas to command the Cubans in Grenada.[95]

According to the CIA, General Austin communicated with officials of St. George's medical school on October 21. The CIA chronology recounts the following:

Austin tells officials of US medical school [St. George's University School of Medicine] that he does not oppose the departure of students but wanted the university to remain open. He promised that the university would be protected by Grenadian forces. He instructed the administrators to consolidate the student body on the main campus. This could be interpreted either as valid assurances, or a move to make it easier to hold the students hostage.[96]

On October 21 and 22, the CIA received "unconfirmed reports that Coard had been killed."[97] The CIA concluded: "Conflicting reports about who was actually in charge indicated that the power struggle was not over."[98] As it turned out, Coard was not dead, but was in hiding. Adding to the confusion were reports received by the CIA on October 23 and 24, indicating divisions in the Grenadian Army over Austin's policies.[99] The job of the CIA in evaluating such reports was not made easier by the absence of CIA agents in Grenada.[100]

On October 21, 1983, the OECS convened a special meeting and recommended joint military action to "restore and maintain law and order" in Grenada. The OECS meeting was called by Tom Adams, the Prime Minister of Barbados, a country which does not belong to the OECS.[101] Prime Minister Adams had been advised by the U.S. State Department that a request for military assistance from the OECS would have to be written.[102] The OECS met in Barbados, requested the assistance of Barbados and Jamaica, and assigned Barbados the task of requesting U.S. and British participation in a joint military action.[103] The request for U.S. military assistance was easy to make if, as one source has it, the U.S. Deputy Assistant Undersecretary of State for Caribbean Affairs was present at the October 21 meeting.[104] Whether or not a representative of the U.S. government was present at the OECS meeting, the results of the meeting were conveyed to U.S. Ambassador Milan Bish on the evening of October 21.[105] Prior to the Grenada coup, OECS member states had enjoyed close relations manifested by a common market, agreements for common defense, and, remarkably, a common currency, and a common judiciary.[106] Following the October 21 OECS meeting, the OECS announced economic sanctions against Grenada and requested U.S. military assistance. This request was granted.[107] On October 22, the OECS Secretariat issued the following statement:

The Member Governments of the Organization of Eastern Caribbean States (Antigua and Barbuda, Dominica, St. Kitts-Nevis, Saint Lucia, St.Vincent and the Grenadines and Montserrat) met at Bridgetown, Barbados on Friday 21st October 1983 to consider and evaluate the situation in Grenada arising out of the overthrow of the Prime Minister Maurice Bishop and the subsequent killing of the Prime Minister together with some of his Cabinet colleagues and a number of other citizens.

The Member States were deeply concerned that this situation would continue to worsen, that there would be further loss of life, personal injury and a general deterioration of public order as the military group in control attempted to secure its position.

Member Governments considered that the subsequent imposition of a draconian 96-hour curfew by the military group in control was intended to allow them to further suppress the population of Grenada which had shown by numerous demonstrations their hostility to this group.

Member Governments have also been greatly concerned that the extensive military build-up in Grenada over the last few years had created a situation of disproportionate military strength between Grenada and other OECS countries. This military might in the hands of the present group has posed a serious threat to the security of the OECS countries and other neighbouring States.

Member Governments considered it of the utmost urgency that immediate steps should be taken to remove this threat.

Under the provisions of Article 8 of the Treaty establishing the OECS concerning Defence and Security in the sub-region, Member Governments of the Organization decided to take appropriate action.

Bearing in mind the relative lack of military resources in the possession of the other OECS countries, the Member Governments have sought assistance for this purpose from friendly countries within the region and subsequently from outside.

Three Governments have responded to the OECS Member Governments' requests to form a multi-national force for the purpose of undertaking a pre-emptive defensive strike in order to remove this dangerous threat to peace and security to their sub-region and to establish a situation of normalcy in Grenada. These Governments are Barbados, Jamaica and U.S.A. Barbados and Jamaica are members of CARICOM and Barbados is linked to some of the OECS Member Governments in a sub-regional security agreement.[108]

On October 22, two representatives of the U.S. Embassy in Barbados and David Montgomery, the British Deputy High Commissioner in Barbados, flew to Grenada to determine the feasibility of evacuating U.S. and British nationals. Grenadian representatives refused to grant permission to the United States to evacuate Americans by charter flight or ocean liner.[109] Montgomery also visited Sir Paul Scoon, Governor-General of Grenada, the official representative of Queen Elizabeth. Under Article 57 of the Constitution of Grenada, the "executive authority of Grenada may be exercised . . . by the Governor-General. . . ." In addition, Article 61 provides that "if the Governor-General, acting in his own deliberate judgment, considers it is impracticable to obtain the advice of the Prime

Minister owing to his absence or illness he may exercise . . . [emergency appointment powers] in his own deliberate judgment."[110] After Operation Urgent Fury, Barbados Prime Minister Tom Adams reported:

> Now that Sir Paul is safe, I can reveal that by the kind offices of a friendly government [Great Britain], albeit a nonparticipating government, his views were sought well before the military operations commenced, on the issuing of an invitation to friendly countries to enter Grenada and restore order. According to my information, Sir Paul agreed to do so as soon as possible.[111]

One commentator has cast doubt on the accuracy of Prime Minister Adams' recollection.[112] Major Mark Adkin, a former British Army officer who served in the Barbados Defense Force in 1983 and participated in Operation Urgent Fury, argues that Sir Paul did not orally request military assistance prior to Operation Urgent Fury. Adkin reports that Sir Geoffrey Howe, British Secretary of State for Foreign and Commonwealth Affairs, advised the United Kingdom Foreign Affairs Committee in June of 1984: "Early on the 24th October the Deputy High Commissioner [Montgomery] in Bridgetown reported, following his brief visit to Grenada, that the Governor General (as the latter has subsequently confirmed) had made no request for Britain to intervene in Grenada."[113] Adkin concludes that President Reagan's decision to provide military assistance was not based on Sir Paul's request, but on "the basis of seizing a fleeting strategic-political advantage."[114] Surely, President Reagan would admit that Operation Urgent Fury provided a strategic opportunity. President Reagan said in a televised speech:

> The events in Grenada and Lebanon, though oceans apart, are closely related. Not only has Moscow assisted and encouraged violence in both countries, but it provides direct support through a network of surrogates and terrorists.
> We got there just in time.[115]

Two facts qualify Adkin's conclusion. First, Sir Geoffrey was the official spokesman for the government of Prime Minister Thatcher, which vigorously protested U.S. military action in Grenada, a Commonwealth nation.[116] Second, Sir Geoffrey's report only referred to requests for British, not American, military assistance. Even ignoring these qualifications, Adkin's conclusion that Sir Paul Scoon never requested military assistance prior to October 25 is contrary to the statement of Deputy Secretary of State Kenneth W. Dam: "Sir Paul Scoon had used a confidential channel to transmit an appeal to the OECS and other regional states to restore order on the island."[117] Former Secretary of Defense Caspar

Weinberger has stated: "On October 23, the Governor-General of Grenada, Sir Paul Scoon, orally requested outside assistance from an OECS peace-keeping force. On October 27, the Barbados Government released the text of the formal request, which was in the form of a letter to Barbados' Prime Minister, John Adams."[118] The Department of Defense reports that Prime Minister Adams advised Milan Bish, the U.S. Ambassador in Barbados, on October 24, that Sir Paul had requested OECS assistance to restore order to Grenada.[119] The question of whether Sir Paul requested military assistance before October 25 is hotly debated.

According to Adkin, the U.S. State Department had required that any request by Sir Paul for military assistance be in writing and had sent a draft letter of request for Sir Paul's signature.[120] Adkin indicates that the draft letter was delivered to and signed by Sir Paul on October 26, when Sir Paul was rescued by U.S. forces, and was backdated to October 24.[121] Another source, however, indicates that Larry Rossin, a State Department representative and the first American to speak with Sir Paul after October 19, received from Sir Paul on October 26 a written request that Sir Paul had already prepared.[122] That is, the written request was not fabricated after the fact.

The text of the letter, addressed to Prime Minister Adams of Barbados, follows:

Government House, St. George's,
Grenada, October 24, 1983

Dear Prime Minister,

You are aware that there is a vacuum of authority in Grenada following the killing of the prime minister and the subsequent serious violations of human rights and bloodshed. I am therefore, seriously concerned over the lack of internal security in Grenada. Consequently I am requesting your help to assist me in stabilizing this grave and dangerous situation. It is my desire that a peace-keeping force should be established in Grenada to facilitate a rapid return to peace and tranquillity and also a return to democratic rule. In this connection I am also seeking assistance from the United States, from Jamaica, and from the Organization of Eastern Caribbean States through its current chairman, the Hon. Eugenia Charles, in the spirit of the treaty establishing that organization to which my country is a signatory.

I have the honor to be
(Signed)
Sir Paul Scoon, Governor-General[123]

The request (if any) of the Governor-General of Grenada, the October 21 vote of the OECS for military action against the Revolutionary Military Council, and the October 22 joint request by the OECS, Jamaica, and Barbados for U.S. military assistance[124] was received by the United States against the backdrop of ongoing and unsuccessful efforts to remove U.S. citizens from Grenada.[125] U.S. officials had held talks with representatives of the Revolutionary Military Council but, "in the absence of a functioning government, credible assurances of . . . [the] well-being and future prospects [of U.S. citizens on Grenada] were impossible to obtain."[126] Representative Dick Cheney, a member of a congressional factfinding delegation, reported that five U.S. Department of State representatives had attempted to arrange evacuation, without success. The medical students, he wrote, were "confined to their quarters on pain of death."[127] One British journalist, however, has reported that U.S. State Department representatives who visited Grenada on October 22 did not advise U.S. citizens to leave Grenada and, indeed, that they found U.S. medical students unwilling to interrupt their studies.[128]

On October 23, President Reagan signed the National Security Decision Directive by which U.S. forces joined the joint military peace-keeping force of the OECS, Jamaica, and Barbados.[129] Former Secretary of Defense Caspar Weinberger reports that by October 24, President Reagan had decided to intervene in Grenada unless the medical students were freed.[130] President Reagan explained U.S. participation in the operation as follows:

> First, and of overriding importance, to protect innocent lives, including up to 1,000 Americans whose personal safety is, of course, my paramount concern. Second, to forestall further chaos [in Grenada]. And third, to assist in the restoration of conditions of law and order and of governmental institutions to the island of Grenada, where a brutal group of leftist thugs violently seized power, killing the Prime Minister, three Cabinet members, two labor leaders and other civilians, including children.[131]

President Reagan further explained his decision to use force in Grenada as follows:

> [W]hen I received reports that a large number of our citizens were seeking to escape the island, thereby exposing themselves to great danger, and after receiving a formal request for help [from the OECS], a unanimous request from our neighboring states, I concluded the United States had no choice but to act strongly and decisively.[132]

From these statements can be culled three justifications offered by the President for military action: to rescue U.S. citizens, to respond to a "formal request for help" from allies, and to restore law and order in Grenada.

On October 25, at about 5:30 a.m. local, U.S. forces commenced "Operation Urgent Fury," consisting of 1,900 U.S. troops and 300 soldiers from OECS nations.[133] The number of U.S. military personnel on Grenada reached 7,355 by October 31.[134] The invading force was opposed (at least on paper) by 500 to 1,200 members of the Grenadian People's Revolutionary Army, several thousand Grenadian militiamen, and 784 Cubans (of whom 53 were regular soldiers and 636 were armed construction workers).[135] Operation Urgent Fury was a joint service operation: among the participants were two battalions of the Army 82d Airborne, two Army Ranger battalions, the Army Delta Force Commandos, Navy SEALS (sea-air-land special forces), and a naval task force including the 22d Marine Amphibious Unit ("MAU"), the Navy's Amphibious Squadron Four (including the amphibious assault ship U.S.S. *Guam,* the amphibious transport dock U.S.S. *Trenton,* the dock landing ship U.S.S. *Fort Snelling,* and the tank landing ships U.S.S. *Manitowoc* and U.S.S. *Barnstable County*), and the battle group of the aircraft carrier U.S.S. *Independence.*

One analyst described Operation Urgent Fury as a "paradigm of limited military actions."[136]

> It featured a "come as you are" scenario typified by critical, time-sensitive mission requirements; minimal planning; employment of joint and combined forces; incomplete intelligence; command, control, and communications intensity; and high political visibility. These critical elements were balanced by several advantages. Among them: The relative proximity of Grenada to the United States; the lack of enemy opposition during deployment; the unsophisticated nature of enemy opposition; access to facilities in Barbados; and availability of a major, established U.S. operational facility at Roosevelt Roads, Puerto Rico.[137]

U.S. forces did not achieve tactical surprise.[138] One source suggests that Grenada had been advised by an ally in CARICOM that an invasion was imminent. On October 23, Radio Free Grenada had broadcast:

> Members of the Organisation of Eastern Caribbean States, along with Barbados and Jamaica, this afternoon took a decision to send military forces to invade Grenada and to call on foreign forces also to invade our country. The decisio[n] was opposed by Guyana, Trinidad and Tobago, the Bahamas and Belize. However, some islands have already sent armed forces to Barbados as a jumping off point for this invasion of Grenada and units from Jamaica and Antigua are on their way to join them. At this time a

warship is only seven and a half miles from Grenada, well inside our territorial waters. An invasion of our country is expected tonight.[139]

The northern half of the island was assigned to the Marines and the Navy, the southern half to the Army and the Air Force.[140] The Marines attacked Pearls Airfield at the northern end of the island at dawn on October 25. The Marines' rules of engagement required restraint: "Disruption to the local economy to be minimized, commensurate with the accomplishment of the mission."[141] The Marines were airlifted by CH-46 helicopter transports escorted by AH-1 Cobra attack helicopters. Pearls was defended ineffectively by Grenadian Army troopers whom one civilian observer described as professional soldiers, "not farm boys with uniforms."[142] Another commentator described the defending force, by contrast, as "a weak platoon, mostly dressed in T-shirts and jeans. . . ."[143] Pearls was secured by 7:30 a.m.[144] By mid-morning, the Marines had also captured, without opposition, the nearby town of Grenville, to the welcoming cheers of its citizens.[145]

As the Marines were attacking Pearls, the Army Rangers parachuted onto the runway at Point Salines Airfield, defended by Grenadians and Cubans. One critic reports that the Rangers parachuted "directly in front of some of the very few antiaircraft guns on the island."[146] Air Force AC-130 gunships, equipped with 20mm, 40mm, and 105mm cannons, fired on the 23mm antiaircraft guns, suppressing them by 6:15 a.m.[147] Other sources note that the Rangers originally planned to land at Point Salines aboard MC-130 transports. They decided to parachute instead because the runway had been obstructed with vehicles and construction equipment.[148] The Rangers jumped from minimum altitude without reserve parachutes.[149] The Rangers encountered significant resistance at the airport, particularly from armed Cuban construction workers. The CIA reported that:

> The Cuban defenders were active at Point Salines airport, where a few advisers and most of the construction workers were assembled, and at adjacent facilities, where most of the military advisers were located. The regular Cuban soldiers fought well, were disciplined, and conducted orderly withdrawals. . . . However, most of them had insufficient arms and ammunition to defend their areas of responsibility, and as a result a large number offered little or no resistance. Most of the Cubans surrendered on the morning of 26 October.[150]

The Cuban Revolutionary Government reported that "[t]he Cuban building workers and the helpers . . . [were] locked . . . in admirable, tenacious resistance in an unequal struggle against Yankee soldiers."[151] On November 14, Castro described the fighting at Point Salines as follows:

> The assertion that the Cubans initiated the acts of hostility is equally false and cynical. The irrefutable truth is that the Cubans were sleeping and their weapons were stored at the time of the airdrop on the runway and around the camps. They had not been distributed. . . . What is strictly historical and strictly true is that the fighting began when the US troops advanced towards the Cubans in a belligerent way. It is also true that when a group of unarmed [Cuban] co-operation personnel was captured, they were used as hostages and forced to lead the way in front of the US soldiers.[152]

By the end of the day, the Rangers had secured the airfield, two Cuban military camps in the vicinity, and the nearby True Blue Campus of the St. Georges University School of Medicine.[153] Five Rangers were killed and five wounded in the battle for the airport.[154] Later on October 25, a contingent from the Army's 82d Airborne arrived at Point Salines by C-130 and C-141. The 82d Airborne continued mop-up operations against Cuban forces in the vicinity of Point Salines Airport. On October 26, the 82d Airborne intercepted radio communications between Cuban forces and Havana. The Cubans on Grenada twice requested permission to surrender. The response: "For the glory of the Revolution, no."[155] By the end of the day on October 26, however, the Cubans near Point Salines, including those in the Morne Rouge complex had surrendered.[156] The leader of the Cuban force, Colonel Pedro Tortolo Comas, escaped capture by finding sanctuary in the Soviet embassy.[157] He was later returned to Cuba, court-martialed, reduced in rank to private, and sent to Angola, where he died in 1986 in an ambush by guerillas led by Jonas Savimbi.[158]

A major target, in addition to the Pearls and Point Salines Airfields, was the Governor-General's mansion near St. George's. The Governor-General, Sir Paul Scoon, was located in the mansion under house arrest. An initial force of Navy SEALS had secured the Governor-General's mansion on October 25, only to be surrounded by elements of the Grenadian People's Revolutionary Army.[159] Sources indicate that the surrounding Grenadian force was supported by Soviet-built BTR-60 armored personnel carriers operated by Cubans.[160] The Governor-General's mansion was within range of an antiaircraft site at Fort Frederick. Marine AH-1 Cobras from the U.S.S. *Guam* attacked this site preparatory to a Marine operation to rescue the commandos and Sir Paul. The Cobras were used for this purpose rather than naval gunfire to minimize collateral damage.[161] One Cobra was hit by antiaircraft fire on its fifth run at the target. Its pilot, Captain Timothy Howard, crash-landed the helicopter despite serious injuries ultimately leading to the loss of his lower right arm. The Cobra's weapons officer, Captain Jeb Seagle, despite his own injuries, pulled Howard from the aircraft. Seagle was shot dead while signalling for help. The second Cobra, piloted by Captain John Giguere and First Lieutenant Jeffrey Scharver, called for Howard's evacuation by CH-46 helicopter. The CH-46 landed, one of the gunners (Gunnery Sergeant Kelly N. Neidigh) pulled Howard aboard, and the CH-46 proceeded over St. George's back to the *Guam*. The remaining Cobra and an Air Force AC-130 attacked the antiaircraft site to provide cover for the CH-46 during the evacuation. However, the Cobra was hit and crashed in St. George's harbor. Giguere and Scharver were lost.[162]

Before dawn on October 26, the Marines launched an amphibious landing at Grand Mal Bay, from which they advanced on St. George's and attacked the Governor-General's mansion.[163] Following a Navy A-7 air strike against antiaircraft sites, the Marines rescued the Governor-General and his party, along with the commandos from the initial attack by 7:30 a.m. Sir Paul was evacuated to the *Guam* at midday. He was returned to Point Salines later on October 26. One commentator reports that it was at Point Salines on October 26 that Sir Paul signed the October 24, 1983 letter requesting military assistance.[164]

By 4:30 p.m. on October 26, the Marines attacked Fort Frederick, the headquarters for the Grenadian Peoples Revolutionary Army and a significant antiaircraft site. The Marines secured the fort without opposition.[165] During a previous Navy A-7 air strike against Fort Frederick, a mental institution (formerly Fort Matthew) next to Fort Frederick reportedly was bombed.[166] Twenty-one patients died. In another accidental bombing, on October 27, a Navy A-7, called in to bomb a building where a sniper had been spotted, reportedly bombed an 82d Airborne command post. One U.S. soldier died and sixteen were wounded.[167]

On October 26, the Marines and the Army Rangers secured the St. George's University Medical School campus at Grand Anse Beach. Military planners did not know that St. George's University Medical School had a second campus (in addition to True Blue) at Grand Anse until October 25.[168] The campus was located near a beach, but the beach was narrow and crowded by dense palm growth.[169] Further complicating matters was small arms and automatic weapons fire as the helicopter approached the beach.[170] Two Marine CH-46 helicopters crash-landed at the beach, after striking overhanging palm branches.[171] One of the aircraft was flown to Salines for repairs, the other was not.[172] The students were evacuated by helicopter by late afternoon.

On the morning of October 27, the Marines captured Richmond Hill Prison, which the Army Delta Force and Army Rangers had tried to secure on October 25, with the loss of at least one helicopter, hit by antiaircraft fire from the prison and from Fort Frederick nearby.[173] On October 27, the Marines captured Fort Rupert, the Pentagon of Grenada.[174] The Marines prepared to assault Fort Adolphus, but cancelled their plans when Fort Adolphus turned out to be the Venezuelan Embassy.[175] The same day, Army Rangers initiated an airborne assault on the Calivigny barracks, where U.S. forces believed 400–600 Cuban troops were located.[176] This assault had been preceded by attacks from A-7 bombers and AC-130 Specter gunships.[177] The third of the flight of eight UH-60 Blackhawk helicopters in the assault crashed into the second. The fourth landed in a ditch in order to avoid the wreckage of the third. Three men died and twelve were injured.[178] No Cubans were discovered at Calivigny.[179]

Over the next several days, U.S. forces established their control of Grenada. On October 29, Bernard Coard and Phyllis Coard were captured.[180] The next day, General Hudson Austin was captured.[181] On November 1, the Marines landed on the nearby island of Carriacou, where they secured a large weapons cache.[182] During Operation Urgent Fury, U.S. forces captured a total of 9,000 automatic and semiautomatic weapons and five million rounds of ammunition.[183]

Operation Urgent Fury was described at first in terms of logistical efficiency, tactical proficiency, and joint services cooperation. U.S. forces were congratulated for evacuating 599 Americans and 80 other nationals from Grenada.[184] The population of Grenada cheered American forces as liberators.[185] On the walls of St. George's Grenadians wrote: "God Bless America."[186] Said Alister Hughes, the Grenadian journalist, "Don't call it an invasion. It was a rescue mission."[187] The Grenada Employer's Federation issued a statement on November 8 "expressing its support for and gratitude to the liberation forces of the Caribbean and United States of America over timely and effective intervention in our time of crisis."[188] Ninety-one percent of the Grenadian people approved Operation Urgent Fury, according to a CBS News poll.[189]

The Army is said to have awarded 8,612 decorations to personnel involved in Urgent Fury.[190] Vice Admiral Joseph Metcalf, the naval task force commander, stated: "We blew them away."[191] President Reagan stated without equivocation: "I can't say enough in praise of our military. Army Rangers and paratroops, Navy, Marine, and Air Force personnel, those who planned a brilliant campaign and those who carried it out."[192]

Over time, such positive views have eroded.[193] One critic has remarked:

> Reminiscent of the attempted rescue of the Iranian hostages and of the Dominican Republic intervention in 1965, the Joint Chiefs of Staff system and interservice rivalry ended up with every service participating, confusions

of command, overkill in the thousands of troops involved, mistakes blamed on faulty communications and Americans shooting Americans.[194]

The Marine Corps reportedly refused to land with Army units, fearing that "Americans from different services who had not trained together would be killing each other by mistake."[195] The Marine Commandant noted the "apparent absence of a detailed, integrated planning process. . . ."[196] As an example, "no maps of any type were available on the ships" from which the Marines embarked.[197] Nautical charts were quite dated.[198] A major source of information about Grenadian waters was Commander Richard A. Butler, the chief staff officer of the amphibious squadron, who had sailed a yacht around Grenada six years prior to Operation Urgent Fury.[199] The CIA reportedly stated that prior to Urgent Fury, it "had no operation on the ground at all."[200]

During the fighting, 18 Americans were killed, 116 Americans were wounded, 25 Cubans were killed, 59 Cubans were wounded, 45 Grenadians were killed (including the 21 civilians killed in the accidental bombing of a mental hospital), and 337 Grenadians were wounded.[201] Six or seven hundred Cubans were captured.[202] The financial cost has been estimated at $134.4 million.[203]

The President's supporters praised Operation Urgent Fury as a decisive step to secure U.S. interests in the Caribbean Basin. Some of the President's natural adversaries, congressional Democrats, joined in the praise. Congressman Thomas Foley (D., WA) stated: "A very large majority of the delegation feels that the President acted correctly to protect American lives."[204] Congressman Michael Barnes (D., MD) stated: "I have reluctantly concluded that U.S. military action was justified in this very unique instance."[205] Others, especially members of Congress who believed the President had failed to consult with Congress under the War Powers Resolution, were critical.[206]

International opinion on Operation Urgent Fury was mixed, but mostly negative.[207] In the United Nations Security Council, eleven nations voted on October 28 to condemn Operation Urgent Fury. The U.S. vetoed the vote; Great Britain and two others abstained.[208] On November 2, the United Nations General Assembly voted to condemn Operation Urgent Fury.[209] On October 26, TASS expressed its "firm condemnation" of Urgent Fury and criticized the U.S. government's stated objectives in Grenada as "'cynical and hypocritical' pretexts for 'outright armed aggression.' . . ."[210] The operation was criticized by West Germany, France, Italy, and Canada.[211] In West Germany, the *General Anzeiger* commented:

[T]he picture of the super power calling the tiny tot on its doorstep to "law and order" by means of force suddenly reveals horrible cracks even in the view of the most loyal allies. There is anger and disapproval especially among the Anglo-Saxon relations. . . . But, even among the Germans there is hardly a hand to applaud the difficult partner. Bonn has explained very clearly its dislike of the American step.[212]

British Prime Minister Thatcher, who had opposed Operation Urgent Fury and had tried to dissuade President Reagan from undertaking it, was reportedly "humiliated" by U.S. actions.[213] Prime Minister Thatcher was particularly enraged because of Grenada's membership in the British Commonwealth.[214] Operation Urgent Fury encouraged Prime Minister Thatcher's political opposition, as exemplified by the question Andrew Faulds, Labour MP, put to Foreign Secretary Sir Geoffrey Howe in the House of Commons:

Does not the Foreign Secretary think that it is time that he and the Prime Minister reconsidered their attitude of underwriting American policies across the world, particularly when that business is conducted by a bunch of ignorant businessmen led by a president who is a dangerous cretin?[215]

On December 19, 1983, elections were held on Grenada, and Herbert Blaize was elected Prime Minister.[216] U.S. forces occupied the island until December 15, 1983, by which date all U.S. combat forces had withdrawn. On December 4, 1986, a Grenadian court sentenced fourteen, including the Coards and Austin, to hang.[217]

Operation Urgent Fury
and the U.S. Constitution

President Reagan offered three justifications for Operation Urgent Fury. First, he sought to rescue the 1,000 Americans on the island. Second, he wished to respond positively to a request from the OECS for military assistance. Third, he wished to restore "law and order" to Grenada. The constitutional legitimacy of each of these justifications should be examined in turn.

Rescue Operation

Approximately one thousand Americans, including 800 medical students at St. George's University School of Medicine, were present on the island of Grenada during October of 1983 when government institutions collapsed. As a consequence of that collapse, former Prime Minister Bishop and other former ministers of the government were executed by the People's Revolutionary Army. The days that followed were characterized by rioting and looting. Prime Minister Coard was nowhere to be found, and General Austin appeared to seize nominal, if not effective, control of the government. Under such chaotic conditions, there arose valid questions about whether and in what form any government existed in Grenada. From the American point of view, the absence of effective government implied the absence of any governmental guarantee of the safety of American citizens in Grenada. As President Reagan reported to Congress: "There was no government ensuring the protection of life and property and restoring law and order."[218]

It will be recalled from Chapter 2 that the President is authorized by the Constitution to undertake unilateral military action to protect the lives of Americans abroad.[219] The basis for this power is the power of the Commander-in-Chief to respond to emergencies and the power of the national chief executive to protect American lives. *The Prize Cases* Court recognized the Commander-in-Chief's discretion to identify and respond to threats to national security. The President is authorized to meet a threat "in the shape it present[s] itself, without waiting for Congress to baptize it with a name."[220] This means that the President is authorized to determine what events threaten national security and what defensive action should be taken. Thus is the Commander-in-Chief empowered to decide that national security is jeopardized by events threatening the physical security of Americans abroad and that the appropriate defensive measure is a rescue operation. Complementing this power of the Commander-in-Chief is the President's generalized power as national chief executive to ensure the safety of Americans abroad. The *Durand v. Hollins* Court expressly recognized the "duty of the president to interpose for the protection of [U.S.] . . . citizens. . . ."[221] This executive power was also recognized by the *In re Neagle* Court in *dictum.*[222] So the constitutional issue about the President's authority for undertaking a military operation to rescue Americans in Grenada is resolved quite easily: since the President believed that Americans were in danger, the President was authorized to undertake the rescue operation.

Critics of Urgent Fury might raise the objection that the characterization of the mission as a rescue operation was a *post hoc* legalism; it was constructed after the fact to produce a legal justification for the operation.[223] This criticism is based on the revelation after Operation Urgent Fury of the fact that officials of St. George's University School of Medicine did not perceive a threat and, indeed, were told by representatives of the Grenadian Revolutionary Military Council that the students were not in danger. Gary Colin, the medical school bursar, stated unequivocally, "Our safety was never in danger. We were used as an excuse by this

[U.S.] government to invade Grenada. They needed a reason to go in, and we were it!"[224]

The pretext criticism is gravely undermined, however, by the absence of any evidence that the President himself was not motivated by a desire to rescue and repatriate the Americans in Grenada. The critics can point to facts that raise doubts about the existence of a threat to students on Grenada. Surely, reasonable minds can differ over the question of whether Americans on Grenada were in danger. But the critics cannot point to any concrete facts to establish that the President manufactured the rescue operation story to obscure his true motivations for undertaking Urgent Fury. No one denies that after Bishop's execution on "Bloody Wednesday," lines of authority on Grenada were blurred. No one denies that "Bloody Wednesday" was the result of profound and violent political collapse on Grenada. Such political upheaval abroad does not necessarily require the initiation by the President of a military rescue operation. Indeed, prior to Operation Urgent Fury, President Reagan had no evidence of an actual plan to harm Americans. However, when anarchy gives rise to politically motivated violence on the scale experienced by Grenada, the President is clearly justified, as a matter of law, in thinking that Americans there are in danger. The President does not require absolute proof of a threat to Americans abroad. It is not necessary for the President to wait until Americans have actually been harmed or taken hostage before he is presented with a reasonable basis for ordering a rescue operation. The President may act on a hunch. So the pretext criticism does not go very far in suggesting the legal invalidity of President Reagan's actions.

Second, the criticism that the President failed to state a sufficient justification for the rescue operation is inconsistent with the legal principle that the President is the party who unilaterally decides whether or not a particular exercise of military force is necessary.[225] The fact that the critics are not of one mind with the President on the necessity of using military force to extract Americans from Grenada is of no legal significance. What is important as a matter of law is that the President thought a military operation was necessary to rescue Americans on Grenada. Having formed such a belief, the President was legally authorized by the Constitution to undertake a military operation. This conclusion, of course, has little to do with the political consequences of the President's actions: the President can undertake a lawful action attended by dire political consequences. The President's decision was initially cheered even by the President's traditional opponents. But as Operation Urgent Fury came under criticism, so did the President. Such increased political opposition had no effect on the legality of the President's actions. The distinction between lawfulness and political attractiveness should be as apparent in context of war powers as in the domestic policy arena.

Third, the critics are hindered in attacking the President's justification for undertaking a military rescue operation by the legal rule that the President is entitled to a presumption of good faith.[226] This means that the critics cannot assert a valid legal argument premised on the assumption that the President is not telling the truth when he identifies the rescue of Americans on Grenada as a justification for Operation Urgent Fury. If the critics wish to pursue this tack, they must overcome the presumption with a showing of presidential bad faith, which is to say, dishonesty. This the critics have not done. As a result, the critics have not articulated a legally coherent attack on the President's actions.

This presumption of presidential good faith is essential to the vitality of the President's legal power to undertake unilateral defensive military action under exigent circumstances. Without this presumption, the legal rule stated in *The Prize Cases* that the President is empowered to determine when he is authorized to use force could be meaningless. If the President's determination of a threat to national security can be trumped by the mere suggestion of bad faith, then the President's power is hollow indeed. This is not, however, the end of the story. It is one thing to describe the President's legal endowments and quite another to translate those endowments into political power. The fact that the President's good faith is difficult to challenge as a matter of law implies nothing about the ability to assail the President's good faith and good judgment in the political arena. President Reagan was called by some the "Teflon President" because accusations of poor judgment and improper motivations did not "stick" to him. This feature of the Reagan presidency is not the result of legal rules but of political forces operating independent of the law. One need only look at the political misfortunes of other presidents such as Presidents Nixon and Johnson, whose constitutional endowments were identical to President Reagan's, to see that constitutional powers do not provide immunity from the political consequences of presidential decisions.

The Requests for Assistance

According to Barbados Prime Minister Tom Adams, Sir Paul Scoon, the Governor-General of Grenada, made an oral request to the OECS for military assistance as well as a written request dated October 24. The Governor-General of Grenada, under Grenada's 1974 Constitution, had been empowered to exercise the "executive authority" of Grenada. So any request by Sir Paul would appear to carry the full authority of the government of Grenada, at least in the absence of a prime minister or other legitimate governmental representative. However, Prime Minister Bishop had suspended the 1974 Constitution by decree on March 25, 1979. Although the suspension of the 1974 Constitution did not eliminate the position of Governor-General, it did suspend the source of the Governor-General's constitutional powers. The legal effect of this suspension on the Governor-General, therefore, is uncertain. Even more difficult to judge is the continuing legal effect of the suspension after the removal from power of Prime Minister Bishop. Since Bishop did not effect a complete elimination of the 1974 Constitution, the legal effect of the suspension might have ended with Bishop's removal from office.

If the suspension of the 1974 Constitution remained in effect, then the Governor-General was not necessarily the authoritative spokesman for the government. On the other hand, by October 22, 1983, no one was obviously the authoritative spokesman for the government of Grenada. Prime Minister Coard could not be found. General Austin purported to be the head of government but did not identify any legitimate basis for this claim. Out of this void came the letter to the OECS from Sir Paul requesting military assistance. Under the totality of circumstances, even assuming the continuing legal vitality of the suspension of Grenada's Constitution, this letter was as authoritative a request for assistance as could be found. The President, empowered by the Constitution to recognize foreign governments,[227] was authorized to decide whom to recognize as the official spokesman for Grenada under these circumstances.[228]

Major Mark Adkin claims that Sir Paul did not request military assistance before October 26, either orally or in writing. This allegation, if true, would eliminate one of the preferred justifications for Operation Urgent Fury. What legal implication would such a change have? Unquestionably, the purported plea for help from Sir Paul had positive public relations value. If there was no such plea, the public relations value disappears. But the absence of a request for military assistance by Sir Paul does not suggest the absence of legal authority for Operation Urgent Fury. The President's interest in rescuing Americans on Grenada, standing alone, justifies the operation.

Similarly, the OECS request for assistance is an independent and sufficient basis for action by the President. The OECS voted to undertake a joint military action and, in turn, to request assistance from the United States. The OECS is a remarkably close alliance. Not only do OECS members pledge a common defense and a common market, but even jointly administer a common system of currency and judicial administration, the latter functions usually reserved exclusively to sovereign nations. This is not to suggest that the OECS is itself a sovereign nation. It is a regional alliance. However, the closeness of the alliance lends credibility to the expression of interest of OECS members in a stable Grenada. The President was entitled to respond unilaterally to the OECS request on the basis of his constitutional power to conduct foreign affairs. Under the foreign affairs power, the President is empowered to undertake unilateral executive agreements, at least when Congress has not objected. "[A]n international compact . . . is not always a treaty which requires the participation of the Senate."[229] If, for the purpose of analysis, the likelihood of armed resistance to U.S. military intervention in Grenada is removed from consideration, the President's decision to deploy armed forces to Grenada was equivalent to his 1982 decision to place Marines in Beirut.[230] The President in his capacity as the "sole organ" of the United States government in external affairs granted the OECS' emergency request for assistance. He thereby committed the United States to a deployment of armed forces pursuant to an executive compact.[231]

Reintroducing to the analysis the possibility of armed resistance, the President was also acting as Commander-in-Chief in granting the request for military assistance. This raises an interesting issue with respect to the powers of the Commander-in-Chief: can an imminent threat to national security that is entirely strategic be treated as an emergency? That is, can chaos on a Caribbean island be an exigent circumstance if the only U.S. national security consequence is a strategic threat such as a larger Soviet-Cuban military presence in the Caribbean? The short answer to this question is "yes": the President makes the determination of exigent circumstances unilaterally.[232] Since a necessary predicate of the President's power to defend is his power to determine when the power to defend may be exercised, the President was authorized to respond to the possibility of hostilities on Grenada by deploying U.S. military forces prepared to do battle.

Suppose that no Americans were on Grenada and that neither Sir Paul nor the OECS had requested American military assistance. Suppose further that the President determined that U.S. national security was endangered by the political turmoil in Grenada because of (1) the possibility that the disruption might spread to other Caribbean islands, disturbing the delicate political equilibrium that has enabled the United States to control Caribbean sea lines of communication, and (2) the possibility that the disruption on Grenada would enable the Soviets or the Cubans (as a proxy for the Soviets) to establish a forward base of operations in Grenada. From Grenada, Soviet and Cuban forces might move to other islands, controlling choke points in the Caribbean, which has long been regarded an American "lake." In fact, this possibility did alarm U.S. officials in early 1983 as they monitored the construction of a 9,000–10,000 foot runway, fuel storage facilities, and housing at the Point Salines airport. Secretary of State Alexander M. Haig, Jr., described the improved airport as a potential base for "every aircraft in the Soviet-Cuban inventory. . . ."[233]

The President is entitled, but not required, to view such developments as threatening to American national security. However, this conclusion is troubling because it appears to prove too much. Therefore, it is important to keep in mind that the President's powers as Commander-in-Chief to act unilaterally are dependent upon the existence of an *imminent* threat to national security. Even assuming that the destabilization of Grenada and subsequent expansion of Soviet and Cuban forces there would be contrary to American national security, was such a threat sufficiently imminent on October 25, 1983 to justify the use of force? This interesting question cannot be answered because the President never addressed the issue. He never said whether or not such developments raised an imminent threat to national security. The reason for his silence on this point undoubtedly was the fact that other factors, such as the presence of 1,000 Americans on Grenada, provided a sufficient legal basis for Operation Urgent Fury.

In the absence of other justifications for Operation Urgent Fury, the President might have articulated an imminent threat to national security by saying that without swift military action, the Soviets would gain a strategic advantage in the Caribbean. The President's critics would have replied that the President's characterization of national security was too vague to justify the action; that *Martin v. Mott,*[234] notwithstanding, the President's justification did not involve a sufficiently concrete imminent threat. As interesting as it is, this legal question probably would not have been judicially resolved as a result of the political question doctrine.[235] A nice legal issue thereby would be lost to the more unruly arena of political debate. If a court did agree to address the issue, it would probably rule for the President. Under *Martin v. Mott,* the President's determination of an imminent threat is entitled to a presumption of good faith. So if the President was able to articulate an imminent threat to the nation's strategic security, his critics would be required to upset the presumption in favor of the President before the court would examine critically the substance of the President's determination. It would not be enough for the President's critics to convince the court that reasonable minds could differ on the question of the President's wisdom; they would have to convince the court that his justification was disingenuous.

Of course, the President was not faced with such an abstract strategic threat. Rather, the President had a formal request for military assistance from the OECS, as well as (according to the President) the request of the Governor-General of Grenada. In agreeing to provide military assistance, the President acted within his constitutional authority.

Law and Order

The President offered as a third justification his interest in imposing law and order in Grenada. As admirable a goal as law and order is, it really serves more as a justification for Sir Paul's request for military assistance rather than as a justification for U.S. accession to the request. The imposition of a regime of law and order on a foreign government is not, of itself, a recognized basis for the exercise of power as the Commander-in-Chief. Of course, the absence of law and order in a foreign nation could serve to foster an imminent threat to U.S. national security. For example, the breakdown of law and order could, and according to the President did, threaten the safety of Americans on Grenada. Thus, the absence of law and order abroad premised the President's decision to use force to protect the safety of Americans there. Similarly, the breakdown of law and order lends credibility to Sir Paul's statement that "there is a vacuum of authority in Grenada."

The fact that law and order were not present on Grenada does not, however, standing alone, justify the President's unilateral use of force. The breakdown of law and order does not of itself present the President with an exigent circumstance threatening the national security of the United States. The entire rationale justifying the President's power to use armed force unilaterally is that, when an emergency does threaten national security, the national executive must be free to respond. This, of course, is why the President has been granted the power to command the armed forces and to determine when he should order the armed forces into combat to prevent an imminent harm. As Alexander Hamilton expressed it, Congress' role in declaring a war is "unnecessary" when a "foreign nation declares or openly and outwardly makes war upon the United States, [because] they are then by the very fact already at war. . . ."[236] But in order to activate these awesome presidential powers, the President must articulate an exigent threat to national security. The absence of law and order states the premise for a justification for presidential war-making, but does not itself justify the unilateral use of force by the President.

This weakness in the President's "law and order" rationale does not, of course, affect the ultimate conclusion that the President's actions were lawful. The valid bases for the President's decision to use force in Grenada were the threat to Americans on that island and the requests for assistance. Each of these two rationales, standing alone, justifies the President's unilateral commitment of U.S. armed forces to Operation Urgent Fury.

Operation Urgent Fury
and the War Powers Resolution

The War Powers Resolution ("WPR") requires pre-conflict consultation by the President with Congress. In order to comply with the WPR, the President convened members of the congressional leadership for a briefing at the White House the night before the commencement of Operation

Urgent Fury on October 25.[237] The President advised those in attendance of the situation in Grenada, the request for military assistance, and his intention to provide such assistance. At the time of this White House meeting, Operation Urgent Fury had not yet begun; the President still could have cancelled it. Members of Congress meeting with the President on the night of October 24 were given an opportunity to ask questions about the situation in Grenada and the military operation and to object or otherwise comment on the wisdom of using military force there. Critics argued that this meeting on the eve of hostilities left too little time for discussion to qualify as consultation under the WPR. The critics' argument was that while a briefing took place, the opportunity for meaningful congressional participation was negligible. Senator Charles McC. Mathias, Jr., (D., MD) of the Senate Foreign Relations Committee complained, "[C]ongressional leaders were simply called to the Oval Office and told that the troops were under way. That is not consultation. The Prime Minister of Great Britain was advised about the invasion before the President told the Speaker of the House of Representatives or the Majority Leader of the Senate."[238] This criticism suggests that the purpose of the WPR was not honored by the President.

The problem with this criticism is that it imports into the WPR a requirement absent from its language: namely, congressional participation. Webster defines the verb "consult" as: "to ask the advice or opinion of" or to "deliberate together."[239] In order to consult with Congress, the President must solicit Congress' point of view and, if one is forthcoming, discuss it. The WPR should be read to import a standard of good faith and reasonableness; that is, to comply with the consultation requirement, the President should pay more than lip service; he should pay attention. But, as admirable a goal congressional participation in the President's decision to use force is, it is not required under the WPR. The President is free under the WPR to decide, without the benefit of congressional advice, that the use of armed force is warranted under a particular set of circumstances and to consult with Congress after making the initial determination. What the President must do, under the terms of the WPR, is give Congress the opportunity to offer an opinion and to engage the President in debate prior to the commencement of hostilities. This is what President Reagan did on October 24.

Just as the WPR does not require congressional participation in the President's initial decision to employ force, it does not require, either implicitly or explicitly, congressional approval of the President's decision. The idea behind the consultation requirement is that the President must speak to Congress. The President must also give Congress the opportunity to comment on the President's intentions. But the WPR does not require a response, either approval or disapproval, from Congress. The WPR does not require the President to change his initial determination if Congress disagrees, although the WPR is intended to make this alternative available to the President. The WPR is most reasonably interpreted as requiring the President to advise Congress of his intention to use U.S. forces and to provide an opportunity for questions and commentary. Otherwise, the consultation requirement would be unlimited in scope. If the President must give Congress as much time as Congress needs to formulate its reaction to the President's plan to use force, then it is Congress and not the President that determines when force will be used. This, of course, is contrary to the constitutional principle that the President, as Commander-in-Chief, is empowered exclusively to make command determinations such as the timetable of a military operation.[240] The President, and not Congress, is the "first General and Admiral."[241]

In addition to the question of how much communication between the President and Congress qualifies as consultation, there is the question of how "Congress" is defined for consultation purposes. Proponents of a literal interpretation of the WPR could argue that it requires the President to convene the entire Congress. However, this is a burdensome requirement. The rules of statutory interpretation, which operate on the assumption that Congress does not mean to require that which is facially unreasonable, would compel a different result: some subset of Congress must be convened. It is also worth noting that to the extent the requirement that the President convene Congress, or a part thereof, is so burdensome that the President, to comply, must compromise his activities as Commander-in-Chief, it is unconstitutional. For example, the WPR cannot be read to require the President to convene such a large number of congressmen together in one place that U.S. adversaries would be alerted to the possibility of future armed conflict. On the whole, the most reasonable interpretation of the WPR's consultation language is that it requires the President to consult with the congressional leadership. This is what the President did. Significantly, this is also the requirement that would be specified in a proposed amendment to the WPR.[242]

So the WPR does not require, by its own terms, more than the President did on October 24 to achieve consultation with Congress. If it did require more, the WPR would be unconstitutional since it would seek to interfere with the President's authority to determine when the armed forces should be used under exigent circumstances.[243] Such a partnership might be politically attractive at any given time, but cannot be compelled consistent with the Constitution's allocation of power to the President. Perhaps it is for this reason that the WPR does not include any requirement of congressional assent.

The second requirement of the WPR is that a report be submitted within 48 hours of the commencement of hostilities. This is a requirement that the President satisfied on October 25, the very day of initial military operations on Grenada. The President's October 25 report to Congress stated:

> On October 12, a violent series of events in Grenada was set in motion, which led to the murder of Prime Minister Maurice Bishop and a number of his Cabinet colleagues, as well as the deaths of a number of civilians. Over 40 killings were reported. There was no government ensuring the protection of life and property and restoring law and order. The only indication of authority was an announcement that a barbaric shoot-to-kill curfew was in effect. Under these circumstances, we were necessarily concerned about the safety of innocent lives on the island, including those of up to 1,000 United States citizens.
>
> The Organization of Eastern Caribbean States (OECS) became seriously concerned by the deteriorating conditions in the member State of Grenada. . . . [T]he OECS formed a collective security force comprising elements from member States to restore order in Grenada and requested the immediate cooperation of a number of friendly countries, including the governments of Barbados, Jamaica and the United States, in these efforts. In response to this call for assistance and in view of the overriding importance of protecting the lives of the United States citizens in Grenada, I have authorized the Armed Forces of the United States to participate along with these other nations in this collective security force. . . .
>
> Although it is not possible at this time to predict the duration of the temporary presence of United States Armed Forces in Grenada, our objectives in providing this support are clear. They are to join the OECS collective security forces in assisting the restoration of conditions of law and order and of governmental institutions to the island of Grenada, and to facilitate the protection and evacuation of United States citizens. Our forces will remain only so long as their presence is required.[244]

The President raised no public objection to the submission of a report, probably because the President was not especially burdened by the requirement that he report to Congress at a time when he was issuing press releases and other public statements about Operation Urgent Fury. Of course, it also makes good political sense to advise Congress on an ongoing military operation for which the President may need congressional support. So, the question of what would happen if the President did not want to report to Congress was not presented. If it had been, an interesting question would have been raised: what happens if the President does not, for security reasons for example, want to report? The answer to this question would, not surprisingly, depend on the facts. If the President did not report for some reason directly related to his command of the armed forces, he would stand on firm constitutional ground. On the other hand, the President would have to recognize that the courts have already held that the President has no inherent, absolute right to withhold information from Congress.[245] Moreover, if he later went to Congress in search of funding for continued military operations, the President might be confronted by the legitimate congressional argument that appropriation of the national treasure cannot occur in a vacuum: in order to make appropriations decisions, Congress needs information.[246] But the President did not explore this theoretical legal landscape because he submitted a report.

By submitting this report, the President did not necessarily start the sixty-day clock, even by the terms of the WPR. His report did not state whether it was made pursuant to the "hostilities" section of the WPR or to the WPR sections pertaining to troops equipped for combat. Only a WPR "hostilities" report starts the sixty-day clock. Of course, it would have been difficult for the President to argue with a straight face that Operation Urgent Fury was not hostile. Congress attempted to start the sixty-day clock by vote, but did not succeed. On November 1, 1983, the House approved a resolution stating that the WPR had become "operative" on October 25.[247] The resolution was placed on the Senate calendar on November 7, but never passed the Senate. On October 28, the Senate approved a rider (to an unrelated bill) to invoke the WPR.[248] The bill containing the rider, however, never passed the Senate. Thus did Congress as a whole fail to invoke the WPR.[249]

As it turned out, the sixty-day clock was of no practical consequence because U.S. combat forces were withdrawn on December 15, 1983, fewer than sixty days after the report was submitted. The President did not say whether he timed the withdrawal to avoid the limitations of the sixty-day clock. Moreover, Congress did not seek a legislative veto of the President's deployment of U.S. armed forces in Grenada.[250]

Had the sixty-day clock expired without congressional approval of Operation Urgent Fury or had Congress passed a legislative veto, the constitutional issue of the President's ability to use the armed forces unilaterally would have been presented. Again, this issue probably would not have been resolved in the courts.[251] Nevertheless, a requirement by Congress that the President withdraw U.S. forces from Grenada following the expiration of a sixty-day period might have been unconstitutional. The reason for this is straightforward: the President was authorized by the Constitution unilaterally to undertake the operation in Grenada in order to counter an imminent threat to U.S. national security. The President, consistent with his constitutional authority, could have determined that national security required the presence of U.S. troops beyond the sixty-day period. Congress cannot limit or otherwise affect the President's constitutional power by its own vote, even a unanimous one.

Congress' argument against this position might be that it proves too much, that the Constitution is too well balanced in general to tolerate the possibility that a presidential power to be exercised under exigent circumstances could continue in effect for sixty days. This argument would be based on the assumption that emergencies "wear out" eventually and certainly lose their vitality within two months. But Congress would encounter two problems with this argument. First, the President is entitled to the benefit of the doubt when he declares an emergency requiring military force.[252] So, if the President states that the original emergency has continued for over sixty days, his statement will be given great credence as a matter of law. As a matter of politics, on the other hand, the President's word is only as good as his last approval rating in the public opinion surveys.

The second problem with the argument against the President's continuing use of force is that one legitimate emergency might lead to another. Suppose that the President, in sending U.S. forces to Grenada to rescue Americans, grossly underestimated the size of the defending army. After U.S. forces have fought for sixty days to a stalemate, the President learns that Cuba plans to send reinforcements to Grenada in Soviet-built transport aircraft. The President determines that to protect the U.S. force, he will order the Navy to intercept the Cuban transport aircraft. If Congress learns of this planned escalation and becomes alarmed, it might be able to offer, depending on all the circumstances, an argument against escalation that is superior to the President's argument for it. It might turn out that all the diplomats, admirals, generals, and voters side with Congress. Such an alignment would have obviously important political implications, but would not be determinative of the legal issue. If the President has the constitutional power to do something, he has the legal authority to do something unpopular. Thus could the President's error in estimating the strength of the opposition during one emergency give rise to a second emergency enabling the President to act unilaterally a second time. Congressmen opposed to the President's use of force would be well advised in such a circumstance to fight the President in the political, rather than the legal, arena.

Of course, in 1983 none of this happened. The President withdrew U.S. forces before sixty days had expired and Congress never executed a legislative veto. Fortunately, an interesting legal question never saw the light of day.

Notes

1. H. O'SHAUGHNESSY, GRENADA: AN EYEWITNESS ACCOUNT OF THE U.S. INVASION AND THE CARIBBEAN HISTORY THAT PROVOKED IT (1984) ("O'SHAUGHNESSY") at 29.

2. J. LEHMAN, COMMAND OF THE SEAS: A PERSONAL STORY (1988) ("LEHMAN") at 293–294. *See also* M. ADKIN, URGENT FURY: THE BATTLE FOR GRENADA (1989) ("ADKIN") at 109.

3. *See generally* Letter to the Speaker of the House and the President Pro Tempore of the Senate on the Deployment of United States Forces in Grenada, II PUBLIC PAPERS OF THE PRESIDENTS OF THE UNITED STATES: RONALD REAGAN, 1983 at 1512–1513 (1985).

4. DEPT. OF DEFENSE, GRENADA: OCTOBER 25–NOVEMBER 2, 1983 ("DOD GRENADA REPORT").

5. DEPT. OF STATE AND DEPT. OF DEFENSE, GRENADA: A PRELIM-INARY REPORT 7 (1983) ("JOINT REPORT"); G. SANDFORD and R. VIGILANTE, GRENADA: THE UNTOLD STORY (1984) ("SANDFORD and VIGILANTE") at Ch. 2.

6. ADKIN at 5; Byron, "Fury From the Sea: Marines in Grenada," 110 U.S. Naval Institute PROCEEDINGS (May 1984) ("Byron") at 119, 122; SANDFORD and VIGILANTE at 25.

7. O'SHAUGHNESSY at 53.

8. LEHMAN at 292; ADKIN at 5; O'SHAUGHNESSY at 75–77; SANDFORD and VIGILANTE at 50; C. WEINBERGER, FIGHTING FOR PEACE 101 (1990).

9. SANDFORD and VIGILANTE at 51; LEHMAN at 292.

10. *E.g.,* ADKIN at 12.

11. SANDFORD and VIGILANTE at 30.

12. Interagency Intelligence Assessment, "Grenada: A First Look at Mechanisms of Control and Foreign Involvement," Annex A at A-1 (December 19, 1983) (obtained from CIA by Freedom of Information Act Request); O'SHAUGHNESSY at 47.

13. JOINT REPORT at 7; SANDFORD and VIGILANTE at 52.

14. J. MOORE, LAW AND THE GRENADA MISSION (1984) ("MOORE") at 6–7 (citing Constitution of Grenada from BLAUSTEIN AND O'LEARY, CONSTITUTIONS OF THE COUNTRIES OF THE WORLD (1974)).

15. *See generally* SANDFORD and VIGILANTE at Chs. 3 and 4.

16. ADKIN at 15.

17. ADKIN at 17.

18. Interagency Intelligence Assessment, "Grenada: A First Look at Mechanisms of Control and Foreign Involvement" (December 19, 1983) at 17 (obtained from CIA through Freedom of Information Act Request).

19. SANDFORD and VIGILANTE at 76.

20. SANDFORD and VIGILANTE at 77.

21. LEHMAN at 292.

22. Byron at 122; ADKIN at 22.

23. LEHMAN at 292.

24. *See* Byron at 119; B. WOODWARD, VEIL: THE SECRET WARS OF THE CIA 1981–1987 (1987) ("WOODWARD") at 287–289.

25. L. RUSSELL and M. MENDEZ, GRENADA 1983 (1985) ("RUSSELL and MENDEZ") at 3.

26. SANDFORD and VIGILANTE at 104.

27. ADKIN at 111.

28. CIA Memorandum, June 15, 1983, re: "Possible Soviet Military Activity in the Caribbean Basin" (obtained from CIA July 25, 1989 by Freedom of Information Act Request).

29. *Id.*

30. *Id.*

31. Message 050537Z FEB 83 (obtained from CIA by Freedom of Information Act Request).

32. "Grenada Chronology 7–25 October 1983" (obtained from CIA by Freedom of Information Act Request).

33. ADKIN at 23; O'SHAUGHNESSY at 10; SANDFORD and VIGILANTE at 93.

34. ADKIN at 23; SANDFORD and VIGILANTE at 93 (total value of 5 million rubles).

35. ADKIN at 24; SANDFORD and VIGILANTE at 93.

36. ADKIN at 24. *See also* SANDFORD and VIGILANTE at 17.

37. ADKIN at 139; Byron at 123; LEHMAN at 298; SANDFORD and VIGILANTE at 16.

38. "Grenada Chronology 7–25 October 1983" (obtained from CIA by Freedom of Information Act Request).

39. Interagency Intelligence Assessment, "Grenada: A First Look at Mechanisms of Control and Foreign Involvement" at 16 (December 19, 1983) (obtained from CIA by Freedom of Information Act Request).

40. Interagency Intelligence Assessment, "Grenada: A First Look at Mechanisms of Control and Foreign Involvement" at 16 (December 19, 1983) (obtained from CIA by Freedom of Information Act Request).

41. *Id.* at 17.

42. *N.Y. Times,* Aug. 7, 1983, p.1, col.6.

43. Interagency Intelligence Assessment, "Grenada: A First Look at Mechanisms of Control and Foreign Involvement" at 7–8 (December 19, 1983) (obtained from CIA by Freedom of Information Act Request).

44. *Id.*

45. Message 050537Z Feb 83 (obtained from CIA by Freedom of Information Act Request).

46. JOINT REPORT at 31; C. WEINBERGER, FIGHTING FOR PEACE 102 (1990).

47. SANDFORD and VIGILANTE at 89.

48. C. WEINBERGER, FIGHTING FOR PEACE 106 (1990).

49. *E.g.,* SANDFORD and VIGILANTE at 148–157.

50. JOINT REPORT at 31.

51. SANDFORD and VIGILANTE at 153.

52. JOINT REPORT at 31. On August 7, 1983, the *New York Times* reported that poor economic conditions were causing a reduction in public support for Bishop. *N.Y. Times,* Aug. 7, 1983, p.1, col.6.

53. JOINT REPORT at 32.

54. ADKIN at 31; O'SHAUGHNESSY at 117.

55. SANDFORD and VIGILANTE at 154.

56. ADKIN at 31.

57. ADKIN at 38–40; SANDFORD and VIGILANTE at 155–156.

58. ADKIN at 40; SANDFORD and VIGILANTE at 156.

59. TASS Statement, Apr. 15, 1983 (obtained from CIA July 25, 1989 by Freedom of Information Act Request).

60. TASS Statement, Apr. 15, 1983 (obtained from CIA July 25, 1989 by Freedom of Information Act Request).

61. ADKIN at 40–41; O'SHAUGHNESSY at 121; SANDFORD and VIGILANTE at 157.

62. JOINT REPORT at 34.

63. ADKIN at 43; DOD GRENADA REPORT at 3; SANDFORD and VIGILANTE at 162.

64. ADKIN at 43.

65. ADKIN at 117.

66. JOINT REPORT at 35.

67. DOD GRENADA REPORT at 3; SANDFORD and VIGILANTE at 163.

68. O'SHAUGHNESSY at 132.

69. "Grenada Chronology 7–25 October 1983" (obtained from CIA by Freedom of Information Act Request); O'SHAUGHNESSY at 134–135.

70. "Grenada Chronology 7–25 October 1983" (obtained from CIA by Freedom of Information Act Request).

71. ADKIN at 69; RUSSELL and MENDEZ at 5; O'SHAUGHNESSY at 138; C. WEINBERGER, FIGHTING FOR PEACE 104 (1990) (Quoting B. PIRNIE, OPERATION URGENT FURY: THE UNITED STATES ARMY IN JOINT OPERATION).

72. O'SHAUGHNESSY at 139; C. WEINBERGER, FIGHTING FOR PEACE 104 (1990) (quoting B. PIRNIE, OPERATION URGENT FURY: THE UNITED STATES ARMY IN JOINT OPERATION); ADKIN at 50; JOINT REPORT at 36; DOD GRENADA REPORT at 4.

73. ADKIN at 73.

74. ADKIN at 76.

75. ADKIN at 76–77; DOD GRENADA REPORT at 4 (Creft beaten to death).

76. RUSSELL and MENDEZ at 5.

77. ADKIN at 77; SANDFORD and VIGILANTE at 165.

78. O'SHAUGHNESSY at 138–139.

79. ADKIN at 78. *See also* SANDFORD and VIGILANTE at 174.

80. O'SHAUGHNESSY at 139 (only Vincent Noel killed in attack).

81. ADKIN at 78.

82. Byron at 124.

83. SANDFORD and VIGILANTE at 4.

84. SANDFORD and VIGILANTE at 4.

85. SANDFORD and VIGILANTE at 4.

86. DOD GRENADA REPORT at 4. *See also* O'SHAUGHNESSY at 148.

87. O'SHAUGHNESSY at 148.

88. O'SHAUGHNESSY at 148.

89. DOD GRENADA REPORT.

90. ADKIN at 90.

91. ADKIN at 160–161.

92. ADKIN at 161. *See also* O'SHAUGHNESSY at 152.

93. ADKIN at 91; O'SHAUGHNESSY at 149.

94. LEHMAN at 291; ADKIN at 119; R. SPECTOR, U.S. MARINES IN GRENADA 1983 (1987) ("SPECTOR") at 2 (amphibious squadron rerouted at midnight October 20).

95. LEHMAN at 296; RUSSELL and MENDEZ at 12 (Col. Comas arrived October 24).

96. "Grenada Chronology 7–25 October 1983" (obtained from CIA by Freedom of Information Act Request). *See also* ADKIN at 87 (on October 19, Austin told Dr. Geoffrey Bourne, medical school vice chancellor, that students were not in danger).

97. "Grenada Chronology 7–25 October 1983" (obtained from CIA by Freedom of Information Act Request).

98. *Id.*

99. *Id.*

100. ADKIN at 116.

101. ADKIN at 96–97.

102. ADKIN at 118; SANDFORD and VIGILANTE at 6–7; WOODWARD at 290.

103. ADKIN at 97.

104. RUSSELL and MENDEZ at 6.

105. SANDFORD and VIGILANTE at 24.

106. SANDFORD and VIGILANTE at 24.

107. *See* Byron at 124.

108. MOORE at App. 2 (reprinted with permission of Professor Moore).

109. SANDFORD and VIGILANTE at 8.

110. *See generally* MOORE at Ch. VI.

111. ADKIN at 114. *See also* SANDFORD and VIGILANTE at 9.

112. ADKIN at 114–115.

113. ADKIN at 114.

114. ADKIN at 115.

115. O'SHAUGHNESSY at 176.

116. ADKIN at 122; C. WEINBERGER, FIGHTING FOR PEACE 119 (1990).

117. *See* "The Origins, Development, and Impact of U. S. Participation in the Grenada Mission," Address of Deputy Secretary of State Kenneth Dam Before the Associated Press Managing Editors' Conference, Louisville, Kentucky, November 4, 1983, AMERICAN FOREIGN POLICY CURRENT DOCUMENTS 1420 (1985).

118. C. WEINBERGER, FIGHTING FOR PEACE 119 n.7 (1990).

119. DOD GRENADA REPORT at 5.

120. ADKIN at 99 and 121.

121. ADKIN at 99.

122. SANDFORD and VIGILANTE at 13.

123. MOORE at 87 (reprinted with permission of Professor Moore); C. WEINBERGER, FIGHTING FOR PEACE 119–120 n.7 (1990).

124. RUSSELL and MENDEZ at 6. The Caribbean Community ("CARI-COM"), the membership of which is comprised of OECS members plus Jamaica, Barbados, the Bahamas, Belize, Guyana, Trinidad and Tobago, and Grenada, was not as belligerent as the OECS. A CARICOM meeting on October 23 had failed to reach a consensus on the advisability of military action. A majority of CARICOM members did vote, however, to suspend Grenada from CARICOM and to support the OECS' non-military sanctions against Grenada. O'SHAUGHNESSY at 164–165.

125. ADKIN at 120.

126. The Honorable Kenneth W. Dam, Deputy Secretary of State, Before the Committee on Foreign Affairs, U.S. House of Representatives, November 2, 1983. *See also* "The Origins, Development, and Impact of U. S. Participation in the Grenada Mission," Address of Deputy Secretary of State Kenneth Dam Before the Associated Press Managing Editors' Conference, Louisville, Kentucky, November 4, 1983, AMERICAN FOREIGN POLICY CURRENT DOCUMENTS 1420 (1985); ADKIN at 100–102; O'SHAUGHNESSY at 153 (two representatives of the U.S. Embassy in Barbados flew to Grenada on October 22).

127. C. WEINBERGER, FIGHTING FOR PEACE 107 n.1 (1990) (quoting D. Cheney opinion editorial, *The Washington Post* (November 14, 1983)).

128. O'SHAUGHNESSY at 166.

129. ADKIN at 106; SANDFORD and VIGILANTE at 9.

130. C. WEINBERGER, FIGHTING FOR PEACE 113 (1990).

131. Statement of President Reagan (October 25, 1983).

132. *Id.*

133. Letter to the Speaker of the House and the President Pro Tempore of the Senate on the Deployment of United States Forces in Grenada, October 25, 1983, II PUBLIC PAPERS OF THE PRESIDENTS OF THE UNITED STATES: RONALD REAGAN, 1983 at 513 (1985).

134. Wright, U.S. Naval Operations in 1983, 110 U.S. Naval Institute PROCEEDINGS 52, 67 (May 1984).

135. Byron at 123; LEHMAN at 298; ADKIN at 139 (1,200 regular Grenadian troops, 2,000–5,000 militiamen, and 300–500 armed police); E. LUTTWAK, THE PENTAGON AND THE ART OF WAR (1984) ("LUTTWAK") at 51 (679 Cubans of whom 43 were regular soldiers); RUSSELL and MENDEZ at 12 (636 Cuban construction workers and 53 Cuban regulars); O'SHAUGHNESSY at 12–13 (a few thousand militia with "rudimentary training"; no more than 43 of 784 "registered" Cubans were regular military); SPECTOR at 3 (pre-landing estimates: 1,200 regular Grenadian troops, 2,000–5,000 militia, 300–400 armed police, 40–50 Cuban military advisors, 600 Cuban construction workers; post-landing estimates: 500–600 regular Grenadian troops, 2,000–5,000 Grenadian militia, 750–800 Cubans of which 25% were regular military).

136. Byron at 119.

137. Byron at 120.

138. SPECTOR at 1.

139. O'SHAUGHNESSY at 169.

140. RUSSELL and MENDEZ at 11.

141. SPECTOR at 5.

142. SANDFORD and VIGILANTE at 11.

143. ADKIN at 239.

144. J. MOSKIN, THE U.S. MARINE CORPS STORY (2d Ed. 1987) ("MOSKIN") at 752; ADKIN at 239; SPECTOR at 7–8.

145. ADKIN at 241; SPECTOR at 8–9.

146. LUTTWAK at 268. *See also* RUSSELL and MENDEZ at 16.

147. RUSSELL and MENDEZ at 16–17.

148. RUSSELL and MENDEZ at 14; ADKIN at 200–203.

149. RUSSELL and MENDEZ at 14; SANDFORD and VIGILANTE at 12 (jumped from 500 feet, the first such combat jumps since World War II); ADKIN at 203, 208–209.

150. Interagency Intelligence Assessment, "Grenada: A First Look at Mechanisms of Control and Foreign Involvement" at 9 (December 19, 1983) (obtained from CIA by Freedom of Information Act request).

151. PRELA, Oct. 25, 1983 (obtained from CIA July 25, 1989 by Freedom of Information Act Request).

152. O'SHAUGHNESSY at 19–20.

153. MOSKIN at 752; SANDFORD and VIGILANTE at 12 (airfield secured by 7:15 a.m., True Blue Campus secured by 8:50 a.m.); ADKIN at 216–219.

154. MOSKIN at 752.

155. RUSSELL and MENDEZ at 23.

156. ADKIN at 262–263.

157. LEHMAN at 298–300.

158. Perry & Fialka, "As Panama Outcome is Praised, Details Emerge of Bungling During the 1983 Grenada Invasion," *The Wall Street Journal* (January 15, 1990) ("*WSJ*") at A-12, col. 6; ADKIN at 313–315.

159. C. WEINBERGER, FIGHTING FOR PEACE 120 (1990); MOSKIN at 752–755; LUTTWAK at 53–54; RUSSELL and MENDEZ at 11; O'SHAUGHNESSY at 18; SANDFORD and VIGILANTE at 10–11; ADKIN at 168–170 (25% of SEALS were lost in initial jump) and at 348 (reprint of Analysis of the Lind Report by the Joint Chiefs of Staff). SEALS also reportedly were involved in the unsuccessful attempt on October 25 to secure the Beausejour transmitting station for Radio Free Grenada. ADKIN at 181–183.

160. SANDFORD and VIGILANTE at 9.

161. SPECTOR at 10.

162. RUSSELL and MENDEZ at 19–20; ADKIN at 242–244; SPECTOR at 9–12.

163. SPECTOR at 13–16.

164. ADKIN at 256.

165. ADKIN at 257; SPECTOR at 16.

166. *WSJ* at col. 4; ADKIN at 245.

167. *WSJ* at col. 4; RUSSELL and MENDEZ at 33–34; ADKIN at 286.

168. ADKIN at 264; SPECTOR at 17.

169. SPECTOR at 17.

170. SPECTOR at 18.

171. SPECTOR at 18; ADKIN at 271. *But see* RUSSELL and MENDEZ at 23 (CH-46 shot down).

172. SPECTOR at 18.

173. LUTTWAK at 54; RUSSELL and MENDEZ at 11 and 19; SANDFORD and VIGILANTE at 15 (Richmond Hill captured on October 26); ADKIN at 186–191. *See also* SPECTOR at 21.

174. O'SHAUGHNESSY at 1–2.

175. SPECTOR at 21.

176. ADKIN at 280.

177. ADKIN at 283.

178. *WSJ* at col. 4 (third helicopter crashed into second and fourth crashed to avoid wreckage); RUSSELL and MENDEZ at 34 (third helicopter hit in tail by antiaircraft fire; only two of eight Blackhawks undamaged in attack); ADKIN at 283–284 (the third crashed into the second and fourth crashed to avoid second and third).

179. ADKIN at 284–285.

180. RUSSELL and MENDEZ at 35 (the Coards and Austin captured October 29); ADKIN at 301; SPECTOR at 22.

181. ADKIN at 308.

182. SPECTOR at 23.

183. SANDFORD and VIGILANTE at 16; ADKIN at 310 (number uncertain: between 4,068 and 9,825 weapons).

184. JOINT REPORT at 1; ADKIN at 318.

185. *E.g.,* RUSSELL and MENDEZ at 33; O'SHAUGHNESSY at 4.

186. O'SHAUGHNESSY at 26.

187. O'SHAUGHNESSY at 26.

188. O'SHAUGHNESSY at 181.

189. SANDFORD and VIGILANTE at 16.

190. LUTTWAK at 33n. (citing *Washington Post,* p.A17 (Mar. 30, 1984); ADKIN at 321–323 (8,500 medals, later rising to 9,802, including 812 Bronze Stars, but not including the Armed Forces Expeditionary Medal, of which 14,000 to 20,000 were awarded for a total of about 30,000 decorations).

191. LUTTWAK at 55.

192. RUSSELL and MENDEZ at 37.

193. *E.g., WSJ* at col. 4; LUTTWAK at 55–57; O'SHAUGHNESSY at Chapter 8.

194. MOSKIN at 748.

195. MOSKIN at 749. *See also* ADKIN at 371 n.2.

196. MOSKIN at 751.

197. SPECTOR at 2; MOSKIN at 751.

198. *WSJ* at col. 2 (1895 British chart); SPECTOR at 2 (1936 British chart).

199. ADKIN at 138; SPECTOR at 2–3.

200. LUTTWAK at 55.

201. JOINT REPORT at 18; LEHMAN at 298–300; Byron at 119; LUTTWAK at 55; RUSSELL and MENDEZ at 35 (350 Grenadians wounded); ADKIN at 308–309 (24 Cubans killed, 67 Grenadians killed, and 19 Americans killed); C. WEINBERGER, FIGHTING FOR PEACE 124 (1990).

202. SANDFORD and VIGILANTE at 16; C. WEINBERGER, FIGHTING FOR PEACE 124 (1990).

203. MOSKIN at 758.

204. ADKIN at 320.

205. ADKIN at 320.

206. *See* Chapter 4.

207. *E.g.,* ADKIN at 318.

208. O'SHAUGHNESSY at 189; ADKIN at 319.

209. ADKIN at 319.

210. Foreign Broadcast Information Service, "Trends in Communist Media," October 26, 1983 at 5 (approved for release December 1, 1987).

211. MOSKIN at 749; O'SHAUGHNESSY at 187.

212. Department of Defense JCS Message 271617Z OCT 83 (obtained from CIA through Freedom of Information Act request).

213. MOSKIN at 749.

214. O'SHAUGHNESSY at 178–179.

215. O'SHAUGHNESSY at 177.

216. ADKIN at 324–325; C. WEINBERGER, FIGHTING FOR PEACE 130 (1990).

217. ADKIN at 330–332.

218. Letter to the Speaker of the House and the President Pro Tempore of the Senate on the Deployment of United States Forces in Grenada, II PUBLIC PAPERS OF THE PRESIDENTS OF THE UNITED STATES: RONALD REAGAN, 1983 at 1512 (1985).

219. *See In re Neagle,* 135 U.S. 1, 64 (1890); *The Prize Cases,* 67 U.S. 635 (1863); *Durand v. Hollins,* 8 F. Cas. 111 (No. 4186) (C.C.S.D. N.Y. 1860); E. CORWIN, THE CONSTITUTION AND WHAT IT MEANS TODAY 60 (8th ed. 1946).

220. 67 U.S. at 666.

221. 8 F. Cas. at 112.

222. 135 U.S. at 64.

223. *E.g.,* ADKIN at 109 and 334; O'SHAUGHNESSY at 3–4 (The Pentagon and State Department had "for four and a half years" sought a way to end "the left-wing government of Grenada."); WOODWARD at 289–290, 295 ("So the Caribbean was a playing field and the Middle East was the real contest.").

224. ADKIN at 109.

225. *The Prize Cases,* 67 U.S. 635, 670 (1863).

226. *Martin v. Mott,* 25 U.S. (12 Wheat.) 1, 28 (1827).

227. *See, e.g., United States v. Belmont,* 301 U.S. 324 (1937).

228. *Cf. Republic of Mexico v. Hoffman,* 324 U.S. 30, 36, 38 (1945); *Ex parte Republic of Peru,* 318 U.S. 578, 589 (1943).

229. *United States v. Belmont,* 301 U.S. 324, 330–331 (1937).

230. *See generally* Chapter 5.

231. *See First National City Bank v. Banco Nacional de Cuba,* 406 U.S. 759, 768 (1972); *United States v. Belmont,* 301 U.S. 324, 330–331 (1937).

232. *The Prize Cases,* 67 U.S. 635, 670 (1863). *See generally* Chapter 2.

233. *Washington Post,* Apr. 21, 1983 at A24, col.1. *See also St. George's Free West Indian,* Mar. 13, 1983 at 16–17 (obtained from CIA July 25, 1989 by Freedom of Information Act Request).

234. 25 U.S. (12 Wheat.) 1, 28 (1827).

235. *See* Chapter 3.

236. 7 WORKS OF ALEXANDER HAMILTON 746–747 (J. Hamilton, ed., 1857) (emphasis omitted).

237. C. WEINBERGER, FIGHTING FOR PEACE 117–119 (1990).

238. Javits, "War Powers Reconsidered," FOREIGN AFFAIRS 130, 137 (1985).

239. WEBSTER'S SEVENTH NEW COLLEGIATE DICTIONARY 179 (1972).

240. *See, e.g., Ex parte Milligan,* 71 U.S. (4 Wall.) 139 (1866).

241. A. HAMILTON, THE FEDERALIST, NO. 69 (1788).

242. *See* Chapter 4.

243. *The Prize Cases,* 67 U.S. 635, 670 (1863).

244. Letter to the Speaker of the House and the President Pro Tempore of the Senate on the Deployment of United States Forces in Grenada, II PUBLIC PAPERS OF THE PRESIDENTS OF THE UNITED STATES: RONALD REAGAN, 1983 at 1512–1513 (1985). *See* Glennon, "The War Powers Resolution Ten Years Later: More Politics Than Law," 78 AM. J. INT'L. L. 571, 572–573 (1984).

245. *See Nixon v. Administrator of General Services,* 433 U.S. 425 (1977); *United States v. Nixon,* 418 U.S. 683 (1974); *United States v. Poindexter,* 1990 U.S. Dist. LEXIS 2881 (March 21, 1990).

246. *But see* Chapter 4 (presentment clause problems with *post hoc* restrictions).

247. H. R. J. Res. 402, 98th Cong., 1st Sess. (1983); 129 CONG. REC. H8933 (Nov. 1, 1983).

248. 129 CONG. REC. S14,876 (daily ed. Oct. 28, 1983).

249. *See Crockett v. Reagan,* 558 F. Supp. 893 (D.D.C.), *aff'd,* 720 F.2d 1355 (D.C. Cir.), *cert. denied,* 467 U.S. 1251 (1982).

250. Of course, any such legislative veto would have been invalid. *See* Chapter 4.

251. *See* Chapter 3.

252. *Martin v. Mott,* 25 U.S. (12 Wheat.) 1, 28 (1827).

U.S. Government Publication

7

Libya, 1986

The Libya Mission[1]

On the morning of December 27, 1985, terrorists attacked and killed civilian travelers, including five Americans, in the Vienna and Rome airports.[2] The Abu Nidal terrorist group was widely suspected of executing the attack. Abu Nidal was also linked by a Department of State study to the government of Libya.[3] Specifically, the study found a "likelihood" of support to Abu Nidal from Libya in the form of "financing, safe haven, and logistical assistance."[4] Libya denied involvement in the Rome and Vienna attacks,[5] even as it praised them. On December 29, the Libyan press agency, JANA, termed the Rome and Vienna attacks "heroic."[6] By contrast, Yasir Arafat, chairman of the Palestinian Liberation Organization, condemned the attacks.[7] The United States persistently accused Libya of participation.[8] A State Department report issued January 8, 1986, stated:

> [Colonel Muammar el-] Qaddafi has used terrorism as one of the primary instruments of his foreign policy and supports radical groups which use terrorist tactics. . . . Qaddafi has provided safe haven, money and arms to these groups—including the notorious Abu Nidal group. . . . Libya's support has broadened to include logistical support for terrorist operations. For example, Libya provided passports to the Abu Nidal members responsible for the attack on the El Al counter in Vienna.[9]

Although Qaddafi at first denied the State Department's allegations, he later proclaimed, "I declare that we shall train [certain groups] . . . for terrorist and suicide missions and . . . place all weapons needed for such missions at their disposal. . . . Libya is a base for the liberation of Palestine."[10] This pronouncement confirmed the conclusions of the Central Intelligence Agency ("CIA").

The Government of Colonel Qadhafi is the most prominent state sponsor of and participant in international terrorism. Despite Qadhafi's repeated public pronouncements that he does not support terrorist groups, there has been a clear and consistent pattern of Libyan aid to almost every major international terrorist group, from the Provisional Irish Republican Army (PIRA) to the Popular Front for the Liberation of Palestine (PFLP). The Libyan Government has also conducted its own terrorist activities, including attacks on the US and French Embassies in Tripoli and plots to assassinate world leaders. . . .

Libya's support for terrorism includes financing for terrorist operations, weapons procurement and supply, the use of training camps and Libyan advisers for guerrilla training, and the use of Libyan diplomatic facilities abroad as support bases for terrorists from Latin America, Western Europe, the Middle East, and East Asia. Qadhafi's major goal involves the Middle East and Africa, particularly the destruction of Israel, the advancement of the Palestinian cause, and the overthrow of conservative and moderate Arab states. Most of his efforts, therefore, are directed toward aiding Middle Eastern terrorism.[11]

The CIA also reported Libyan patronage of the Baader-Meinhof Gang/ Red Army Faction, Latin American terrorist groups, Carlos, Polisario, pre-Khomeini Iranian terrorists, and the Moro National Liberation Front in the Philippines.[12]

The United States brought punitive measures against Libya, imposing trade restrictions and freezing Libyan government assets held by U.S. banks.[13] Rumors ran high about the possibility of military operations,[14] Secretary of State George P. Shultz and Secretary of Defense Caspar W. Weinberger disagreeing over the advisability of such action. Secretary Weinberger disputed the suggestion of Secretary Shultz that military action against Libya should be undertaken even in the absence of data absolutely confirming a direct connection between specific terrorist acts and Libya.[15] Secretary Shultz said that the United States "cannot wait for absolute certainty and clarity as a precondition for military action."[16] He added, "A nation attacked by terrorists is permitted [by international law] to use force to prevent or preempt future attacks, to seize terrorists or to rescue its citizens when no other means is available."[17] Secretary Weinberger, on the other hand, criticized those pursuing "instant gratification from some kind of bombing attack without being too worried about the details."[18] He raised "the basic question of whether what we are doing will discourage and diminish terrorism in the future."[19]

The Navy commenced freedom of navigation exercises in the central Mediterranean on January 24, 1986.[20] By the middle of March, three U.S. aircraft carriers, the *Coral Sea,* the *Saratoga,* and the *America,* and their battle groups were operating in the Mediterranean, and the Pentagon was announcing plans for naval air operations over the Gulf of Sidra.[21] Libya considered these activities to be provocative because it claimed the entire 150,000-square-mile Gulf south of 32R30' north latitude (the so-called "Line of Death") as part of Libyan territorial waters.[22] This territorial dispute had led, in August of 1981, to the downing of two Libyan SU-22 FITTER fighters by two U.S. Navy F-14 fighters.[23]

On the morning of March 24, 1986, during U.S. naval air operations over the Gulf of Sidra south of the "Line of Death" but north of the internationally recognized twelve-mile territorial limit, Libyan forces launched two SA-5 surface-to-air missiles ("SAM"s) at U.S. aircraft from a site near Sirte.[24] During the same morning, two more SA-5 missiles and one SA-2 missile were fired.[25] The missiles missed, and U.S. naval forces retaliated by attacking the radar installation at the SAM site with high-speed antiradiation missiles ("HARM") launched from naval aircraft. Naval forces operating in the Gulf of Sidra had been issued rules of engagement that "provided that if there were some indications of hostile intent by Libyan ships or planes in the areas where we had told the Libyans and others our naval exercises were to be held, then *all* Libyans present would be presumed to be hostile, and our ships and planes were to open fire."[26]

Naval aircraft also launched Harpoon missiles against a LaCombattante-class fast attack craft, sinking it. U.S. Navy aircraft also attacked and damaged a Nanuchka-class corvette proceeding toward the carrier task force.[27] In addition, the guided missile cruiser U.S.S. *Yorktown* launched missiles against a second LaCombattante fast attack craft that had proceeded to within ten miles of the task force. On March 25, Navy aircraft attacked a second Nanuchka-class corvette, leaving the vessel dead in the water and afire.[28] Former Secretary of the Navy John F. Lehman, Jr., reports that a total of three Libyan craft were destroyed.[29] On March 27, President Reagan reported to Congress by letter that the naval exercises in the Gulf of Sidra had ended.[30] The same day, the Arab League's Council of Ministers denounced U.S. actions in the Gulf of Sidra.[31] Colonel Qaddafi claimed victory.[32]

On April 5, terrorists bombed a West Berlin nightclub frequented by U.S. military personnel, killing a civilian woman and an American soldier, Army Sergeant Kenneth T. Ford, and wounding scores of other Americans.[33] American officials in West Berlin declared a "definite, clear connection" between the bombing and Libya.[34] One source has reported that on March 25, 1986, the CIA intercepted a message from the head of the Libyan Intelligence Service in Tripoli to eight Libyan People's Bureaus (or embassies) directing them, ominously, to execute the "plan" against American targets.[35] Robert B. Oakley, head of the State Department's counterterrorism office, stated that the bombing "fit the pattern" of Libyan-sponsored terrorism.[36] West German officials focussed their investigation on reports that the Libyan People's Bureau in East Berlin had used its embassy status to provide logistical support to terrorists operating in West Berlin.[37] France expelled two Libyan diplomats accused of participating in the planning of terrorist attacks against Americans in Europe.[38] On April 9, President Reagan held a press conference during which he announced that the U.S. had "considerable evidence" indicating Libyan support for terrorism against Americans.[39] The President may have been referring to a communication from the Libyan People's Bureau in East Berlin to Tripoli one source has reported as intercepted on April 4, the day before the bombing. The communication reportedly read: "Tripoli will be happy when you see the headlines tomorrow."[40] Another communication from East Berlin to Tripoli reportedly stated on April 5 that the operation was "happening now."[41] At his April 9 press conference, the President announced his intention to act militarily if further intelligence established a direct connection between Libya and the terrorists. "We're going to defend ourselves," he said.[42]

Late on April 14 (early April 15 local), 1986, U.S. forces executed air strikes against Libyan targets. The targets were selected either because of their association with terrorism or for tactical defense purposes.[43] As a State Department spokesman put it, the targeting objective was to "stop Qaddafi's direction of and support of international terrorism."[44] Former Secretary of Defense Caspar Weinberger summarizes:

> The President's goal was to preempt, or disrupt, and discourage further Libyan operations abroad and to teach Qaddafi a lesson that the practice of state-sponsored terrorism carried a high cost.[45]

Air Force F-111 aircraft bombed targets in and around Tripoli: the military side of the Tripoli airport, the Libyan External Security building, the el-Azziziya military barracks (including the compound of Libyan leader Colonel Muammar el-Qaddafi), and the Libyan commando and terrorist training center at Sidi Bilal.[46] The F-111s flew from bases in Great Britain. Because France refused permission to overfly its territory, the round trip for the F-111s was 6,000 miles and required four refuelings en route.[47]

The Air Force F-111s caused heavy damage to the el-Azziziya barracks.[48] Colonel Qaddafi was not injured in the attack on el-Azziziya, but Libyan sources claimed Qaddafi's adopted daughter was killed.[49] The F-111s also damaged the Sidi Bilal training center and destroyed five IL-76 Candid transport aircraft at Tripoli airport.[50] For undetermined reasons, one F-111 was lost, including its two crewmen, Captain Paul F. Lorence and Captain Fernando L. Ribas-Dominicci of the U.S. Air Force. A residential neighborhood in Tripoli was damaged in the attack.[51] Ironically, the French Embassy was located there.

Navy attack aircraft bombed military targets in and around Benghazi, including the Benina air base and the Jamahiriya barracks.[52] Like the Air Force F-111s, U.S. naval aircraft encountered significant resistance from SAM batteries and antiaircraft artillery.[53] Libyan antiaircraft capability was reduced by means of HARM and Shrike missiles and electronic jamming.[54] The Libyans launched no fighters during the air strike.[55] U.S. naval aircraft inflicted substantial damage, destroying four MiG shipping crates (and damaging a fifth), damaging or destroying a MiG assembly warehouse, and destroying three or four MiG-23s, two Mi-8 HIP helicopters, one F-27 transport, and one other small aircraft. U.S. naval aircraft also damaged one Mi-8 helicopter, two Boeing 727 transports, and other aircraft. Hangers and support buildings at Benina were damaged or destroyed.[56]

Secretary Shultz stated at the press conference reporting the operation that the strikes had been ordered as the result of "irrefutable" evidence of Libyan involvement in the bombing of the Berlin club.[57] He said that the strike was necessary to deter future Libyan support of terrorism.[58] "If you raise the costs [of terrorism]," he stated, "you do something that should eventually act as a deterrent. And that is the primary objective, to defend ourselves both in the immediate sense and prospectively."[59] Director of Central Intelligence William J. Casey echoed Secretary of State Shultz' argument in September, 1986:

> Our military raid on Libya had some very therapeutic effects. Terrorist organizations and their state sponsors must now factor into their equation the certainty of swift and painful retaliation. This already has had an inhibiting effect on international terrorism and a galvanizing effect on the resolve of our friends and on their willingness to act in concert with us.[60]

President Reagan addressed the nation on April 14 to confirm that Libya had played a role in the Berlin bombing; he said that "Libya's agents . . . planted the bomb."[61] "Our evidence is direct; it is precise; it is irrefutable."[62] President Reagan stated[63] that the air strikes were conducted in retaliation for the Libyan role in the Berlin bombing and were "pre-emptive" in nature.[64] He reported that the United States had "solid evidence about other attacks Qadhafi has planned against the United States installations and diplomats and even American tourists. Thanks to close cooperation with our friends, some of these have been prevented."[65] "Self-defense is not only our right, it is our duty," the President said.[66]

The Libya Mission
and the U.S. Constitution

The United States and Libya engaged in two violent clashes in 1986. The first occurred on March 24 when Libyan shore batteries launched SAMs against U.S. Navy aircraft. The initial response of the United States was to destroy the SAM sites. The President's constitutional power to defend unambiguously allows him to use armed force to neutralize a proximate threat. When the Libyans launched the SAMs, they launched an attack on U.S. forces. The Constitution allows the President under such circumstances to respond by eliminating the threat. This much is not controversial.[67] However, critics might argue that the President did not attack the SAM sites to eliminate a threat so much as to show "resolve"; that is, the attack against the SAM site was more a diplomatic "statement" than a tactically necessary defensive reaction. There are two responses to this criticism. The first is that, since the SAM sites had actually been used against U.S. forces and since SAMs are unquestionably a threat to aircraft, the President was responding to a real threat from a real enemy.

The second response is that for the President to make the "statement" he made on March 24 is to seek deterrence. The President is empowered to use force to deter hostile actions against the United States.[68] This conclusion flows from the Supreme Court's pronouncement that the President is "bound to resist force by force . . . without waiting for any special legislative authority."[69] Since the determination of whether a threat requires a military response is to be determined by the President,[70] the President may "resist force" by using force to dissuade adversaries from continuing the use of force. So the diplomatic "statement" was that hostile acts against U.S. naval vessels would result in the use of military force. President Reagan acted within the bounds of his authority even if the attack on the SAM sites was a diplomatic "statement."

Hostilities intensified on March 24 and March 25 as U.S. and Libyan forces engaged in a naval battle, resulting in the loss of three Libyan attack vessels. The President was on equally firm constitutional ground in undertaking this military action. When U.S. aircraft and the cruiser *Yorktown* fired on closing Libyan naval vessels, they did so to protect the task force from a perceived threat. Admittedly, the on-scene commander was not operating with the benefit of certainty as he divined the hostile intent of the Libyan vessels. Even if his assessment was incorrect, however, his actions (on behalf of the President) did not stray beyond the constitutional limits of defensive war-making. Nothing about the President's power to defend depends upon the wisdom or correctness of on-scene tactical decisions or the accuracy of intelligence. The President need not resolve ambiguity in favor of the enemy.

The second phase of the U.S.-Libya confrontation occurred on April 14. Unlike the March engagement, the April 14 air strikes were premeditated and carefully planned. The only formal contact between the President and Congress on the question of the April 14 air strikes against Libya took place several hours before commencement of operations and did not result in any form of congressional approval, either express or implied.[71] The air strikes against Libya thus provide an unambiguous factual situation against which to test the scope of the President's constitutional war-making authority. If some form of pre-strike congressional authorization (whether or not a declaration of war) was required by the Constitution, the President's conduct on April 14, 1986, was brazenly unconstitutional. If not, then the President's action was undertaken within the bounds of his constitutional authority.

By 1986, President Reagan had been advised that the government of Libya had supported attacks on Americans abroad. A State Department report had linked the government of Libya and the Abu Nidal terrorist organization.[72] Abu Nidal, in turn, was believed responsible for the terrorist attacks on December 27, 1985 at the Rome and Vienna airports that had left Americans dead.[73] As if to resolve any question about Libya's involvement in terrorist activities, Qaddafi declared his support, both spiritual and logistical, for terrorist missions.[74] Libya confirmed its hostility toward the U.S. by means of the April 5, 1986 nightclub bombing in West Berlin. The President stated that "orders were sent from Tripoli to the Libyan People's Bureau in East Berlin to conduct a terrorist attack against Americans to cause maximum and indiscriminate casualties."[75] The Secretary of State described the evidence linking Libya directly to the bombing as "irrefutable."[76]

This pattern of aggression by Libya against American citizens supported the inference that Libya had undertaken a course of action that not only had harmed Americans in the past but also would harm Americans in the future. In response to this information, President Reagan undertook a military action he characterized in defensive,[77] as opposed to offensive,[78] terms.

Chapter One examined the analogous decision by President Thomas Jefferson to order the Navy to defend American commercial vessels in the Mediterranean against the Barbary pirates[79] without a congressional declaration of war. The similarities between Jefferson's Libya problem and Reagan's are striking: two presidents used the Navy to deal with dangerous political forces in Libya. Americans had already been attacked, and the U.S. government had received threats of future attacks. Following Jefferson's order, the twelve-gun tender U.S.S. *Enterprise* engaged and

captured a fourteen-gun corsair of the Bey of Tripoli. The mission of
the naval squadron was described in clearly preemptive terms by the
Secretary of the Navy.[80]

The U.S. squadron's mission was overtly hostile to the Barbary powers:

> But should you find on your arrival at Gibraltar, that all the Barbary
> powers have declared war against the United States, you will then distribute
> your force in such a manner, as your judgment shall direct, so as best to
> protect our commerce and chastise their insolence—by sinking, burning,
> or destroying their ships and vessels wherever you shall find them.[81]

Although President Jefferson described the engagement to Congress as
a response to a sudden attack upon U.S. naval forces,[82] he was undertaking
the same sort of military action as that ordered by President Reagan.
He wished not only to respond to past attacks against the U.S. but also
to deter and preempt future attacks.

Jefferson was not a delegate to the Constitutional Convention but his
position in the political mainstream of the Framers' thinking cannot be
denied. Thus can Jefferson's use of force be viewed as a model of
constitutionally authorized presidential war-making. Jefferson used the
Navy to "show the flag" in the Mediterranean, much as Reagan did in
the Gulf of Sidra in March, 1986. As a result, naval forces were used
to punish the Tripolitan adversary for past bad acts and to deter future
ones. President Reagan's actions thus lie well within the scope of the
model established by Jefferson.

President Reagan's use of force against Libya is similarly consistent
with that of President Lincoln, who ordered the Navy to impose a blockade
on southern ports during the Civil War. Like President Reagan, President
Lincoln used naval forces in an unambiguous act of war without the
benefit of a congressional declaration of war. However, unlike President
Reagan's, President Lincoln's unilateral use of naval force enjoyed the
express blessing, after the fact, of the Supreme Court.[83] In *The Prize
Cases*,[84] the Supreme Court noted that even as Commander-in-Chief and
the chief national executive, the President "has no power to initiate or
declare a war. . . ."[85] Nevertheless, the Court characterized the President's
power to defend in the broadest terms, even imposing on the President
a *duty* to defend:

> If a war be made by invasion of a foreign nation, the President is not only
> authorized but bound to resist force by force. He does not initiate the
> war, but is bound to accept the challenge without waiting for any special
> legislative authority.[86]

The Court elaborated on the President's power and duty to defend by expounding on the uncertainties of conflict and the impossibility of predicting *a priori* the form of the threat to which the President might have to respond. Whatever its form, the Supreme Court stated, the President must meet the threat.[87] Again, the Supreme Court in *The Prize Cases* provides guidance by finding that "[w]hether the President in fulfilling his duties, as Commander-in-Chief, . . . has met with such armed hostile resistance, . . . as will compel him to accord to them the character of belligerents, is a question to be decided *by him*. . . ."[88]

It is clear then that the Constitution grants to the President the power to defend the nation's security (including the lives of Americans abroad). Few doubt the existence of this constitutional power of defense. The question debated among commentators is when the President's power to act unilaterally is activated. The critics would point out that *The Prize Cases* Court's ruling that the President determines when to activate his power to defend is a "slippery slope." The Constitution grants the President the power to defend and also the power to determine when a use of force is defensive, as opposed to offensive. That is, the Constitution places the President on the unilateral use of force "slope," and, by allowing him to decide when to use force, allows him to "slip" to an apparently undetermined point. Since the Constitution did not predetermine any limit beyond which the President may not "slip," the courts could discover that point by legal analysis on a case-by-case basis. However, since the courts have generally declined to review presidential decisions to use force,[89] extensive case-by-case analysis has not taken place. As a result, the point on the "slope" beyond which the President may not "slip," if there is one, might never be discovered, and the President might be free to "slip" forever.

One response to this criticism is that the President is not free to slip forever. Congress may rein in the President by means of its impeachment and appropriation powers, not to mention its political influence. But within the scope of the President's defensive war-making power, the slope is slippery indeed. The President may conduct defensive military operations that he judges necessary. His decision to use force is not subject to congressional oversight in terms of the war powers themselves, although Congress may review the President's actions with respect to other constitutional powers such as those of appropriation. The difficulty of establishing an enduring distinction between offensive and defensive war undermines (but does not erase) that distinction as a basis for congressional oversight.

When the Framers recognized the necessity of empowering the President to use force unilaterally for defensive purposes, they granted the President broad discretion. The breadth of the President's power to make war has been recognized by the courts as a necessary consequence of the original

grant of power to defend the nation from armed attack. The recognition
of such broad presidential war powers necessarily raises the question of
whether such powers will be exercised wisely. Indeed, if the President
is empowered to determine whether he is constitutionally authorized to
exercise his war powers, is the temptation to act guilefully too overwhelming to resist? The Supreme Court, in *Martin v. Mott,* rejected the
idea that the President's war powers could be challenged on the basis of
imputed guile. The Court said: "It is no answer, that such a power may
be abused, for there is no power which is not susceptible of abuse."[90]
The fact that power might be abused does not mean that it will be. If
it is abused, the Constitution provides remedies, including impeachment.

In April, 1986 President Reagan could have presented his information
about Libya to Congress seeking a declaration of war. He did not do
so, considering the threat of harm to Americans sufficiently imminent
to justify the use of force without congressional authorization. The
President knew that Libya had materially supported the Rome and Vienna
airport attacks. He not only knew of Libya's concrete assistance to terrorists
in the form of arms, passports, and safe harbor, but also was aware of
Qaddafi's public declarations of support for terrorism and his intention
to provide terrorists with training and arms in the future. The President
even knew of communications to East Berlin from Tripoli regarding
terrorism against Americans.[91]

Critics of the President's decision to use force against Libya might
argue that the lack of "smoking gun" evidence of Libyan direction of
a specific future attack suggests the unconstitutionality of the air strikes.
The President's determination of imminent threat, they would say, was
too tenuous to be entitled to constitutional sanctification. They would
argue that what the President had, at most, was a generalized indication
that a terrorist attack against Americans might be executed sometime in
the future. The critics would argue that for the President to characterize
such a future attack as inevitable would be hyperbolic justification; a
standard of inevitability would grant the President *carte blanche* to use
his defensive powers to initiate a military offense. The air strikes against
Libya, they would reason, were labelled defensive but were in fact offensive
since they were preemptive. As unauthorized presidential offensive war-
making the air strikes were, they would conclude, unconstitutional.

The critics would be wrong, however, to conclude that uncertainty
about the likelihood of a future Libya-supported terrorist attack against
Americans means that the constitutional question should be resolved
against the President. Nothing in the Framers' debate or the judicial
analyses suggests this. To the contrary, the President is entitled to the
benefit of the doubt.[92] Given his power to determine whether a situation
requires a military response,[93] the President may determine that, although

the date of a future attack is unknown, it should be preempted with military force. In short, the President is entitled to be cautious.

The President's critics would be correct in their assertion that the President's power to wage war unilaterally is not without limit. Since Congress has the power of appropriation,[94] Congress can refuse to fund disapproved military activity undertaken by the President. Indeed, Congress did just this on several occasions during the Vietnam War.[95] Congress, of course, also possesses the ultimate weapon: impeachment of the President for "high crimes and misdemeanors."[96]

Although Congress' power to declare war has been read by at least one commentator to incorporate a veto-like power to "declare *against* a war,"[97] the Framers unanimously rejected a proposal to grant Congress the power to declare war "and peace."[98] Moreover, no court has ever identified such a congressional power. Indeed, the only Supreme Court opinion ever to lay down an absolute legal constraint on presidential war powers was *Youngstown Co. v. Sawyer*,[99] the famous steel seizure case. In that case, the Court could have ruled against the President on the basis of his failure to obtain a congressional declaration of war against Korea, but it did not. Thus the steel seizure case has come to stand for the proposition that the Supreme Court will not allow the President's war-making power to extend beyond the scope of military action into the arena of domestic policy-making. But the steel seizure case does not suggest that the Court is likely to challenge the President's decision to commit forces to combat.

As a result, a guileful President would experience little difficulty identifying or even creating a threatening incident abroad sufficiently provocative to justify the use of force. Similarly, a cynical President might find it expedient to undertake an offensive military campaign and simply label it a defensive, preemptive action. This is just the reading given to the air strikes by critics who viewed the anti-terrorism justification as a pretext for overthrowing Qaddafi's regime.[100] Although Congress might have the power under such a circumstance to bar the use of federal funds for combat, it might lack the political will to do so. The President's power to commit forces to combat in the name of national defense thus would present Congress with a *fait accompli*, a war to be terminated by a congressional vote for withdrawal short of victory.[101] War would become in such a situation, as Madison noted, "the true nurse of executive aggrandizement."[102]

But such a scenario is based on the premise of a fundamentally dishonest President, contemptuous of the Constitution and the political process. The premise of the law is not so hard-bitten, as the *Martin v. Mott* Court stated: "When the president exercises an authority confided to him by law, the presumption is, that it is exercised in pursuance of law."[103]

Of course, the President need not be cynical to be wrong. The President's decision to use force might be based on inaccurate intelligence. The President's decision to strike against Libya was based on reports linking Libya and terrorist operations against Americans. Had these reports been incorrect, the President's decision would have been misinformed. Such an error would have resulted in adverse diplomatic and domestic political consequences and needless death and destruction. However, an error would not render the President's actions unconstitutional. The *Mott* Court was clear about this when it granted the President the benefit of the doubt.[104] But even if the Supreme Court had not made things so easy for the President by means of *dicta* in the *Mott* decision, the same result would obtain. If the President is free under the Constitution to determine the existence of exigent circumstances and then act on that determination,[105] he must be free to err. This conclusion is the inescapable inference from the premise that the President is empowered to respond to threats. He might not fully understand the extent or nature of the threat, but to deprive him of the power to respond when his understanding is incomplete is to deprive him of the power entirely. The basis for the power is the exigency of threatening circumstances, which do not always present themselves in full blown and obvious form.

Exigency itself is not subject to absolute specification *a priori*. It is easy to see how a critic might accept the legal conclusion that the President is free to respond militarily to exigent circumstances and reject the President's finding that he faced an exigent circumstance in 1986. After all, if the President had time to plan the air strikes, he also might have had time to seek congressional authorization. The answer to those not satisfied with President Reagan's determination of exigency in 1986 is that the Constitution does not assign a wooden standard to determine when a threat is sufficiently imminent to justify presidential war-making. The Constitution did not require President Reagan to certify to Congress that Libya would have attacked Americans abroad in May, for example, but for his preemptive strike in April. If anything is clear from the Framers' debates and the judiciary's infrequent clarifications of the constitutional war-making powers, it is that the Constitution establishes no such fixed standard to mark the limit of presidential war-making authority. Rather, the Constitution allows the President wide latitude to decide if a threat, however characterized, is too imminent to await a congressional declaration of war and to determine whether a military action has created a state of undeclared *de facto* war requiring the use of force in response.[106] President Reagan thus was authorized to identify the threat posed by Libya in 1986 and to order a defensive response.

To require more of the President would be to render his defensive powers merely nominal. If the President is required by the Constitution to wait for an attack, he may not preempt. If he may not preempt, then he must accept casualties from hostile forces before undertaking a response. The sort of strike-and-run tactic favored by terrorists, and indeed employed in guerrilla warfare in general, is perfectly suited to such a limitation on presidential war-making; if an enemy strikes and withdraws, the President may not respond because the enemy has withdrawn. Such an encumbrance on the President's ability to make war, of course, nullifies any meaningful ability of the President to undertake a swift military response to a threat.

In ordering the air strike, President Reagan sought to accomplish two stated defensive purposes: deterrence, in the form of retaliation for past attacks, and preemption, in the form of neutralizing command and control facilities used by Libya to conduct terrorist operations. Critics could argue that such purposes are actually offensive and therefore unauthorized. The critics would have a point to the extent that a legally meaningful distinction between offensive and defensive force is not always self-evident.[107] But the Constitution resolves this ambiguity in the President's favor: it is the President who decides when the national security is jeopardized; it is the President who decides on the appropriate defensive reaction. President Reagan's decision to employ air power to the end of deterrence and preemption was a decision to use military force defensively to address a threat to national security. His actions were therefore undertaken within the limits of his constitutional authority.

Those who assert the unconstitutionality of the President's use of force on April 14 must concede the existence of his power to defend. Their argument is that the threat from Libya did not justify the President's exercise of his power. However, discretion is at the very heart of all power; to be granted power is to be enabled to act wisely or unwisely. The critics would concede that the President could use military force to rescue kidnapped Americans from Libya. For them to suggest that the President may not undertake a preemptive strike to prevent kidnapping or other harm from befalling Americans abroad is unsupportable. What they really mean to say is that, although the President's actions were lawful, they were unwise. If this is what they mean to say, they should say it, and thus avoid a constitutional debate when a political debate would be more fruitful.

The Libya Mission
and the War Powers Resolution

Following the military operations against Libya, critics questioned whether the President had complied with the War Powers Resolution ("WPR").[108] Some members of Congress, including House Republican

Leader Robert Michel, protested that the President had failed to comply with the WPR's consultation provision. The President had advised congressional leaders of the strike three hours before it commenced, an amount of notice Representative Michel considered insufficient for meaningful consultation.[109]

These objections raised the question of how early discussion must commence to qualify as consultation. If the President had convened congressional leaders during the April 14 strikes, consultation obviously would not have been achieved. On the other hand, the WPR does not require congressional involvement in the entire operational planning process. Were such congressional participation contemplated, the WPR undoubtedly would have said so.

But the WPR did not say so, probably because Congress doubted it had the constitutional authority to require such participation. After all, the Constitution confers on the President both the ultimate command of the armed forces and foreign affairs powers.[110] In addition, the power to respond to emergencies with military force is in the hands of the President. The WPR does not require the President to obtain congressional permission before employing military force.

Although the WPR rules out the extremes, it provides little guidance to the President on his conduct in between. The most reasonable position is that which the White House offered congressional critics in April of 1986: since the President was able to call off the attack at the time of his meeting with congressional leaders and since the meeting fulfilled the WPR objective of pre-hostilities communication between the President and Congress, consultation occurred. The President had the power and the responsibility to determine the appropriate response to Libya under emergency conditions. By consulting with Congress, he was not inviting their participation in the command of the armed forces but asking for any point of view members of Congress might wish to offer before the fact. It is probably the case that more extensive discussions with Congress would have been politically beneficial. Ideally, the President would obtain congressional assent before undertaking military operations. But if the President determines that such interaction is not advisable, he is not legally required to cancel or delay military operations.

The exigency of the circumstances of the March, 1986 naval engagements apparently precluded consultation between the President and Congress. When the SAMs were launched, the President faced an immediate threat to naval aircraft. Even more urgent was the use of force against Libyan naval vessels approaching the task force. The WPR by its own terms requires consultation only "in every possible instance." In these instances, consultation was not possible.

Prior to the April 14, 1986 air strike, the President convened congressional leaders to advise them of his plans and solicit their views. Some members of Congress, such as Representative Michel, considered this meeting to be inadequate because, occurring just hours before the air strike, congressional leaders lacked the opportunity to formulate meaningful comments and questions. This criticism was reminiscent of the remark of Senator Hugh Scott, Republican Minority Leader, following the *Mayaguez* rescue operation: "We were informed. We were alerted. We were advised. We were notified. We were telephoned. It was discussed with us. I don't know whether that's consultation or not."[111]

Those asserting the inadequacy of President Reagan's consultation with Congress would find comfort in the House report on the WPR rejecting "the notion that consultation should be synonymous with merely being informed." According to the report, the President must ask members of Congress for "advice and opinions and, in appropriate circumstances, their approval of action contemplated."[112] Contrary to the position taken by congressional critics, however, the President was not required to do more than he did. As a constitutional matter, Congress may not interfere in the decisions of the Commander-in-Chief as Commander-in-Chief; that is, Congress cannot involve itself in command decisions.[113] One such command decision is the timing of an attack. For Congress to ask that the attack be delayed so it can consider whether to comment or ask questions is to interfere in the timing of the attack. This Congress may not do. Congress would be on firmer ground in requesting that the President conduct consultation as soon as he has decided to undertake a specific military action. But no evidence indicates that the President decided on the April 14 attack far in advance and then purposely delayed consultation until the last minute.

When the President convened congressional leaders on the eve of the air strikes against Libya, he did not commit himself necessarily to additional interactions with Congress. One could argue that by consulting with Congress in compliance with the WPR, the President admitted the applicability of the WPR to the Libya situation. This argument, however, has the shortcoming of elevating form over substance: for the President formally to undertake a consultation with Congress does not necessarily imply that he believes himself legally required to do so. Indeed, it would be ironic if the true effect of the WPR was to increase the President's wariness in discussing matters of war and peace with Congress for fear of implying a lack of confidence in his constitutional authority.

The second WPR requirement, that of notification within 48 hours of introducing U.S. forces into imminent or actual hostilities, is of legal consequence primarily because the making of a report starts the WPR's sixty-day "clock." In fact, the President reported by letter to Congress on March 26, 1986.[114] He also submitted a report "consistent with" the WPR on April 16.[115] In it, he stated:

> These strikes were conducted in the exercise of our right of self-defense under Article 51 of the United Nations Charter. This necessary and appropriate action was a preemptive strike, directed against the Libyan terrorist infrastructure and designed to deter acts of terrorism by Libya, such as the Libyan-ordered bombing of a discotheque in West Berlin on April 5. Libya's cowardly and murderous act resulted in the death of two innocent people—an American soldier and a young Turkish woman—and the wounding of 50 United States Armed Forces personnel and 180 other innocent persons. This was the latest in a long series of terrorist attacks against United States installations, diplomats and citizens carried out or attempted with the support and direction of Muammar Qadhafi. Should Libyan-sponsored terrorist attacks against United States citizens not cease, we will take appropriate measures necessary to protect United States citizens in the exercise of our right of self-defense.
>
> In accordance with my desire that Congress be informed on this matter, and consistent with the War Powers Resolution, I am providing this report on the employment of the United States Armed Forces. These self-defense measures were undertaken pursuant to my authority as Commander in Chief of United States Armed Forces.[116]

In a situation such as the operation against Libya, the reporting requirement does not limit the President's power to use force. Such operations do not necessarily contemplate a strategy of attrition. Rather, by definition, they are designed to deal with current exigencies, the long-term implications of which will not appear until the emergency has ended. The air strike against Libya offers an especially clear example of this principle: because the April 14 tactical air strike did not necessarily contemplate a second strike, the sixty-day clock stopped running when the aircraft returned to their respective bases.

The April 14 air strikes against Libya can be described fairly as "hostilities," as the term is used by the WPR. The President's intentional use of armed force in order to inflict physical damage must amount to "hostilities" if the term has any meaning. Thus the WPR required the President's report within 48 hours of the air strikes. The President submitted a report "consistent with" the WPR on April 16. The consequence of the President's report is that it started the sixty-day clock, according to the WPR. However, since "hostilities" started and U.S. forces withdrew on April 14, the sixty-day clock stopped running almost as soon as it started.[117] Thus the report had no meaningful consequence in the sense of activating the most substantial and constitutionally infirm mechanism of the WPR: automatic termination. This conclusion is not controversial so many years after the fact; after all, everyone knows that the April 14 air strike was not followed by another. So "hostilities" really did end. Five days after April 14, however, one could not have been so certain about the eventual outcome. Another air strike on, for example, April 20 would have encouraged the President's critics to argue that the sixty-day clock was still running. Alternatively, they would argue that the President had undertaken an attrition strategy involving periodic tactical air strikes against Libya. This strategy, they would argue, meant that the President had introduced armed forces "into situations where imminent involvement in hostilities is clearly indicated by the circumstances."[118] However, the force of this argument depends on the President's express selection of a strategy of attrition. In fact, the April 14 air strike did not contemplate a follow-on, either strategically or tactically. Indeed, critics actually argued at the time that it was this very wait-and-see approach that rendered the President's policy against terrorists *ad hoc*. In the absence of a necessary military follow-on to the April 14 air strikes, there was no clear indication of imminent hostilities. Therefore, there was no basis for the sixty-day clock to run after April 14.

Conclusion

In the spring of 1986, the President believed that Libya would continue its campaign to harm U.S. citizens. He sought to defend against such attacks by means of a preemptive strike on April 14, 1986. As a defensive measure undertaken without a declaration of war by Congress, the strike against Libya was within the scope of the President's constitutional war-making authority. Moreover, he complied with the requirements of the WPR, despite the WPR's dubious constitutional grounding.

Notes

1. This chapter is based on Hall, "The Constitution and Presidential War Making Against Libya," 42 NAVAL WAR COLLEGE REV. 30 (1989), with the permission of the Naval War College.

2. *N.Y. Times,* Dec. 28, 1985, at 1, col. 5. The airport massacres followed the October 3, 1985 hijacking of the cruise ship *Achille Lauro,* during which an American, Leon Klinghoffer, was murdered, the November 23, 1985 hijacking of an Egyptian airliner, during which an American was murdered, and the November 24, 1985 bombing of a Frankfurt, West Germany shopping mall, which wounded 23 Americans. J. LEHMAN, COMMAND OF THE SEAS: A PERSONAL STORY 364–367 (1988).

3. *N.Y. Times,* Jan. 1, 1986, at 1, col. 3.

4. *Id.,* Jan. 1, 1986, at 4, col. 4 (Text of State Department Report).

5. *Id.,* Jan. 1, 1986, at 5, col. 1; *id.,* Jan. 6, 1986, at 1, col. 4.

6. *Id.*, Jan. 1, 1986, at 6, col. 1.

7. *Id.*, Jan. 1, 1986, at 6, col. 2.

8. *Id.*, Jan. 9, 1986, at 6, col. 1; *id.*, Mar. 23, 1986, at 1, col. 5.

9. *Id.*, Jan. 9, 1986, at 6, col. 1 (Text of State Department Report).

10. *Id.*, Jan. 16, 1986, at 8, col. 1.

11. Central Intelligence Agency assessment, approved for release April 25, 1986 (obtained from CIA July 25, 1989 by Freedom of Information Act Request).

12. *Id.* For a longer list of Qaddafi patrons, *see* Parks, "Crossing the Line," 112 U.S. Naval Institute PROCEEDINGS 40, 41 (November 1986) ("Parks").

13. *N.Y. Times,* Jan. 9, 1986, at 1, col. 6.

14. *See, e.g.,* "Targeting Gaddafi," TIME 18 (April 21, 1986).

15. *N.Y. Times,* Jan. 17, 1986, at 1, col. 4.

16. *Id.*, Jan. 16, 1986, at 1, col. 5.

17. *Id.*, Jan. 16, 1986, at 8, col. 2.

18. *Id.*, Jan. 17, 1986, at 1, col. 4.

19. *Id.*, Jan. 17, 1986, at 1, col. 4.

20. Wright, "U.S. Naval Operations in 1986," 113 U.S. Naval Institute PROCEEDINGS 30, 33 (May 1987). *See also* Stumpf, "Air War With Libya," 112 U.S. Naval Institute PROCEEDINGS 42 (August 1986).

21. *N.Y. Times,* Mar. 19, 1986, at 1, col. 5; *id.*, Mar. 20, 1986, at 7, col. 1; *id.*, Mar. 22, 1986, at 3, col. 2.

22. Parks at 40, 42.

23. Parks at 43.

24. Letter to the Speaker of the House of Representatives and the President Pro Tempore of the Senate on the Gulf of Sidra Incident, March 26, 1986, I PUBLIC PAPERS OF THE PRESIDENTS OF THE UNITED STATES: RONALD REAGAN, 1986 at 406–407 (1988).

25. C. WEINBERGER, FIGHTING FOR PEACE 186 (1990).

26. C. WEINBERGER, FIGHTING FOR PEACE 183 (1990) (emphasis original).

27. *N.Y. Times,* Mar. 25, 1986, at 1, col. 6; Text of Secretary of Defense Weinberger's statement at *id.*, Mar. 25, 1986, at 10, col. 1. *See also* Stumpf, "Air War With Libya," 112 U.S. Naval Institute PROCEEDINGS 42, 46–47 (August 1986) (one LaCombattante-class boat sunk, one Nanuchka-class corvette sunk, a second Nanuchka-class corvette damaged); Parks at 45 (one LaCombattante and two Nanuchkas damaged); Rausa, "Sea Service Aviation Operations in 1986," 113 U.S. Naval Institute PROCEEDINGS 98 (May 1987) (one Libyan missile patrol boat destroyed); B. WOODWARD, VEIL: THE SECRET WARS OF THE CIA 1981–1987 ("WOODWARD") at 442–443 (1987).

28. *N.Y. Times,* Mar. 26, 1986, at 8, col. 1; *id.*, Mar. 27, 1986, at 8, col. 1.

29. J. LEHMAN, COMMAND OF THE SEAS: A PERSONAL STORY 370 (1988). *But see* C. WEINBERGER, FIGHTING FOR PEACE 186 (1990) (one patrol boat destroyed and one missile boat damaged).

30. *N.Y. Times,* Mar. 28, 1986, at 1, col. 2. *See also* Parks at 45.

31. *N.Y. Times,* Mar. 28, 1986, at 12, col. 4.

32. *Id.,* Mar. 29, 1986, at 3, col. 1.

33. *Id.,* Apr. 6, 1986, at 1, col. 5–6.

34. *Id.,* Apr. 6, 1986, at 1, col. 6.

35. WOODWARD at 444.

36. *N.Y. Times,* Apr. 7, 1986, at 6, col. 2.

37. *Id.,* Apr. 6, 1986, at 1, col. 5–6.

38. *Id.,* Apr. 6, 1986, at 19, col. 1.

39. *Id.,* Apr. 10, 1986, at 1, col. 6; *id.,* Apr. 10, 1986, at 22, col. 1.

40. WOODWARD at 444. *See also* Address to the Nation on the United States Air Strike Against Libya, April 14, 1986, I PAPERS OF THE PRESIDENTS OF THE UNITED STATES: RONALD REAGAN, 1986 at 468 (1988).

41. WOODWARD at 444.

42. *N.Y. Times,* Apr. 10, 1986, at 1, col. 6.

43. Parks at 47–49.

44. *N.Y. Times,* Apr. 16, 1986, at 20, col. 5 (remarks of State Department Spokesman Bernard Kalb). *See also* J. LEHMAN, COMMAND OF THE SEAS: A PERSONAL STORY 371–374 (1988); C. WEINBERGER, FIGHTING FOR PEACE 189–192 (1990).

45. C. WEINBERGER, FIGHTING FOR PEACE 193 (1990).

46. *N.Y. Times,* Apr. 15, 1986, at 1, col. 5. *See id.,* Apr. 15, 1986, at 13, col. 1 (transcript of Weinberger/Shultz press conference). *See also* Parks at 47–48; Rausa, "Sea Service Aviation Operations in 1986," 113 U.S. Naval Institute PROCEEDINGS 98 (May 1987).

47. Parks at 51.

48. Parks at 51.

49. WOODWARD at 446; Parks at 52 (Qaddafi not a target but possibly injured); C. WEINBERGER, FIGHTING FOR PEACE 196 (1990).

50. Parks at 51 (also reporting numerous aborted F-111 attacks); C. WEINBERGER, FIGHTING FOR PEACE 198 (1990).

51. *N.Y. Times,* Apr. 16, 1986, at 1, col. 5; *id.,* Apr. 16, 1986, at 15, col. 3; *id.,* Apr. 17, 1986, at 22, col. 1; Parks at 52; C. WEINBERGER, FIGHTING FOR PEACE 197–198 (1990).

52. *N.Y. Times,* Apr. 15, 1986, at 1, col. 5; *id.,* Apr. 16, 1986, at 15, col. 3 (remarks of Vice Admiral Frank Kelso, Jr., USN); *id.,* Apr. 15, 1986, at 1, col. 3. *See also* Rausa, "Sea Service Aviation Operations in 1986," 113 U.S. Naval Institute PROCEEDINGS 98 (May 1987).

53. *N.Y. Times,* Apr. 16, 1986, at 15, col. 3.

54. Stumpf, "Air War With Libya," 112 U.S. Naval Institute PROCEEDINGS 42, 48 (August 1986); Parks at 51.

55. Parks at 51.

56. Parks at 51; C. WEINBERGER, FIGHTING FOR PEACE 198 (1990).

57. *N.Y. Times,* Apr. 15, 1986, at 10, col. 1. *See also* transcript of Press Secretary Speakes' press conference, *id.,* Apr. 15, 1986, at 13, col. 1. *See also* President Reagan's Address to American Business Conference, *id.,* Apr. 16, 1986, at 20, col. 1.

58. *Id.,* Apr. 15, 1986, at 1, col. 3.

59. *Id.,* Apr. 15, 1986, at 1, col. 3.

60. Remarks of William J. Casey before the *Washington Times* Advisory Board and Editorial Board, The International Club, Washington, D.C. (September 25, 1986) (text provided by Central Intelligence Agency July 25, 1989 through Freedom of Information Act Request).

61. Address to the Nation on the United States Air Strike Against Libya, April 14, 1986, I PUBLIC PAPERS OF THE PRESIDENTS OF THE UNITED STATES: RONALD REAGAN, 1986 at 468 (1988).

62. *Id.*

63. National Security Agency ("NSA") officials dissented from the President's decision to use NSA data, including decoded Libyan diplomatic message traffic, to prove Libyan involvement in terrorism. *N.Y. Times,* Apr. 17, 1986, at 24, col. 1.

64. Address to the Nation on the United States Air Strike Against Libya, April 14, 1986, I PUBLIC PAPERS OF THE PRESIDENTS OF THE UNITED STATES: RONALD REAGAN, 1986 at 469 (1988).

65. *Id.* at 468–469.

66. *Id.* at 469.

67. *See* Chapter 2.

68. *See, e.g., Durand v. Hollins,* 8 F. Cas. 111 (No. 4186) (C.C.S.D. N.Y. 1860) (Nelson, J.).

69. *The Prize Cases,* 67 U.S. 635, 668 (1863).

70. *Id.* at 670.

71. For testimony on the lawfulness of the air strikes, *see* WAR POWERS, LIBYA, AND STATE SPONSORED TERRORISM: HEARINGS BEFORE THE SUBCOMMITTEE ON ARMS CONTROL, INTERNATIONAL SECURITY, AND SCIENCE OF THE HOUSE COMMITTEE ON FOREIGN AFFAIRS, 99th Cong., 2d Sess. (1986).

72. *N.Y. Times,* Jan. 1, 1986, at 1, col. 3, and at 4, col. 1; *id.,* Jan. 9, 1986, at 6, col. 1.

73. *Id.,* Dec. 28, 1985, at 1, col. 5.

74. *Id.,* Jan. 16, 1986, at 8, col. 1.

75. Address to the Nation on the United States Air Strike Against Libya, April 14, 1986, I PUBLIC PAPERS OF THE PRESIDENTS OF THE UNITED STATES: RONALD REAGAN, 1986 at 468–469 (1988).

76. *N.Y. Times,* Apr. 15, 1986, at 10, col. 1. *See also* transcript of Press Secretary Speakes' press conference, *id.,* Apr. 15, 1986, at 13, col. 1; President Reagan's address to American Business Conference, *id.,* Apr. 16, 1986, at 20, col. 1.

77. *See, e.g.,* Emerson, "The War Powers Resolution Tested: The President's Independent Defense Power," 51 NOTRE DAME LAWYER 187, 192 (1975) (implications of defensive presidential war-making).

78. *See* E. KEYNES, UNDECLARED WAR: TWILIGHT ZONE OF CONSTITUTIONAL POWER (1982) (implications of offensive presidential war-making). *See also* testimony of John Norton Moore, CONGRESS, THE PRESIDENT, AND THE WAR POWERS: HEARING BEFORE THE HOUSE

COMMITTEE ON FOREIGN AFFAIRS, 91st Cong., 2d Sess. (June 25, 1970); Moore, "The National Executive and the Use of Armed Forces Abroad," 21 NAVAL WAR COLLEGE REV. 28 (1969).

79. H. NASH, THE FORGOTTEN WARS, 1798–1805, 287–289 (1961); S. BLYTH, HISTORY OF THE WAR BETWEEN THE UNITED STATES AND TRIPOLI AND OTHER BARBARY POWERS, 115–125 (1806).

80. W. GOLDSMITH, I GROWTH OF PRESIDENTIAL POWER: A DOCUMENTARY HISTORY 373–376 (1974) (citing I STATE PAPERS AND DOCUMENTS OF THE UNITED STATES 75–78 (1814)); I NAVAL DOCUMENTS RELATED TO THE UNITED STATES WARS WITH THE BARBARY POWERS, 465–467 (1939); Sofar, "The Presidency, War and Foreign Affairs: Practice Under the Framers," 40 L. & CONT. PROB. 12 (1976).

81. *Id.*

82. I MESSAGES AND PAPERS OF THE PRESIDENTS 1789–1897 at 326–327 (J. Richardson, ed., 1898).

83. *See generally* C. BERDAHL, WAR POWERS OF THE EXECUTIVE IN THE UNITED STATES 58–77 (1921).

84. 67 U.S. 635 (1863).

85. 67 U.S. at 668.

86. 67 U.S. at 668. *See also U.S. v. Curtiss-Wright Corp.,* 299 U.S. 304 (1936); *Myers v. U.S.,* 272 U.S. 52 (1926).

87. 67 U.S. at 669.

88. *The Prize Cases,* 67 U.S. 635, 670 (1863) (emphasis original). *See also Martin v. Mott,* 25 U.S. (12 Wheat.) 19, 30 (1827).

89. *See* Chapter 3.

90. 25 U.S. (12 Wheat.) 19, 32 (1827).

91. *See* C. WEINBERGER, FIGHTING FOR PEACE 188 (1990) (describing evidence against Qaddafi as a "smoking gun").

92. *Martin v. Mott,* 25 U.S. (12 Wheat.) 19, 32–33 (1827).

93. *The Prize Cases,* 67 U.S. 635, 668–670 (1863).

94. U.S. CONST., Art. I, Sec. 8.

95. *See, e.g.,* Defense Procurement Authorization Act, P.L. 91-121, 83 Stat. 204 (1969); Defense Appropriations Act, P.L. 91-171, 83 Stat. 469 (1969); Foreign Military Sales Act Extension, P.L. 91-672, 84 Stat. 2053 (1970); Supplemental Foreign Aid Authorization Act, P.L. 91-652, 84 Stat. 1942 (1971); Defense Procurement Act, P.L. 91-441, 84 Stat. 905 (1970); Supplemental Appropriations Act, 87 Stat. 134 (1973).

96. U.S. CONST., Art. II, Sec. 4.

97. Van Alstyne, "Congress, the President, and the Power to Declare War: A Requiem for Vietnam," 121 U. PA. L. REV. 1, 5 (1972).

98. II RECORDS at 319.

99. 343 U.S. 579 (1952). For further discussion, *see* Chapter 2.

100. *E.g.,* WOODWARD at 444. *See also id.* at 94–97, 184–186, 363–368, 409–412, 417 (planning against Qaddafi prior to 1986).

101. This is the problem the War Powers Resolution was intended to solve. However, the War Powers Resolution's only pre-conflict requirement on the

President is "consultation" with Congress. *See* Hall, "War Powers By The Clock," 113 U.S. Naval Institute PROCEEDINGS 36 (1987).

102. Letters of Helvidius (1793), 6 THE WRITINGS OF JAMES MADISON 138, 174 (G. Hunt, ed., 1906).

103. 25 U.S. at 32–33.

104. 25 U.S. at 32–33.

105. *The Prize Cases,* 67 U.S. at 668–670.

106. *The Prize Cases,* 67 U.S. 635 (1863).

107. *See, e.g.,* Watkins, "The Maritime Strategy," U.S. Naval Institute PRO-CEEDINGS, Supplement (January 1986); "Maritime Strategy: Sea Power in a Changing World," AVIATION WEEK AND SPACE TECHNOLOGY 38–54 (February 27, 1989); J. LEHMAN, COMMAND OF THE SEAS: A PERSONAL STORY (1988).

108. 50 U.S.C. §§ 1541–1548. *See* Chapter 4.

109. *See* C. WEINBERGER, FIGHTING FOR PEACE 193 (1990).

110. U.S. CONST., Art. II, Sec. 2, Cls. 1 and 2.

111. R. TURNER, THE WAR POWERS RESOLUTION: ITS IMPLEMEN-TATION IN THEORY AND PRACTICE 62 (1983). Such short notice would not have satisfied the late Senator Jacob Javits, the WPR's chief Senate sponsor. *Id.* at 54.

112. *Id.* at 55–56.

113. *E.g., Ex parte Milligan,* 71 U.S. (4 Wall.) 139 (1866).

114. Letter to the Speaker of the House of Representatives and the President Pro Tempore of the Senate on the Gulf of Sidra Incident, March 26, 1986, I PUBLIC PAPERS OF THE PRESIDENTS OF THE UNITED STATES: RONALD REAGAN, 1986 at 406–407 (1988).

115. Letter to the Speaker of the House of Representatives and the President Pro Tempore of the Senate on the United States Air Strike Against Libya, April 16, 1986, I PUBLIC PAPERS OF THE PRESIDENTS OF THE UNITED STATES: RONALD REAGAN, 1986 at 478 (1988).

116. *Id.*

117. The same argument can be made with respect to the hostilities in the Gulf of Sidra on March 24, 1986.

118. 50 U.S.C. § 1544(a)(1).

8

Persian Gulf, 1987–1988

The U.S. Middle East Task Force

The Iran-Iraq war began in September of 1980. In the eight years that followed, as many as 1,000,000 casualties were suffered by both sides. In 1984, Iraq commenced attacks against Iranian-owned, Iranian-flagged, or Iranian-leased vessels, particularly oil tankers, in the Persian Gulf. Iran responded by attacking all non-Iranian shipping in the Gulf.[1] The Senate Committee on Foreign Relations reported that, from January 1981 to March 1987, 314 ships had been attacked by Iran or Iraq in the Persian Gulf. By the end of 1988, the total was 539.[2] Attacks on merchant shipping were significant not only to the belligerents (Iran exports almost all of its oil by tanker) but also to the United States and its allies.[3]

In September of 1986, Iran began attacking Kuwait's shipping and territory in response to Kuwaiti support for Iraq.[4] On November 1, 1986, Kuwait announced to the Gulf Cooperation Council its intention to seek protection from attacks on its merchant fleet. On January 13, 1987, Kuwait requested U.S. protection for Kuwaiti vessels, which would fly the U.S. flag.[5] Kuwait advised the U.S. at that time that it had already received an offer of protection from the Soviet Union. On March 7, 1987, the U.S. offered protection to eleven Kuwaiti tankers reflagged under U.S. registry.[6] This offer was accepted by Kuwait on April 2, 1987. Thus did eleven Kuwaiti ships come under the protection of the U.S. Middle East Force, which had provided protection to U.S.-flagged vessels in the Persian Gulf since 1949.[7]

Assistant Secretary of State for Near Eastern and South Asian Affairs Richard W. Murphy told the Senate Committee on Foreign Relations:

> In the context of these developments, Kuwait asked to register a number of ships in its tanker fleet under the U.S. flag. We informed Kuwait that if the vessels in question met ownership and other technical requirements under U.S. laws and regulations, they could be registered under the U.S.

U.S. Government Publication

flag. This is in accordance with our established position on qualifications for U.S.-flagged registration of commercial vessels in general. We also informed the Kuwaiti that by virtue of the fact that these vessels would fly the American flag, they would receive the U.S. Navy protection given any U.S.-flagged vessel transiting the gulf. The U.S. Navy has always had the mission to provide appropriate protection for U.S. commercial shipping world-wide within the limits of available resources and consistent with international law.[8]

Secretary of Defense Caspar W. Weinberger summarized the purpose of the reflagging operation, named Operation Earnest Will, in terms of reducing Soviet influence in the Persian Gulf region and reducing "Iran's ability to gain effective dominance over navigation and energy resources in the . . . Gulf. . . ."[9]

Secretary Weinberger offered the following description of U.S. interests in the Persian Gulf, by way of justifying the reflagging operation.

There is no basic dispute about American interests in the Persian Gulf. This area is vital to the United States for three reasons:

- Because of western dependence on Gulf oil, we have a significant interest in limiting the Soviet Union's influence in the region, which is also an area of great strategic interest to the Soviets because of its enormous economic potential and its location near Soviet borders (and Afghanistan).
- The security and stability of the moderate states of the area are important to our political and economic goals; we have a major interest in standing by our friends in the Gulf, because of their importance in their own right, because of their influence in the Gulf and beyond, and because of the profoundly negative impact in the Gulf and elsewhere of a U.S. withdrawal or refusal to meet its commitments any longer.
- The unimpeded flow of oil through the Gulf is critical to [the] economic health of the western world, and we have an important stake in non-belligerent freedom of navigation there; we have a vital economic stake in seeing that this supply of oil continues, given Western reliance upon Gulf oil imports, the overwhelming proportion of world oil reserves held by the Gulf countries, and the deep and growing interdependence of Western economies.[10]

On April 4, 1987, Secretary Weinberger directed the Navy to increase its Persian Gulf strength. The Navy extended the U.S.S. *Kitty Hawk's* deployment by three months and determined that a carrier battle group would be on station near the Gulf at all times.

On May 17, 1987, the frigate U.S.S. *Stark* was on patrol in international waters in the Persian Gulf, about 85 miles northeast of Bahrain.[11] The *Stark* is a *Perry*-class frigate equipped to defend against cruise missile attack with Standard missiles, MK-75 76mm guns, SLQ-32 radar, chaff dispensers, and a Phalanx antimissile system for close-range defense.[12] At about 8 p.m. local, an Iraqi F-1 Mirage fighter took off from Shaibah air base in Iraq. The Mirage was tracked by a joint U.S./Saudi Airborne Warning and Control System ("AWACS") aircraft. The Mirage proceeded south along the Saudi coast and then suddenly proceeded east, toward the *Stark*. The *Stark* tracked the Mirage's southerly progress and noted its eastward turn. Shortly after 9:00 p.m. local, the Mirage was proceeding toward the *Stark* at 5,000 feet at 550 m.p.h. The Mirage's air-intercept radar locked on the *Stark* for several seconds.[13] The *Stark* broadcasted: "Unknown aircraft this is U.S. Navy warship on your 078, for 12 miles, request you identify yourself, over."[14] The Mirage did not respond. By the time of this first broadcast, the Mirage had already fired on the

Stark.[15] The *Stark* broadcasted a second warning: "Unknown aircraft, this is U.S. Navy warship on your 076 at 12 miles, request you identify yourself and state your intentions, over."[16]

At about 32.5 nautical miles range from the *Stark,* the Mirage turned east toward the *Stark,* then circled back toward Iraq.[17] The *Stark* did not detect the launch of two Exocet AM39 air-to-surface missiles. The first Exocet was fired 22.5 nautical miles and the second 15.5 nautical miles from the *Stark*.[18] The *Stark,* not considering the Mirage a threat, did not arm its Super Rapid Blooming Offboard Chaff (SRBOC) system until seconds before the first Exocet hit. Therefore, the SRBOC did not dispense any chaff to "confuse" the Exocets. The MK-15 Phalanx Close In Weapon System (CIWS) (an antimissile Gatling gun) and the MK-92 STIP fire control radar were in stand-by mode. The *Stark's* fire control radar did not lock on the Mirage prior to the impact of the first missile.[19] The *Stark* never fired in its own defense or in retaliation for the attack.[20]

The *Stark's* first confirmation of an inbound missile came from a topside look-out.[21] The first Exocet missile struck the *Stark's* port side above the water line and travelled into the crew's quarters, spraying flaming fuel through the ship's interior. Many crewmembers died in their bunks. The second missile struck about thirty seconds later.[22] Only one of the two warheads detonated, but the effect was disastrous. The ship's aluminum frame superheated and ignited, spreading flames and toxic gas through the ship. Thirty-seven sailors died.

Iraq's President, Saddam Hussein, admitted Iraqi responsibility for the attack and stated, "I hope this unintentional accident will not affect relations between Iraq and the United States of America." President Reagan interpreted this statement as an apology.[23] Assistant Secretary of State Richard W. Murphy testified before Congress that the Iraqi government had agreed to pay reparations for damages, including loss of life, resulting from the attack.[24]

The *Stark's* skipper, Captain Glenn Brindel, stated that all combat systems were operational, but that he had lacked the time to activate them. He interpreted the rules of engagement permitting him to fire on a target demonstrating "hostile intent" as limited to targets actually "shooting a weapon at you." Naval analyst Norman Polman remarked: "The problem was the unclear circumstances of the *Stark's* mission. The captain didn't know whether he was at war or peace."[25] The formal investigation into the attack on the *Stark* produced some harsh assessments. The investigators found that the "Persian Gulf was, on and prior to 17 May 87, a relatively uncomplicated air threat environment and STARK was, during the evolving action, confronted with a single air problem."[26] Nevertheless, the report identified serious lapses in the *Stark's* defenses that contributed to the tragedy.[27]

The day after the attack on the *Stark*, new rules of engagement were issued, permitting attacks on any Iranian or Iraqi aircraft approaching in a threatening manner.[28] Secretary of Defense Weinberger summarized the Persian Gulf rules of engagement as follows:

> The ROE [Rules of Engagement] provide authority to the on-scene commander to declare a threat hostile and engage that threat (i.e., a force demonstrating hostile intent or committing a hostile act) with all forces available to him in self-defense of his unit and U.S.-flagged vessels. Only that force which is required to neutralize the threat or prevent a hostile act is authorized. Further, any use of force beyond that used against the immediate threat or in response to a specific hostile act must be approved by the National Command Authority.[29]

No Iraqi aircraft were attacked under these rules of engagement, although on February 12, 1988, an Iraqi aircraft fired two missiles at the destroyer U.S.S. *Chandler*. Fortunately, they missed.[30] The rules of engagement remained unclear to some. A Pentagon official said to TIME magazine. "They need to tell us what they want us to do. Do you want us to shoot down planes that come too close? Do you want us to wait until we're attacked and then turn somebody to ashes?"[31] These questions would return to haunt the U.S. on July 3, 1988, when the U.S.S. *Vincennes* shot down an Iranian airliner.

The *Stark* incident prompted the following exchange of letters between Senator Claiborne Pell, Chairman of the Senate Committee on Foreign Relations, and the Department of State. Senator Pell wrote:

> Dear Mr. Secretary: I am writing to you with respect to the Administration's Persian Gulf policy and its War Powers implications.
>
> The facts that a U.S. naval vessel has been attacked by Iraqi aircraft and that, since September, 24 vessels serving Kuwaiti ports have been assaulted by Iranian aircraft vividly illustrate that U.S. troops are being placed in a situation "where imminent involvement in hostilities is clearly indicated by the circumstances." Moreover, the Administration has recently announced: (a) that it will protect Kuwaiti tankers and provide them with U.S. registration; and (b) that U.S. naval forces in the Gulf have been instructed to fire on all aircraft exhibiting hostile intent.
>
> These developments clearly activate the provisions of the War Powers Resolution. The Administration should take immediate steps to comply with the law and submit a report in accordance with Section 4(a)(1) of the War Powers Resolution. I would appreciate your response at the earliest possible date.

The Department of State replied:

Dear Mr. Chairman: I am responding to your letter dated May 21 to the Secretary concerning developments in the Persian Gulf and the provisions of the War Powers Resolution.

We are paying close attention to the question of the possible applicability of the War Powers Resolution to the situation in the Gulf and remain committed to full and continued consultation with the Congress. In our view, the War Powers Resolution is not applicable under present circumstances. This is not a situation where imminent involvement of U.S. Armed Forces in hostilities is clearly indicated by the circumstances. Prior to the attack on the U.S.S. Stark, there had never been an attack on a U.S. vessel in the Gulf, and the attack on the U.S.S. Stark was evidently the result of a targeting error rather than a deliberate decision to attack a U.S. vessel. The object of the escorting of the reflagged tankers will be to deter, not to encourage, hostile action. We do not believe that there is a basis for concluding at this time that "imminent involvement in hostilities is clearly indicated by the circumstances."

We will continue to keep the situation under active review from this standpoint and will continue to consult with the Congress on significant developments.[32]

This correspondence exemplifies the practical consequences of the sort of statutory ambiguity found in the WPR. The question unresolved by these letters (but discussed further in this chapter) is who resolves the ambiguity? As if to underscore this ambiguity, House Joint Resolution 295 was introduced on May 28, 1987.[33] It would have provided that the requirements of the WPR became operative as a result of the attack on the U.S.S. *Stark*. Therefore, it sought to compel the withdrawal of U.S. forces from the Persian Gulf within sixty days of the enactment of the resolution by Congress. The resolution was never enacted.

In the aftermath of the *Stark* tragedy, President Reagan declared, "Mark this point well. The use of the vital sea lanes of the Persian Gulf will not be dictated by the Iranians. These lanes will not be allowed to come under the control of the Soviet Union. The Persian Gulf will remain open to navigation by the nations of the world."[34] The President, however, delayed implementation of the Kuwaiti reflagging operation.

By mid-June, when the President planned to commence the reflagging, both the House and Senate had considered resolutions opposing the reflagging policy, at least pending receipt of a report outlining the objectives and risks of the policy. On June 4, 1987, Senators Pell (D., RI), Hatfield (R., OR), and Cranston (D., CA) introduced Senate Bill 1327 to prohibit the reflagging of any vessel owned by a nation in the Persian Gulf or any "national of such a country."[35] The bill sought to prohibit the use of appropriated funds for the reflagging operation and to encourage a "United Nations Peacekeeping Force to protect nonbelligerent shipping."[36] Senate Bill 1327 was reported to the Senate with considerable amendment. The amended version contained a finding that the reflagging operation "could risk involving United States forces in the conflict between Iraq and Iran." The amended bill would have reaffirmed U.S. neutrality, encouraged diplomatic effort, particularly through the United Nations, and forbidden the use of federal funds to "implement" the reflagging operation. Senate Bill 1327 died on the Senate calendar.

On June 9, 1987, Senators Hatfield, Bumpers (D., AR), Pell, Harkin (D., IO), and Matsunaga (D., HI) introduced Senate Bill 1343[37] requiring that Persian Gulf operations comply with the War Powers Resolution ("WPR"). Senate Bill 1343 contained a finding that the reflagging operation "requires the transmittal to the Congress" of a WPR report and that the sixty-day "clock" would start 48 hours after commencing escort operations, whether or not a report was submitted. After amendment, the Committee on Foreign Relations, by a 10-to-9 vote, favorably reported Senate Bill 1343 to the full Senate.[38] Senate Bill 1343 also died on the Senate calendar.

On June 10, 1987, House Joint Resolution 310 was introduced.[39] It declared that the reflagging operation "constitutes the introduction of United States Armed Forces into hostilities or situations where imminent involvement in hostilities is clearly indicated by the circumstances. . . ." House Joint Resolution 310, therefore, sought the submission to Congress of a WPR report from the President. House Joint Resolution 310 died in the House Foreign Affairs Committee.

During the summer of 1987, 110 congressmen filed suit to compel the President's compliance with the WPR.[40] This suit, like the proposed bills and resolutions to invoke the WPR, did not result in a legal restraint on the President.

On July 21, 1987, the reflagging policy was finally implemented. Three days later, on July 24, 1987, a convoy composed of the U.S.-flagged Kuwaiti tankers *Bridgeton* and *Gas Prince,* the frigate U.S.S. *Crommelin,* the cruiser U.S.S. *Fox,* and the destroyer U.S.S. *Kidd* proceeded north about 18 miles west of Iran's Farsi Island. At 6:55 a.m., the *Bridgeton* hit a mine that had been placed in the sea lanes, according to Iranian Prime Minister Mir Hussein Mousavi, by "invisible hands."[41] The damage to the *Bridgeton* was reparable, and no members of her crew were injured. Secretary of Defense Weinberger said, "We did not look for mines in that area [of the Gulf] because there have never been any."[42]

The *Bridgeton* incident induced a controversy over the readiness of the Navy in the area of antimine warfare. Only three ocean-going minesweepers were on active duty, none in the Gulf. This compares with 125 minesweepers then employed in the Soviet Navy. Of course, because the U.S.

relies on NATO allies to provide minesweeping, it was not actually the case that Soviet minesweeping capabilities exceeded those available to the U.S. by a ratio of 125 to 3. The Navy was also criticized for failing to deploy minesweeping RH-53D Sea Stallion helicopters to the Gulf. When the Navy tried to ferry them to Saudi Arabia and Kuwait, the U.S. reportedly was unable to obtain landing rights.[43]

Another post-*Bridgeton* controversy was over the issue of retaliation. Former National Security Advisor Zbigniew Brzezinski said, "We should have pulverized Farsi Island. All this power cringing in the area is a terrible embarrassment."[44] Secretary Weinberger's reply: "[W]hoever laid the mines didn't leave fingerprints."[45] That is, the U.S. was not entirely certain who laid the mines, so was correspondingly uncertain of how to retaliate.

Tensions increased as Iran staged war games, named "Martyrdom," in the Gulf in early August. On August 10, a Navy F-14 Tomcat fired two Sea Sparrow missiles at two U.S.-made Iranian F-4 Phantom fighters. The Phantoms had flown a course from Iran toward a U.S. Navy P-3C ORION, a maritime patrol aircraft, which was escorted by F-14 Tomcat fighters. The Tomcat's missiles missed, and the Phantoms departed.[46] By mid-August, the Gulf's mine warfare had spread south to the Gulf of Oman where a cluster of mines was discovered on August 10, when the tanker *Texaco Caribbean* hit a mine eight miles from the port of Fujairah, United Arab Emirates. Ironically, the U.S.-owned, Panama-flagged *Texaco Caribbean* was loaded with Iranian oil. On August 24, the destroyer U.S.S. *Kidd* fired across the bows of two unidentified vessels approaching within two-and-a-half miles of Kuwaiti tankers under escort.[47]

On August 29, Iraq attacked the tanker *Alvand* as it loaded at Iran's Sirri Island. Iraq attacked other merchantmen, as well as Iran's oil terminal at Kharg Island. Iran responded by attacking neutral shipping en route to or from Kuwait and Saudi Arabia. In addition, Iran launched a Silkworm missile toward Kuwait. It splashed into the Gulf, short of its apparent target.

On September 21, U.S. forces attacked the Iranian naval landing craft *Iran Ajr*. The *Iran Ajr* had been suspected for at least a month of laying mines in the Gulf. Prior to the attack, Saudi AWACS aircraft and U.S. Navy P-3 aircraft monitored the progress of the *Iran Ajr* from the Iranian port of Bandar Abbas to a position in the shipping lane 50 miles northeast of Bahrain.[48] Rear Admiral Harold Bernsen, commander of the U.S. Joint Task Force Middle East, previously had obtained OH-6A Cayuse helicopters and crews from the U.S. Army. Based aboard the frigate U.S.S. *Jarrett*, the Army helicopters were equipped with infrared optical equipment for night operations. Admiral Bernsen, aboard the flagship U.S.S. *LaSalle*, ordered two of the Army helicopters to observe the *Iran*

Ajr. Hovering 500 yards abeam, at least one of the helicopters observed crewmen on the deck "dropping objects overboard which appear to be mines."[49] The area in which the *Iran Ajr* was observed dropping objects overboard was an anchorage for the merchant and naval vessels of the U.S. and other neutrals. Admiral Bernsen ordered the two Army helicopters to fire their rockets and 7.62mm Gatling guns. The *Iran Ajr* was left disabled and afire.

At dawn on September 22, SEALS from the Navy amphibious assault ship U.S.S. *Guadalcanal* boarded the *Iran Ajr* and found three bodies. The SEALS determined that the *Iran Ajr* had been manned by Iranian Navy regulars.[50] They also found nine mines, seven of which were live. Six mines had been placed in the water. The *Jarrett* recovered twenty-six Iranian sailors adrift on rafts or flotsam. They were later released in Oman to the International Red Crescent. Following examination and documentation of her cargo, the *Iran Ajr* was scuttled.[51] President Reagan justified the military action in terms of self-defense.

> The actions taken by U.S. forces were conducted in the exercise of our right of self-defense under Article 51 of the United Nations Charter. Mining of the high seas, without notice and in an area of restricted navigation, is unlawful and a serious threat to world public order and the safety of international maritime commerce. These Iranian actions were taken despite warnings given to the Government of Iran, subsequent to the recent mine damage done to the U.S.-flag vessel BRIDGETON, that the U.S. Government would take the action necessary to defend U.S. vessels from attacks of this nature.[52]

The President used the occasion of his announcement of the military operation to reiterate U.S. objectives in the Persian Gulf.

> [W]e must continue steadily to pursue our established, three-part policy in the Gulf:
>
> 1. Bringing ever-increasing international pressure to bear for a negotiated end to the war and to stop its spillover;
> 2. Steadfastly continuing to help our friends, the nonbelligerent nations of the Gulf, to defend themselves against Iranian threats; and
> 3. Prudently pursuing cooperative efforts with the Gulf Cooperation Council (GCC) States and other friends to protect U.S.-flag ships and to prevent Iran from seriously jeopardizing freedom of nonbelligerent navigation.[53]

Iran claimed that the *Iran Ajr* was an unarmed merchant ship carrying a cargo of foodstuffs. Secretary Weinberger replied, with the confidence of one armed with photographs and other incriminating evidence recovered from the *Iran Ajr,* "These things certainly weren't fruits and vegetables."[54] Some congressmen renewed their claim that the President had violated the WPR by using the military in the Persian Gulf. Democrats in the Senate drafted an appropriations bill amendment, never implemented, to end financing of naval operations in the Persian Gulf after 90 days.[55] The President attacked the proposal in September of 1987, warning of "disastrous effects for the U.S. commitment to the Persian Gulf and to our strategic interests in keeping those waters safe for navigation."[56]

On October 8, 1987, a force of 60 Iranian gunboats proceeded from Kharg Island toward Khafji, an oil facility 110 miles away operated jointly by Saudi Arabia and Kuwait. Saudi aircraft overflew the Iranian gunboats, inducing their return to Iran.[57] Later that day, at least one helicopter flying a "routine patrol"[58] observed a Corvette-class attack craft and three small gunboats, all armed, about 15 miles southwest of Farsi Island.[59] At 9:50 p.m. local time, the Iranian boats opened fire on the U.S. aircraft. Two or three U.S. AH-6 helicopters, armed with 7.62mm Gatling guns and 2.75-inch rocket launchers and equipped with infrared scopes, responded and attacked the Iranian vessels. The Corvette escaped,[60] but one to three gunboats were sunk.[61] The incident encouraged the President's critics in Congress to demand invocation of the WPR. Representative Dante Fascell (D., FL), Chairman of the House Foreign Affairs Committee, said, "Hostilities in the Persian Gulf can no longer be called imminent. We are in them."[62] Senator Paul Simon (D., IL) stated that "this conflict reads like a case study" for the WPR.[63]

On October 16, 1987, a missile, reportedly an Iranian Silkworm launched from the Fao Peninsula, north of the Gulf, struck the U.S.-flagged Kuwaiti tanker *Sea Isle City* in Kuwaiti waters. Eighteen crew members were injured, including her American captain, who was blinded. The attack followed by one day a similar attack in the same area against the U.S.-owned Liberian supertanker *Sungari.* No one aboard the *Sungari* was injured.[64]

On October 19, 1987, in response to these attacks, four destroyers, the U.S.S. *Kidd, Hoel, John Young,* and *Leftwich* approached the Rashadat oil platforms, 75 miles off Iran in the Persian Gulf. They transmitted the following message:

> Rashadat. Rashadat. This is the U.S. Navy. We will commence firing on your position at 1400 hours [2 p.m. local]. You have 20 minutes to evacuate the platform.[65]

The Iranians did not reply, but did evacuate. Then the destroyers sent over 1,000 rounds of five-inch shells into the platforms.

The Rashadat platforms, according to Secretary of Defense Weinberger, had not been used for oil loading since November of 1986. Since then, the Iranians had used the facility as a command, control, and communications ("C3") center.[66] Specifically, Secretary Weinberger said that Rashadat had been used "to mount radar surveillance, to report on convoy movements, and to launch small-boat attacks against non-belligerent shipping."[67] A U.S. Navy helicopter had reported taking antiaircraft fire from the platform on October 8, 1987.

Following the shelling, a Navy SEAL team boarded one platform to destroy its supporting pilings with explosives. Another SEAL team boarded a different platform five miles away to destroy C3 equipment. Iran retaliated by firing a Silkworm missile from the Fao Peninsula 50 miles to Kuwait's Sea Island oil loading facility. The missile struck its target, damaging loading docks but causing few injuries.

Chairman of the Joint Chiefs of Staff Admiral William Crowe told *Time* magazine that the U.S. had rejected the idea of attacking Iranian Silkworm sites in retaliation for the attack on the *Sea Isle City,* since Silkworm launchers are mobile. "All we'd do there [the Fao Peninsula] is kill a lot of date trees."[68] *Time* also reported that targets such as the Iranian bases at Farsi Island and Bandar Abbas were rejected for fear of inciting Congress to invoke the WPR.[69]

On October 21, 1987, the Senate passed Senate Joint Resolution 194.[70] The resolution was sent to the House on October 26, 1987, but died in the House Foreign Affairs and Rules Committees. Senate Joint Resolution 194 expressed the ambivalence of the Senate about the reflagging operation. On the one hand, the resolution stated that circumstances in the Persian Gulf, especially the September 21, October 8, and October 19, 1987 operations, justified a report from the President to Congress.[71] On the other hand, the resolution provided that nothing in the resolution "shall be construed as complying with, modifying or negating" the WPR.[72] On the one hand, the resolution expressed the Senate's "support for a continued United States presence in the Persian Gulf region and the right of nonbelligerent shipping to free passage in this region."[73] On the other hand, the resolution expressed the Senate's "reservations about the convoy and escort operations of United States naval vessels in connection with tankers registered under the United States flag."[74]

The resolution would have required a report from the President on the President's Persian Gulf policy. The resolution also would have provided for expedited consideration of the President's Persian Gulf policy, following receipt of the report. The Senate expressed in the resolution its approval of the October 19 Rashadat operation and noted that nothing in the resolution "should be construed as limiting the President's constitutional powers as Commander-in-Chief to utilize American military force in self-defense operations, or as urging the withdrawal of American military forces from the Persian Gulf region."[75] The resolution further recognized that "the United States, as a maritime power, has a preeminent interest in the freedom of the seas and in taking such actions as are necessary to maintain such freedom."[76]

On October 22, 1987, House Joint Resolution 387 was introduced into the House.[77] The purpose of the resolution was to provide specific authorization under the WPR for the "continued presence of the United States Armed Forces in the Persian Gulf,"[78] given a finding that the WPR became applicable to Persian Gulf operations on October 16, 1987, the date when the *Sea Isle City* was struck by a Silkworm missile.[79] Although the authorization to be granted the President was indefinite in term, the resolution would have required presidential reports at least every three months.[80] The resolution died in the House Foreign Affairs and Rules Committees.

Following the Rashadat operation was a period of calm in the Gulf. Even the Iran-Iraq war slowed in tempo. The *Economist* asked, "Has Iran abandoned that ritual of the Gulf war, its winter offensive against Iraq's second city, Basra?"[81] In February, 1988, the U.S.S. *Okinawa* left the Gulf and was not replaced. At about that time, the battleship U.S.S. *Iowa* departed the northern Arabian Sea. This left a naval force in the Gulf of "one command ship, one amphibious transport ship, eight major surface combatants (mostly . . . [*Perry*-class] frigates), six . . . [oceangoing minesweepers], roughly 14 smaller patrol craft (mostly Mk-III 65-foot patrol boats), and two or three mobile sea bases carrying Marines and special forces personnel."[82] At the same time, the carrier U.S.S. *Enterprise* and her battle group were operating in the northern Arabian Sea.[83]

In late February, 1988, Iraq resumed the "war of the cities" with missile strikes against Tehran. On March 5, 1988, the frigate U.S.S. *John A. Moore* fired on radar contacts identified as Iranian speed boats. The next evening, helicopters from the frigate U.S.S. *Simpson* reported taking machine gun fire from an oil platform and from patrol boats.[84] On March 19, Iraq struck Kharg Island's oil facility, prompting Iranian strikes against neutral shipping. In mid-March, Iran captured the Kurdish town of Halabja in northeastern Iraq. Days later, Iraq bombed the town with chemical weapons.

On April 14, 1988, the *Perry*-class frigate U.S.S. *Samuel B. Roberts* struck a 385-pound mine 65 miles east of Bahrain, wounding ten sailors. The *Roberts* was severely damaged with a nine-foot hole below the water line. Rear Admiral George N. Gee, Director of the Surface Combat Systems Division, said, "Her crew was able to save the ship and most knowledgeable people would say that we probably should have lost her."[85] The mine was identified as Iranian on the basis of information obtained from the *Iran Ajr* in September of 1987. The mine was determined to have been laid recently on the basis of the absence of marine growth on other Iranian mines located in the immediate area of the *Roberts*.[86] The Joint Task Force Middle East was directed to respond to the *Roberts* mining by sinking the Iranian *Saam*-class frigate *Sabalan* (or a similar surface target). If sinking a ship was not possible, U.S. forces were directed to attack two oil/gas separation platforms, Sasson and Sirri, used by Iran to provide C3 for antishipping operations.[87]

On April 18, 1988, naval forces commenced Operation "Praying Mantis" by broadcasting a radio warning in English, Farsi, and French to the Sasson platform: "You have five minutes to abandon the platform; I intend to destroy it at 0800."[88] Two tugs evacuated crew members. Five minutes later, the destroyers U.S.S. *Merrill* and U.S.S. *Lynde McCormick* fired airbursts with their five-inch guns. This induced the evacuation by tug of the remaining crew members. Next, while Cobra helicopter gunships delivered covering fire, U.S. Marines boarded the Sasson from helicopters. Two hours later, demolition teams destroyed the Sasson with 1,500 pounds of plastic explosive. At about the same time, the Sirri crew was advised to abandon the platform. Most crew members departed on a tug. The cruiser U.S.S. *Wainwright,* the frigate U.S.S. *Bagley,* and the frigate U.S.S. *Simpson* commenced firing. One round hit a compressed gas tank, igniting the platform, which was destroyed.[89]

Following the attacks on Sasson and Sirri, U.S. Navy surface action groups patrolled the area. The *Bagley's* LAMPS-I helicopter identified an approaching patrol boat as the Iranian Combattante-II-class *Joshan*. The surface action group commander sent a radio broadcast to the *Joshan:* "Stop your engines and abandon ship; I intend to sink you." In response, the *Joshan* fired a Harpoon missile. The *Bagley's* LAMPS launched chaff to "confuse" the Harpoon, which passed close aboard down the starboard side of the *Wainwright*. The *Wainwright* and the *Simpson* launched five SM-1 missiles and one Harpoon in response. The SM-1 missiles hit and the Harpoon missed. The listing *Joshan* was then sunk with five-inch and 76mm guns. During the attack on *Joshan,* an Iranian F-4 made a high-speed approach on the *Wainwright,* which fired SM-2 missiles. The F-4 was hit, but managed to land at Bandar Abbas.[90]

On the same day, armed Iranian Boghammar attack boats attacked the U.S. tug *Willi Tide,* a British merchant ship, and the *Scan Bay,* a U.S.-operated Panamanian oil barge. Two U.S. Navy A-6s from the U.S.S. *Enterprise* attacked the Boghammars with Rockeyes, sinking one and chasing the others to their base at Abu Musa Island, where they ran aground. The surface action group then detected the Iranian frigate *Sahand* proceeding in its direction at high speed. When an A-6 overflew the *Sahand* to confirm her identity, the *Sahand* fired her antiaircraft guns and infrared (IR) missiles. The A-6 defeated the IR missiles with flares and responded by launching a Harpoon missile, Skipper bombs, and a laser-guided bomb. The *Sahand* was left dead in the water and afire. The U.S.S. *Joseph Strauss* and one A-6 each launched a Harpoon missile on the burning *Sahand*. A-6s then launched Skipper, Walleye, and 1,000-pound bombs on the *Sahand,* which sank a few hours later.[91]

During the attack on *Sahand,* the flight of A-6s that had attacked the Boghammars was advised by the *Strauss* of the presence of a second *Saam*-class frigate, the *Sabalan*. The A-6s identified the *Sabalan* with forward-looking infrared radar and attacked it. The lead A-6 scored a direct hit, dropping a laser-guided MK-82 500-pound bomb down the *Sabalan's* stack. The *Sabalan* launched three IR surface-to-air missiles during the attack. The *Sabalan* was left dead in the water, Secretary of Defense Frank C. Carlucci having decided not to sink her.[92] She was towed back to Bandar Abbas by an Iranian vessel.

On April 29, 1988, the United States announced that the Navy would "respond to requests of assistance to neutral ships in distress in the Persian Gulf/Strait of Hormuz," in addition to U.S.-flagged ships.[93] Secretary of Defense Carlucci announced:

> Aid will be provided to friendly, innocent, neutral vessels flying a non-belligerent flag outside declared war-exclusion zones that are not carrying contraband or resisting legitimate visit and search by a Persian Gulf belligerent. Following a request from the vessel under attack, assistance will be rendered by a U.S. warship or aircraft if this unit is in the vicinity and its mission permits rendering such assistance.[94]

This represented a significant change in U.S. policy. In June of 1987, Secretary of Defense Weinberger had expressly denied any "American commitment to defend all non-belligerent shipping in the Persian Gulf."[95] On July 2, 1988, pursuant to the new policy, the frigate U.S.S. *Elmer Montgomery* responded to a distress call from a Danish tanker under attack by three Iranian speedboats. The *Montgomery* fired a warning shot. The speedboats departed, and no one was hurt.

The Iranians continued to suffer military setbacks in the Spring of 1988. In April, the Iraqis drove Iranian troops from the Fao Peninsula, loosening Iran's hold on the Shatt-al-Arab waterway. On May 25, Iraq expelled Iranian troops from the area of Shalamcheh, southeast of Basra. Iran had held this position for 18 months. Although Iran continued to hold Iraqi territory in Kurdistan and the Majnoon Islands in the Shatt-al-Arab waterway, Iraq's victory encouraged speculation about the possibility of a ceasefire, since Iraq had been unwilling to consider one while Iran was poised to seize Basra, its second largest city.

On the morning of July 3, 1988, the *Montgomery* observed seven Iranian gunboats approaching a Pakistani merchant vessel. A short time later, the *Montgomery* detected five to seven explosions from the north. A LAMPS-III helicopter from the cruiser U.S.S. *Vincennes,* which is equipped with the Aegis weapons system and electronically scanned SPY-1A radar, was vectored north to investigate. At 10:10 a.m. local, an Iranian gunboat fired on the helicopter.[96] The *Vincennes* and the *Montgomery* proceeded to the helicopter's position. En route, two Iranian gunboats turned toward and closed on the *Vincennes* and the *Montgomery*.[97] The *Vincennes* later discovered bullet damage on the starboard bow. At 10:43 a.m. local, the *Vincennes* and the *Montgomery* responded with five-inch guns, sinking two Iranian boats and damaging a third.[98] At approximately 10:47, Iran Air Flight 655, an Airbus 300, with 290 aboard, took off from the Bandar Abbas airport, which serves both military and civilian aircraft, flying toward the *Vincennes.* At 10:47 a.m., the *Vincennes'* AN/SPY-1A radar detected the Airbus and designated it "unidentified, assumed enemy."[99] The unidentified aircraft was broadcasting identification friend or foe ("IFF") in civilian Mode III. At 10:48 a.m., an officer aboard the *Vincennes* consulted an airline schedule, but matching the aircraft with a scheduled commercial flight was hampered by at least two facts: the Airbus took off 27 minutes late and Gulf time is one-half hour later than the time in Bandar Abbas.[100]

At 10:49 a.m., the *Vincennes* started to broadcast warnings over Military Air Distress ("MAD") channels. At 10:50 a.m., the *Vincennes* started to broadcast warnings over civilian International Air Distress ("IAD") channels. A total of five MAD and four IAD warnings were made.[101] Simultaneously, the *Vincennes* commenced radical maneuvers (thirty-degree rudder at thirty knots) as it continued to battle the Iranian gunboats.[102]

At about the same time, the Airbus was misidentified as an Iranian F-14 at a range of 30 miles.[103] The *Vincennes* mistakenly believed the target's transponder was broadcasting IFF in both civilian Mode III and military Mode II, thus confounding identification.[104] The radar "signature" was identified as that from an F-14 fighter.[105] This identification of an attacking F-14 seemed to be confirmed by the presence of an Iranian P-3 forty nautical miles away, flying a targeting profile.[106] However, the nearby frigate U.S.S. *Sides* did not receive any Mode II signal, only a Mode III signal. In fact, the Airbus was not broadcasting in Mode II.[107] It is possible the Mode II signal was transmitted by the P-3. Admiral William J. Crowe, Jr., Chairman of the Joint Chiefs of Staff, however, stated that these "errors or mistakes were not crucial to the fateful decision."[108]

At 10:51 a.m., the *Vincennes* requested and received permission to fire at the aircraft if it approached within 20 miles. Additional warnings were broadcasted on civilian and military channels: "Your identity is not known, your intentions are not clear. You are standing into danger and may be subject to U.S.N. defensive measures. Request you alter course immediately. . . ."[109] At 10:53 a.m., the *Vincennes'* tactical information coordinator informed the skipper, Captain William C. Rogers 3d, that the aircraft was descending, when it was actually ascending.[110] At 10:54 a.m., the aircraft was eight miles from the *Vincennes,* and the *Vincennes* fired two standard SM-2 surface-to-air missiles.[111] The Airbus was destroyed.

Naval analyst Norman Friedman summarized the factors leading to the decision to fire:

> The most important consideration was the expectation that the Iranians would mount a major attack on the "Great Satan," which they blamed for their misfortunes. All the pieces seemed to be present: the speedboats deployed to disrupt AAW cover; the targeting P-3; and the attacking F-14, which was clearly not transmitting so as to avoid alerting the target and which was flying along an airline corridor so that its intentions would be discovered only at the last possible moment. The potential for damage to the *Vincennes* was so great, given this context, that Captain Rogers had to react when he was told that the target was diving to attack.[112]

Dr. Friedman concluded that the misperception of a Mode II signal, which contributed to an incorrect identification of an F-14, was not critical because Captain Rogers could have perceived a threat from a correctly identified Airbus, broadcasting in Mode III, flying a possible suicide mission, loaded with high explosive rather than passengers.[113] The critical error was the tactical information coordinator's misreading of a console which indicated an ascending aircraft: his report to Captain Rogers of a descending aircraft with constant bearing and decreasing range fit the profile for an air attack.

Iran promised retaliation. "We will not leave the crimes of America unanswered. We will resist the plots of the Great Satan and avenge the blood of our martyrs from criminal mercenaries."[114] The Ayatollah Ruhollah Khomeini called for a "real war . . . against America and its lackeys."[115] Secretary of Defense Carlucci refused to rule out the possibility of escalation.[116]

On July 20, 1988, the Ayatollah Ruhollah Khomeini announced his acceptance of a ceasefire with Iraq.[117] On July 22, Iran and Iraq announced they would send their foreign ministers to the United Nations to negotiate a peace. The foreign ministers had been invited by the Secretary General of the United Nations to discuss the implementation of United Nations Resolution 598.[118] Resolution 598 was passed in July of 1987 and called for a ceasefire, exchange of prisoners, withdrawal of forces, peace talks, and a commission to investigate the cause of the war.

Also on July 22, Iraq announced a new offensive along the central border region between Iran and Iraq.[119] Diplomatic discussions were held through July and August of 1988, even as Iran and Iraq continued fighting along their border. On August 9, as prospects for an August 20 ceasefire improved, Secretary of Defense Carlucci suggested the possibility of a U.S. force reduction in the Persian Gulf following a ceasefire.[120] "If it appears that things have quieted down," he said, "we will revert to the normal posture that we've had in the Gulf, which is generally about five or six ships."[121] The same day, the Pentagon announced the arrival in Kuwait of the 54th convoy through the Gulf under U.S. escort.[122] On August 20, 1988, the ceasefire between Iran and Iraq went into effect.[123]

Gulf operations in 1987 required about $69 million in expenditures. In 1988, the cost was $116 million.[124] Of this $116 million, $100 million was appropriated by Congress for Gulf operations and $16 million was derived from reductions in other areas of the operating budget.[125] In addition to these expenses, Gulf operations led to other costs: $90 million to repair the *Stark*, $60–96 million to repair the *Roberts,* the loss of four helicopters (a SH-3 Sea King, UH-1 Huey, AH-1T Cobra, and SH-2 Seasprite) at several million dollars apiece, and the loss of one $45 million EA-6B aircraft. In addition, during a flight deck accident aboard the carrier U.S.S. *Nimitz,* six aircraft worth $200 million were destroyed or damaged: four A-6s, one EA-6B, and one KA-7 Corsair II tanker. The ultimate cost was the loss of 53 lives, 37 aboard the *Stark.*[126] From July 1987 through December 1988, the U.S. Navy escorted 259 ships through the Persian Gulf in 127 convoys.[127]

The U.S. Middle East Task Force and the U.S. Constitution

The President's decision to undertake the reflagging operation to protect Kuwaiti shipping must be examined from a perspective unlike that used to evaluate the constitutionality of the air strikes against Libya in 1986. Although the air strikes against Libya and the reflagging operation were strategically similar in that each sought to deter fanatical third world regimes from continuing hostility, the two military operations differed tactically. The air strikes against Libya were conducted during one day, whereas the Persian Gulf operations were conducted for well over a year.[128] Even counting the March 24, 1986 naval skirmish in the Gulf of Sidra, the Libya operation was much more brief than the Persian Gulf deployment.

Furthermore, the President undertook the air strikes against Libya with the specific intention of causing physical damage to predetermined targets in Libyan territory. By contrast, the mission of the naval forces in the Persian Gulf was to prevent damage from being inflicted upon neutral U.S.-flagged vessels. U.S. forces in the Persian Gulf undertook the defense of U.S.-flagged merchant shipping but were not directed initially to undertake any military activities beyond that plainly defensive scope. In short, while U.S. forces went to Libya intending to shoot, U.S. forces in the Persian Gulf hoped that their presence would discourage shooting.

As a result of these distinctions, the commencement of the reflagging operations did not raise the constitutional war powers issue in the way that the Libya air strikes did. Even the President's critics would admit that the President's decision to reflag Kuwaiti merchant ships was less provocative than his decision to execute an air strike against Libya. As time went on, however, events in the Persian Gulf gave rise to constitutional war powers questions. Indeed, in retrospect one might be tempted to look at the large number of violent exchanges between the United States and Iran during the Persian Gulf deployment and conclude that the United States and Iran were involved in an undeclared low intensity war. Under this retrospective view of the facts, the issue of constitutional war powers is presented in full bloom.[129]

The best place to begin is the beginning. When, on March 7, 1987, the President offered to protect Kuwaiti merchant vessels flying the U.S. flag, he did not do so as Commander-in-Chief of the United States. Rather, he did so pursuant to his power to conduct foreign affairs.[130] The President made a diplomatic commitment that could lead, as many diplomatic activities can, to the use of military force. Even diplomatic commitments requiring military action under certain circumstances (such as invasion by a common enemy) are undertaken pursuant to the President's foreign affairs powers, rather than the powers of the Commander-in-Chief. The first question, then, is whether the foreign affairs powers of the President can justify President Reagan's unilateral decision to reflag and protect Kuwaiti shipping.

The agreement with Kuwait was not a treaty but an executive diplomatic agreement.[131] The President, as the chief diplomatic agent of the United States, is empowered to act as the "sole organ" of the government.[132] This does not mean that the President's power to enter into executive agreements is coextensive with the Senate's treaty ratification power. Certainly, the more an executive agreement encroaches on domestic matters, the more likely it is to require Senate ratification.[133] An executive agreement involving the commitment of military forces abroad, however, is a prime example of the sort of executive agreement the President may enter unilaterally, particularly where Congress does not object.[134] Diplomatic arrangements involving the military might, of course, require appropriations, for which Congress is responsible. Although there were several efforts to muster a congressional objection to the reflagging policy, either through appropriations or otherwise, none was successful. The President was authorized, therefore, unilaterally to enter into the reflagging agreement with Kuwait.[135]

The military implications of the President's actions pursuant to his foreign affairs powers were manifested on May 17, 1987, when the *Stark* was struck by two Exocet missiles. The attack on the *Stark,* by emphasizing the Navy's role in the Persian Gulf, caused attention to be focused on the constitutional war powers issue. However, the *Stark* tragedy did not, of itself, raise the constitutional stakes of the President's decision to increase U.S. forces in the Persian Gulf. Indeed, as a legal (as opposed to political) matter, the attack on the *Stark* had no constitutional implications. By all accounts, the attack was an accident. So the tragedy was no more provocative from a constitutional point of view than any other operating accident at sea. Even if the attack had not been an accident, the *Stark* was not engaged in the employment of force at the time of the attack. Unlike U.S. forces in the Gulf of Sidra in 1986, U.S. forces in the Persian Gulf in 1987 were not seeking to inflict damage on anyone. The *Stark* was passively occupying a space in international waters into which two Exocet missiles were sent. So even if Iraq had meant to attack the *Stark,* the incident would not have formed the basis for a challenge to the President's war powers. The President's war powers apply to the President's deliberate use of military force, not to the use of force by other nations. The simple fact of the matter is that the *Stark* never fired a shot. Thus, while it is clear that the attack on *Stark* was tragic in human terms and provocative in diplomatic and political terms, the attack did not of itself provide the basis for a constitutional challenge to the President's decision to increase the naval presence in the Persian Gulf.

The *Stark* incident, of course, occurred before the President's reflagging policy was actually implemented. The actual implementation took place on July 21, 1987 when a convoy of U.S.-flagged Kuwaiti tankers proceeded up the Persian Gulf with a U.S. naval escort. One of these tankers, the *Bridgeton,* was damaged by a mine in the sea lanes. The attack on the *Bridgeton,* like the attack on the *Stark,* did not undermine the President's authority to use the Navy in the Persian Gulf.[136] Both the *Stark* and the *Bridgeton* were victims of military attacks, the former accidental and the latter intentional. But neither the *Stark* nor the *Bridgeton* (or its escorts) initiated any exercise of military force. Since neither incident was caused by the initiation of hostilities by U.S. forces, neither opened the door to a challenge of the President's war powers.

Incidents such as the attack on the *Stark* and the mining of the *Bridgeton* focus political attention dramatically. But constitutional issues do not appear and disappear as a function of political intensity. It is simply not the case that the issue of presidential war powers is determined by the success or failure of military activities. The President's constitutional authority to pursue the reflagging operation was not diminished by the attacks on *Stark* and *Bridgeton*.

The essentially passive nature of U.S. Persian Gulf activities ended on September 21, 1987, when U.S. forces attacked the Iranian naval landing craft, *Iran Ajr.* This operation was a deliberate response to the discovery of the minelaying activities by the *Iran Ajr.* Since military force was applied intentionally to cause physical damage to a military asset of a foreign power, the constitutional issue of presidential war powers was squarely presented by the attack. The central question raised by this use of force is whether the President undertook the action within the scope of his defensive powers.[137]

The critical fact about the *Iran Ajr* incident is that U.S. forces actually witnessed the Iranian ship mining shipping lanes. In light of the previous discovery by U.S. naval forces in the Persian Gulf of mines in the shipping lanes and the damage sustained by the *Bridgeton* and the *Texaco Caribbean,* the President had a reasonable basis for believing that these mines could damage U.S. ships, whether military or civilian. Thus it is clear that the President's actions were undertaken within the scope of his constitutional authority to protect U.S. property and citizens.

An inescapable ambiguity of mine warfare is that mines are not specifically targeted. Rather, they float or are moored in a particular area, waiting to damage any vessel coming within a critical proximity. To the extent that mine warfare is random in its targeting, it is not necessarily the case that the *Iran Ajr* sought to damage U.S. property in particular. However, nothing about the President's constitutional power to defend suggests that he should resolve such ambiguities against taking protective action. The President, as Commander-in-Chief, is empowered to undertake defensive military action he believes necessitated by the circumstances.[138] There is no requirement that such threatening circumstances be presented with certainty. Indeed, if anything, the inherent randomness of Iran's mining of the sea lanes enlarges rather constricts the President's power to defend by broadening the scope of the threat. The mining of sea lanes threatened a large number of U.S. ships, thereby providing the President a justification for undertaking prophylactic military measures.

Having detected Iran in the act of undertaking violent steps against vessels, including those of the United States, the President was authorized to use force both to prevent Iran's actions and to deter future actions. This conclusion follows *a fortiori* from the conclusion that the President was authorized to attack Libya. It will be remembered that the President had evidence in hand to suggest that Libya was involved in terrorist operations against United States citizens. The President, having caught the *Iran Ajr* in the act, had even better evidence against Iran on September 21.[139]

An even more obviously justified exercise of the President's power to defend occurred on October 8, when U.S. helicopters fired on Iranian gunboats which had attacked a U.S. helicopter on patrol. The President is authorized to allow U.S. forces to respond in kind to a military attack, if for no other reason than tactical self-defense. An argument could be made that by shadowing the Iranian gunboats, the helicopter provoked Iran's attack. But this argument is meritless since the attack took place in international waters and in international air space. The U.S. helicopter had a right to be where it was. Furthermore, the helicopter did not display hostile intent by flying an attack profile or launching weapons. There is nothing necessarily provocative about one nation's military forces observing the activities of another's.

The October 19, 1987 attack by U.S. naval forces against the Rashadat oil platforms should be viewed in a constitutional analysis as virtually identical to the April 14, 1986 air strikes against Libya.[140] The fact that the scale was smaller than the Libya air strikes is not relevant to the constitutional analysis. The October 19 operation, like the Libya air strikes, was not a tactical response necessitated by a sudden attack by hostile forces. Indeed, the U.S. waited three days before undertaking the operation in response to the Iranian Silkworm missile attack against the tanker *Sea Isle City*.

What the President did on October 19 was order a deliberate attack against Iranian C3 facilities to deter future attacks against U.S. property and to reduce the capability of Iran to attack shipping in the future. He did so on the basis of intelligence establishing Iranian responsibility for the attack on the *Sea Isle City* and his belief that future attacks against U.S.-flagged shipping were likely. He chose his target to reduce Iran's capability to attack neutral shipping. He did not attack a Silkworm site because, as Admiral Crowe explained, Silkworm launchers are mobile, so such attacks would yield little in the way of measurable military results. Thus does the operation fall into the constitutional category occupied by the Libya air strikes: a use of force by the President for the purposes of deterrence and reduced enemy capability to harm U.S. lives and property in the future.

Operation Praying Mantis, the April 18, 1988 attack by U.S. forces against two Iranian oil platforms, the Sasson and the Sirri, falls into the same category as the October 19, 1987 attack against the Rashadat oil platforms. The purpose of Operation Praying Mantis was to deter Iran's mining of sea lanes, which had caused the April 14, 1988 damage to the U.S.S. *Roberts.* One could argue that since the mining of the *Roberts* was not an act absolutely determined to have been caused by Iran and because of the essentially random nature of minelaying activity in general, the President lacked sufficient constitutional grounds for ordering the attacks against the Sasson and the Sirri. However, the determination that Iran was responsible for the mining of the *Roberts* was reasonable, having been based on data obtained from the *Iran Ajr.* In any case, the only nation known to be mining in the Persian Gulf was Iran, so the President's conclusion that Iran was responsible was almost certainly correct.[141]

In retaliation for the attack against the Sasson and the Sirri, Iran launched a naval attack against U.S. naval forces. In response, U.S. forces sunk one Iranian frigate, disabled a second frigate, and sank one Iranian patrol boat. This use of force belongs to the category easiest to justify in constitutional terms: the use of force to repel an ongoing enemy attack against U.S. military personnel. No one seriously questions the President's constitutional authority to allow a response to such attacks. Critics might, however, suggest that the defensive military action was unlawful because it was provoked by U.S. attacks on the Sasson and the Sirri. This argument does not take the critics very far. If their characterization is assumed to be correct, then the constitutional validity of the naval engagement depends on the constitutional validity of Operation Praying Mantis. However, as already shown, Operation Praying Mantis was undertaken by the President within the scope of his constitutional authority.

On July 3, 1988, an Iranian gunboat fired on a U.S. Navy helicopter, inducing an exchange of naval gunfire that left two Iranian boats sunk and a third damaged. The skirmish also led to the destruction by the U.S.S. *Vincennes* of an Iranian Airbus. The *Vincennes* incident should be examined from two perspectives in a constitutional analysis. Under the first perspective, the fact that the Airbus was a civilian airliner apparently not involved in any military activity is eliminated, for a moment, from consideration. Net of that fact, the incident can be analyzed as if the *Vincennes* had shot down an Iranian military aircraft during an ongoing military engagement. Under this version of the facts, the constitutional analysis would produce the conclusion that the use of force was justified. In such a circumstance, the *Vincennes* would be viewed as having eliminated a perceived threat at a time of ongoing hostilities, an action plainly within the scope of presidential power.

The only ambiguity created by this reconstruction of the facts is the aircraft's manifestation of hostile intent. The aircraft was closing on the

Vincennes at a high rate of speed. The *Vincennes* made two key identification errors: she mistakenly detected a broadcast from the Airbus of a military Mode II signal and she mistakenly perceived that the aircraft was descending in attack profile when it was, in fact, ascending. These errors do not undermine the President's constitutional authority. Tactical decisions by on-scene commanders may be good or bad: the constitutional issue is whether the President is authorized to allow such decisions to be made. In the context of an ongoing attack by military forces against the U.S., the answer clearly is that the President may allow a military response, even a bad one.

Under the second perspective, the fact that the Airbus was full of civilians is reintroduced, but does not alter the conclusion of the constitutional analysis. Like the attack on the *Stark,* the attack on the Airbus produced a result terrible in human terms but unrelated to any constitutional war powers issue. The constitutional war powers of the President are only invoked when the President undertakes a purposeful, deliberate, and intentional action. One could argue that whenever the President undertakes an activity that can lead to accidents of the kind experienced by the *Stark* and the Airbus, the President's war powers should be challenged. Such an argument, however, proves too much: any time the President deploys U.S. forces, an accident can occur that will lead to loss of life, whether American or not. The fact of an accident does not affect the underlying constitutionality of a presidential order to deploy forces. If a President deploys forces in violation of the Constitution, then his action is unconstitutional even if the deployment is successful. Conversely, when the President is authorized to use force, an unfavorable outcome does not act retroactively to eliminate the constitutional authority. Critics raising this issue, once again, confuse the issue of whether the President's actions are constitutional and the question of whether they are wise.

The U.S. Middle East Task Force and the War Powers Resolution

Throughout the Persian Gulf deployment, some members of Congress argued for the application of the War Powers Resolution ("WPR") to restrain the President.[142] In addition, Representative Neal (D., NC) introduced in the House a resolution proposing amendments to the WPR, "to make rules governing certain uses of the Armed Forces of the United States in the absence of a declaration of war by the Congress."[143] The resolution apparently was drafted with the Persian Gulf in mind, for it limited the President's unilateral use of armed force to four situations: (1) to "repel an attack on the United States" (including preemption of and retaliation for such attacks); (2) to repel attacks on U.S. forces outside the United States (including preemption and retaliation); (3) to protect U.S. citizens during evacuations abroad; and (4) pursuant to statutory authority.[144] The resolution would not have authorized presidential war-making in other circumstances, such as freedom of navigation operations in the Persian Gulf. Indeed, the resolution would not have authorized the preemption of terrorist attacks, which lies within the scope of presidential authority. Thus did the resolution illustrate the difficulty of *a priori* statutory specification of the circumstances under which the President may wage war.

Even under the circumstances where the resolution would have allowed the President to use force, the President would have been limited to thirty days of unilateral action.[145] This, of course, would have represented a reduction from the sixty days allowed by the WPR. More importantly, the thirty-day limitation ostensibly would have applied to situations where the President is plainly authorized by the Constitution to act unilaterally. So, the proposed amendment of the WPR sought to amend the Constitution by a majority vote of Congress. The proposal would have also allowed Congress to terminate presidential action within the thirty-day period or to authorize action beyond thirty days. The resolution also proposed the prohibition of any appropriation or treaty from being interpreted as implicit authorization for presidential war-making.[146] The resolution was passed by the House but was not sent to the Senate.

The threshold issue raised by congressional demands for the invocation of the WPR was whether the President's decision to offer naval escorts to reflagged Kuwaiti merchant shipping activated the terms of the WPR. Under WPR Section 3, the President must consult with Congress before introducing U.S. forces into "hostilities or into situations where imminent involvement in hostilities is clearly indicated by the circumstances."[147] The President's critics argued that the Persian Gulf was a war zone and that, therefore, the circumstances clearly indicated imminent hostilities.[148] However, it was not necessarily clear in early 1987 that hostilities involving U.S. forces were "imminent," even though hostilities between Iran and Iraq were ongoing. In June of 1987, after the *Stark* attack, Secretary of Defense Weinberger described the "risks to U.S. naval forces in the Gulf" as "low."[149] The United States was not a belligerent in the Iran-Iraq war; indeed, the United States was a declared neutral and thus was entitled to free navigation of international waters. The only purpose served by the naval escort was to protect neutral U.S.-flagged merchant shipping. That purpose is defensive and not inherently provocative.

The other flaw in the critics' argument is that, even accepting that the Persian Gulf situation could have been described in 1987 as presenting imminent hostilities, the circumstances did not present this indication "clearly," as required by the WPR. Since the purpose of the reflagging operation was to deter violence, optimists would argue that the U.S.

presence in the Persian Gulf reduced the likelihood of hostilities. Thus imminent hostilities were not clearly indicated, under an optimistic interpretation of the facts. When Congress required in the WPR that imminent hostilities be "clearly" indicated, it did not do so idly. The word "clearly" means something: what it means is that consultation is not required when hostilities are a mere possibility. The WPR does not require that the President be a pessimist.

The reporting requirement of WPR Section 4[150] was also inapplicable to the President's decision to reflag and escort Kuwaiti vessels. A report is required whenever consultation is required, but as we have seen, consultation was not required. A report is also required when U.S. forces are introduced into foreign territory, including territorial waters or airspace, "while equipped for combat."[151] However, the naval escorts were limited to international waters. Therefore, by the plain language of Section 4, a report was not required. The WPR does not express more than it says: the WPR simply does not apply to the President's decision to increase the size of the U.S. naval presence or increase the tempo of naval operations in international waters. Since the reporting requirement did not apply, the President's decision to increase the size of the naval force operating in the Persian Gulf did not cause the sixty-day "clock"[152] to start running. No possibility of automatic termination loomed as the convoy escort operation commenced.

When the *Stark* was attacked on May 17, the debate about the applicability of the WPR intensified. Senator Pell argued in his May 21, 1987 letter to Secretary of State George P. Shultz that the attack on the *Stark* was proof of the presence in the Gulf of imminent hostilities. Senator Pell was asking, essentially, what more proof do you want? Hostilities are not only imminent, they are present and 37 sailors are dead as a result. The Department of State disagreed with Senator Pell's interpretation of the WPR and had the better part of the legal debate. The Department of State argued correctly that the attack on the *Stark* was not an act of hostility against the United States. Rather, it was an accident. The Secretary of Defense summarized the situation succinctly:

> There is at this time, no clear indication of imminent involvement of our forces in hostilities. Prior to the attack on the USS STARK, there had been no attack on U.S. vessels in the Gulf. The attack on the USS STARK was apparently the result of an error in targeting, and not the result of any decision by Iraqi forces to attack U.S. vessels. We have no reason to believe that such an attack will be repeated. The objective of our Naval presence will be to deter, not encourage, hostile action.[153]

The fact that U.S. sailors aboard a man-of-war were killed by a missile fired by a foreign nation did not suggest the presence of imminent hostilities because the missile was fired in error. As terrible as the accident was, it did not suggest that the United States and Iraq necessarily had been or were about to become involved in hostilities.

The existence of a war between Iran and Iraq suggested the possibility of imminent danger to U.S. forces operating in the Persian Gulf. The presence of danger was proved by the *Stark* incident and by the July 21 mining of the *Bridgeton*. Each of these incidents induced members of Congress to demand presidential compliance with the WPR.[154] However, if the WPR was designed to require the President to consult and report whenever U.S. forces were involved in dangerous activities, it would have said so. If it had said so, the WPR's consulting and reporting requirements would have exceeded the statement of its purpose and policy in WPR Section 2.[155] Naval deployments are always dangerous, even when nominally routine. The WPR does not apply to all such naval deployments. The word chosen by Congress in enacting the WPR was "hostilities," not "danger." Imminent hostilities were not clearly indicated by virtue of the attack on the *Stark*. Therefore, the President was not required to report to Congress on the Middle East Task Force either before or after the *Stark* attack.

On May 28, 1987, House Joint Resolution 295 was introduced to invoke the WPR.[156] On June 4, 1987, Senators Pell, Hatfield, and Cranston introduced a bill to prohibit the U.S. reflagging operation.[157] A few days later, on June 9, Senators Hatfield, Bumpers, Pell, Harkin, and Matsunaga introduced a bill to apply the WPR to the Persian Gulf operations.[158] On June 10, 1987, House Joint Resolution 310 was introduced to invoke the WPR.[159] The House passed House Resolution 508 on August 8, 1988, but never sent it to the Senate. On October 21, 1987, the Senate passed Senate Joint Resolution 194, which would have required a WPR report.[160] On October 22, 1987, House Joint Resolution 387 was introduced to apply the WPR to Persian Gulf operations.[161] None of these resolutions was enacted. There were other proposals as well. The amount of legislative activity on the war powers issue was significant.

As already discussed, the WPR, by its own terms, did not apply to the President's decision to increase naval forces in the Persian Gulf. But more importantly, the legislative activities following the *Stark* attack showed how the existence of the WPR served to confuse the policy debate over the wisdom of the Persian Gulf operation. The debate over the procedural requirements of the WPR tended to obscure the substantive debate over the wisdom of the reflagging policy itself. The reflagging operation raised a number of serious questions, not the least of which was whether it would eventually lead the United States into a war with Iran or Iraq. The legal war powers debate did not inform any of the substantive issues raised by the reflagging operation. Therefore, even if the legal debate over the war powers had yielded a resolution of the inter-branch dispute over war powers, it would not have contributed to a resolution of the differences between the President and members of Congress concerning the President's policy in the Persian Gulf.

The procedural details of the WPR are easier to debate than the merits of the policy. The debate over the President's compliance with the WPR involved arguments about the meaning of "imminent hostilities" and other statutory terminology. By contrast, the debate on the wisdom of the reflagging operation involved much broader issues of international law, the capabilities of U.S. forces, military threats in the Persian Gulf, and the strategic implications of using a "blue water" navy to conduct what some believed to be "brown water" operations. The debate on the merits was rich with variety and important issues. Reasonable and capable minds differed sharply over the President's wisdom. Even the Secretary of the Navy objected to the operation.[162] The debate on the WPR tended to divert attention from issues of geopolitical substance toward issues of legal procedure.

The September 21 attack against the *Iran Ajr* raised anew the question of the applicability of the WPR to the Persian Gulf. There is no doubt but that U.S. forces were involved in "hostilities" when they fired on the *Iran Ajr*. Even so, the President was not required to consult. The consultation requirement of the WPR is limited to "every possible instance" where consultation can be undertaken before hostilities. Clearly, the circumstance of suddenly discovering the *Iran Ajr* laying mines in the sea lanes precluded any such consultation. The President is not required, even by the terms of the WPR, to delay a military response while he consults with Congress.

The next question is whether the WPR required a report on the *Iran Ajr* attack. In fact, the President did report to Congress on the *Iran Ajr* incident.[163] In this communication, the President made reference to his unilateral power to conduct such operations even as he adopted a tone of conciliation with Congress.

> These limited defensive actions have been taken by our Armed Forces in accordance with international law, and pursuant to my constitutional authority with respect to the conduct of foreign relations and as Commander-in-Chief. While being mindful of the historical differences between the Legislative and Executive Branches of government, and the positions taken by all of my predecessors in office, with respect to the interpretation and constitutionality of certain of the provisions of the War Powers Resolution, I nonetheless am providing this report in a spirit of mutual cooperation toward a common goal.[164]

Thus did the President seek to calm the inter-branch dispute on war powers, while staking his claim to unilateral authority in the Persian Gulf. The President reported to Congress, but did not concede that he was required to do so.

One could argue that the meaning of "hostilities" in the WPR is limited to continuing hostilities, not isolated hostile incidents. Under this interpretation, no report was required because the military action against the *Iran Ajr* did not lead to continuing hostilities. While there might be merit to this argument, it is not worth pursuing because the operational consequences of the WPR report were nil. That is, although a WPR report would have started the sixty-day "clock," the clock would have stopped when the use of force terminated; that is, when the *Iran Ajr* was in U.S. hands (or, at the latest, when she was scuttled). Therefore, the automatic-termination provision would not have restricted the President.

Had the President wished to make an issue of the WPR report, he could have refused to comply, thereby raising a constitutional issue about Congress' authority to require a report.[165] If the report was required so that Congress could participate in the President's command of the armed forces, then Congress clearly was acting beyond the scope of its constitutional authority. Congress may not involve itself in the President's command decisions. The President, as Commander-in-Chief, has been granted the power to use force for defensive purposes.[166] The President (as represented by the Joint Task Force Middle East) was constitutionally authorized to fire on the *Iran Ajr*. Congress may not impair this authority by statute. This not to say, however, that Congress could not have required a report from the President eventually. Congress might be able to require a report as a condition to the exercise by Congress of a legitimate constitutional power, such as appropriations.[167]

Like the *Iran Ajr* attack, the October 8, 1987 engagement between U.S. forces and Iranian naval vessels developed too quickly for the President to consult with Congress. But the action was clearly hostile, ostensibly requiring a WPR report to Congress. But, once again, the WPR's requirement that the President report within 48 hours is constitutionally problematic. Congress' demand that the President submit a report within 48 hours of a military activity undertaken for self-defense against an unprovoked and sudden attack could interfere with the President's command of the armed forces. Congress in such a circumstance might not be participating in policy-making so much as in the President's command decision to use force to repel a sudden attack. The President's power to use the military for this purpose is unquestionably unilateral.

This conclusion, of course, does not inform the distinct question of whether the President would be wise, as a political matter, to inform

Congress formally that U.S. forces had been engaged in hostilities. The President apparently believed that, although he was not constitutionally required to submit a report, he was well advised to do so for political reasons.[168] He sought to split the difference by submitting a report "consistent with" the WPR, rather than required by it.[169] The report was similar in this regard to the President's report concerning the *Iran Ajr* incident.[170]

In contrast to the October 8 naval engagement, the October 19, 1987 attack on the Rashadat oil platforms was not an instantaneous response to sudden Iranian aggression. It was a deliberate and premeditated military operation.[171] Therefore, unlike the *Iran Ajr* attack and the October 8 engagement, the attack on Rashadat ostensibly activated the consultation requirement of the WPR. The President did consult with congressional leaders on October 18.[172] But, again, the WPR risks running afoul of the President's constitutional power to use armed force for defensive purposes. Prior to October 19, Iran had undertaken military aggression against United States ships. By ordering the attack on Rashadat in retaliation for Iran's attack against the *Sea Isle City,* the President sought to deter further aggression by Iran against the United States and to reduce Iran's ability to undertake such actions by eliminating Rashadat's C3 capability. The President's power as Commander-in-Chief to defend U.S. lives and property is unilateral.

Similarly, the WPR, by its terms, required a report within 48 hours of the October 19, 1987 Rashadat operation. But, just as consultation was constitutionally problematic, so was the requirement of a report to be submitted within 48 hours. Since the President was undertaking an action as Commander-in-Chief to defend U.S. lives and property, he was constitutionally empowered to act unilaterally. No act of Congress can amend this constitutional authorization. The President did submit a report to Congress within 48 hours "consistent with" the WPR about the attack on Rashadat. He did so, apparently, to satisfy political, rather than legal, requirements.[173]

Operation Praying Mantis, the April 18, 1988 attack by U.S. forces against the Iranian platforms Sasson and Sirri, falls into the same category as the October 19, 1987 Rashadat operation for WPR purposes. The President undertook a military action that was hostile and, therefore, involved the WPR. But if Congress required a report within 48 hours to participate in the President's command decision to employ force, it exceeded its Article I powers. Furthermore, the report's initiation of the sixty-day clock did not restrain the President since "hostilities" ended in one day.[174]

The President did advise Congress of the April 18 military operations within 48 hours of their initiation.[175] But in so doing, he noted that, although he wished to inform Congress of U.S. military activities "consistent with" the WPR, he did not intend to withdraw U.S. forces from the Persian Gulf until U.S. objectives had been achieved.[176] Thus did the President advise Congress that he did not consider himself limited by the WPR sixty-day clock.

The July 3, 1988 downing by the U.S.S. *Vincennes* of the Iranian Airbus was an accident. Pre-hostilities consultation with Congress was, of course, impossible. As he had done with respect to other military actions in the Persian Gulf, the President sent Congress a report "consistent with" the WPR, in which he reminded Congress of his past cooperation in the form of "letters, reports, briefings, and testimony" and his continuing desire to cooperate with Congress "in pursuit of our mutual, overriding aim of peace and stability in the Persian Gulf region."[177] Although the President did report to Congress about the *Vincennes* incident, the WPR's requirement that he do so within 48 hours raised constitutional questions. In shooting down what he thought was a hostile target, the captain of the *Vincennes* (representing the President) was attempting to do something clearly within the scope of the President's authority: protecting U.S. forces from armed aggression. The WPR cannot limit this constitutional authority. The *Vincennes,* of course, made a tragic mistake. But the consequences of the mistake, as profound as they may be in geopolitical and moral terms, do not change the constitutional balance of war powers. The President is constitutionally empowered to make mistakes.

By examining each instance of the use of force by the President in the Persian Gulf it becomes clear that the WPR either did not apply by its own terms or, if it did apply, was based on dubious constitutional authority. Taken as a whole, the naval operations in the Persian Gulf in 1987 and 1988 seem to suggest ongoing hostilities between the United States and Iran. But this characterization can only be made with the benefit of hindsight, a power not enjoyed by the President in early 1987. Thus does it appear that attacks on the President's compliance with the WPR win little for his critics. A more productive approach for those critical of the President's Persian Gulf policy is to criticize the policy itself.

Notes

1. Secretary of Defense Caspar W. Weinberger, "A Report to the Congress on Security Arrangements in the Persian Gulf" (June 15, 1987) ("Weinberger Report") at ii. *See also* O'Rourke, "The Tanker War," 114 U.S. Naval Institute PROCEEDINGS 30 (May 1988).

2. Data for 1981–1986 from SEN. COMM. ON FOREIGN RELATIONS, PERSIAN GULF AND THE WAR POWERS RESOLUTION at 2 (1987). Data for 1987–1988 from O'Rourke, "Gulf Ops," 115 U.S. Naval Institute PROCEEDINGS (May 1989) ("O'Rourke") at 42, 43.

3. 70% of the world's oil reserves are located in the Persian Gulf Region. Weinberger Report at i. The Persian Gulf is the source of 6.8 percent of U.S. oil, 54 percent of Japan's oil, and 41 percent of Western Europe's oil. SEN. COMM. ON FOREIGN RELATIONS, PERSIAN GULF AND THE WAR POWERS RESOLUTION 2 (1987).

4. Weinberger Report at ii.

5. C. WEINBERGER, FIGHTING FOR PEACE 387 (1990).

6. *See generally* Weinberger Report. *See also* O'Rourke at 42; McDonald, "The Convoy Mission," 114 U.S. Naval Institute PROCEEDINGS 36 (May 1988).

7. Weinberger Report at 15.

8. Testimony of May 19, 1987, quoted in SEN. COMM. ON FOREIGN RELATIONS, PERSIAN GULF AND THE WAR POWERS RESOLUTION 4 (1987).

9. Weinberger Report at iii. *See also* C. WEINBERGER, FIGHTING FOR PEACE Ch. 13 (1990).

10. Weinberger Report at 2.

11. *N.Y. Times,* May 18, 1987, p.1, col.6. *See generally* Vlahos, "The *Stark* Report," 114 U.S. Naval Institute PROCEEDINGS 64 (May 1988) ("Vlahos"); SEN. COMM. ON FOREIGN RELATIONS, PERSIAN GULF AND THE WAR POWERS RESOLUTION 3–4 (1987); Department of Defense, "Formal Investigation into the Circumstances Surrounding the Attack on the U.S.S. *Stark* (FFG 31) on 17 May 1987," Vol. I (Report of Investigation) (1987) ("*Stark* Report").

12. J. LEHMAN, COMMAND OF THE SEAS 393 (1988).

13. Vlahos at 64, 66.

14. *Stark* Report at 12. *See also* TIME, Jun. 1, 1987, p.16.

15. *Stark* Report at 12.

16. *Stark* Report at 13.

17. *Stark* Report at 2, 12.

18. *Stark* Report at 12. The Exocet's nominal range is 38 nautical miles. *Stark* Report at 2.

19. *Stark* Report at 2–3, 7, 13–14; Vlahos at 66.

20. *Stark* Report at 16.

21. *Stark* Report at 14; Vlahos at 66.

22. *Stark* Report at 15.

23. *N.Y. Times,* May 19, 1987, p.1, col.6.

24. *Id.,* May 20, 1987, p.1, col.5.

25. TIME, Jun. 1, 1987, p.16–23.

26. *Stark* Report at 31.

27. *Stark* Report at 31.

28. *N.Y. Times,* May 20, 1987, p.12, col.1.

29. Weinberger Report at 17–18.

30. O'Rourke at 44.

31. TIME, Jun. 8, 1987, p.23.

32. SEN. COMMITTEE ON FOREIGN RELATIONS, PERSIAN GULF AND THE WAR POWERS RESOLUTION at 7–8 (1987).

33. H.J. Res. 295, 100th Cong., 1st Sess. (1987).

34. TIME, Jun. 8, 1987, p.23. *See* Hawkins, "Strategy and 'Freedom of Navigation,'" 12 THE NATIONAL INTEREST 48 (1988). *See also* Speech of Rear Admiral Harold J. Bernsen, USN, December 1, 1988, Union League, Philadelphia, Pennsylvania.

35. S.1327, 100th Cong., 1st Sess. (1987).

36. *Id.*

37. S.1343, 100th Cong., 1st Sess. (1987).

38. SEN. COMM. ON FOREIGN RELATIONS, PERSIAN GULF AND THE WAR POWERS RESOLUTION at 8 (1987).

39. H.J. Res. 310, 100th Cong., 1st Sess. (1987).

40. *Lowry v. Reagan,* 676 F. Supp. 333 (D.D.C. 1987).

41. TIME, Aug. 3, 1987 at 25.

42. TIME, Aug. 10, 1987 at 8.

43. *Id.*

44. TIME, Aug. 17, 1987 at 39.

45. *Id.*

46. *Id. See also* N.Y. *Times,* Sept. 22, 1987, p.6, col.1.

47. N.Y. *Times,* Oct. 9, 1987, p.8, col.1.

48. N.Y. *Times,* Sept. 22, 1987, p.1, col.6 (statement of White House Spokesman, Marlin Fitzwater).

49. TIME, Oct. 5, 1987 at 22.

50. Letter to the President Pro Tempore of the Senate and the Speaker of the House, September 24, 1987, 23 WEEKLY COMPILATION OF PRESIDENTIAL DOCUMENTS, September 28, 1987 at 1066. *See also* C. WEINBERGER, FIGHTING FOR PEACE 414–417 (1990).

51. *Id. See also* TIME, Oct. 5, 1987 at 22; N.Y. *Times,* Sept. 23, 1987, p.1, col.6.

52. Letter to the President Pro Tempore of the Senate and the Speaker of the House, September 24, 1987, 23 WEEKLY COMPILATION OF PRESIDENTIAL DOCUMENTS, September 28, 1987 at 1066.

53. Statement by the President, September 24, 1987, 23 WEEKLY COMPILATION OF PRESIDENTIAL DOCUMENTS, September 28, 1987 at 1067.

54. TIME, Oct. 5, 1987 at 20.

55. N.Y. *Times,* Sept. 24, 1987, p.1, col.6.

56. N.Y. *Times,* Sept. 26, 1987, p.5, col.1.

57. N.Y. *Times,* Oct. 9, 1987, p.8, col.1. *See also* C. WEINBERGER, FIGHTING FOR PEACE 418 (1990).

58. N.Y. *Times,* Oct. 9, 1987, p.8, col.1. *See also* C. WEINBERGER, FIGHTING FOR PEACE 418 (1990).

59. N.Y. *Times,* Oct. 9, 1987, p.1, col.6 (one unarmed OH-6 helicopter); Letter to President Pro Tempore of the Senate and the Speaker of the House,

October 10, 1987, 23 WEEKLY COMPILATION OF PRESIDENTIAL DOC-UMENTS, October 19, 1987 at 1159 (three U.S. helicopters).

60. TIME, Oct. 19, 1987 at 13.

61. *N.Y. Times,* Oct. 9, 1989, p.8, col.2 (two U.S. helicopters sank all three Iranian gunboats); Letter to the President Pro Tempore of the Senate and the Speaker of the House, October 10, 1987, 23 WEEKLY COMPILATION OF PRESIDENTIAL DOCUMENTS, October 19, 1987 at 1159 (three U.S. heli-copters caused damage to three Iranian boats, sinking one).

62. TIME, Oct. 19, 1987 at 13.

63. *N.Y. Times,* Oct. 9, 1987, p.8, col.1.

64. TIME, Oct. 26, 1987 at 42–43.

65. TIME, Nov. 2, 1987 at 62.

66. C. WEINBERGER, FIGHTING FOR PEACE 420 (1990).

67. TIME, Nov. 2, 1987 at 64. *See also* Letter to the Speaker of the House of Representatives and the President Pro Tempore of the Senate on the United States Reprisal Against Iran, October 20, 1987, II PUBLIC PAPERS OF THE PRESIDENTS OF THE UNITED STATES: RONALD REAGAN, 1987 at 1212 (1987).

68. TIME, Nov. 2, 1987 at 63.

69. *Id.* at 63–64.

70. S.J. Res. 194, 100th Cong., 1st Sess. (1987).

71. *Id.,* Sec. 1(a)(1)

72. *Id.,* Sec. 6.

73. *Id.,* Sec. 1(a)(2).

74. *Id.,* Sec. 1(a)(3).

75. *Id.,* Sec. 1.

76. *Id.,* Sec. 7.

77. H.J. Res. 387, 100th Cong., 1st Sess. (1987).

78. *Id.,* Sec. 2(b).

79. *Id.,* Sec. 2(a).

80. *Id.,* Sec. 4

81. *Economist,* Feb. 13, 1989 at 40.

82. O'Rourke at 44.

83. *Id.*

84. *Id.*

85. *Id.*

86. Letter to the Speaker of the House and the President Pro Tempore of the Senate on the United States Military Strike in the Persian Gulf, April 19, 1988, 24 WEEKLY COMPILATION OF PRESIDENTIAL DOCUMENTS, April 25, 1988 at 493.

87. Perkins, "The Surface View: Operation Praying Mantis," 115 U.S. Naval Institute PROCEEDINGS 66, 68 (May 1989) ("Perkins"). *See also* Langston and Bringle, "The Air View: Operation Praying Mantis," 115 U.S. Naval Institute PROCEEDINGS 54 (May 1989) ("Langston and Bringle"); Letter to the Speaker of the House and the President Pro Tempore of the Senate on the United States

Military Strike in the Persian Gulf, April 19, 1988, 24 WEEKLY COMPILATION OF PRESIDENTIAL DOCUMENTS, April 25, 1988 at 493.

88. Perkins at 68.

89. Perkins at 69.

90. Perkins at 69–70. *See also* Letter to the Speaker of the House and the President Pro Tempore of the Senate on the United States Military Strike in the Persian Gulf, April 19, 1988, 24 WEEKLY COMPILATION OF PRESIDENTIAL DOCUMENTS, April 25, 1988 at 493.

91. Langston and Bringle at 58–59. *See also* Letter to the Speaker of the House and the President Pro Tempore of the Senate on the United States Military Strike in the Persian Gulf, April 19, 1988, 24 WEEKLY COMPILATION OF PRESIDENTIAL DOCUMENTS, April 25, 1988 at 493; C. WEINBERGER, FIGHTING FOR PEACE 424–425 n.9 (1990).

92. O'Rourke at 47. *See also* Langston and Bringle at 59.

93. Department of State, Gulf Advisory No. 1/88 (May 22, 1988) (obtained from Department of State through Freedom of Information Act request).

94. O'Rourke at 47.

95. Weinberger Report at i.

96. Letter to the Speaker of the House and President Pro Tempore of the Senate on the Downing of an Iranian Jetliner by the United States Navy in the Persian Gulf, July 4, 1988, 24 WEEKLY COMPILATION OF PRESIDENTIAL DOCUMENTS, July 11, 1988, at 896.

97. *See generally* DEPARTMENT OF DEFENSE, INVESTIGATION REPORT: FORMAL INVESTIGATION INTO THE CIRCUMSTANCES SURROUND-ING THE DOWNING OF IRAN AIR FLIGHT 655 ON 3 JULY 1988 ("VINCENNES REPORT") 5 (1988). *See also* Friedman, "The *Vincennes* Incident," 115 U.S. Naval Institute PROCEEDINGS 72 (May 1989) ("Friedman").

98. *N.Y. Times,* Aug. 20, 1988, p.5, col.2; Letter to the Speaker of the House and President Pro Tempore of the Senate on the Downing of an Iranian Jetliner by the United States Navy in the Persian Gulf, July 4, 1988, 24 WEEKLY COMPILATION OF PRESIDENTIAL DOCUMENTS, July 11, 1988, at 896.

99. *N.Y. Times,* Aug. 20, 1988, p.5, col.2.

100. *Id.*

101. VINCENNES REPORT at 7.

102. Radical maneuvers were necessary because the forward five-inch gun had malfunctioned. The *Vincennes* maneuvered to keep the after five-inch gun bearing on the surface targets. Friedman at 74.

103. *N.Y. Times,* Aug. 20, 1988, p.5, col.3. The U.S.-made F-14 is an air-to-air fighter, ordinarily not configured for surface attacks. However, Norman Friedman reports: "It was known that Iran's F-14s could drop unguided (iron) bombs, if they could approach to within two nautical miles of a target, and U.S. crews in the region suspected that the F-14s had been wired to launch Harpoon missiles. . . ." Friedman at 73.

104. *N.Y. Times,* Jul. 5, 1988, p.1, col.6.

105. *Id.,* Jul. 11, 1988, p.1, col.1 and p.10, col.2.

106. Friedman at 74.

107. VINCENNES REPORT at 31–33. *See also* Letter of Commander D.R. Carlson, USN (Commanding Officer, U.S.S. *Sides*), 115 U.S. Naval Institute PROCEEDINGS 87 (September 1989) ("Carlson").

108. *N.Y. Times,* Aug. 20, 1988, p.1, col.6.

109. VINCENNES REPORT at 33.

110. *N.Y. Times,* Aug. 20, 1988, p.5, col.4–6. *See also* VINCENNES REPORT at 6.

111. VINCENNES REPORT at 6.

112. Friedman at 76.

113. *Id.* Dr. Friedman's account was described as "yet another apologia" by the skipper of the U.S.S. *Sides.* Carlson at 87.

114. *N.Y. Times,* Jul. 4, 1988, p.4, col.5.

115. *Id.,* Jul. 5, 1988, p.9, col.3.

116. *Id.* at p. 10, col.6.

117. *Id.,* Jul. 21, 1988, p.1, col.1.

118. *Id.,* Jul. 23, 1988, p.1, col.1.

119. *Id. See also id.,* Jul. 25, 1988, p.1, col.3.

120. *Id.,* Aug. 10, 1988, p.8, col.6.

121. *Id.*

122. *Id.*

123. *Id.,* Aug. 21, 1988, p.6, col.1.

124. O'Rourke at 49.

125. O'Rourke at 49.

126. O'Rourke at 50.

127. O'Rourke at 89. (source: Department of Defense, January 17, 1989).

128. The U.S. Navy has protected U.S.-flagged vessels in the Persian Gulf since 1949, and continues to do so. This legal analysis focuses on naval operations on April 2, 1987 until the August 20, 1988 ceasefire between Iran and Iraq.

129. Thus are the Persian Gulf operations analogous to operations in Lebanon in 1982–1984. *See* Chapter 5.

130. U.S. CONST., Art. II, Sec. 2, Cl. 2.

131. *See generally* Chapter 2. *See also, e.g., Republic of Mexico v. Hoffman,* 324 U.S. 30 (1945); *ex parte Peru,* 318 U.S. 578 (1943); *United States v. Belmont,* 301 U.S. 324 (1937).

132. *See, e.g., United States v. Belmont,* 301 U.S. 324 (1937); *United States v. Curtiss-Wright Export Corp.,* 299 U.S. 304 (1936).

133. *See United States v. Curtiss-Wright Export Corp.,* 299 U.S. 304 (1936); *Myers v. United States,* 272 U.S. 52, 118 (1926).

134. L. TRIBE, AMERICAN CONSTITUTIONAL LAW 170–171 (1978); L. HENKIN, FOREIGN AFFAIRS AND THE CONSTITUTION 177 (1972).

135. By offering to reflag Kuwaiti vessels, the President did not enlarge the mission of the United States Navy, which was already responsible for the protection of U.S.-flagged merchant vessels.

136. The same can be said for the damage sustained by the U.S.-owned *Texaco Caribbean,* which was damaged by a mine on August 10, 1987.

137. *See* Chapter 2.

138. *The Prize Cases,* 67 U.S. 635, 668–670 (1863).

139. *See* Chapter 7.

140. *See* Chapter 7.

141. As discussed in Chapter 7, the Constitution does not require certainty in the President's intelligence as a predicate to military force.

142. *E.g.,* H.J. Res. 295, 100th Cong., 1st Sess. (1987); S.1343, 100th Cong., 1st Sess. (1987); H.J. Res. 310, 100th Cong., 1st Sess. (1987); S.J. Res. 194, 100th Cong., 1st Sess. (1987); H.J. Res. 387, 100th Cong., 1st Sess. (1987). *See also* H.R. 2520, 100th Cong., 1st Sess., Sec. 2(a) (1987) (repeal WPR); H.R. 2525, Sec. 2, 100th Cong., 1st Sess. (1987) (repeal WPR).

143. H.R. 508, 100th Cong., 1st Sess. (1987).

144. *Id.* at Sec. 3.

145. *Id.,* Sec. 5.

146. *Id.,* Sec. 8(a).

147. 50 U.S.C. § 1543.

148. SEN. COMM. ON FOREIGN RELATIONS, PERSIAN GULF AND THE WAR POWERS RESOLUTION (1987). *See also* C. WEINBERGER, FIGHTING FOR PEACE 400–401 (1990).

149. Weinberger Report at iii.

150. 50 U.S.C. § 1544.

151. 50 U.S.C. § 1543(a)(2).

152. 50 U.S.C. § 1545.

153. Weinberger Report at 21.

154. C. WEINBERGER, FIGHTING FOR PEACE 406 (1990).

155. 50 U.S.C. § 1542.

156. H.J. Res. 295, 100th Cong., 1st Sess. (1987).

157. S.1327, 100th Cong., 1st Sess. (1987).

158. S.1343, 100th Cong., 1st Sess. (1987).

159. H.J. Res. 310, 100th Cong., 1st Sess. (1987).

160. S.J. Res. 194, 100th Cong., 1st Sess. (1987).

161. H.J. Res. 387, 100th Cong., 1st Sess. (1987).

162. C. WEINBERGER, FIGHTING FOR PEACE 401–403 (1990). *Cf. also* O'Rourke, "Our Peaceful Navy," 115 U.S. Naval Institute PROCEEDINGS 79 (1989).

163. Letter to the President Pro Tempore of the Senate and the Speaker of the House, September 24, 1987, 23 WEEKLY COMPILATION OF PRESIDENTIAL DOCUMENTS, September 28, 1987 at 1066. *See also* "Communication from the President of the United States Transmitting a Report on the September 21, 1987 Engagement of United States Armed Forces and Iranian Mine Laying Craft in the Persian Gulf," H. Doc. No. 100-112, 100th Cong., 1st Sess. (1987).

164. Letter to the President Pro Tempore of the Senate and the Speaker of the House, September 24, 1987, 23 WEEKLY COMPILATION OF PRESIDENTIAL DOCUMENTS, September 28, 1987 at 1066.

165. *See* Chapter 4.

166. *See generally* Chapter 2; *The Prize Cases,* 67 U.S. 635, 668–669 (1863).

167. *See* L. TRIBE, AMERICAN CONSTITUTIONAL LAW 247–249 (1978). *See also Nixon v. Administrator of General Sciences,* 433 U.S. 425 (1977); *United States v. Nixon,* 418 U.S. 683 (1974); *United States v. Poindexter,* 1990 U.S. Dist. LEXIS 2881 (March 21, 1990).

168. Presidents Ford and Carter drew similar conclusions. *See generally* R. TURNER, THE WAR POWERS RESOLUTION: ITS IMPLEMENTATION IN THEORY AND PRACTICE (1983).

169. Letter to the President Pro Tempore of the Senate and the Speaker of the House, October 10, 1987, 23 WEEKLY COMPILATION OF PRESIDENTIAL DOCUMENTS, October 19, 1987 at 1159–1160. *See also* "Communication from the President of the United States Transmitting a Report on the October 8, 1987 Engagement Between United States Armed Forces and Iranian Naval Vessels in the Persian Gulf," H. Doc. No. 100-113, 100th Cong., 1st Sess. (1987).

170. Letter to the President Pro Tempore of the Senate and the Speaker of the House, September 24, 1987, 23 WEEKLY COMPILATION OF PRESIDENTIAL DOCUMENTS, September 28, 1987 at 1066. *See also* "Communication from the President of the United States Transmitting a Report on the September 21, 1987 Engagement of United States Armed Forces and Iranian Mine Laying Craft in the Persian Gulf," H. Doc. No. 100-112, 100th Cong., 1st Sess. (1987).

171. It is interesting to note that the Rashadat platforms were chosen, at least in part, to avoid inciting Congress to invoke the WPR. TIME, Nov. 2, 1987 at 63–64. Apparently, the President believed a target not located on Iranian soil would be more palatable to Congress.

172. Letter to the Speaker of the House of Representatives and the President Pro Tempore of the Senate on the United States Reprisal Against Iran, October 20, 1987, II PUBLIC PAPERS OF THE PRESIDENTS OF THE UNITED STATES: RONALD REAGAN, 1987 at 1212 (1989).

173. Letter to the Speaker of the House of Representatives and the President Pro Tempore of the Senate on the United States Reprisal Against Iran, October 20, 1987, II PUBLIC PAPERS OF THE PRESIDENTS OF THE UNITED STATES: RONALD REAGAN, 1987 at 1212 (1989). *See also* "Communication from the President of the United States Transmitting a Report on the October 19, 1987 Actions by U.S. Armed Forces in the Persian Gulf," H. Doc. No. 100-120, 100th Cong., 1st Sess. 1 (1987).

174. *See* Chapter 5.

175. Letter to the Speaker of the House and the President Pro Tempore of the Senate on the United States Military Strike in the Persian Gulf, April 19, 1988, 24 WEEKLY COMPILATION OF PRESIDENTIAL DOCUMENTS, April 25, 1988 at 493–494.

176. Letter to the Speaker of the House and the President Pro Tempore of the Senate, April 19, 1988, 24 WEEKLY COMPILATION OF PRESIDENTIAL DOCUMENTS, April 25, 1988 at 494.

177. Letter to the Speaker of the House and President Pro Tempore of the Senate on the Downing of an Iranian Jetliner by the United States Navy in the Persian Gulf, July 4, 1988, 24 WEEKLY COMPILATION OF PRESIDENTIAL DOCUMENTS, July 11, 1988, at 896–897.

Conclusion

The Framers of the Constitution did not foresee the Vietnam War, the deaths of 241 U.S. servicemen in their Beirut barracks in 1983, or the deaths of 37 sailors aboard the U.S.S. *Stark* in the Persian Gulf in 1987. Lacking perfect foresight, they left the ultimate question of whether a war should be fought to the realm of political, as distinct from legal, debate. They knew that, even in triumph, war is tragic. They did not seek to encumber with legal doctrine the political issue of whether to fight.

The Constitution does not tell Congress, the President, or the people when war should be waged. It reserves to the political process the question of whether the exercise of military force is good and right, addressing instead the question of how the legal power to wage war should be allocated.[1] To say that the President may wage war under certain circumstances is not, therefore, to say that he should. The legal standard in the war powers context, as in others, establishes a minimum standard, not a goal.

This book has pursued the objective of describing, in terms of the Constitutional Convention of 1787 and subsequent judicial decisions, the President's war powers. These judicial decisions have been infrequent as a result of the political question doctrine. What illumination the courts have provided establishes that the scope of the President's power to defend national security is broad, and is complemented by his executive and foreign affairs powers. These constitutional powers cannot be compromised by the War Powers Resolution, which, in any case, is flawed by ambiguous language.

The measure of this book's success is not whether the reader believes that President Reagan's decisions to use military force in Lebanon, Grenada, Libya, and the Persian Gulf were sound morally, strategically, or politically. The correct measure is whether the reader is persuaded that these unilateral actions by the President were lawful.

The conclusion that the President acted lawfully does not suggest that all presidential decisions to use force are lawful. The Constitution did not grant the President *carte blanche*. The Constitution does not permit the President to use the military to abridge the Bill of Rights, for example, or to invade Canada to increase the federal tax base. Nothing about the President's unilateral power to make war allows the President to use force to achieve goals unrelated to national defense. When the President does use force toward a national defense objective, he is not required as a matter of law to meet Congress' standard of proportionality. However, a grossly disproportionate military action might amount to an atrocity, which might be adjudicated in the courts or in the Senate as an impeachment proceeding.

The Constitution does grant the President the power to decide unilaterally whether national security requires the use of military force under exigent circumstances. This of course is an exception to the general rule that the President does not act unilaterally, as for example in the process of enacting domestic policy. It is important to remember that this exception only applies when exigent circumstances threaten national security.

In the long term, the constitutional balance favors Congress, which enjoys the power of appropriation. This is no idle entitlement; what is required of Congress is the collective will to exercise the power. Ultimately, the House of Representatives has the power of impeachment, which it might exercise in a case of presidential abuse of the war powers. Impeachment proceedings in the Senate might create the forum where a clash between Congress and the President over war powers is resolved, especially if the courts have refused to consider the issue.

Congress, of course, also possesses the power to declare war. Because the President has initiated armed conflict so many times in our history, some feel that Congress' power to declare war has become mere ornamentation. But this point of view ignores the serious legal implications of a declaration of war in terms of treaty obligations, the law of the seas, the treatment of prisoners of war,[2] and other matters. That Congress has not exercised this awesome power since the second world war does not suggest its wane; indeed, it might suggest the opposite.

Ideally, the President would obtain a congressional declaration of war prior to every use of military force. Democratic principles make this conclusion inescapable. The best way to go to war is with a congressional declaration. In the aftermath of the Vietnam War, many have come to believe that the failure of successive presidents to obtain a declaration of war against North Vietnam and to obtain the corresponding popular approval for our military involvement contributed to our national anguish over that war. To say the least, U.S. involvement in Vietnam lasted long enough to provide many opportunities for war to be declared. But where circumstances do not provide such opportunities for a declaration, the President is entitled to act unilaterally. When the President does so, Congress does not have, by virtue of its power to declare war, the power to veto the President's decision. The Framers considered this possibility and rejected it.

Members of Congress had every right to object to President Reagan's employment of the military from 1982 through 1988. Congressional complaints about the lawfulness of the President's actions, however, were less productive than criticisms based on geopolitical and military concerns. Arguments about the lawfulness of the President's actions did not inform the separate debate on whether each employment of force was in the national interest. A lawful use of force might, after all, be a very bad idea in terms of national security.

One purpose of this book is to discourage Congress from sitting on the political "fence" during armed conflicts. If Congress objects to the President's use of force under circumstances such as those presented to President Reagan, it should focus on the substantive issues rather than the procedural ones. If Congress will do so, the clash of wills between Congress and the President hopefully will encourage wise decisions on the use of force.

Notes

1. Legal principles determine whether a war should be fought only in the sense that a violation of U.S. rights might lead to a use of military force. *See, e.g.,* Tarcov, "Principle and Prudence in Foreign Policy: The Founders' Perspective," 76 THE PUBLIC INTEREST 45 (Summer 1984).

2. American prisoners of war in Vietnam were told by their captors that they were imprisoned as common criminals, not prisoners of war, because the U.S. Congress had not declared war. Brief by Commander Timothy Sullivan, USNR, Naval Air Station Brunswick, Maine, June 8, 1988.

About the Book and Author

Ronald Reagan's term in office was punctuated by four significant employments of military force: the deployment of Marines to Lebanon; the intervention in Grenada; the air strikes against Libya; and the deployment of naval forces to the Persian Gulf. In the aftermath of each of these military operations, critics questioned the constitutional basis for such unilateral presidential war-making, arguing that Congress alone is empowered to declare war. Debates over whether the President failed to comply with the statutory requirements of the War Powers Resolution further complicated these constitutional disagreements.

In *The Reagan Wars*, David Hall seeks to overcome a key source of confusion in these heated debates—the failure to distinguish between the wisdom of Reagan's actions and their legality. He demonstrates that the circumstances under which the Constitution permits unilateral presidential war-making were present when President Reagan waged war between 1980 and 1988. Hall first considers the thinking of the Constitution's Framers on the question of war powers and the subsequent two hundred years of judicial interpretation regarding the proper balance between congressional and presidential authority to make war. In light of this historical background, he then closely examines the facts and the legal circumstances of each of the four "Reagan wars." Hall's thought-provoking conclusions deserve the attention of anyone interested in the role of the Constitution in U.S. foreign policy-making.

David Locke Hall is a member of the Pennsylvania Bar and holds an A.B. from Dartmouth College, an M.P.P.M. from Yale, and J.D. and M.A. degrees from the University of Pennsylvania. He has written articles for *Proceedings*, *Naval War College Review*, and various law journals and reviews.

Index